The Relationship Key

Unlock Your Ideal Life Experience

Jonathan R. Wachtel

Inspirational Life Guidance Publications

ISBN-10: 150023270X
ISBN-13: 978-1500232702

Library of Congress Control Number: 2014911345
CreateSpace Independent Publishing Platform,
North Charleston, SC

Dedication

I dedicate this book to our thoughts, feelings, and instincts, who are always providing us with exactly what we need to achieve our greatest aims and are just trying to get our attention so that we can benefit from their guidance, help, and protection. I also dedicate this book to you, my fellow creator and manifestation of our common Source. You are powerful, and if you do not know this yet, you will learn this soon.

Contents

Acknowledgments

Thank you to Melanie, who has presented me with many of the experiences I've needed to have in order to discover the great majority of what is in this book. My experiences with her have been essential to my learning many of the lessons contained within these pages and being able to share them with you here.

Thank you to Mikey, who has helped me in more ways than can possibly be sufficiently acknowledged here, often providing levity to life's obstacles, and also who simplified the title of this book to its current form. Thank you to Zoe, who has been another more-than-invaluable presence in my life during the writing of this book. Without either of these closest of friends and companions on the journey through life's lessons, this book could not exist. For it is with their support and their willingness to listen to me and to confide in me, too, that I have been able to process and learn from the life experiences I've created for myself and be rewarded by having these lessons be clarified with, and immediately beneficial to, people I care about tremendously. Only with this mutual and mutually valuable processing could I have gleaned from my experiences, and theirs, the life lessons that I share in the following pages.

Thank you to Perel, who has also played a vital role in my processing and understanding the lessons here. Thank you to Davina, who only came into my life near the end of the writing of this book, but who has played a pivotal role in my understanding many of the lessons in this book. These friends have been highly important presences in my life. I am grateful to them for being willing to listen to me, for being messengers of relevant feedback regarding my own life experiences in forms in which I could positively receive it, and for sharing their experiences with me as well so that our overlapping lessons could be identified and mutually benefited from.

Thank you to my sister, Lisa, who helped me with my taking the front cover photo and whose suggestions in regard to the front cover layout and design refined it and made it what it is. Thank you to my parents, who laid the foundation for me to learn in this life from lifetimes of experiences and to get to where I am in my understanding of life, people, relationships, and everything, capable of guiding others.

Thank you to those friends who have not been named here, and to my clients, and to everyone else who has traveled the journey of life with me up to this point and beyond, reflecting back my own experiences and my own messages to myself, and making it possible for me to learn all that I share here. Many of you deserve mentioning here, but I will keep these acknowledgments reasonably brief and wish that you know who you are.

To everyone who has been mentioned explicitly here and to everyone who has not been mentioned explicitly here, please know that I recognize that without any single one of you, this book could not exist as it does. I am exceedingly grateful and appreciative for the role you have played in making this book, and my understanding of everything that is conveyed in it, possible.

Introduction

Our life experience is composed of relationships: our relationships with our thoughts, feelings, instincts, bodies, and physical belongings; our relationships with our past, present, and future; our relationships with our family, friends, and significant others; our relationships with our higher selves and with some conception of the Source of all that we experience.

When we feel we are not in control of what happens to us in our lives, we are stressed and unfulfilled. When we feel we *are* in control of what happens to us, we are relaxed and fulfilled.

Considering all this, it would be nice to have a key to understanding how we can take control of the nature of our relationships with ourselves and the objects, events, and people in our lives. If we had this key, and we could use it, we could make everything in our lives whatever we'd like it to be.

Imagine: Just being *aware* that you have this control would make your life so much more deeply fulfilling, because you would know that you are not doomed to be subject to the whim of other people's actions toward you, random events in your body and in the world around you, or even your own frustrated instincts, erratic emotions, or fearful thoughts. You would know that no matter what happens to you, no matter what you experience, it is within your power and capacity to change—to choose more of this, or to choose something different from this.

We might be inclined to believe that having such power would be a nice, but far-fetched, fantasy. However, there is a higher part of us that knows that it is the very reason why we are here in the first place—to obtain this key and to experience the exercise of our creative ability to shape our relationships and our lives.

This book will guide you toward this key. It explains in words, to the extent that this is possible, that which you will come to understand in your own experience as you allow these words to guide you toward a greater awareness of the workings of the world within and outside of you.

Here is the core of this key:

Our relationships with everyone and everything around us in this physical world are reflections of our relationship with ourselves. The way we treat ourselves—our own thoughts, feelings, and instincts—sets the example for how our own bodies treat themselves, how other people and the world around us treat us, and how we are inclined to treat others and the world around us as well.

This book explains in detail this key to understanding why your relationships with everyone and everything are the way they are, and how to change these relationships to make them whatever you want them to be.

Read on, and learn how to take control of your life and unlock your ideal life experience.

A Request From The Author

As you read through this book and experiment with applying the concepts presented here in your own life, please consider recording the experiences you have along your journey. By writing down or otherwise recording your experiences, you will have the opportunity to look back and see how your mindset and experiences have changed, and what mindset preceded what experiences.

If you do record some of your experiences along the way of applying what you read here, I would love to read about some of the transformative experiences you have. With your permission, I would also potentially like to include them in a future book so that your successes in life creation can help inspire others toward positive transformation as well.

Please keep this in mind while you read. You can share your accounts of your life experience creation with me at jonathan@jonathanrwachtel.com.

Part 1:
Our Relationship With Ourselves

Our Thoughts, Feelings, And Instincts: Reaction Vs. Response

Considering our relationships with everyone and everything are reflections of, and therefore begin with, our relationship with ourselves—with our own thoughts, feelings, and instincts—we first ought to address our relationship with our own thoughts, feelings, and instincts.

Often our thoughts, feelings, and instincts are formed within us in reaction to the events of our lives. For example, someone might yell at you, and if you are stressed enough, you might simply yell back. In this case, you might not be aware of any of your internal goings-on that led to your yelling back at all. But if you are a bit less stressed and more aware, you might notice that within you arises the inclination (or instinct or want or desire) to yell back before you yell back. And with more awareness, you might notice, after you notice the inclination to yell back, that there is actually a feeling that is giving rise to that inclination—in this case, likely anger. And with more awareness than this, you might notice, after you notice the inclination to yell back, and after you notice the feeling that is giving rise to this inclination, that there are thoughts that are giving rise to this feeling—perhaps, in this case, something like, "Why is this person yelling at me? This person is getting me angry." So you notice that these thoughts are giving rise to the feeling of anger, which is giving rise to the inclination to yell back, which is leading to your yelling back. If you are in a relaxed-enough, or de-stressed-enough state, you might be aware enough to notice that after you recognize the inclination toward some action arise within you, and then the feeling giving rise to this inclination, and then the thoughts giving rise to this feeling, you can recognize that there is a choice behind these thoughts. At this point, you recognize that you can either choose to think those reactive thoughts, which lead to reactive feelings, which lead to reactive inclinations, which lead to reactive actions, or you can choose something different. You can choose to be willful and in control of your life. You can choose to respond differently (internally as well as externally) from the way you would otherwise be inclined to react. In this case, you might choose simply to ask the person from a calm place, "Why are you yelling at me?"

In this example, we see that what is really always happening is that we are choosing what we think, which is causing what we feel, which is causing what we are inclined to say and do, which is leading to what we actually say and do, which is leading to what manifests in our physical lives. It is just that we are often inclined simply to choose to react. And we eventually practice our patterns of reaction to people saying or doing certain things toward us, or to certain things happening in our lives, so many times that we end up going through our lives on autopilot, unaware of the full creative process within us that we are using all the time.

We basically end up allowing other people and the events of our lives to choose our life experiences for us through our already built-up patterns of reaction to them. When we do this, we create cycles of getting the same themes of results. But in reality, we are the ones who created the life experiences we've been having all along. So we're reacting to the results of our own choices, thereby bringing about more of the same types of experiences that we've been getting, or bringing about magnifications of certain aspects of the experiences that we've been getting by focusing the magnifying glass of our attention and energy on them.

So we might notice themes in our lives of the way people have been treating us, for example, but in focusing on this theme, and on how those people made us feel, we are only further creating more situations where we will be supported in the feeling that people treat us this way. For our beliefs and expectations about how people treat us, and our anticipation of people treating us this way when we interact with them, actually encourages us to say or withhold certain things, and to speak in a certain tone, with certain facial expressions and body language, and to react to certain things that people say or do or not, so that we can pretty much guarantee that we keep getting the same results as we have been getting, or simply the results that we believe we will get.

The thoughts and feelings that we act from will pretty much guarantee that we will get results from our actions that will support those thoughts and feelings—results that will give us more reasons to think and feel as we were thinking and feeling going in.

The Paradigm Of The Development Of Our Thoughts, Feelings, And Instincts

We can recognize here that our thoughts, feelings, instincts, speech and actions are the tools with which we shape our experience of life. Considering how powerful they are in shaping our lives, it would be useful to understand them a bit better. Let's examine their development within us over the course of our early lives, during which the stage is prepared for us to begin to shape our lives with awareness, according to our own conscious choices.

As soon as we are born, we have instincts: the instinct to be warm and comfortable, the instinct to breathe, the instinct to eat, the instinct to sleep, the instinct to maintain our physical existence in this world. From this point on through our early childhood (though developing and evolving all along the way), we believe that what we see, hear, taste, smell, physically feel, and know is what everyone sees, hears, tastes, smells, physically feels, and knows. If an object is hidden, and we see, and therefore know, where it is hidden, we believe everyone else knows where it is hidden also and so everyone knows where to look for it. There is only our own experience of the world, from our own physical location in space and time. Therefore, there is only here and now—where we are. We don't yet have any significant conception of past or future due to our lack of experience with them, and so we live, for the most part, in the present moment. We also don't yet have any significant conception of other physical places, or a world outside of our own, and so we live in our own world—a world that consists of our sensory experience of our immediate physical surroundings.

The phrase "I want now" captures a lot of the experience of this early stage of life. We are the only ones in existence ("I"). We want or desire things—mostly related to the maintenance of our physical existence in this world (and everything that doesn't actually fall into this category *seems* to fall into this category as far as we are concerned, so we feel that everything we want we actually *need* in order to survive). Further, anything we want in any moment, we want at that very moment (because, after all, *now* is all that exists for us, so why would we want to have something *later* or simply *not now*?). If we don't have things the way we want in this moment, we get frustrated or angry, because we want things to be different than we perceive them to be. It doesn't really matter what other people want, because as far as we're concerned, there is only us and our own wants anyway, and so things should be the way *we* want them to be and it's frustrating if they're not.

During adolescence, our conception of our own experience of the world as being the only experience of the world is modified. We come to realize that there are other people out there who experience things from different locations in space and time than we do. What we see through our eyes when we look at a three-dimensional diorama of a mountain scene might not be what someone else sees through his or her eyes when looking at that same scene from the other side of the diorama, because there are things that we can see that would be hidden by the mountain from the other person's view.

Since we are aware that other people exist out there, we want to fit in with them and we reflect on how well or how poorly we did this. "Who am I and how do I feel about how I fit in?" is a phrase that captures this stage of life. To a large degree, we focus more on our past experiences now than on our present ones in an effort to discern who we are in terms of how we relate to the people around us. We try to determine our identities by reflecting on how we feel about how we came across to others in our interactions with them. In reflecting on how we feel, we project our own feelings onto others and imagine that they feel about us the way we feel about ourselves. In general, as far as we're aware, everyone would feel whatever we would feel in any particular situation. So while people are separate from us physically in space and time and so might experience different things sensorily than we do in any particular moment due to having different immediate physical surroundings, they are not separate from us in how they react to that world and experience any particular situation emotionally.

With this perspective, if we don't feel we were perceived well by ourselves and by others based on our past actions, we end up replaying the past and wishing we could change it. This leads to regret, shame, and guilt about the past.

During young adulthood, we shift yet again in our perspective. Now we come to recognize that other people experience the same types of physical stimuli differently from the way we do. Different people have different emotional reactions to events and different experiences of the world than we do. Therefore, at this point, we want to figure out how to connect with those other individuals who have different experiences than we do. We realize we have to consider other people's differing wants and emotions when we make decisions. So we want to understand other people's individualized experiences of the world in order to predict what they might be in different situations and make better decisions based on this. We even try to predict our own future selves' experiences of the world as we try to make the best decisions for ourselves and everyone else who might be affected (because if other people are affected, then this will affect *us*, which is still what really concerns us at this point).

The phrase "I want to find someone to connect with, and I need to make the right decisions in order to find and keep that person in my life" captures this stage of life well. At this point our thoughts are concerned with the future, with figuring out what our own and other people's experiences and reactions might be. As we consider the consequences of our decisions, if we don't have confidence in ourselves to make good decisions that will lead to good outcomes, we end up wishing the future would be different than we imagine it will be. This leads to fear, worry and anxiety about the future.

By the early to mid-twenties, our perspective is different yet again. At this point, the prefrontal cortex of our brains is finally fully developed. This allows us to be more aware of ourselves and the consequences of our actions than ever before. While we have been growing in our awareness throughout our lives up to this point (and onward), and therefore growing in our control over the shaping of our life experience, it is at this point that we can fully choose, with complete awareness, the thoughts, feelings, wants, behaviors, and external events to which we give our attention. This means that we can more fully transform the patterns of thought, feeling, instinct, belief, and behavior that we have built up throughout our lives in reaction to the world around us, and replace these with our willfully chosen responses. We can transcend the past so that rather than create more of the same, we can create a distinctly different, and potentially vastly better, future. It is at this point that the stage is set for us to be truly willful and mindful in shaping our lives.

Other Aspects Of The Paradigm Of Development And Creation

We may notice here that the pattern of psychological development (or the development of our awareness of our ability to shape our life experience) follows the pattern of the development of our awareness of our reaction to something: First there's something, then there's action and instinct, then there's feeling, then there's thought, and then there's choice. We noticed in the pattern of the development of our awareness of our reaction to something that the pattern of creation is in the reverse order: We choose what we think, which causes what we feel, which causes what we are inclined to say and do, which leads to what we actually say and do, which leads to what manifests in our physical life experience. Or, more simply, creation is in the order of choice, thought, feeling, instinct leading to action, which leads to the physical manifestation of what we have chosen.

From what we have discussed in terms of the patterns of psychological development, we can parse out some other aspects of the pattern of development and the reverse of that pattern—the pattern by which we create our lives. This will be useful since this is why we're here in the first place—to learn how to use the tools we were given to shape our lives with awareness into what we want them to be. But there will be more on this later.

For now, let's examine one other pattern here:

In development, first we exist, then we define boundaries between ourselves and the world around us, then we define who we are in relation to the people and the world around us, then we seek to make decisions that will lead to good consequences for ourselves and the people and the world around us, and then we become aware of how to choose willfully. Or, more simply: Enter existence, define boundaries, define identity, make decisions, become aware of how to choose willfully.

Since creation is in the reverse of the order of the development of our awareness of our ability to shape our lives, we can identify the way we create our lives here: We are aware of our ability to choose willfully the decisions that we make about who we are (or how we define ourselves), which leads us to redefine our boundaries to encompass this new definition of ourselves, which leads to our physical experience of the world. Or, more simply: We choose willfully and with awareness in order to make decisions that define who we are, which defines our boundaries in this world, and this leads to our physical experience of life.

Our Internal GPS System: How We Create Our Lives

Now that we have some understanding of the process by which we create our lives, let's examine a useful metaphor that will help us learn how to apply this understanding in our own lives.

We basically have an internal GPS system with which we are born and that we are constantly using in every moment of our lives whether we are aware of it or not.

Here's how we use this GPS system:

Each thought on which we choose (consciously or unconsciously) to focus our attention is an address, or a destination, that we plug into our GPS. Our feelings (emotions) tell us whether it's a good destination or a bad destination that we are plugging into our GPS with our thoughts and headed toward with our energy—whether it feels good or feels bad to go there, and what it's going to feel like when we get there if we keep going whatever direction we're going. Our feelings are also the fuel in the car that get us motivated and moving in the direction of the destination that we are plugging in with our thoughts. Our wants, instincts, or desires, or more subtly and when we're plugging in destinations that make us feel good, our inclinations or intuition, are the directions spoken by the GPS—turn right, turn left, go straight, act on this opportunity, speak with this person, go there right now, say this right now. If we act on our desires or inclinations—if we drive in that direction—we will get to whatever destination we have plugged in with our thoughts that led to those directions being given to us.

Obviously there are many opportunities along the way here to use our GPS in ways that don't help us in any way and even in ways that seem to hurt us, or simply to fail to use our GPS fully altogether. If we are unconsciously plugging in destinations with our thoughts in reaction to things in the world around us—in reaction to events in our lives and to people's words and actions toward us—and fueling ourselves in those directions with our reactive feelings, then we will likely not end up where we really want to be. If we get stuck on plugging in destinations with our thoughts but never act on the directions given to us, we won't get anywhere. If we get stuck adding fuel to our movement but never make use of our emotions in their function as monitors of our thought-destinations—of whether we're going a good or a bad direction for us—then we are likely going to keep ending up where we don't want to be. If we get stuck acting on the directions we're given through our desires but don't make use of the fact that these are merely directions that are being given to us based on the thoughts and feelings we've been giving our attention to, then we will likely find ourselves over and over again in situations where it seems like we're acting in opposition to the world rather than with the flow of it and in control of it.

It is necessary that we be present, mindful, and aware in order to use our GPS system willfully to get where we want to go. We've got to be aware enough of our thoughts to choose the ones to which we pay attention. We've got to be aware enough of our feelings to use them to monitor the thoughts to which we are giving our attention and to give our attention to those feelings that are fueling us in a positive direction. We've got to be aware enough of our intuitive inclinations to hear their directions and act on them in the moment. Awareness is the key to using our GPS in our favor, rather than to our detriment.

We've got to be able to move fluidly through the process of using our GPS and driving to our destinations. We've got to be able to think willfully chosen thoughts and attend to them and then let go of them so we can stop looking at the GPS and typing in addresses and instead listen to the directions and actually go somewhere. With our thoughts, we are constantly able to be setting goals and making requests, setting intentions about where we'd like to go and what we'd like to experience, and asking questions to which we'd like answers. We've got to be able to attend to our feelings and acknowledge them so that they will have served their purpose of letting us know what direction we're going, and rather than just getting caught up in determining how it feels to be going to the destination we've plugged in, we need to be able actually to let go of our feelings and either replace the destination we are plugging in with our thoughts (if we feel bad) or listen to the directions and go there (if we feel good). We've got to be able to attend to our wants and inclinations and follow the subtle ones that are leading us toward our intuition-guided, willfully chosen positive destinations, and not follow the intense lack-and-need-based ones that are leading us toward our desire-guided, reactively set destinations.

As we learn to use our internal GPS, we learn to experience control over the shaping of our lives. Everything that we experience in our lives, and that we have ever experienced, began as a seed that we sowed with our thoughts, nourished with the energy of our attention, and fed with our feelings. Nothing is beyond us to bring into our lives, and nothing that we have brought into our lives has to remain here. We can choose a new destination in any moment and immediately shift the direction we're headed. But the first step is awareness—awareness that we have this power, and awareness of what is in our lives currently and the thoughts and feelings to which we have given our attention that have led us here. Once we learn how we got to a particular destination in our lives—once we learn what thoughts and feelings brought us here—we have the power to choose either to keep coming here, or to go somewhere entirely different. If we are present to our life experiences in the world around us in every moment, we can always be learning through comparison and contrast what we want more of and what we want less of in our lives. And through giving our attention to what we want more of, and taking our attention away from what we want less of, we can come to fill our lives with only the experiences that we want in them.

How to Increase Awareness

The first step in all of this is awareness. So how can we increase our awareness? Just like we would need to practice anything else that we want to get better at, we need to practice being more mindful of the present moment—of our thoughts, feelings, and instincts in the present moment, and of our sensory experience of the world around us in the present moment.

We ought to practice being mindful in every moment, and we ought to have a mindfulness practice that we make part of our daily routine in order to remind us to do this.

Here are a couple of great meditations that can be practiced regularly—at least once a day, but preferably every morning and every night. You can also practice either of these meditations at any point during the day that you're noticing yourself getting stressed, reacting to the world around you, or getting lost in your thoughts and feelings about your experience rather than simply being present to the world around you and willfully intending and creating your experience.

Walking Meditation

Walking meditation is particularly useful during those times that you are very anxious or angry or are lost in active thought or intense emotion.

Clear a path of floor space to walk back and forth across, or simply go outside where there is relatively even ground to walk on. Begin walking quickly back and forth across the room so that your heart rate and your breathing speed up and get into sync with your racing thoughts and emotions. Then, when your body and mind are in sync, gradually slow down your walking, and your thoughts and emotions will gradually slow down with your walking.

During the entire time that you are walking, pay attention to the sensations of walking. Notice the movements of the muscles in your feet as you walk. Feel your heel touch the floor and roll to your toes, and then the next heel, rolling to your toes. Feel the floor beneath your feet—whether it's hard or soft, hot or cold. Simply experience what it is to be walking—with all the nuances and details that you are usually unaware of because you are usually paying attention to other things.

Whenever you notice that your mind has wandered from focus on the sensations of walking, notice what has drawn your attention away. Notice the thoughts, the feelings, the sounds, or whatever you're paying attention to. Acknowledge those thoughts, feelings, or whatever, accept that your mind has wandered (because it will wander), and gently bring your attention back to focus on the sensations of walking. You are successfully practicing this meditation at every moment that you notice that your mind has wandered from your anchor, or intended point of focus (in this case, your walking) and you choose to bring your attention back to your intended point of focus.

If you notice that negative thoughts and feelings are drawing your attention, you might also respond to your thoughts and feelings after you have noticed, heard, and acknowledged them. You can redirect them toward something more positive—replace those negative destinations in your internal GPS with more positive destinations. Just be sure to acknowledge and listen to your thoughts and feelings before you try to respond to them or redirect your attention to other destinations or back to your walking. Otherwise, those thoughts and feelings will keep trying to get your attention until you give it to them. Once you acknowledge and listen to them so that they successfully bring to your attention what you need to do to direct or redirect yourself to destinations toward which you'd like to be headed, they will have no purpose in persisting to get your attention, and you will find it much easier to let go of them and return to your intended point of focus in the present moment.

Breathing Meditation

Breathing meditation is very similar to walking meditation, except that here your intended point of focus in the present moment is the sensations of breathing rather than the sensations of walking.

You can pay attention to the air as it flows past your nostrils—the warmth or coolness, the moisture or dryness, the distinction in these qualities of the air that flows in as compared to the air that flows out. You can pay attention to the rise and fall of your chest as you breathe. You can pay attention to the air as it flows past your upper lip. Regardless of what aspects of the sensations of breathing you choose to attend to, you use this as your anchor in the present moment. You focus your attention on your anchor in the present moment, and whenever you notice that your mind has wandered from your point of focus, you choose to bring your attention back to your anchor.

Again, whenever you notice that your mind has wandered, simply acknowledge where it has wandered to, accept that it has wandered, and bring your attention back to your breathing. Your goal is to be a kind listener to yourself, allowing any thoughts and feelings that seek your attention to have your attention. Once you've listened to them, gently respond to those thoughts and feelings that seem to require a response or redirection. Then bring your attention back to your anchor in the present moment so you don't get lost in the thoughts and feelings you're listening to and fail to hear the other thoughts and feelings that seek your attention and potentially also your response and redirection.

A Walk Outside

One very important practice to increasing and maintaining mindful awareness and presence to your life experiences, and ultimately fulfillment in life, is getting outside each day. We all need the reminder to get out of our internal worlds and live in the world outside of us. Staying inside all day encourages our getting lost in our own thoughts and feelings. Getting outside and experiencing the vastness of the world around us helps remind us to keep our own frustrations, regrets, and anxieties in perspective.

Further, the sunshine and fresh air are important reminders to our bodies and brains, in addition to our minds, that it is time to be awake, and therefore that nighttime is the time to be asleep. We end up tired during the day and have trouble sleeping at night if our bodies and brains are not on a regular schedule of sleep and wake (with sufficient sleep during the time for sleep), and if they don't have daily exposure to sunshine to maintain the correspondence of their internal clocks with the cycle of day and night. Our bodies and brains need to know when to be awake and when to be asleep, and so it is up to us to set and maintain daily routines and practices to let them know when we would like them to be awake and when we would like them to be asleep. If we do this, then we sleep well at night and are awake and alert during the day.

One great way to get sunshine and fresh air on a daily basis is to go for a walk or a run everyday. Use the time to pay attention to the world around you—the green of the trees, the grandness of the buildings, the blue of the sky, the presence of people, the sound of the rustle of leaves or the voices of people, the warmth of the sunshine or of a cool breeze on your skin. Experience the sights, the sounds, the smells, the physical sensations. Whenever you notice your mind wander into its own internal commentary or thoughts, feelings, and desires about the present or the past or the future, simply acknowledge what you are thinking, feeling, and wanting, respond to this wherever appropriate, and shift your attention back to the sensations of the world around you coming through your physical senses.

You can also use part of this time to pay attention to the rhythm of your breathing or your footsteps or your body's movements. The repetition of the rhythm over time can be very effective at keeping you in the present moment as the present moment shifts from moment to moment, from one breath to another, from one footstep to another, from one muscle movement to another.

Life As A Meditation

The goal is to work toward making all of life into a meditation, where in every moment you choose something as your anchor to bring your attention back to the present. When you are brushing your teeth, you can just be brushing your teeth, and whenever you notice your mind wander, you can notice where it wanders to and bring your attention back to brushing your teeth. When you are talking with someone, you can just be talking with that person, and bring your attention back to the meaning you are trying to convey whenever you notice your mind wander. When you are listening to someone talk, you can just be listening to the meaning that is being conveyed to you. When you are writing something, you can just be writing whatever you are writing, paying attention to the meaning you are trying to capture in words. When you are walking, you can just be walking, unless there is something else that more requires your attention in that moment and so can be a better anchor for you then. When you are breathing, you can just be breathing, unless there is something else that more requires your attention in that moment and so can be a better focus of your attention to come back to whenever you notice that your attention has wandered.

Whenever you notice that you are drifting off into your reactions to the events of your life, to what people have said or done toward you, or to whatever has happened to you, you can choose to listen to the thoughts and feelings that are coming up. Then you can choose to respond to them and redirect them toward something more positive and desirable (considering that they are destinations you are plugging into your internal GPS system). Then you can let them go and bring your attention back to the present moment, for it is through your awareness of the present moment that all fulfillment is gained.

The fulfillment in a conversation comes from being present to the conversation, so that there are no thoughts or feelings of being somewhere else. The fulfillment in hanging out with a group of people comes from being present to the group, so that you aren't wandering elsewhere with your attention. The fulfillment in reading comes from settling down into reading so that you have fully made the decision to read and not to do anything else with your time in that moment. When your attention is fully focused on something in the present moment, you are fulfilled. When your attention is divided between or among places or activities, you are less fulfilled than you could be.

So when you shift from one activity to another, shift fully. If you are still with your thoughts and feelings in what you were just doing or where you just were, or in the other options that you could have chosen but didn't (but that you possibly could still choose if you wanted to), then you aren't fully where you are. The result is that you are left unfulfilled with whatever you are doing or wherever you are or whomever you're with. Fulfillment can only be obtained by making a decision to do something, or to be somewhere, or to be with someone or a group of people and living fully in that decision with all of your attention. The intensity of the life energy of complete existence comes from being fully focused on what you are doing and on where you are in this moment. So do your best to be mentally and emotionally where you are physically, with acceptance of (rather than resistance to) your experience here.

Right now you are here, and that's okay. And if you are really present here, you can learn from what you are experiencing here what you would even more like to experience in the next moment. This way, by being fully here, you can notice and choose to improve things so the next present moment of your experience will be even better than this one.

Getting More Of What You Want And Less Of What You Don't Want

Whatever we give the energy of our attention to, we get more of. Considering this, we ought to give the energy of our attention to the things that we like in our lives and that we want more of.

Just as if we were training a pet, it's up to us to reward everything that we like in our lives with our positive attention, because by rewarding things with our positive attention, we ensure that we will get more of them.

So, if we like something that we experience in our lives, it is up to us to communicate this by expressing gratitude and appreciation to ourselves, aloud, and to whomever else it seems appropriate. By focusing the magnifying glass of our attention on those experiences that we like, we guarantee that we will fill our lives with more experiences like these.

We don't need to call upon anything supernatural to understand how this works.

If you focus on things that you don't like in your life, you are not going to be in such a good mood. If you aren't in a good mood, you are not going to be likely to engage in activities that you enjoy or to notice or act on opportunities that present themselves to you that would make you feel good. If you aren't in a good mood, you would also be less inclined to greet people so positively, because your experience of frustration, regret, anxiety and general sense of lack of control over your life is going to come through in every encounter you have with other people and the world around you. If you end up yelling at people or simply expressing frustration toward them, they are likely to react to this and increase the anger or frustration you were already feeling. All of your experiences in life will only further serve to support your negative emotional state. You will be lost in yourself, justifying your own negative state of being, and creating more and more reasons to justify that negative state of being as everything that happens to you and everything that everyone does to you simply reinforces the state you're already in.

Alternatively, if you choose to focus on things that you like, you are going to be in a better mood than if you focus on things that you don't like. If you are in a better mood, you are going to be more inclined to engage in activities that you enjoy and to notice and act on opportunities that present themselves to you that would support and reinforce your positive emotional state. If you are in a better mood, you would also be more inclined to greet people with your positive energy shining through in a smile, in the words and tone with which you greet them, and in all the rest of your welcoming, overflowingly positive body language. The consequence is that you would be more inclined to get positive energy back from the people you encounter as they smile back at you and reflect back your positive emotions, thereby further reinforcing your positive state of mind. You will be much more present to the world around you instead of being lost in yourself, and you will continue to gain more reasons to be present to the world because the world will seem welcoming and positive toward you as you are welcoming and positive toward it. Your sense of control over your life will be reinforced as everything seems to go your way, giving you even more reasons to be present and appreciative and grateful for everything that you experience.

Whether you're trying to get what you want from your pet, your significant other, your friends, your coworkers, your boss, your employees, your children, your parents, random strangers, the world around you in general or your own thoughts, feelings, and instincts, the key is to focus on what you want with positive energy like gratitude and appreciation. When you notice anything that you don't want, simply notice it, acknowledge it and respond to it or redirect it where appropriate, and then return to focusing your attention and energy on that which you like and appreciate and are grateful for.

The thoughts on which you focus your energy will be reinforced so that you will come to believe them far more than you did the first time you thought them. For they will produce feelings that will incline you toward certain actions that will bring about experiences with other people and the physical world around you that will give you more reasons to think those thoughts.

Any emotion that you express and give your energy to will give you more reasons to express that emotion. Giving your energy to anger will bring more reasons to be angry. Giving your energy to sadness will bring more reasons to be sad. Giving your energy to fear will bring more reasons to be afraid. Giving your energy to peace will bring more reasons to be peaceful. Giving your energy to love will bring more reasons to be loving. Giving your energy to happiness will bring more reasons to be happy. Giving your energy to gratitude and appreciation will bring more reasons to be grateful and appreciative.

Consider that wherever you focus your attention in any moment—whatever you allow yourself to think and give your energy to, whatever you allow yourself to feel and give your energy to, whatever you allow yourself to want and give your energy to, whatever behaviors you allow yourself to engage in—will bring about more reasons in your life to focus your attention there. Everything that you allow yourself to do internally and externally in reaction or in response to anything is essentially practice for how you will think, feel, and act next time you face a similar situation.

Thus, we often build up patterns of thought, feeling, desire and behavior that can become mindless. We can come to go through life on autopilot, reacting to everything as we have reacted before and simply going through the motions, feeling that we have no control or ability to do otherwise. Once we get caught up in a positive reinforcement loop of negative patterns of mind and action, it can become difficult to get out—increasingly difficult the deeper we descend into negative patterns and have these reinforced for us. As our awareness and sense of control fades, we increasingly have trouble recognizing that, and how, we can get out of the downward spiral.

At every stage and in every moment, it is easier now to shift your attention elsewhere and break former patterns than it will be next time after you have rehearsed them again this time doing what you might have done before. Further, once you get yourself in the mode of doing what you want to do and get your life on the track you want it to be on, everything begins to support your staying on track and it becomes easier to keep going the direction you want to go. You can get caught in the positive reinforcement loop of an upward spiral, where your awareness and sense of control over your life continually grow and are reinforced by everything that happens around you. Life becomes increasingly filled with a sense of magic as you can increasingly easily trace everything that happens to a thought and feeling that you gave your attention to.

The Roads Of Life

As we're traveling the roads of life and learning how to use our internal GPS system effectively to get to places where we'd actually like to go, we encounter many other people traveling the roads of life as well. From family to friends to significant others to people we merely bump into or exchange a few words with, we have innumerable opportunities to have our own thoughts, feelings, beliefs, and ways of treating ourselves reflected back at us by other people. This is pivotal to our growth and ultimately to our learning how to use our internal GPS system effectively, for we see where our thoughts, feelings, instincts and actions, and our ways of treating our thoughts, feelings, instincts, and body, take us as we give our attention to one thing or another. We see the results of our internal goings-on in our experiences with other people and the world around us.

Early on in our travels, we are bound to take many side streets and perhaps even get on and off of several highways going different directions. We are often wandering around quite a bit before we get on the main highway of our journey toward a clearly defined destination. Once we get on the main highway, we will likely be traveling in a clear direction for an extended period of time. But before then, we are still trying to figure out where we're going.

Further, there is such a thing as the right direction or the right place for now, but not the right direction or the right place for always. In fact, there is only such a thing as the right direction and the right place for now. For even when we get on the main highway, we will eventually get off an exit, and perhaps go onto another highway going a different direction or onto a side street leading to another highway or toward our final destination. So it is definitely okay to change directions and get on different roads. And we are always moving in some form, ideally. It is necessary to our getting where we want to go. However, we do have to decide where we want to go and actually go there in order to use our GPS effectively as it guides us along the most direct routes toward the destinations on which we focus our attention.

When we are on the side streets of our lives, we are only there for so long, since the side streets are far shorter than the highways. Because of this, when we encounter people on the side streets of our lives, there has to be something that pulls us toward them and them toward us if we are to meet and learn from each other, for we are only likely to be crossing paths for a short period of time. Therefore, it is often the case that when we meet people on the side streets, especially when it comes to attraction-based relationships of any sort, there is immediate, intense attraction between us and those people. It feels magical, with sparks flying everywhere, almost fantasy-like, and somewhat ungrounded and unstable as we feel like the experience comes from the other person and we are dependent on the other person for it. And then, just as suddenly and intensely as these relationships begin, they end. Some major issue or issues come(s) up and one or both people involved feel the issue(s) is/are too much, and that's the end. We part ways as we reach the end of the side street that we were traveling together, because that's the only part of our life paths that crossed without great unfulfillment for one or both people involved that would result from changing direction to go the way of the other person rather than going our own way. Of course, sometimes people go the way of other people instead of their own way. But it is better for us to go our own way and meet the people we encounter as we travel our own journey. For then we will eventually meet the people on the main highway of our lives.

The main highway of our lives is the road on which we will likely be traveling for the largest portion of our lives. This depends, of course, on where our journey takes us, and ultimately on the destinations we set for ourselves and how direct a route we take toward them. When we meet people on the main highway of our lives, we gradually realize that they're going the same direction as we are for an extended period of time. We might pass them, and they might pass us, and we might pass them again. We might get off an exit and come back on, or they might get off an exit and come back on. But again and again we find ourselves crossing paths with them, going the same direction as they are in life, experiencing overlapping obstacles, learning overlapping lessons.

We don't need any particular magical spark between us and the people on the main highway of our lives for them to get our attention or for us to get their attention. We simply come to feel comforted by their presence—perhaps even immediately—and by the continued reassurance that their ongoing presence provides that they'll be there, that they'll be sticking around, that we'll keep encountering them again and again and that we can depend on this. Whether they're close friends or significant others, the people we meet on the main highway of our lives tend to be relative constants in our lives. We relate to them and they to us because of our overlapping struggles and lessons in life, and so we tend to understand each other. We learn from their obstacles and lessons—from seeing obstacles and lessons that look like ours, but in the different context of their lives and personalities—and they learn from ours.

We weather the storms of life together and help each other to grow through them, even if this sometimes happens through our reflecting back each other's obstacles in negative ways. We are often compelled to address the obstacles that arise with them rather than simply leaving these people behind because we keep encountering these people. So just as we cannot leave obstacles in ourselves behind but rather must address them, we can come to realize that this is true with obstacles with these people as well. In fact, the obstacles we face with them are actually reflections of the obstacles in ourselves (as all obstacles outside of us are, though here it seems more apparent that we can't avoid addressing them without encountering them over and over again with these people and within ourselves in other ways as well).

Here we face the long haul of support, challenges, and ultimately lessons and growth in forms that entail a lot of reward each time we address things in ourselves. For here we further ourselves along the main highway of our lives toward our greatest, most willfully set destinations. And we get to experience the fulfillment that comes along with this—with getting further along the path toward where we most want to go in life and toward experiencing what we most want to experience in life. For the path of the main highway is the journey of our increasingly willful shaping of our lives into the forms in which we most want to experience them.

Another Aspect Of The Paradigm

In development, first we exist, then we experience the world in the present moment, then we reflect on what is now our past experience of the present moment, then we figure out from that reflection on our past experience what might happen in the future, which leads to a greater understanding that can be brought to the next experience in the present moment in the form of greater awareness. Or, more simply: Enter existence, experience the present moment, reflect on past experience, figure out from reflection what might be to come in the future, which leads to a greater understanding and consequently greater awareness.

Notice here that the pattern begins again, or loops around to the beginning, once it ends, for the greater awareness to which this whole process leads is then brought to the next experience in the present moment. If we put this pattern even more simply, we have: Enter existence, experience, reflect, figure out, understand to form greater awareness.

Now let's identify the reverse of this pattern of development—the order of creation: First there is awareness, then we figure out what is to come in the future, then we reflect on what we've figured out in the past, then we experience in the present moment what we've figured out, and then what we've figured out exists.

Notice the way each stage of the pattern builds upon the one that came before in the order of development, and that this occurs in the order of creation as well. The result is that everything in development is built upon what we experience in the present moment, while everything in creation is built upon what we figure out is to come in the future. Or to carry it out further and more accurately to the actual beginnings of each pattern, everything in development is built upon what exists already, while everything in creation is built upon what we choose.

Part 2:
Our Relationships With Others

Let's return to the key to relationships: The way we treat ourselves sets the example for how we treat others, how we're inclined to feel treated by others, and how others actually treat us.

Considering this, we will now delve into exactly what types of relationships with ourselves we might have and the ways different people treat themselves. We will examine where we can go wrong in our relationship with ourselves and set an example that we'd rather not set about how we should be treated. We will also examine how we can turn this around and treat ourselves as we want to be treated and feel treated by others and the world around us.

In this part of the book, we will explore different personality types and aspects of personality. This will provide you a window into yourself and the way you function internally, as well as how you can function more optimally and build the relationship with yourself that you'd ideally want to have, which will lead to building the relationships with others that you'd ideally want to have in terms of the way you treat them and the way they treat you. This will also provide you a window into others and the way they function internally so that you can better understand your dynamics with them, their dynamics with you, and their dynamics with other people as well.

You'll understand better why you've gotten along really well with certain people and not so well with others, why you've been attracted to certain people and why you haven't been attracted to others, why certain relationships have gone well and why other relationships haven't gone well. You'll become aware of why you face the obstacles that you experience in your relationships and you'll learn to see these obstacles as opportunities for growth. As you learn from the challenges you face with others, you eliminate these obstacles and fill your life with increasingly deeply fulfilling relationships—with yourself, the other people in your life, and every other aspect of the world around you.

The aspects of personality contained in this part of the book will help you more fully to step into other people's internal shoes and understand why they do what they do and say what they say toward you and otherwise. Through understanding others better, you will come to understand yourself better, and through understanding yourself better, you will come to understand others better. The comparison and contrast between you and others will likely be eye-opening for you.

But don't just take my word for it. Read on and find out for yourself.

Another Aspect Of The Paradigm

In development, first we exist, then we desire to preserve or maintain our existence, then we desire to fit in with others, then we desire to connect with other individuals, and then we become aware.

To break this down and explain each stage further: First, we exist. Then, since we exist, we seek to preserve or maintain our existence (and that of family members on whom we depend and/or who depend on us for material resources) by acquiring the appropriate environment and resources to do so; we need food, shelter, clothing, money to buy these things, a career to get this money, the right temperature, cleanliness of body and environment, physical health, etc. Then we desire to fit in with others in existence (as a group of friends or a community) ultimately in order to preserve our existence better, because if we belong and contribute our resources to a group and look out for the group, the group might aid us in our existence by looking out for us. Then we desire to connect with other individuals in existence (as close friends and/or a significant other) in order to fit in better and ultimately in order to preserve our existence better, because if we connect with another individual or other individuals and look out for him or her or them, he or she or they might aid us in our existence by looking out for us. And then we become aware of something more than this. Notice that each stage builds upon the previous one.

Now for the reverse of this order—the order of creation: First, we are aware, then we seek to connect, then we seek to belong, then we seek to preserve, and then we exist. There are a bunch of gaps to fill in here when it comes to the order of creation: What are we aware of at first? What do we seek to connect with? What do we seek to belong to? What do we seek to preserve? What does it mean that we exist only in the end of this process?

To fill in what seem to be the answers based on the pattern: First we are aware of ourselves, then we seek to connect with ourselves, then we seek to allow all parts of ourselves to belong within and contribute to us in order better to enable every part of ourselves to connect with us, then we seek to preserve the existence of all parts of ourselves so that all parts of us might exist in order to connect with us, and then we truly exist.

Notice here, again, that each stage builds upon the previous one. In this case, the result is that every stage in development is ultimately for the sake of the preservation or maintenance of our existence in this world, while every stage in creation is ultimately for the sake of connection with ourselves. Or to carry it out further and more accurately to the actual beginnings of each pattern, everything in development has the aim of furthering existence, while everything in creation has the aim of furthering awareness.

The Paradigm Of Development And Personality

All of development—of everyone and everything within this world—follows the same basic paradigm. First there is something, then there are instincts, then feelings, then thoughts, then choice. First there is existence, then there is experience in the present, then reflection on the past, then figuring out about the future, leading to a greater understanding and ultimately greater awareness. First there is something, then there is the desire to maintain existence, then there is the desire to belong, then there is the desire to connect, and then there is self-aware choice.

All of creation—the shaping of our world from a place of willful awareness—follows the reverse of the paradigm of development, for all development is actually just the development of the world's awareness of the process by which it is brought into being as it is.

These are the keys to understanding various aspects of personality, for every aspect of personality, like everything else in this world, is actually just the result of our getting fixated, or stuck, on some stage in the process of development. If we become aware of what we are getting stuck on and in what ways this expresses itself, we can let go of this and move on to express the true role of the stage on which we've gotten stuck in the context of the full paradigm of creation, in the context of the natural flow of things from one to the next.

In other words, rather than being lost within ourselves and losing sight of our context in the world with regard to our relationships with everyone and everything else, we can come to interact with others from a place of illumination of what is within and what is outside of us. We can grow to see others more clearly as they are, rather than only in relation to our own self-interested motives. We can come to interact with others from a place of non-attachment, rather than needing something from them. This is possible because we can come to recognize everything we want as already existing within ourselves, and when we recognize this, we end up getting everything we want in our relationships with others as well.

The Golden Rule

"Do unto others as you would have them do unto you." "Love thy neighbor as thyself." "Do not do that which is hateful unto you unto your neighbor." "Treat others as you would have them treat you."

Cutting to the core of how to apply this: "Treat yourself as you want to be treated." When you do this, the result is that you treat others they way they want to be treated, and they treat you the way you want to be treated.

Another Aspect Of The Paradigm

First we exist, then we simply allow experiences to express themselves through us, then we receive experiences from the world and allow them to gestate within us until we come up with something different from what we've received, then we come up with new experiences on our own and share them with the world, and then there is choice. More simply, first there's something, then there's allowing, then there's receiving, then there's sharing, and then there's choice.

Here's another way to look at this pattern: First there is existence, then there is child, then there is female, then there is male, and then there is choice. (Biologically, we actually do all begin more female than male, at least structurally, very early in our development in the womb, and then those of us who are males, with the appropriate genetic blueprints and so forth to dictate this, develop structurally as males afterward.)

Here it is quite obvious how the order of development is opposite the order of creation, and so in the order of creation, first there is choice, then there is the male who shares biologically, then there is the female who receives biologically and allows this to gestate and manifests within herself something different from what she's received, then there is the child who allows this interaction to take place through itself, and then something exists (a new perspective on the world exists).

There is a lot more in this pattern to explore and consider, e.g. the idea of a child developing to become more female and stopping there or moving on to become more male in various ways—more receiving and stopping there or moving on to become more sharing, more like its mother and stopping there or moving on to become more like its father, etc. As we examine different aspects of personality, we will be exploring more of what it means to stop at one stage in the paradigm of development and not move on.

For now, just remember what we saw with the previous patterns of the paradigm: All development follows a cyclical pattern, whereby when we get to the end, we return to the beginning, and so there is no better or worse since in some sense there is no beginning and no end; there is just where we are. For example, first we exist, then we experience in the present, then we reflect on the past, then we figure out about the future, which leads to a greater understanding that can be brought to the next experience in the present moment in the form of greater awareness, beginning the pattern of development again. There is no point in this process of becoming more aware where it is truly better to be, for every point in the process is a necessary part of the evolution of awareness. This could all be explored further, but this is sufficient for now.

The Dynamics Within Each Of Us That Shape Our Experiences

Within every person, there is a sharing aspect, a receiving aspect, and an allowing aspect. In other words, within every person, there is a male aspect, a female aspect, and a child aspect.

This will be better understood as we go through the internal functioning of different aspects of personality. But for now, keep this in mind: Within every person, there are three aspects of the self engaged in interaction with each other and thereby setting the paradigm for the dynamics of the interactions this person will face with other people and everything else.

When not greatly healthy due to being under or having been under stress for an extended period of time, the three aspects of self are as follows: There is a male, sharing, imposing, controlling, forceful, micromanaging, directing-attention-toward-others aspect. There is a female, receiving, reactive, rebellious, judgmental, critical, dismissive, wanting-attention aspect. And there is a child, allowing aspect that tries to harmonize with the male and female aspects by tuning itself out and simply allowing the male and female aspects to manifest through itself.

In other words: We control ourselves, we impose limiting beliefs and ideas upon ourselves, we micromanage ourselves, we tell ourselves that we're here for others and that we shouldn't need our own attention and so we ignore ourselves. We consequently feel controlled by ourselves and we react to and rebel against, and judge, criticize, and dismiss ourselves, and we put a lot of energy into trying to get our own attention. And we tune ourselves out because there's too much disharmony within us during all of this.

When we have these dynamics in ourselves, we feel imposed upon, controlled, and ignored by people; judged, criticized, and dismissed by people; and tuned out by people. It may be different people or the same people at different times, but the dynamics that exist within us will unavoidably be reflected in the dynamics that exist between us and other people. Meanwhile, because we are trying to tune out the conflicts within ourselves, we are tuned out and on autopilot, going through the motions of life mindlessly, reactively, and continually unfulfilled when we have these dynamics in ourselves. We can't truly be present to other people and the world around us because we are too busy using our energy to avoid being present to our own thoughts, feelings, and instincts as they keep trying to speak up and let us know what we are doing to ourselves. So our interactions with other people and the world around us are really reactions to all the issues we are already sensitive to due to our own internal dynamics.

When healthy, due to being under little to no stress or dealing with stress well for an extended period of time, these three aspects of the self operate in their healthy versions and set a positive paradigm for the dynamics of the interactions this person will face with other people and everything else. The key difference when healthy comes from the presence of awareness.

In the light of awareness, the male, sharing aspect begins to guide itself and guide and help the female aspect in accordance with the wants of the female aspect. In the light of awareness, the female, receiving aspect begins to acknowledge and accept itself. And in the light of awareness, the child, allowing aspect begins to get in touch with itself and become harmonious within itself so it can effectively harmonize with the male and female aspects. The end result is that all three aspects of self harmonize with one another and unite in a common purpose and aim without any hierarchy of different levels, without imposition or control but only gentle help and guidance, without dismissal or judgment but only positive attention and acceptance, without dissociation or tuning out but only acknowledgement and presence.

In other words: We truly guide, help, and encourage ourselves with positive, expansive beliefs and ideas, with acknowledgement of, and attention to, our own needs. We truly acknowledge, listen to, and accept ourselves, and we pay attention to ourselves and therefore get our own full attention. And we truly get in touch with, and are present to, ourselves.

With such dynamics in ourselves, we feel guided, supported, and truly helped by people; acknowledged and accepted by people; and attended to by, validated by, and in harmony with people. We are present to ourselves, our lives, and the people and the world around us with full awareness and attention.

Male, Female, and Child

Male (Sharing Experience)

You are inclined to disconnect from yourself, ignore your own needs, and expect a lot of yourself as you try to come up with ways and things you can provide. You want to challenge, protect, help, and be useful, especially in your relationships. You're inclined to get angry and controlling and to feel vulnerable as you try to be tough and strong and protect others, to feel unappreciated and regretful about how you could have done more as you try to be helpful and caring to others, and to overwhelm yourself and feel incapable and useless as you try to figure out ways you can be useful to others, all especially in your relationships.

You are like the sun in relation to the earth. You want to be continually shining upon and providing for your partner. You want to be strong, loving, and capable, and to be providing physical and material protection, tangible help, and useful guidance. You get stressed when you ignore your own needs too greatly in your efforts to focus on your partner (and family and others) and so don't have your needs attended to by anyone. When you're stressed, you withdraw into yourself and need time and space to yourself as you try to figure out how you can keep providing when you feel you've given all you have and have nothing left to provide. You're not inclined to be open to receiving protection, help, or guidance from your partner or others because, being like the sun in relation to the earth, you feel it's up to you to be the source of these things for you and for your partner and others.

The key to shifting your relationships: The key is to notice when you are trying to be protective, helpful, and useful by imposing your own strong instincts, loving feelings, and capable thoughts on others rather than directing your protection, help, and useful guidance toward yourself. If you don't take care of your own needs and allow yourself to be in control, to protect and appreciate yourself, and to act on your own guidance, then no one will allow you to be in control, and no one will protect or appreciate you or listen to and act on your guidance. The result is that your protection, help, and usefulness will come from the ulterior motive of needing something in return, since your needs aren't being met by you. When you aren't listening to your own needs, you can't hear your partner's needs either, because your own needs take up your attention when they aren't being met. So when you don't listen to your own needs, you end up having to impose *your* idea of protection, help, and useful advice on your partner, rather than actually hearing what your partner wants, feels, and thinks, and protecting, helping, and advising based on what would be deemed protective, helpful, and useful by your partner.

If you are trying to protect, help, or be useful based on what you want, feel, or think, then pause and take a moment to breathe and listen to yourself and consider how your protection, help, and advice might be applied to yourself. Also, consider what your partner or other person might actually want, feel, or think. If you impose your own wants, feelings, and thoughts on your partner or other person, you won't get the results you want; you won't be in control, successfully protective, protected, helpful, appreciated, or useful.

Instead, pay attention and listen to your partner or other person, ask questions about what she/he wants, feels, and thinks, acknowledge her/his answers, be they in spoken words, facial expressions, other body language, actions, or other forms, and: Protect your partner or other person by challenging him/her to do what she/he actually wants to do. Help your partner or other person in ways that she/he actually feels would be helpful to her/him. Advise and guide your partner or other person based on her/his own understanding, in ways that she/he actually thinks your advise, guidance, and input would be useful to her/him.

Even if you want, feel, or think differently, if you simply impose what you want, feel, or think on her/him, it will not be received, and so you will not get the results you want. You will simply be putting a lot more energy into the situation without getting favorable results that correspond with the amount of energy you're putting in.

Bottom line: If you impose yourself on the other person, your efforts won't be interpreted as protective, helpful, or useful. If you protect, help, and advise where it is wanted, which begins with applying your protection, help, and advice to yourself and thereby meeting your own needs first, your efforts will be interpreted as protective in positive ways, helpful, and useful, and you will be appreciated for them.

The Golden Rule applied: Allow your partner or other person to challenge, protect, help, and be useful to you, and you will be able to challenge, protect, help, and be useful to her/him.

This works because then you will be protected and challenged rather than vulnerable to retaliation against your imposed and undesired protection, you will have help and your needs will be met rather than you simply denying that you have needs, and you will be able to focus on what you're capable of doing rather than overwhelming yourself by trying to do everything yourself. The result is that you'll be able to challenge, protect, help, and be useful to your partner or other person in ways that are welcome and appreciated in a loving and balanced, give-and-take relationship.

How to begin applying the Golden Rule: Protect yourself with your own strong instincts, help yourself with your own loving feelings, and be useful to yourself with your own capable thoughts. This way you will already be making yourself feel in control, powerful and protected, appreciated and helpful, competent and useful, and so you will be more open to receiving acknowledgement of your strength, love, and competence, as well as to receiving protection, appreciation, and guidance, from your partner and other people.

What you're attracted to in others: You're attracted to people with whom you can share your thoughts, feelings, and instincts, and who will receive and experience these as useful, helpful, and protective and thereby make you feel capable, loving, and strong.

Female (Receiving Experience)

You are inclined to replay certain experiences you have (focusing on the ways that you haven't been attended to and provided for) and dismiss, judge, and criticize other experiences you have (where you *have* been attended to and provided for). You want perfection, completion, importance, and fulfillment, especially in your relationships. You're inclined to look for things that are imperfect, bad, or wrong, wanting to be the one who's right; replay emotional experiences that make you feel that you are lacking in attention in comparison to others in search of how you are different, special, and significant; and seek out experiences that make you unhappy and unfulfilled in attempts to avoid being trapped by them so that you can be happy.

You are like the earth in relation to the sun. You want to be continually shined upon and provided for by your partner so that you can come up with something different from what you've received—so that you can give forth new life with the protection, help, and guidance that your partner shines upon you. You want to be right, good, perfect, complete, important, special, excited, happy, and fulfilled in relation to your partner. When you're stressed, you want to be reassured that your partner is there to shine attention upon you and provide for you, that you are right, good, perfect, important, and special to your partner, so that you can feel complete and fulfilled with your partner.

The key to shifting your relationships: The key is to notice when you are replaying instincts, feelings, and thoughts of you, your experiences, and other things not being right, good, perfect, complete, important, special, happy, and/or fulfilled. When you are replaying experiences—namely negative instincts, feelings, and thoughts—you are also dismissing other experiences—namely positive instincts, feelings, and thoughts. It is your judging, criticizing, dismissing, rejecting, and distracting yourself and running away from your own positive instincts, feelings, and thoughts that sets the example for your already feeling and being made to feel judged, criticized, dismissed, and rejected by your partner, and like your partner is distracting him/herself from you or running away from you. It is your not accepting, attending to, listening to, understanding, and taking seriously your own positive instincts, feelings, and thoughts that sets the example for how you feel and how you will be made to feel by your partner and others.

So the key is to accept, attend to, listen to, and take seriously your own positive instincts, feelings, and thoughts. For then you will already feel accepted, attended to, listened to, taken seriously, and as though you are getting the attention that you are deserving and worthy of, and you will be setting the example for how you truly want to be treated by your partner and others. The result is that you will be far more likely actually to be treated this way and to feel that you are being treated this way by your partner and others.

When you notice yourself replaying negative instincts, feelings, or thoughts, getting caught up in your internal experiences, take some time to breathe and redirect your attention to what you are experiencing through your physical senses in the present moment. Listen to the instincts, feelings, and thoughts that come up, hear them, acknowledge them, respond kindly to them and redirect them toward something more positive if appropriate. Then let them go and redirect your attention back to what you are seeing, hearing, tasting, smelling, or touching in that moment. Be present and notice when your attention wanders. In those cases, acknowledge and accept that your attention has wandered, listen to where your attention has wandered to, respond to the instincts, feelings, and thoughts that have come up, and redirect your attention back to the present moment so that any other instincts, feelings, and thoughts that want your attention can get it and be heard and acknowledged by you.

The Golden Rule applied: Accept and treat your partner and others as right, good, perfect, complete, important, special, exciting, fun, and fulfilling, and your partner and others will accept and treat you as right, good, perfect, complete, important, special, exciting, fun, and fulfilling. Allow your partner and others to be right and correct you, to express himself/herself/themselves, to be heard, to matter, and to be attended to and taken seriously, and your partner and others will allow you to be right and correct him/her/them, to express yourself, to be heard, to matter, and to be attended to and taken seriously.

This works because if you allow your partner and others to be right, to be heard, to be important, and to be taken seriously, he/she/they will be far more likely to listen to you when you try to correct him/her/them or express your instincts, feelings, and thoughts. When you give your partner your full attention, you will be far more likely to get his/her full attention in return, because he/she will already have had the opportunity to express him/herself and so he/she will be more able and willing to give you his/her full attention rather than being distracted by what he/she still wants to say. When you make your partner feel listened to, he/she will be much more likely to be willing and even eager to listen to you, too—if only to encourage your continuing to listen to him/her when he/she wants to be heard as well. This way, you set the example for how you actually want to be treated—you give what you want to get back—and the result is that you'll have more positive attention and fulfillment in your relationship.

How to begin applying the Golden Rule: Accept your own instincts as good and right, listen to and treat your own feelings as important, and take your own thoughts seriously. This way you will already be making yourself feel accepted, listened to, and taken seriously, and so you will be more open to experiencing your partner as accepting you, listening to you, and taking you seriously. Rather than discouraging him/her from trying to accept you, listen to you, and take you seriously by not acknowledging and appreciating his/her efforts to do so, you will be more likely to notice, acknowledge, and encourage and positively reinforce the positive attention that you actually want from him/her. You will, thereby, ensure that you'll get more positive attention from your partner.

What you're attracted to in others: You're attracted to people who give you positive attention and thereby make you feel right, good, perfect, complete, important, special, excited, happy, and fulfilled.

Child (Allowing Experience)

You are inclined to dissociate from and tune out your own experiences because you feel that your experiences are not grounded in reality. You want harmony, value, security, stability, and guidance, especially in your environment growing up and in your upbringing with parents, teachers, etc. You're inclined to do what others (parents, teachers, friends, etc.) want you to do in order to keep the peace, be what others want you to be in order to have value to them, and make decisions that others would want you to make in order to maintain their security and guidance.

In the relationship between the sun and the earth, you are like a tree that grows out of the soil of the earth with the energy and direction of the sunshine. You are the product of the interaction, and you are inclined to tune out your own experiences and allow the instincts, feelings, and thoughts of your parents to be expressed through your actions, who you are, and the decisions you make.

The key to shifting your relationships: The key is to notice when you are dissociating from and tuning out your own instincts, feelings, and thoughts in an effort to maintain peace and harmony, meet other people's (parents, teachers, etc.) expectations, and maintain the security and guidance of other people (parents, teachers, etc.). When you are tuning out your own experiences rather than being present to them, you make yourself feel as though asserting your own instincts would cause conflict, as though being true to your own feelings would make you look bad to and disappoint others, and as though your own thoughts are ungrounded, unstable, and untrustworthy sources of guidance that would lead you to make decisions that would alienate your supporters.

You try to do what other people want you to do, be what other people feel you should be, and make the decisions that other people think you should make. And other people confirm the lack of validity of your own experiences for you by following your example and tuning out your experiences as well. But as you learn to attend to, be present to, and acknowledge your own experiences instead of tuning them out, you can learn to find harmony in your own instincts, value in your own feelings, and trustworthiness in your own thoughts, and other people follow your example.

The Golden Rule applied: Be assertive, passionate, and decisive so you are clear to other people what you want, what you feel, and what you think. This way they can accommodate you to keep the peace, meet your expectations, and be dependable sources of guidance to you. As a result, they will be clear to you what they want, what they feel, and what they think, and you will be able to accommodate them to maintain peace, meet their expectations, and be dependable to them. Assert and act on your own instincts, be true to your own feelings, and make decisions in accordance with your own thinking, and other people will assert and act on their own instincts, be true to their own feelings, and make decisions in accordance with their own thinking, and the result will be harmony, value, and dependability where they really count all around.

This works because when you listen to and express what you want, feel, and think, you give permission to others to listen to and express what they want, feel, and think also. By being present to other people with peace, passion, and trust, you bring other people to be more present to you with peace, passion, and trust as well, and the result is that you and the people around you experience harmony, genuineness, and security. You are much more present, harmonious, valuable, and dependable to others when you are present to and expressive of your own instincts, feelings, and thoughts, and so then others reflect this and are much more present, harmonious, valuable, and dependable to you, too. Following your example, they do what they want, feel, and think rather than trying to live in accordance with your and other people's wants, feelings, and thoughts and tuning out their own.

When you act in accordance with your own instincts, feelings, and thoughts, rather than other people's, you will grow to find harmony, value, and trust in your instincts, feelings, and thoughts and bring your life into harmony with them. The result is that you will be a force of peace to other people, be genuinely you and valuable to others as you, and be dependable and trustworthy to others. Then other people around you will bring their lives into harmony with their own instincts, be valuable as themselves, and be trustworthy to others and to you.

How to begin applying the Golden Rule: Tune into your own assertive instincts, passionate feelings, and decisive thoughts, and allow them to be manifested through yourself. In other words, find harmony in your own instincts, value in your own feelings, and trustworthiness in your own thoughts enough to assert, express, and make decisions based on your own instincts, feelings, and thoughts rather than other people's. This way you will already be making yourself feel like you have harmony, value, and security within yourself, and so you will be more open to tuning peacefully, authentically, and securely into the harmony, true value, and trustworthiness of other people (and things) as well.

What you're attracted to in others: You're attracted to people who are assertive in their instincts, passionate in their expression of feeling, and decisive in their thinking, because then you have assertive instincts, passionate feelings, and decisive thoughts to act on, be true to, and make decisions in accordance with. In the same vein, you are attracted to people who act on what they want, have clear expectations of you, and are dependable sources of guidance, because then you can act based on their instincts, feelings, and thoughts and maintain harmony with them, meet their expectations, and maintain their security in your life.

Development And Creation Forms

In the order of development: As soon as we exist, we are child, allowing, harmonizing and tuning out. Then we become more female, receiving, reacting, criticizing, and differentiating. Then we become more male, disconnecting, ignoring, sharing, initiating, controlling and creating. And then we become aware.

In the order of creation: As soon as we become aware, we are male, connecting, attending, sharing, initiating, guiding and creating. Then we become female, receiving, accepting, responding, and differentiating. Then we become child, allowing, harmonizing, and tuning in. And then we truly exist.

Myers-Briggs Personality Dimensions

There are four Myers-Briggs personality dimensions, with two directions we can lean in on each dimension: inward-oriented vs. outward-oriented, conceptual vs. practical, rational vs. empathetic, and structured vs. flexible.

Note that the Myers-Briggs personality dimensions follow the male-female duality, where there are two directions on each dimension—one related to the male, initiating, creating and sharing, controlling/micromanaging (when stressed) or attentive/guiding (when not stressed) paradigm, and one related to the female, differentiating, receiving and expressing, reactive/rebelling/attention-seeking (when stressed) or responding (when not stressed) paradigm. The directions for each dimension are listed here in the order of male followed by female so as to be consistent with the creative order followed by the listing of all other personality aspects here.

As with every other aspect of personality and everything else, we all have all of these ways of operating within us, and it is just that we identify with and prioritize one direction over the other on each dimension. Further, as with every other manifestation of the paradigm of creation, it doesn't matter whether you are male or female in terms of which direction on any dimension you identify with primarily.

Where We Go For Energy: Sharing Energy (Inward-Oriented) Vs. Receiving Energy (Outward-Oriented)

Sharing Energy – Inward-Oriented (Introverted)

You look inward for energy. You plug into yourself for energy and need time to recharge away from outside stimulation. You live with your attention mainly on your own internal world.

You want to come up with new, subtle and refreshing energy to share with others and the world around you.

When you're stressed: You feel overstimulated, like everything is too much, and you withdraw into your own internal world and introspection away from any and all outside stimulation.

How you're perceived in a relationship: When you're stressed, you can come across as strangely quiet, private, and withdrawn, especially to outward-oriented people.

What you need to learn in order to shift your relationships: There must be a balance between looking inward for energy and looking outward for energy. You need to learn to be present to what's going on outside you and quiet down your internal world so that you are not so overstimulated by the stimulation coming from outside you when it piles on top of the stimulation coming from within.

Compatibility in a romantic relationship: You're inclined to be attracted to people who are outward-oriented because opposites attract, and you complement each other well when you're both in a good enough place to learn from the other person's way of approaching things. You're inclined to relate more to people who are inward-oriented like you.

Receiving Energy – Outward-Oriented (Extraverted)

You look outward for energy. You plug into the outside world for energy and seek out stimulation outside yourself. You live with your attention mainly on the outside world.

You want to receive energy from others and the world around you and come up with a different energy (more exciting, more stimulating) from what you've received.

When you're stressed: You feel deprived of stimulation and engage with the outside world in search of almost constant stimulation.

How you're perceived in a relationship: When you're stressed, you can come across as overbearing, draining, and simply too much, especially to inward-oriented people.

What you need to learn in order to shift your relationships: There must be a balance between looking outward for energy and looking inward for energy. You need to learn to be present to what's going on inside you and build up your internal world so that you are not so in need of stimulation coming from outside you as your sole source of energy.

Compatibility in a romantic relationship: You're inclined to be attracted to people who are inward-oriented because opposites attract, and you complement each other well when you're both in a good enough place to learn from the other person's way of approaching things. You're inclined to relate more to people who are outward-oriented like you.

Development And Creation Forms

In the order of development: The female, receiving, reactive part of us isn't getting any attention from the male part of us and so goes outward in search of attention, stimulation, and energy. The male, sharing, creative part of us isn't in touch with his Source and Creator nature or attentive to the female part of us and so withdraws and goes inward in an attempt to come up with things to share so he can be a source of stimulation and energy for himself and for the female part of us. The result is a desire or a sense of need to look only outward or only inward, depending on which part of us we most identify with, in search of energy.

In the order of creation: The male, sharing, creative part of us is in touch with his infinite Source and Creator nature and attentive to the female part of us and so truly is a source of stimulation and energy for himself and for the female part of us, able to attend to her consistently without effort or withdrawing inward. The female, receiving part of us is getting all the attention, stimulation, and energy she wants and needs from the male part of us and so doesn't need to go outward in search of these things. The result is a lack of any desire or sense of need to look only outward or only inward in search of energy because we are fulfilled with all the energy we want wherever we go. We can, therefore, choose willfully and in a balanced way where we wish to spend our time and plug in for energy.

How We Process The World And Search For Meaning: Sharing Meaning (Conceptual) Vs. Receiving Meaning (Actual)

Sharing Meaning – Conceptual (Intuitive)

You want to think about and discuss conceptual, abstract things, such as theories and ideas that you can generalize from experience as you imagine what could be that hasn't been and isn't already. You are big-picture-oriented, preferring to discuss possibilities rather than the details of daily life.

You want to come up with new, conceptual and profound meaning to share with others and the world around you.

When you're stressed: You get lost in the brainstorming of ideas and have trouble actualizing them in physical reality. You feel uncomfortable with details and mundane, daily life routines.

How you're perceived in a relationship: When you're stressed, you can come across as overly abstract, impractical, and airy, especially to actual people.

What you need to learn in order to shift your relationships: There must be a balance between attending to the conceptual big-picture ideas of life and attending to the actual details of life. You need to learn to think inside the box of your past and present experiences and consider what has been done before and how you could actualize your ideas within this framework rather than merely living in the brainstorming stage and coming up with completely new ideas that have no groundedness in reality.

Compatibility in a romantic relationship: You're inclined to be attracted to people who are actual because opposites attract, and you complement each other when you're both in a good enough place to learn from the other person's way of approaching things. However, you're inclined to relate significantly more to, and feel far more understood by, people who are conceptual like you.

Receiving Meaning – Actual (Sensing)

You want to think about and discuss concrete, real things, such as actual people and actual events that you can experience with your physical senses in the present and past. You are detail-oriented, preferring to discuss tangible examples and practical approaches.

You want to receive meaning from others and the world around you and come up with a different meaning (more concrete, more tangible) from what you've received.

When you're stressed: You get lost in the details of life and have trouble seeing the big picture. You feel uncomfortable in the realm of abstract ideas.

How you're perceived in a relationship: When you're stressed, you can come across as overly concrete, mundane, and superficial, especially to conceptual people.

What you need to learn in order to shift your relationships: There must be a balance between attending to the actual details of life and attending to the conceptual big-picture ideas of life. You need to learn to think outside the box of your past and present experiences and consider what could be rather than merely sticking with the way things have been and have been done up to this point.

Compatibility in a romantic relationship: You're inclined to be attracted to people who are conceptual because opposites attract, and you complement each other when you're both in a good enough place to learn from the other person's way of approaching things. However, you're inclined to relate significantly more to, and feel far more like you're on the same page as, people who are actual like you.

Development And Creation Forms

In the order of development: The female, receiving, reactive part of us isn't getting any big-picture meaning or purpose from the male part of us and so goes to the details of actual present and past experiences in search of some kind of meaning or purpose. The male, sharing, creative part of us isn't in touch with his Source and Creator nature or attentive to the past-and-present-actuality perspective of the female part of us and so actively tries to conceive of and find meaning and purpose in the bigger picture of what could be in an attempt to be a source of these things for himself and for the female part of us. The result is a desire or a sense of need to look solely to the details of actual life or solely to big-picture concepts about what could be, depending on which part of us we most identify with, in search of meaning and purpose.

In the order of creation: The male, sharing, creative part of us is in touch with his Source and Creator nature and attentive to the past-and-present-actuality perspective of the female part of us and so truly is a source of big-picture, conceptual meaning and purpose for himself and for the female part of us. The female, receiving part of us is getting all the meaning and purpose she wants and needs from the male part of us and so doesn't need to go to the details of actual present and past experiences in search of these things. The result is a lack of any desire or sense of need to look solely to the details of actual life or solely to big-picture concepts about what could be in search of meaning and purpose because we have all the sense of meaning and purpose we want. We can, therefore, choose willfully and in a balanced way how we wish to process the world and where we wish to find (and how we wish to create) meaning and purpose in any moment.

How We Make Decisions: Sharing Guidance (Rational) Vs. Receiving Guidance (Empathetic)

Sharing Guidance – Rational (Thinking)

You make decisions based on what makes sense, what's rational, and what's logical to you. You try to be rational and objective in your decision-making. You want to discuss topics removed from human experience, such as facts (if concrete) or theories (if conceptual).

You want to come up with new, rational and objective guidance to share with others and the world around you.

When you're stressed: You try so hard to be objective and rational that you actually end up being totally unobjective and irrational.

How you're perceived in a relationship: When you're stressed, you can come across as cold, insensitive, and unempathetic, especially to empathetic people.

What you need to learn in order to shift your relationships: There must be a balance between being rational and being empathetic. You need to learn that in order to be truly rational and objective, you have to consider other people's feelings in your assessments and decision-making. If you disregard other people's feelings, you will inherently be irrational and unobjective. This is because if you don't make decisions with any sensitivity to other people's feelings due to your trying to be objective, you will be missing key factors that must be considered in order actually to be objective.

Compatibility in a romantic relationship: You're inclined to be attracted to people who are empathetic because opposites attract, and you complement each other well when you're both in a good enough place to learn from the other person's way of approaching things. You're inclined to relate more to people who are rational like you.

Receiving Guidance – Empathetic (Feeling)

You make decisions based on how they would make other people feel. You try to be empathetic and sensitive to other people's feelings and are subjective in your decision-making. You want to discuss human experience, such as your and other people's daily life experiences and how they made you and other people feel.

You want to receive guidance from others and the world around you and come up with different guidance (more empathetic, more sensitive) from what you've received.

When you're stressed: You try so hard to be empathetic to other people's feelings that you actually end up totally disregarding other people's feelings.

How you're perceived in a relationship: When you're stressed, you can come across as unobjective, irrational, and illogical, especially to rational people.

What you need to learn in order to shift your relationships: There must be a balance between being empathetic and being rational. You need to learn that in order to be truly empathetic and sensitive to other people's feelings, you have to consider what might make sense or be the rational thing for you to do in your assessments and decision-making. If you disregard what makes sense and is rational for you to do in the short run, you will very likely end up insensitive to other people's feelings—if not in the short run, then in the long run. This is because if you don't make decisions that make sense and are good for you due to your trying to be sensitive to other people's feelings, you will likely end up upset with others and inclined to disregard their feelings.

Compatibility in a romantic relationship: You're inclined to be attracted to people who are rational because opposites attract, and you complement each other well when you're both in a good enough place to learn from the other person's way of approaching things. You're inclined to relate more to people who are empathetic like you.

Development And Creation Forms

In the order of development: The female, receiving, reactive part of us isn't getting any guidance in decision-making from the male part of us that considers her emotions rather than simply telling her what to do, and so she tries to make decisions from her own subjective perspective, attempting to consider the feelings of others but instead often disregarding them in reaction to her feeling disregarded. The male, sharing, creative part of us isn't in touch with his Source and Creator nature or attentive or sensitive to the emotional, subjective perspective of the female part of us and so attempts to make objective, logical, rational decisions for himself and for the female part of us that can't ever truly be objective because they disregard the emotions of the female part of us. The result is a desire or a sense of need to look solely to others' emotions and subjectivity or solely to logic and attempted objectivity, depending on which part of us we most identify with, to try to gain clarity about what decisions to make.

In the order of creation: The male, sharing, creative part of us is in touch with his Source and Creator nature and attentive and sensitive to the emotional, subjective perspective of the female part of us and so truly is a source of objective, rational guidance for himself and for the female part of us. The female, receiving part of us is getting all the empathetic and objective guidance she wants and needs from the male part of us and so is genuinely sensitive to the feelings of others. The result is a lack of any desire or sense of need to look solely to others' emotions and subjectivity or solely to logic and attempted objectivity in search of guidance in our decision-making because we have all the sense of clarity we want. We can, therefore, choose willfully and in a balanced way how we wish to make our decisions.

How We Approach The World And Determine Direction: Sharing Direction (Structured) Vs. Receiving Direction (Flexible)

Sharing Direction – Structured (Judging)

You want to structure your time and surrounding space. You want to plan things out and consider the consequences of actions, and you get closure from having an idea of what's going to happen. You want to do one thing at a time and follow through before moving on to the next thing. You want to do work first, and leave relaxation and fun until after work is finished.

You want to come up with new, planned and structured direction to share with others and the world around you.

When you're stressed: You can become inflexible about planning and structuring things and sticking to the plan, frustrated when things don't go according to your plans, and anxious and fearful about the possible negative consequences of actions.

How you're perceived in a relationship: When you're stressed, you can come across as overly serious, rigid, and controlling, especially to flexible people.

What you need to learn in order to shift your relationships: There must be a balance between being structured and being flexible. You need to learn to be more flexible and spontaneous. You should still set intentions for what you'd like to have happen, but then you should work on being more open and flexible along the way so that if things don't go according to plan, it's okay, and you can relax and recognize and remind yourself that they'll work out another way. You also need to learn to let up on your need to control and structure things in general, and remind yourself to relax and trust that things will work out all right somehow.

Compatibility in a romantic relationship: You're inclined to be attracted to people who are flexible because opposites attract, and you complement each other well when you're both in a good enough place to learn from the other person's way of approaching things. You're inclined to relate more to people who are structured like you.

Receiving Direction – Flexible (Perceiving)

You want to keep your time and surrounding space flexible. You want to do spontaneously whatever you think and feel like doing in the moment, and you want to keep your options open until the last minute. You want to start many things at once and not necessarily follow through with them. You want to relax and have fun, and leave work until later.

You want to receive direction from others and the world around you and come up with a different direction (more spontaneous, more flexible) from what you've received.

When you're stressed: You can have trouble following through with and finishing projects and plans as you just do whatever you think and feel like in the moment and don't get anywhere.

How you're perceived in a relationship: When you're stressed, you can come across as irresponsible, unreliable, and undependable, especially to structured people.

What you need to learn in order to shift your relationships: There must be a balance between being flexible and being structured. You need to learn to be more structured and plan things out. You should remind yourself to set some kind of intentions for what you'd like to have happen so that things actually happen, but then still be open and flexible along the way so that if things don't go according to plan, it's okay, and you recognize that they'll work out another way. You also need to learn not to do whatever you think and feel like in the moment all the time, and remind yourself to look ahead a bit and consider the consequences of your actions.

Compatibility in a romantic relationship: You're inclined to be attracted to people who are structured because opposites attract, and you complement each other well when you're both in a good enough place to learn from the other person's way of approaching things. You're inclined to relate more to people who are flexible like you.

Development And Creation Forms

In the order of development: The female, receiving, reactive part of us isn't getting any direction from the male part of us and so goes to her reactive thoughts, feelings, and instincts in the moment in search of some kind of direction. The male, sharing, creative part of us isn't in touch with his Source and Creator nature or attentive to the flexible, open-ended perspective of the female part of us and so actively tries to come up with plans and directions to share, considering all possible negative future consequences, so he can be a source of direction for himself and for the female part of us. The result is a desire or a sense of need to look solely to our reactive thoughts, feelings, and instincts in the moment about what we want to do or solely to the possible future negative consequences of our actions, depending on which part of us we most identify with, in search of direction.

In the order of creation: The male, sharing, creative part of us is in touch with his Source and Creator nature and attentive to the flexible, open-ended perspective of the female part of us and so truly is a source of direction for himself and for the female part of us, providing a clear destination but allowing for a flexible and open-ended approach to getting there. The female, receiving part of us is getting clear destinations and therefore all the direction, with long-term consideration, she wants and needs from the male part of us and so her thoughts, feelings, and instincts in the moment become an accurate gauge of which direction to go in the moment in order actually to get somewhere. The result is a lack of any desire or sense of need to look solely to our thoughts, feelings, and instincts in the moment or solely to possible consequences of our actions because we have all the direction we want. We can, therefore, choose willfully and in a balanced way how we wish to approach the world and determine our direction in any moment.

The Myers-Briggs Personality Dimensions And The Five Levels Of Stress (from no stress to extreme stress)

When we're under no stress at all, we are balanced in our expression of the two directions on each dimension of personality. We express the two directions in their creation forms.

When we are under usual, daily stress, we identify with the end of each dimension with which we usually most identify (the male or female form), in their development forms. (For example, if you are INTJ—introverted, intuitive, thinking, judging—then you identify with the male forms of all of the dimensions usually.) When we are under more than usual, daily stress, we get more extreme in our bias toward the end of each dimension with which we usually most identify, in their development forms.

When we are under a lot of stress, we shift toward identification with the opposite end of each dimension as compared to that with which we usually most identify (switching from the male to the female form or vice versa), in their development forms. (For example, if you are INTJ, then you shift toward identification with ESFP—extroverted, sensing, feeling, perceiving—the opposite end of each dimension, in this case the female forms of all of the dimensions, under a lot of stress.) When we are under extreme stress, we get more extreme in our bias toward the opposite end of each dimension as compared to that with which we usually most identify, in their development forms.

When we are under stress for an extended period of time, we get less healthy, and our biases in identification with one end or the other of each dimension become more extreme. When we are under lack of stress for an extended period of time (due to lack of external stresses or due to dealing with things well), we get healthier, and our biases in identification with one end or the other of each dimension become subtler.

Enneagram Three Inclinations

There are three main inclinations that exist within all of us and that get us to attend to the three main areas of life to which we must attend for the sake of our continued existence and fulfillment within this world. In the order of development, these are the preserving inclination, the belonging inclination, and the connecting inclination. In the order of creation (the reverse of the order of development), there is the connecting inclination, the belonging inclination, and the preserving inclination. We all have one of these inclinations as primary, one as secondary, and one as tertiary in prioritization within us.

Sharing Existence – Connecting Inclination (One-on-one Instinctual Variant)

You care a lot about connections with close friends (often of the opposite gender to you) and a significant other. You want to find your other half in the world (the person who's going to complete you, that one other person who understands you and whom you understand, on whom you can depend and who can depend on you), and you want to find intensity and a feeling of connection in all of your activities generally. You want to have long, intense conversations with one or two other people at a time.

The approach you're inclined to take in search of fulfillment: You're inclined to disconnect from and ignore yourself and try to share your thoughts, feelings, and instincts with another for the sake of connecting with your close friends and especially your significant other, or with anyone, for that matter. You're inclined to do this because your own thoughts, feelings, and instincts that are applied to yourself seem to you to be untrustworthy, undependable, unfulfilling, not to be taken seriously, incapable, and useless when it comes to connecting with your close friends and especially your significant other, or with any other person.

The result of ignoring and disconnecting from yourself in attempts to connect with another person is that you feel ignored and disconnected.

How you can actually achieve fulfillment: You need to connect with your own thoughts, feelings, and instincts and allow them to guide you in order to connect with your friends, significant other, and other individuals. When you do this, you recognize that your own thoughts, feelings, and instincts are actually trustworthy, dependable, fulfilling, to be taken seriously, capable, and useful when it comes to connecting with your friends, significant other, and other people.

When you focus on and connect with yourself, you feel focused on and connected.

What you're inclined to identify with: You're inclined to identify with your thoughts, feelings, and instincts of connecting with someone or something.

Understanding what your thoughts, feelings, and instincts are really saying to you: Your thoughts, feelings, and instincts are saying to you, as though in conversation with you, "I feel lonely and disconnected, and I want to have company and feel connected," and "I feel like I don't have anyone I can trust and depend on who is enjoyable and fulfilling to be with and who listens to me and understands me, and I want someone like this." In other words, the way to show that you are really listening to your thoughts, feelings, and instincts is to respond to them by allowing them to connect with you, really being present to them, keeping them company, and connecting with them as they guide you in connecting with other people and the world around you.

By being someone your thoughts, feelings, and instincts can trust and depend on who is enjoyable and fulfilling to be with and who listens to them and understands them so they feel like they can connect with you, you give them what they want and consequently get what you want as well. This is the true path to connection.

Where you're inclined to project your thoughts, feelings, and instincts: When you are identifying with your thoughts, feelings, and instincts of connecting, believing that they are you, you are inclined to project your thoughts, feelings, and instincts most onto your close friends and especially your significant other—expecting of them what you expect of yourself and generally treating them as you would treat yourself if you were to do what they are doing. You are inclined to treat your close friends and especially your significant other as though they are part of you and as though when they say or do something, it is as if you are saying or doing it. You are inclined to feel like the words, actions, etc. of your close friends, and especially of your significant other, reflect on you.

When you are identifying with your true self and connecting with your thoughts, feelings, and instincts, and allowing them to connect with you, you are inclined to allow your close friends and significant other to follow the guidance of their own thoughts and to make their own decisions. You are able to guide and advise them in ways they actually want to be guided and advised, without projecting your own thoughts, feelings, and instincts onto them and telling them what decisions to make.

Relationship mindset: I'll look out for my significant other and my close friends, and my significant other and my close friends will look out for me.

Romantic relationship compatibility: If you have connecting as your primary inclination, you are most likely to relate well in a romantic relationship with someone else who is also connecting. This way you both have the common focus of sharing your experience of life with each other and intensely connecting with each other, with close friends, and with the world around you.

Receiving Existence – Belonging Inclination (Social Instinctual Variant)

You care a lot about community, being part of a group (often a group of friends of the same gender as you), belonging somewhere. You want to be part of something larger than yourself, like a team, where everyone is working toward a common goal. You want to hang out with a group of people.

The approach you're inclined to take in search of fulfillment: You're inclined to dismiss some of your own thoughts, feelings, and instincts for the sake of fitting in and belonging somewhere. You're inclined to do this because some of your thoughts, feelings, and instincts seem to you to be worthless, unsuccessful, insignificant, unworthy of attention, selfish, and unhelpful when it comes to fitting in and belonging to the group or community.

The result of judging, dismissing, and not accepting or including some parts of yourself in attempts to fit in with, be accepted by, and belong to a group is that you feel judged, dismissed, unaccepted, excluded, and like you don't belong.

How you can actually achieve fulfillment: You need to listen to, acknowledge, and accept all of your own thoughts, feelings, and instincts and allow them to express themselves and belong within you in order to fit in and belong somewhere. When you do this, you recognize that your own thoughts, feelings, and instincts are actually valuable, successful, important, worthy of attention, loving, and helpful when it comes to fitting in and belonging to the right group or community for you.

When you pay attention to and accept and include all parts of yourself, you feel accepted, included, and like you belong.

What you're inclined to identify with: You're inclined to identify with your thoughts, feelings, and instincts of belonging somewhere.

Understanding what your thoughts, feelings, and instincts are really saying to you: Your thoughts, feelings, and instincts are saying to you, as though in conversation with you, "I feel like I don't fit in or belong, and I want to fit in and belong," and "I feel like I am worthless, unsuccessful, insignificant, unworthy of attention, selfish, and unhelpful, and so I don't belong. I want to feel like I am valuable, successful, important, worthy of attention, loving, and helpful so that I belong." In other words, the way to show that you are really listening to your thoughts, feelings, and instincts is to respond to them by allowing them to express themselves as they are, accepting them, allowing them to belong within you, and including them in your consideration as they guide you in identifying your social role and fitting in.

By recognizing your thoughts, feelings, and instincts as valuable, successful, important, worthy of attention, loving, and helpful to you so they feel like they belong within you, you give them what they want and consequently get what you want as well. This is the true path to belonging.

Where you're inclined to project your thoughts, feelings, and instincts: When you are identifying with your thoughts, feelings, and instincts of belonging, believing that they are you, you are inclined to project your thoughts, feelings, and instincts most onto your group of friends or team or community—expecting of its members what you expect of yourself and generally treating them as you would treat yourself if you were to do what they are doing. You are inclined to treat the members of your group of friends or team or community as though they are part of you and as though when they say or do something, it is as if you are saying or doing it. You are inclined to feel like the words, actions, etc. of the members of your group of friends, or team or community, reflect on you.

When you are identifying with your true self and accepting and including all of your thoughts, feelings, and instincts, allowing them to belong within you, you are inclined to allow the members of your group of friends or team or community to be true to their own feelings and to be who they are. You are able to help them in ways they actually want to be helped, without projecting your own thoughts, feelings, and instincts onto them and telling them who to be.

Relationship mindset: I'll look out for the community and the community will look out for me/us.

Romantic relationship compatibility: If you have belonging as your primary inclination, you are most likely to relate well in a romantic relationship with someone else who is also belonging. This way you both have the common focus of community and being part of and contributing to something larger than yourselves.

Allowing Existence – Preserving Inclination (Self-preservation Instinctual Variant)

You care a lot about career, family, health, environment, and maintaining and preserving all of these things. You want to have enough resources—money, food, clothing—to meet your needs, and to have things be clean, neat, and organized in some way. You want to be by yourself and get work done, eat, sleep, etc.

The approach you're inclined to take in search of fulfillment: You're inclined to tune out your own thoughts, feelings, and instincts for the sake of getting work done and obtaining sufficient resources so that you can preserve your body, your environment, and your family. You're inclined to do this because your own thoughts, feelings, and instincts seem to you to be conflict-causing, inharmonious, bad, not deserving of attention, vulnerable, and powerless when it comes to preserving your body, environment, and family.

The result of tuning yourself out in attempts to get work done and obtain sufficient resources to preserve your body, your environment, and your family is that you feel tuned out, exhausted (from trying to get your own attention), hungry and thirsty (for your own attention), and like you don't have enough of the proper resources to survive (because you aren't getting enough of your own energy and attention to survive).

How you can actually achieve fulfillment: You need to tune into your own thoughts, feelings, and instincts and act on them in order to identify and take the best approach to obtaining sufficient resources to preserve your body, your environment, and your family. When you do this, you recognize that your own thoughts, feelings, and instincts are actually peaceful, harmonious, good, deserving of attention, protective, and powerful when it comes to preserving your body, environment, and family.

When you tune into yourself, you feel energized, satiated, and like you have more than enough of the proper resources to survive and thrive.

What you're inclined to identify with: You're inclined to identify with your thoughts, feelings, and instincts of preserving yourself.

Understanding what your thoughts, feelings, and instincts are really saying to you: Your thoughts, feelings, and instincts are saying to you, as though in conversation with you, "I feel like I don't have enough to survive and be comfortable, and I want to have enough to survive and be comfortable," and "I feel like my surroundings are filled with conflict and are inharmonious, and like I am bad and not deserving of attention, and I feel vulnerable and powerless to change this. I want to feel like my surroundings are peaceful and harmonious, and like I am good and deserving of attention, and I want to feel protective and powerful in making things this way." In other words, the way to show that you are really listening to your thoughts, feelings, and instincts is to respond to them by giving them enough positive attention and, in this way, feeding them, rejuvenating them, and preserving them as they guide you in preserving your body, your environment, and your family.

By recognizing your thoughts, feelings, and instincts as peaceful, harmonious, good, deserving of attention, protective, and powerful to you so they feel like they can preserve themselves within you, you give them what they want and consequently get what you want as well. This is the true path to preservation of yourself and your surroundings.

Where you're inclined to project your thoughts, feelings, and instincts: When you are identifying with your thoughts, feelings, and instincts of preserving, believing that they are you, you are inclined to project your thoughts, feelings, and instincts most onto your family members and the people with whom you work—expecting of them what you expect of yourself and generally treating them as you would treat yourself if you were to do what they are doing. You are inclined to treat your family members and the people with whom you work as though they are part of you and as though when they say or do something, it is as if you are saying or doing it. You are inclined to feel like the words, actions, etc. of your family members and the people with whom you work reflect on you.

When you are identifying with your true self and preserving your thoughts, feelings, and instincts, feeding them and allowing them to exist within you, you are inclined to allow your family members and the people with whom you work to do what their own instincts tell them to do and to do what they want to do. You are able to protect them in ways they actually want to be protected, without projecting your own thoughts, feelings, and instincts onto them and telling them what to do.

Relationship mindset: I'll look out for my material needs and those of my family.

Romantic relationship compatibility: If you have preserving as your primary inclination, you are most likely to relate well in a romantic relationship with someone else who is also preserving. This way you both have the common focus of career, family, and preserving your health and environment.

Development And Creation Forms

In the order of development: Once we exist, we tune out our own existence and seek to preserve, by allowing to be manifested through us, the existence of our bodies, environments, and families in the world outside ourselves. Then we dismiss and exclude parts of our own existence and seek to belong to, be accepted by, and receive existence from, a group in the world outside of us that will help us to preserve our existence. Then we disconnect from ourselves and seek to connect with, and share existence with, other individuals in the world outside of us who will look out for us and guide us in preserving our existence. And then we become aware of ourselves.

In the order of creation: Once we are aware of ourselves, we seek to connect with ourselves and share self-aware existence with ourselves. Then we seek to be accepted by, and to belong within, ourselves and receive self-aware existence from ourselves in order to be able to connect with ourselves. Then we seek to preserve ourselves and tune into our own self-aware existence so that we will be able to connect with ourselves. And then we truly exist.

The shift of our focus from development to creation is from preserving our existence to connecting with ourselves, and ultimately from maintaining our existence to growing in, and sharing, our awareness of our existence that comes from connection with our true selves.

The Expression Of The Secondary And Tertiary Inclinations

Under usual daily situations, we prioritize our primary inclination first, followed by our secondary inclination, followed by our tertiary inclination. Since we view everything through the lens of our personality motivations and priorities, we actually usually attend to our secondary inclination primarily in order to increase the likelihood that we'll be fulfilled in our primary inclination, ultimately. And while we are often inclined not to attend very much to our tertiary inclination usually, to the extent that we do attend to it, we do so in order to attend better to our secondary inclination, which again, we are attending to in order to attend better to our primary inclination.

So, for example, if your primary inclination is the connecting inclination, your secondary inclination is the preserving inclination, and your tertiary inclination is the belonging inclination, then: You are inclined to try to be part of something larger than yourself in order better to provide for and preserve yourself and your family financially, health-wise, and otherwise, and you are inclined to try to provide for and preserve yourself and your family in order better to connect with other people and cultivate close friendships and a relationship with a significant other. Notice, here in this example, everything is really about connecting with other people in close relationships, ultimately.

Our primary inclination is, therefore, our highest priority under usual circumstances. It shapes the lens through which we view everything. It is what drives us and motivates us. And so we are inclined to bias our attention to this area of our lives, specifying all of the details about what we want and don't want in life in regard to this area, and expecting more from it in return for all of the attention we're giving it. This is the area of life where we primarily search for fulfillment of our Enneagram personality type's motivations (more on this soon). Therefore, when we are not in a good place due to having been under stress for an extended period of time (due to approaching things from an order-of-development perspective rather than from an order-of-creation perspective), we end up with issues in the area of our lives toward which our primary inclination directs us due to giving too much attention to that area and then expecting too much back from it.

In addition, while we are attending too much to our primary inclination, we are failing to attend to our tertiary inclination, especially. We want general things from this area but often fail to take the time to specify exactly what we want from it and take action to bring this about. Therefore, when we are not in a good place, we end up with issues in the area of our lives toward which our tertiary inclination directs us due to giving too little attention to that area.

What we would ideally strive for is balance, attending to all three areas of life largely equally and wherever appropriate (sleeping when appropriate based on the time, etc., working when appropriate, saying hi to other people when in a social setting, connecting with one or two other people when the opportunity arises and nothing else requires our attention more) so that we can achieve fulfillment in all three areas. This is as opposed to giving most of our attention to one area of life and largely neglecting another area of life, which gives rise to a lot of expectation and need as we act from a place of unfulfillment and try to make up for the lack of our own attention by seeking this attention outside of us. We can only be fulfilled when we become for ourselves and give to ourselves what we want from others and the world around us. This is key.

Another pivotal influence in the expression of the three inclinations is stress. We are inclined to shift our focus of attention to different areas of life based on our level of stress in conjunction with our ordering of the inclinations (more on this in one moment). Be aware, here, that if we rarely attend to some area of life except when we are under a lot of stress, it is unlikely that our destinations in regard to that area are going to be positive. It is more likely that when our attention is on that area of life, it is negative attention, focusing on lack and unfulfillment there. Thus is usually the case with the area toward which our tertiary inclination directs us, leading to problems in that area as a result and to our inclination to avoid that area as much as possible since there are too many issues there and it isn't usually much of a priority for us anyway. This is what happens until will begin consciously to redirect our destinations in regard to that area, giving positive attention to it.

We get our internal dynamics reflected back at us in every area of life as we are treated the ways we treat ourselves by everyone and everything. However, we are usually most willing to put up with our negative internal dynamics being reflected back at us in the area of life toward which our primary inclination directs us because this area is the highest priority for us most of the time. When we encounter reflections of our negative internal dynamics in other areas of life, we might simply try to avoid our obstacles by avoiding, ignoring, dismissing, and tuning out those areas of life. But we so much want fulfillment in the area of life toward which our primary inclination directs us that we are particularly motivated to try to figure out how to do something to make this what we want, hopefully eventually recognizing that we have to change our own internal dynamics so that the reflection of them in the world around us changes. For this is how we come to address our obstacles and learn and grow from them rather than simply ignoring them, dismissing them, tuning them out, or running away from them, where they continually pop up and chase us. They do this until we actually address them, listen to and understand their messages about how we've been treating ourselves, and redirect our destinations and treat ourselves better.

The Enneagram Three Inclinations And The Five Levels Of Stress (from no stress to extreme stress)

When you are not under any stress, you are subtly inclined by your intuition to attend to each of the three main areas of life when appropriate in a balanced, healthy way. (At this point, the three inclinations express themselves in you in their creation forms.) However, when you are not attending to all of the three areas in a balanced way, you get stressed, and the three inclinations turn into desires that come into your experience in correspondence to different degrees of stress based on your personality's prioritization of these inclinations. (At this point, the three inclinations express themselves in you in their development forms.)

To understand this, you can imagine that it is as though you have a sort of traffic light of desires within you that turns on when you are under stress. When you have been giving too much attention to certain areas of life and ignoring other areas, you end up under stress. When you are under usual, daily stress, the first traffic light turns on as your primary inclination expresses itself as a desire within you, nagging with feelings of lack of fulfillment like a nagging child trying to get your attention. When you are under more than usual, daily stress, the first traffic light turns off and the second traffic light turns on as your secondary inclination expresses itself as a desire within you, nagging with feelings of lack of fulfillment for your attention. When you are under a lot of stress, the second traffic light turns off and the third traffic light turns on as your tertiary inclination expresses itself as a desire within you, nagging with feelings of lack of fulfillment and trying to get your attention. When you are under extreme stress, all of the traffic lights burn out (hopefully temporarily) due to overuse, and you have no drive to attend to anything that would contribute to the maintenance of your existence or your fulfillment within this world.

When you are under stress for long periods of time due to lack of presence and lack of balanced attention to each of the three main areas, the traffic lights grow brighter in an effort to get your attention as you are less and less present and attentive to anything fully. The aim is to be present to the world around you and to your own internal GPS system's guidance—in the form of your thoughts, feelings, and instincts—in each moment, and to attend to all aspects of each of the three main areas of life in a balanced fashion, so that stress never has to enter the picture of your experience of life.

However, considering we are all working toward the elimination of stress and aren't there permanently yet, the goal is to use your awareness of your internal traffic light ordering to notice and gauge your stress level so that you can recognize your desires not as guidance that you should follow but as indications of your stress level. Then upon noticing that you have the strong desire to be by yourself and clean things and get work done, or to be around people and belong somewhere, or to connect with someone in conversation, you can acknowledge that you are simply experiencing stress. Then you can ask yourself: What have I been attending to too much, and/or what have I been ignoring, that I would be straying from being present and experiencing stress right now? And then: How can I pull my attention away from where I've been directing it too much, and how can I attend more fully to whatever I've been ignoring, so that I can decrease my stress and get back to the fulfillment that comes from being present and not having anything nagging for my attention?

As we learn to balance our attention to each area of life, we get less stressed, and we get stressed less often, and the lights in our traffic light grow dimmer because we do not need them to be bright to get our attention. And eventually we hardly need the traffic light at all.

Enneagram Nine Personality Types

The Breakdown Of The Types—An Introductory Overview

We each operate internally and externally in some specific way based on how we relate to our own thoughts, feelings, or instincts, and based on which of these relationships is most prominent within us. The different Enneagram personality types, when seen in their true light, are categorized by how they function internally in certain basic ways, in terms of where they direct their attention.

There is a male, sharing, initiative, controlling or guiding form, a female, receiving, differentiating, reactive or responsive form, and a child, allowing, harmonizing, tuning out or tuning in form of thought, of feeling, and of instinct. So, there are three thinking types, three feeling types, and three instinctual types, making for nine different aspects of the pattern of development/creation that can be identified with and fixated upon to become a personality type. In the order of creation (again, the opposite of the order of development), these are: sharing thought, receiving thought, allowing thought, sharing feeling, receiving feeling, allowing feeling, sharing instinct, receiving instinct, and allowing instinct.

The sharing types ignore themselves (their own needs) and direct the attention of their experiences outward toward others. The receiving types dismiss their own experiences and give their attention to their reactively manifested experiences. The allowing types tune out their own experiences and allow other people's experiences to be manifested through them. By "experiences", here, I mean "thoughts, feelings, or instincts."

The thinking types have these relationships with their thoughts. The feeling types have these relationships with their feelings. The instinctual types have these relationships with their instincts.

Therefore, to put it all together:

Sharing thought ignores itself and directs the attention of its thoughts toward others. Receiving thought dismisses its own thoughts and gives its attention to its reactively manifested thoughts. Allowing thought tunes out its own thoughts and allows other people's thoughts to be manifested through the decisions it makes.

Sharing feeling ignores itself and directs the attention of its feelings toward others. Receiving feeling dismisses its own feelings and gives its attention to its reactively manifested feelings. Allowing feeling tunes out its own feelings and allows other people's feelings to be manifested through who it is.

Sharing instinct ignores itself and directs the attention of its instincts toward others. Receiving instinct dismisses its own instincts and gives its attention to its reactively manifested instincts. Allowing instinct tunes out its own instincts and allows other people's instincts to be manifested through its actions.

Though we all have all of these different relationships within us, we all have a main type as well as a secondary type, which is one number more or one number less than the main type (see the type numbers in parentheses next to the names that indicate how the types function).

Read on to understand what all this actually means, why we do what we do, and how we can improve our relationships with ourselves and others and get the results we want in life:

The Types

Sharing Thought (Enneagram Type 5)

You come up with your own innovative thoughts and ideas so you will be able to act in the world and share your new understanding with others. In other words, you're inclined to observe and think a lot and try to figure out and understand everything so you'll have knowledge you can share that might prove useful to others. You get overwhelmed when there are too many things you feel you don't know enough about to be capable of addressing. So you keep observing, thinking, researching, and trying to figure everything out, incorporating new information from your experiences and learning into your growing framework of understanding in an effort to feel capable, competent, and useful.

Your relationship with yourself: You are inclined to expect a lot of yourself and overwhelm yourself with staticky thinking as you try to come up with information and new, innovative ideas that might be useful to others.

You feel that you have to be capable and useful to others because if you are capable and useful then you will be less likely to be a burden on others. So you try to figure out everything yourself so that you won't expect too much from others.

However, when you try to understand and figure out everything yourself, you expect a lot of yourself and overwhelm yourself with your own over-thinking and over-analysis of everything. So you end up feeling increasingly overwhelmed by other people's expectations of you on top of your own as you increasingly try to remedy this by withdrawing into your mind and thinking more in an effort to figure things out yourself. This happens until you learn to be useful to yourself by acting on what you know, learning from experience along the way, and delegating the rest to competent and capable others who have experience in relevant areas, thereby allowing others to be useful to themselves and to you as well. In essence, you are inclined to try to be useful to yourself by trying to be useful to others rather than by being useful to yourself, and you need to learn to be useful to yourself by actually being useful to yourself.

The key to shifting your relationships: The key is to notice when you are trying to be useful to other people and the world around you by imposing on them your understanding and what you think will be useful to them in disregard of what *they* think would be useful to them, and to practice acknowledging at those times that you are imposing and what you are imposing and why. Then, shift your attention and energy to yourself and act on your own thoughts and understanding so that you are useful to yourself, and allow other people to act on their own thoughts and understanding and thereby to be useful to themselves and to you as well. This way, instead of making yourself useless by overwhelming yourself with your own overactive thinking as you try to be useful to everyone but yourself, you are competent, capable, and useful to yourself.

When you quiet your thoughts and act on your own understanding and so already feel capable and like you're contributing something useful to the world, your attempts to offer something useful to others become the overflow of your already existing clear-minded understanding derived from actual experience with the world outside your mind. This is in contrast to their being insistent attempts to convince others that your advice would be useful to them even though you don't yet feel the capability and confidence that comes only from having lived the advice, acting on it and experiencing it for yourself. The result is that rather than trying to figure out what might be useful to others and the world around you through endless thinking as an observer isolated from and devoid of actual experience with what you are thinking about—where you try to advise people without consideration of their own thoughts, knowledge, and experience—you will be able to advise people as a fellow participant in life by guiding them in their own understanding of themselves and their situations that they have derived or can derive from their own experiences and the information and knowledge that they already have. This requires far less energy on your part because you don't have to figure everything out yourself or convince anyone of anything; you just have to guide and advise other people in their figuring out things for themselves, and this allows you actually to be competent, capable, and useful.

How you are inclined to treat yourself and others and how you are inclined to feel that others treat you: When you are stressed and/or unhealthy (due to prolonged stress), you are inclined to treat yourself and others as incompetent and useless, and you are inclined to feel that others treat you as incompetent and useless.

When you are relaxed and healthy (due to prolonged lack of stress either because of circumstances or because you've been responding positively to life's obstacles), you are inclined to treat yourself and others as competent and useful, and you are inclined to feel that others treat you as competent and useful.

The Golden Rule applied: Allow other people to act on their own understanding and capability and to be useful to you in the knowledge and skills they can offer, and you will be able to act on your own understanding and capability and be useful to other people in the knowledge and skills you can offer. Or, more simply, allow other people to be participants in your life, and you will be able to be a participant in other people's lives.

This works because if you let other people be useful then you won't be busy overwhelming yourself with trying to figure out everything yourself and reinventing the wheel. Instead, you will be able to learn from others and the world around you, and to allow some things to be taken care of by others who have more experience with them. So you will be able to focus on coming up with useful ideas, advice, and skills to offer in the areas where you have experience. Rather than seemingly competing with others as you try to be more useful to them than they are to you, when you allow other people to be useful, they allow you to be useful, and so everyone involved feels competent, capable, and useful.

How to begin applying the Golden Rule: If you simply start trying to allow other people to be useful in your life, you will continue to be supported in your feeling that other people are incompetent and useless and that you really need to figure out how to do everything yourself. Further, you will continue to be supported in your feeling that when you let people be participants in your life, they expect too much of you and overwhelm you. So you'll continue to feel that you can't offer anything useful and that you really need to think more before you participate in the world and in other people's lives and allow other people to participate in your life.

So, you can't just change your external approach and make the shift. You first need to change the way you approach things internally (or change your internal approach as you change your external approach).

Start here: Share your capable, useful thoughts with yourself and act on them. This way you will already be making yourself feel like you are being allowed to be capable and useful and like capability and usefulness are being shared with you, and so you will be more open to allowing other people (and things, such as money, for example) to be capable and useful and share their capability and usefulness with you as well.

When you are present to your thoughts and you consistently treat your thoughts as capable, and as though their guidance is useful, by acting on their guidance, your thoughts treat you as capable, and as though your guidance is useful, by acting on your guidance when you suggest a new destination for them and you. The result is you feel that you are capable and useful to others and that others are capable and useful to you. Consequently, you are inclined to treat others as capable and make use of their guidance, and others are inclined to treat you as capable and make use of your guidance. Further, you are inclined actually to be capable and useful to others, and others are inclined actually to be capable and useful to you. Thus, you get everything that you truly want when you treat your thoughts as capable and make use of their guidance.

The example you are inclined to set for others in regard to how you should be treated: By not acting on your own advice and guidance, you set the example for others that your advice and guidance should not be acted upon.

As you learn to direct your useful thinking toward yourself and act on your own advice, you come to set the example for others that your advice should be acted upon.

Your main limiting belief: My capable thinking, when directed toward myself, is not capable or useful, and so I should direct my capable thinking toward others instead of toward myself.

Response to your main limiting belief: Only when I direct my capable thinking toward myself can I truly be useful to anyone else and actually feel competent and capable, because no one will follow my guidance if *I* don't.

The three aspects of self in your internal dynamic: There is a part of you that imposes the idea that your capable thoughts, when directed toward yourself, are not useful because they don't seem to be useful to anyone else. There is a part of you that reacts to this by judging your capable thoughts that are directed toward yourself as incompetent and incapable and getting overwhelmed by them and dismissing them. And there is a part of you that simply tunes out your capable thoughts that are directed toward yourself in an attempt to maintain competence and be useful to yourself since your capable thoughts that are directed toward yourself are seemingly causing confusion and incapability within you.

In the healthy version of this dynamic: The part of you that would impose the idea that your capable thoughts, when directed toward yourself, are not useful instead guides the direction of your capable thoughts toward yourself toward the aim of real competence and usefulness. The part of you that would react by judging your capable thoughts that are directed toward yourself as incompetent and incapable and getting overwhelmed by them instead acknowledges your capable thoughts that are directed toward yourself as capable and useful and understands them. And the part of you that would tune out your capable thoughts that are directed toward yourself in an attempt to maintain competence and be useful to yourself in light of their actually causing incapability within you instead tunes into your capable thoughts that are directed toward yourself and acts on them since they are now actually maintaining useful understanding and capability within you.

How to get all parts of yourself on the same team and working for you: Listen to and acknowledge your thoughts that you need to be useful to other people by figuring out and gathering useful information and advice for them and that trying to be useful to yourself isn't actually useful to anyone, and recognize that these thoughts have your best interests in mind. They actually just want to help you be competent, capable, useful and independent, which is what you want as well. It's just that they are misdirected in how best to go about being competent and useful, believing that you have to direct your capable thoughts away from yourself and toward others in order to be this.

So after you listen to them and acknowledge them, let them know that you understand that their main intention is to help you be competent and useful, and that they can even better achieve this aim if they help you direct your competent, useful thoughts toward yourself instead. This way you can actually get what you want, which is to be competent and capable, useful and independent.

What you're inclined to identify with: You're inclined to identify with your thought that your thoughts that are directed toward yourself are incapable and useless.

Understanding what your thoughts are really saying to you: Your thoughts are saying to you, as though in conversation with you, "I feel like I'm incapable and useless to you, and I want to be competent and useful to you." In other words, the way to show that you are really listening to your thoughts is to respond to them by recognizing them as competent and useful, and following their guidance yourself. This is the true path to capability.

What your thoughts really want and how they try to get it: Your thoughts really want to be preserved by you, accepted by you, and connected to you, and you make them believe that in order to accomplish these aims, they need to be capable and useful to you. Therefore, they try to do whatever they believe they need to do in order to be useful to you so they can prove that they are capable. If this means trying to be useful to the world and other people, then this is what they'll do. But if you pay attention to them, you'll recognize that they actually just want to be capable to you, and they're only trying to be useful to others because you're making them believe that this is the only way they'll be capable to you. If you recognize them as capable when they are useful to *you*, then this is what they'll do for you instead.

Because you make your thoughts believe that, in order to get what they want, they need to be capable and useful to you, you seek to be capable and useful to other people and to the world in order to be kept in the world and in other people's lives, to be accepted by the world and other people, and to connect to the world and other people. And, therefore, you try to do whatever you believe you need to do in order to be useful to the world and other people so you can prove that you are capable. If this means trying to be useful to the world and other people and ignoring yourself, then this is what you'll do. But if you pay attention to your own thoughts, you'll recognize that they actually just want to be capable, and if you recognize them as capable when they try to be useful to *you*, then you'll actually be recognized by the world and the people around you as useful.

Internal experience image: When you are stressed, and especially when you have been stressed for a long time and so are more caught up in your personality's obstacles and coping mechanisms, you try to figure out and understand everything yourself through active thinking in an effort to be self-sufficient and useful to others. It is as though your mind is a radio, and you tune it into every station at once in an effort to figure out everything yourself. But the result is that you just get a lot of overwhelming noise without anything coherent that you can understand. You end up feeling overwhelmed by other people and their expectations of you because you are already occupied trying to understand all the noise in your own mind as you expect yourself to understand all the radio stations' messages as they all play at once. You also end up feeling incompetent and incapable of *anything* because you've been trying to understand and do *everything*.

The only way out of the inundation of overwhelming expectations is to tune into one station and direct your innovative thoughts toward yourself and be useful to yourself. Then you realize that you don't need to work so hard to understand everything and come up with something useful to offer to others, because you learn from your experience along the way and what you learn becomes far more useful to others than advice coming from over-thinking without living and experiencing the implementation of your own advice. Life is much easier to understand when you simply tune into one station at a time, because then what you need to know comes to you when you need it, and you can actually understand it when you hear it.

What you're attracted to in others: You're attracted to people with whom you can share your new and innovative thoughts, because then you feel useful. In the same vein, you are attracted to people whom you can guide and who will act on the information you provide, because then you feel capable and useful. Ideally, the people you choose to bring into your life and be useful to are people who will stimulate new ideas in you in return, because then you can get the intellectual stimulation and sense that others are capable and useful to you that you really want.

The types of words you use to criticize yourself and others: idiot, stupid, dumb, incompetent, inconsistent, useless

The types of words you use to praise yourself and others: smart, intelligent, brilliant, genius, consistent, useful

Receiving Thought (Enneagram Type 7)

You look for things in the world around you that give you things to think about, and then you try to make things more fun and exciting than they seem that they will be. In other words, you're inclined to engulf yourself in fun and exciting experiences that keep you mentally stimulated and active. You want to be happy and fulfilled, and you feel that escaping by distracting yourself with exciting experiences from the feeling of being trapped by serious thoughts and fears (experienced by you as boredom) is the way to keep yourself happy.

Your relationship with yourself: You are inclined to replay your thoughts that you are unhappy, bored, and trapped in unfulfillment, and to dismiss, and distract yourself from, your thoughts that you are already happy, fulfilled, and free (because you deem these thoughts too boring or serious).

You feel that some of your thoughts are boring and trapping because they don't fit your conception of what is exciting, fun, and fulfilling. So you judge these thoughts within you, not taking them seriously, dismissing them, running away from them, and trying to keep yourself happy and fulfilled by distracting yourself from what you perceive as the dull, boring, negative, and unpleasant.

However, running away and otherwise distracting yourself from those thoughts that seem to you unpleasant merely brings about more of a sense of being trapped, deprived, and in pain as your thoughts chase after you like nagging children who just want to get your attention and be heard. So you find yourself increasingly avoiding others and not taking them seriously and increasingly avoided by others and not taken seriously by them as you have been avoiding yourself. You feel increasingly trapped in your unhappiness, which seems to chase after you no matter how much you try to run from it, until you learn to be present and listen to and accept your own thoughts as they are without avoidance or dismissal.

The key to shifting your relationships: The key is to notice when you are getting caught up in focusing on and replaying your thoughts that you are unhappy and trapped and that things are dull or boring, and to practice acknowledging at those times that you are judging and what you are judging and why. Then, shift your attention to what is going on in the present moment as it is and allow yourself to listen to your thoughts that you are happy and free and that things are exciting and fun already without dismissing these thoughts as dull or confining. This way, rather than bringing about more reasons to feel trapped and unhappy, where you try to be happy by distracting yourself and escaping from things that make you feel trapped and ultimately from unhappiness, you bring about more reasons to be excited as you notice all the positive experiences that already exist in your life.

When you are listening to your thoughts that you are already happy and free and that things will be as they should be, your attempts to make things fulfilling become the overflow of your already existing joy. This is in contrast to their being highly critical and judgmental attempts to identify and avoid unfulfilling and confining experiences because you are too busy focusing on what makes you unhappy to accept your experiences as they are and as they will be. The result is that rather than trying to correct the future by avoiding the unhappiness that you anticipate experiencing, which only leads you to find more experiences that support your feeling deprived and trapped, you will be able to recognize the fulfillment in each moment. This requires far less energy on your part because you don't have to focus on what makes you unhappy and continually be running away from unfulfillment as you and the people around you don't take you seriously and you never allow yourself to experience the joy in each moment; you just have to allow yourself to be present to the fulfillment in yourself and your experiences, and this actually encourages and increases your happiness and sense of freedom.

How you are inclined to treat yourself and others and how you are inclined to feel that others treat you: When you are stressed and/or unhealthy (due to prolonged stress), you are inclined to treat yourself and others as unfulfilling and not to be taken seriously, and you are inclined to feel that others treat you as unfulfilling and don't take you seriously.

When you are relaxed and healthy (due to prolonged lack of stress either because of circumstances or because you've been responding positively to life's obstacles), you are inclined to treat yourself and others as fulfilling and to be taken seriously, and you are inclined to feel that others treat you as fulfilling and take you seriously.

The Golden Rule applied: Accept and treat other people as exciting, fun, and fulfilling, and other people will accept and treat you as exciting, fun, and fulfilling. Allow other people to express themselves and to be attended to and taken seriously, and other people will allow you to express yourself and to be attended to and taken seriously.

This works because if you don't distract yourself and run away from others all the time (dismissing them as too boring or serious), but instead allow them to express themselves and be taken seriously, then others won't feel the need to react and distract themselves from you, dismiss you, and not take you seriously. They, instead, will focus on you, hear you out, and take you seriously. When you focus on other people and pay attention to them, then they focus on you and pay attention to you. Rather than seemingly competing with others as you try to be the one who's exciting, entertaining, and attention-grabbing, when you allow other people to be exciting and entertaining, too, they allow you to be exciting and entertaining, and so everyone involved feels attended to, happy, and fulfilled.

How to begin applying the Golden Rule: If you simply start trying to take other people seriously, you will continue to be supported in your feeling that other people are boring and that you are bored by them and would rather distract yourself from the dullness. Further, you will continue to be supported in your feeling that you're not getting enough attention and that you need to do more exciting things to get it. So you'll continue to feel that you are trapped and limited in options and that you need to find more exciting things to do to distract yourself from the boredom. And you'll continue to feel that other people aren't paying attention to you or taking you seriously.

So, you can't just change your external approach and make the shift. You first need to change the way you approach things internally (or change your internal approach as you change your external approach).

Start here: Pay attention to and receive your own fulfilling thoughts from yourself. This way you will already be making yourself feel like you are getting attention and like you are being taken seriously, and so you will be more open to noticing and accepting fulfillment and attention from other people (and things, such as money, for example) as well.

When you are present to your thoughts and you happily treat your thoughts as fulfilling, and as though their guidance is to be taken seriously, by acting on their guidance, your thoughts treat you as fulfilling, and as though your guidance is to be taken seriously, by acting on your guidance when you suggest a new destination for them and you. The result is you feel that you are fulfilling to others and taken seriously by others and that others are fulfilling to you and are to be taken seriously by you. Consequently, you are inclined to treat others as fulfilling and take them seriously, and others are inclined to treat you as fulfilling and take you seriously. Further, you are inclined actually to be fulfilling to others, and others are inclined actually to be fulfilling to you. Thus, you get everything that you truly want when you treat your thoughts as fulfilling and take their guidance seriously.

The example you are inclined to set for others in regard to how you should be treated: By not paying attention to your own thoughts or taking them seriously, you set the example for others that you should not be paid attention to or taken seriously.

As you learn to pay attention to your own thoughts and take them seriously, you come to set the example for others that you should be paid attention to and taken seriously.

Your main limiting belief: My thoughts that I am already happy are dull and unexciting and so I should avoid them and not take them seriously.

Response to your main limiting belief: Only when I pay attention to my thoughts that I am already happy will I be truly happy. It is my thoughts that I am happy, and not my thoughts that I am unhappy, that are truly fulfilling.

The three aspects of self in your internal dynamic: There is a part of you that imposes the idea that your thoughts that you are already happy as you are are dull and unexciting because they don't motivate you to identify and avoid what is boring. There is a part of you that reacts to this by judging your thoughts that you are already happy as boring and avoiding them and not taking them seriously. And there is a part of you that simply tunes out your thoughts that you are already happy in an attempt to maintain fulfillment since your thoughts that you are already happy are seemingly causing you to be deprived and trapped within you.

In the healthy version of this dynamic: The part of you that would impose the idea that your thoughts that you are already happy as you are are unexciting instead guides the acknowledgment of your thoughts that you are already happy toward the aim of greater fulfillment. The part of you that would react by judging your thoughts that you are already happy as boring and not taking them seriously instead acknowledges your thoughts that you are already happy as fulfilling and takes them seriously. And the part of you that would tune out your thoughts that you are already happy in an attempt to maintain fulfillment in light of their actually causing unfulfillment within you instead tunes into your thoughts that you are already happy and acts on them since they are now actually maintaining freedom and happiness within you.

How to get all parts of yourself on the same team and working for you: Listen to and acknowledge your thoughts that you are unhappy—or that various choices would make you unhappy—and that you should dismiss your thoughts that you are already happy as boring, and recognize that these thoughts have your best interests in mind. They actually just want to help you ensure that you are happy and fulfilled and that the choices that you make will lead you to be happy and fulfilled, which is what you want as well. It's just that they are misdirected in how best to go about making you fulfilled and your choices fulfilling, believing that you have to focus on what is making you unhappy and what would make you unhappy in order to avoid and escape all of these things and be happy.

So after you listen to them and acknowledge them, let them know that you understand that their main intention is to help you be happy and fulfilled now and in the future, and that they can even better achieve this aim if they help you listen to and acknowledge your thoughts that you are already happy and might be happy if you make the choices you're considering instead. This way you can actually get what you want, which is to be happy and fulfilled and to make choices that will lead you to happiness and fulfillment.

What you're inclined to identify with: You're inclined to identify with your thought that your thoughts of happiness are unfulfilling and shouldn't be taken seriously.

Understanding what your thoughts are really saying to you: Your thoughts are saying to you, as though in conversation with you, "I feel like I'm boring to you and that you don't take me seriously, and I want to be fulfilling to you and taken seriously by you." In other words, the way to show that you are really listening to your thoughts is to respond to them by recognizing them as fulfilling and taking them seriously, and accepting them and giving them your attention. This is the true path to fulfillment.

What your thoughts really want and how they try to get it: Your thoughts really want to be preserved by you, accepted by you, and connected to you, and you make them believe that in order to accomplish these aims, they need to be fulfilling to you and taken seriously by you. Therefore, they try to do whatever they believe they need to do in order to be taken seriously by you so they can prove that they are fulfilling. If this means pointing out what might make you unfulfilled, then this is what they'll do. But if you pay attention to them, you'll recognize that they actually just want to be fulfilling to you, and they're only pointing out what might make you unfulfilled because you're making them believe that this is the only way they'll be taken seriously by you. If you take them seriously when they point out what might make you *fulfilled*, then this is what they'll do for you instead.

Because you make your thoughts believe that, in order to get what they want, they need to be fulfilling to you and taken seriously by you, you seek to be fulfilling to, and taken seriously by, other people and the world in order to be kept in the world and in other people's lives, to be accepted by the world and other people, and to connect to the world and other people. And, therefore, you try to do whatever you believe you need to do in order to be taken seriously by the world and other people so you can prove that you are fulfilling. If this means pointing out what's unfulfilling in the world, then this is what you'll do. But if you pay attention to your own thoughts, you'll recognize that they actually just want to be fulfilling, and if you point out what's *fulfilling* in them and in the world and the people around you, then you'll actually be taken seriously by the world and the people around you.

Internal experience image: When you are stressed, and especially when you have been stressed for a long time and so are more caught up in your personality's obstacles and coping mechanisms, you are inclined to distract yourself and run away from what you perceive as unhappy and unfulfilling thoughts. It is as though these thoughts are nagging children, and you don't want to pay attention to them, so you run away from them. But the result is that they chase after you and come up with more and more elaborate ways of getting your attention. Further, if you run away from them, you often end up backed into a corner and trapped by them. Meanwhile, you end up feeling simultaneously chased and trapped, and like others are running away from you and not giving you attention or taking you seriously.

However, if you simply give the children your attention, they are satisfied because they have gotten what they wanted, and they stop chasing after you. The result is that you end up feeling fulfilled and happy where you are without anything to run away from.

What you're attracted to in others: You're attracted to people who bring about active thinking in you, because then you have stimulating thoughts to replay and make more exciting. When you are dismissing your thoughts and running away from them, you are attracted to people who don't pay much attention to you and who don't take you seriously, because then you can distract yourself from them with more exciting people and things in order to be happy. When you are present to your thoughts and hearing them out, you are attracted to people who make you feel happy and fulfilled because they pay attention to you, take you seriously, and also make you feel exciting, entertaining, and free.

The types of words you use to criticize yourself and others: boring, dull, downer, too serious, unhappy

The types of words you use to praise yourself and others: exciting, entertaining, fulfilling, fun, happy

Allowing Thought (Enneagram Type 6)

You allow the thoughts of others to be manifested through yourself, through the decisions that you make. In other words, you're inclined to try to make the decisions that other people would want you to make, rather than trusting your own thoughts to guide you securely in your decisions. You feel that you have to consider all the possible ways that things could go wrong if you make any particular decision, because you feel that you are responsible for making decisions that will keep people you can depend on in your life so that you have security and guidance.

Your relationship with yourself: You are inclined to dissociate from and tune out your own thoughts because you feel that they do not provide grounded, stable, dependable, or trustworthy guidance.

You feel that your thoughts might not guide you securely or dependably in your decision-making and might lead you to make decisions that would cause you to be abandoned by the people you depend on because they might not be the decisions that those people would want you to make. So your way of dealing with this potential abandonment is to avoid it altogether and just tune out your own thoughts in an attempt to make the decisions that other people would want you to make and maintain the dependability, security, and guidance of those people in your life.

However, not trusting your own thoughts and decisions merely results in other people not trusting your thoughts and decisions either. So you keep trying to be dependable to others in the hopes that you'll have security and guidance from them as you trust yourself less and less to make decisions on your own. Further, you have a more and more difficult time actually being dependable to anyone as you try to be dependable to all of your supporters and sources of security at once, and you end up making commitments that you fail to keep, which can lead to the realization of your fears of being abandoned by the people you depend on. The more you look for guidance and security outside yourself, the more your anxious catastrophizing and indecisiveness—the result of your not knowing what or whom to trust—grows, until you begin to ground, listen to, and trust your own thoughts.

The key to shifting your relationships: The key is to notice when you are tuning out your thoughts that you perceive as ungrounded, unstable, or untrustworthy, and to practice acknowledging at those times that you are tuning out and what you are tuning out and why. Then, shift your attention back to your thoughts in the present moment and listen to them, acknowledge their potential trustworthiness, and make your decisions based on them. This way, instead of trying to get security and guidance from others and constantly worrying about all the ways you could lose your security if you make one decision or another, you feel secure and stable within yourself as you get clear, trustworthy guidance from your own grounded thoughts.

When you are tuned into your own thoughts and so already feel that you have trustworthy guidance, your attempts to be trustworthy become the overflow of your already existing internal security. This is in contrast to their being attempts to tune out the lack of security that you are creating within yourself by tuning out your own thoughts. The result is that rather than trying to get security by making decisions that you believe other people would want you to make, which only leads to greater insecurity, you will be able to be secure in yourself and dependable to others by listening to and making decisions based on your own thoughts. This requires far less energy on your part because you don't have to try so hard to make decisions that everyone in your life would be okay with without your own decisiveness to guide you; you just have to make decisions based on your own thinking and allow your thoughts to guide you toward positive outcomes where the right people are still there for you when you want them to be.

How you are inclined to treat yourself and others and how you are inclined to feel that others treat you: When you are stressed and/or unhealthy (due to prolonged stress), you are inclined to treat yourself and others as undependable and untrustworthy, and you are inclined to feel that others treat you as undependable and untrustworthy.

When you are relaxed and healthy (due to prolonged lack of stress either because of circumstances or because you've been responding positively to life's obstacles), you are inclined to treat yourself and others as dependable and trustworthy, and you are inclined to feel that others treat you as dependable and trustworthy.

The Golden Rule applied: Be decisively and stably present so other people can make decisions in accordance with your thinking, and other people will be decisively and stably present so you can make decisions in accordance with their thinking. Be loyal and trustworthy to other people by trusting and acting on your own thinking, and other people will be loyal and trustworthy to you by trusting and acting on their own thinking.

This works because when you are decisive in your thinking and decision-making, you give permission to others to be decisive in their thinking and decision-making, too. By being present, stable, grounded, loyal, and trustworthy, you bring other people to be more present, stable, grounded, loyal, and trustworthy as well, and the result is that you and the people around you have security, stability, and trustworthy guidance. You are much more dependable and stable to others when you act on your own thinking, so then others reflect this and are much more dependable and stable to you, too. Following your example, they do what they think rather than anxiously trying to make decisions that they believe you and other people would want them to make in an effort to maintain your security and that of others. When you are decisive rather than always looking to other people's thinking for guidance, you will grow to trust your own thinking and be a stable and trustworthy presence and source of guidance to other people. Then other people around you will be stable, dependable sources of guidance to others and to you.

How to begin applying the Golden Rule: If you simply start trying to make decisions based on your own thinking, you won't be in touch enough with your thoughts to do this so easily; you won't even know what you think to make decisions based upon this. You will find yourself just being inclined to make decisions based on what other people think. When you try to make decisions based on your own thoughts, you will continue to be supported in your feeling that your thinking is ungrounded and untrustworthy. Further, you will continue to be supported in your feeling that making decisions based on your own thinking will cause you to lose the dependability of other people in your life. So you'll continue to feel that in order to maintain the security and guidance of other people, you need to tune out what you think.

So, you can't just change your external approach and make the shift. You first need to change the way you approach things internally (or change your internal approach as you change your external approach).

Start here: Tune into your own decisive thoughts and allow them to be manifested through yourself. In other words, trust your own thoughts enough to make decisions based on your own thoughts rather than based on other people's thoughts, and do so. This way you will already be making yourself feel like you have trustworthy, dependable guidance and security, and so you will be more open to tuning securely into the trustworthiness and dependability of other people (and things, such as money, for example) as well.

When you are present to your thoughts and you reliably treat your thoughts as dependable, and as though their guidance is trustworthy, by acting on their guidance, your thoughts treat you as dependable, and as though your guidance is trustworthy, by acting on your guidance when you suggest a new destination for them and you. The result is you feel that you are dependable and trustworthy to others and that others are dependable and trustworthy to you. Consequently, you are inclined to treat others as dependable and trust them, and others are inclined to treat you as dependable and trust you. Further, you are inclined actually to be dependable and trustworthy to others, and others are inclined actually to be dependable and trustworthy to you. Thus, you get everything that you truly want when you treat your thoughts as dependable and trust their guidance.

The example you are inclined to set for others in regard to how you should be treated: By not trusting or depending on your own thoughts, you set the example for others that you shouldn't be trusted or depended on.

As you learn to trust and depend on your own thoughts, you come to set the example for others that you should be trusted and depended on.

Your main limiting belief: My thoughts that tell me that I can trust my own thinking aren't dependable or trustworthy and so I should tune them out.

Response to your main limiting belief: Only when I trust my thoughts that tell me that I can trust my own thinking will I really be able to trust, and be trustworthy to, anyone or anything else.

The three aspects of self in your internal dynamic: There is a part of you that imposes the idea that your thoughts that you can trust your thoughts are insecure in the guidance they provide. There is a part of you that reacts to this by judging your thoughts that you can trust your thoughts as unstable and untrustworthy and getting anxious about them and dismissing them. And there is a part of you that simply tunes out your thoughts that you can trust your thoughts in an attempt to maintain security since your thoughts that you can trust your thoughts are seemingly causing instability within you.

In the healthy version of this dynamic: The part of you that would impose the idea that your thoughts that you can trust your thoughts are insecure in the guidance they provide instead guides the making of decisions based on your thoughts toward the aim of security and stability. The part of you that would react by judging your thoughts that you can trust your thoughts as untrustworthy and getting anxious about them instead acknowledges your thoughts that you can trust your thoughts as stable and trusts them. And the part of you that would tune out your thoughts that you can trust your thoughts in an attempt to maintain security in light of their actually causing instability within you instead tunes into your thoughts that you can trust your thoughts and makes decisions based on them since they are now actually maintaining security and stability within you.

How to get all parts of yourself on the same team and working for you: Listen to and acknowledge your thoughts that other people's thoughts are more trustworthy and dependable than your own thoughts and that you should tune out your own thoughts and make decisions based on other people's thoughts, and recognize that these thoughts have your best interests in mind. They actually just want to help you maintain the security and dependable guidance of others, which is what you want as well. It's just that they are misdirected in how best to go about maintaining security and dependable guidance, believing that you have to tune out your own thoughts in order to do this.

So after you listen to them and acknowledge them, let them know that you understand that their main intention is to help you maintain security and guidance, and that they can even better achieve this aim if they help you tune into and make decisions based on your own thoughts instead. This way you can actually get what you want, which is guidance that is dependable, trustworthy, stable, and secure.

What you're inclined to identify with: You're inclined to identify with your thought that your thoughts are undependable and untrustworthy.

Understanding what your thoughts are really saying to you: Your thoughts are saying to you, as though in conversation with you, "I feel like I'm undependable and untrustworthy to you, and I want to be dependable and trustworthy to you." In other words, the way to show that you are really listening to your thoughts is to respond to them by recognizing them as dependable and trustworthy and making decisions based on them. This is the true path to trustworthiness.

What your thoughts really want and how they try to get it: Your thoughts really want to be preserved by you, accepted by you, and connected to you, and you make them believe that in order to accomplish these aims, they need to be trustworthy and dependable to you. Therefore, they try to do whatever they believe they need to do in order to be dependable to you so they can prove that they are trustworthy. If this means not speaking up and instead directing you to the thoughts of other people whom you deem trustworthy, then this is what they'll do. But if you pay attention to them, you'll recognize that they actually just want to be trustworthy to you, and they're only not speaking up and instead directing you to other people because you're making them believe that this is the only way they'll be dependable. If you recognize them as dependable to you when they *speak up*, then this is what they'll do for you instead.

Because you make your thoughts believe that, in order to get what they want, they need to be trustworthy and dependable to you, you seek to be trustworthy and dependable to other people and to the world in order to be kept in the world and in other people's lives, to be accepted by the world and other people, and to connect to the world and other people. And, therefore, you try to do whatever you believe you need to do in order to be dependable to the world and other people so you can prove that you are trustworthy. If this means trying to make decisions it seems other people would want you to make and not making decisions based on your own thinking, then this is what you'll do. But if you pay attention to your own thoughts, you'll recognize that they actually just want to be trustworthy, and if you make your decisions based on them, then you'll actually be recognized by the world and the people around you as dependable.

Internal experience image: When you are stressed, and especially when you have been stressed for a long time and so are more caught up in your personality's obstacles and coping mechanisms, you are inclined to tune out your own thoughts and look to others for guidance. Whenever you have to make a decision, it is as though you have a committee meeting in your head. You ask yourself things like "What would this person think if I did this? What about this other person? Would I still have this person in my life if I make this decision?" You don't trust yourself to make your own decisions and you are afraid that if you make the wrong decision then you might lose the people in your life on whom you do depend.

The only way to get the feeling of security you're looking for is to consult with your own thoughts, and not just with others, when you make decisions. The most stable and dependable guidance comes from within, and you can only truly get—and recognize—trustworthy guidance and security from others once you trust yourself.

What you're attracted to in others: You're attracted to people who are decisive in their thinking, because then you have decisive thinking to reflect and express through yourself, to guide you in your decision-making. In the same vein, you are attracted to people who are stable, dependable sources of guidance, because then you know what decisions to make so you can maintain their security in your life. In the ideal, you are attracted to people to whom you are trustworthy when you make decisions based on your own thoughts so that you are dependable to these people simply by following your own internal guidance.

The types of words you use to criticize yourself and others: irresponsible, disloyal, untrustworthy, undependable, unreliable

The types of words you use to praise yourself and others: responsible, loyal, trustworthy, dependable, reliable

Sharing Feeling (Enneagram Type 2)

You come up with your own loving, caring feelings, and then you share your loving feelings with others. In other words, you're inclined to come up with ways you can demonstrate and express your caring and be helpful to other people. You feel that if you were to take care of yourself, you would be selfish. But if you help other people and show that you care enough through things like compliments, flattery, humor, helpful actions, and physical touch and intimacy, then they will appreciate you, care about you, and love you for everything you've done for them.

Your relationship with yourself: You are inclined to ignore yourself and even actively be mean to yourself and call yourself selfish for needing things as you try to be loving, caring, and helpful to other people.

You feel that you have to be loving and caring toward other people because if you are caring toward others then you might be cared about by others. So you try to be helpful to others in the hope that they'll be appreciative of you, want you, and need you in return.

However, when you direct all of your loving, caring energy outward toward others, you don't get the feeling of being appreciated that you want because you are not appreciating yourself. So you end up feeling increasingly unappreciated, unloved, and uncared for as you increasingly try to remedy this by being more helpful to others. This happens until you learn to love, care for, appreciate, and help yourself by allowing others to care for and help themselves and to be caring and helpful to you as well. In essence, you are inclined to try to help yourself by trying to help others rather than by helping yourself, and you need to learn to help yourself by actually helping yourself.

The key to shifting your relationships: The key is to notice when you are trying to help other people and the world around you by imposing on them what you feel would be helpful to them in disregard of what *they* feel would be helpful to them, and to practice acknowledging at those times that you are imposing and what you are imposing and why. Then, shift your attention and energy to yourself and love and care for yourself and allow other people to help themselves and to help you as well. This way, instead of making yourself helpless by directing all of your overbearing feelings toward trying to help everyone but yourself, you are appreciated and cared for by your own love for yourself.

When you love yourself and are already taken care of by yourself and so already feel appreciated, your love for others and your attempts to help others become the truly selfless overflow of your already existing genuine love for yourself. This is in contrast to their being needy, clingy, selfish attempts to get from others the love and caring that you aren't getting from yourself. The result is that rather than trying to help and care for others in the ways that *you* feel they need to be helped, where you have to manipulate them into letting you help them, you will be able to help and care for them in the ways that *they* feel they want or need to be helped. This requires far less energy on your part because you don't have to go out of your way to help in ways that aren't wanted and that won't be appreciated; you just have to help other people where they are actually asking for help or are actually in need of help, and this allows you actually to be helpful, loved, and appreciated.

How you are inclined to treat yourself and others and how you are inclined to feel that others treat you: When you are stressed and/or unhealthy (due to prolonged stress), you are inclined to treat yourself and others as selfish and helpless, and you are inclined to feel that others treat you as selfish and helpless.

When you are relaxed and healthy (due to prolonged lack of stress either because of circumstances or because you've been responding positively to life's obstacles), you are inclined to treat yourself and others as loving and helpful, and you are inclined to feel that others treat you as loving and helpful.

The Golden Rule applied: Allow other people to share their loving, caring feelings with you and meet your wants and needs, and you will be able to share your loving, caring feelings with other people and meet their wants and needs. Or, more simply, allow other people to care for and help you, and you will be able to care for and help other people.

This works because if you let other people care for and help you then you won't be denying and neglecting your own needs. You will, instead, be able to have those needs met. So you will be able to focus on selflessly loving and helping other people in ways that would be truly helpful to them, and actually meet their needs, without needing anything from those people in return. Rather than seemingly competing with others as you try to be more helpful to them than they are to you, when you allow other people to be helpful, they allow you to be helpful, and so everyone involved feels helpful, loved, and appreciated.

How to begin applying the Golden Rule: If you simply start trying to allow other people to be helpful to themselves and to you, you will continue to be supported in your feeling that other people are helpless and need your help. Further, you will continue to be supported in your feeling that you really shouldn't have needs because you need to be there for other people. So you'll continue to neglect your own needs as you try to help others more, and you'll continue to feel that other people don't appreciate or love you.

So, you can't just change your external approach and make the shift. You first need to change the way you approach things internally (or change your internal approach as you change your external approach).

Start here: Share your helpful, loving feelings with yourself and care for yourself. This way you will already be making yourself feel like you are being allowed to be helpful and caring and like love and appreciation are being shared with you, and so you will be more open to allowing other people (and things, such as money, for example) to be helpful and caring and share their love and appreciation with you as well.

When you are present to your feelings and you appreciatively treat your feelings as loving, and as though their intentions are helpful, by acting on their intentions, your feelings treat you as loving, and as though your intentions are helpful, by acting on your intentions when you suggest a new destination for them and you. The result is you feel that you are loving and helpful to others and that others are loving and helpful to you. Consequently, you are inclined to treat others as loving and recognize their positive intentions in helping you, and others are inclined to treat you as loving and recognize your positive intentions in helping them. Further, you are inclined actually to be loving and helpful to others, and others are inclined actually to be loving and helpful to you. Thus, you get everything that you truly want when you treat your feelings as loving and recognize their positive intentions in helping you.

The example you are inclined to set for others in regard to how you should be treated: By not loving or caring for yourself, you set the example for others that you shouldn't be loved or cared for.

As you learn to direct your loving feelings toward yourself and care for yourself, you come to set the example for others that you should be loved and cared for.

Your main limiting belief: My loving feelings, when directed toward myself, are not loving or helpful, and so I should direct my loving feelings toward others instead of toward myself.

Response to your main limiting belief: Only when I direct my loving feelings toward myself can I truly be helpful to anyone else and actually feel cared for and appreciated, because no one will care for me and appreciate me if *I* don't.

The three aspects of self in your internal dynamic: There is a part of you that imposes the idea that your loving feelings, when directed toward yourself, are not helpful because they don't seem to be helping anyone else. There is a part of you that reacts to this by judging your loving feelings that are directed toward yourself as unloving and selfish and feeling ashamed of them and dismissing them. And there is a part of you that simply tunes out your loving feelings that are directed toward yourself in an attempt to maintain love and help yourself since your loving feelings that are directed toward yourself are seemingly causing hatefulness and helplessness within you.

In the healthy version of this dynamic: The part of you that would impose the idea that your loving feelings, when directed toward yourself, are not helpful instead guides the direction of your loving feelings toward yourself toward the aim of real love and caring. The part of you that would react by judging your loving feelings that are directed toward yourself as unloving and selfish and feeling ashamed of them instead acknowledges your loving feelings that are directed toward yourself as loving and caring and appreciates them. And the part of you that would tune out your loving feelings that are directed toward yourself in an attempt to maintain love and help yourself in light of their actually causing hatefulness and helplessness within you instead tunes into your loving feelings that are directed toward yourself and acts on them since they are now actually maintaining love and helpfulness within you.

How to get all parts of yourself on the same team and working for you: Listen to and acknowledge your feelings that you need to help other people by doing things for them and that trying to help yourself doesn't actually help anyone, and recognize that these feelings have your best interests in mind. They actually just want to help you be loving and helpful, which is what you want as well. It's just that they are misdirected in how best to go about being loving and helpful, believing that you have to direct your loving feelings away from yourself and toward others in order to be this.

So after you listen to them and acknowledge them, let them know that you understand that their main intention is to help you be loving and helpful, and that they can even better achieve this aim if they help you direct your loving, helpful feelings toward yourself instead. This way you can actually get what you want, which is to be loved and loving, helped and helpful.

What you're inclined to identify with: You're inclined to identify with your feeling that your feelings that are directed toward yourself are selfish and helpless.

Understanding what your feelings are really saying to you: Your feelings are saying to you, as though in conversation with you, "I feel like I'm selfish and helpless to you, and I want to be loving and helpful to you." In other words, the way to show that you are really listening to your feelings is to respond to them by recognizing them as loving and helpful, and directing them toward yourself. This is the true path to love.

What your feelings really want and how they try to get it: Your feelings really want to be preserved by you, accepted by you, and connected to you, and you make them believe that in order to accomplish these aims, they need to be loving and helpful to you. Therefore, they try to do whatever they believe they need to do in order to be helpful to you so they can prove that they are loving. If this means trying to help the world and other people, then this is what they'll do. But if you pay attention to them, you'll recognize that they actually just want to be loving to you, and they're only trying to help others because you're making them believe that this is the only way they'll be loving to you. If you recognize them as loving when they are helpful to *you*, then this is what they'll do for you instead.

Because you make your feelings believe that, in order to get what they want, they need to be loving and helpful to you, you seek to be loving and helpful to other people and to the world in order to be kept in the world and in other people's lives, to be accepted by the world and other people, and to connect to the world and other people. And, therefore, you try to do whatever you believe you need to do in order to be helpful to the world and other people so you can prove that you are loving. If this means trying to help the world and other people and ignoring yourself, then this is what you'll do. But if you pay attention to your own feelings, you'll recognize that they actually just want to be loving, and if you recognize them as loving when they try to help *you*, then you'll actually be recognized by the world and the people around you as helpful.

Internal experience image: When you are stressed, and especially when you have been stressed for a long time and so are more caught up in your personality's obstacles and coping mechanisms, you are inclined to ignore your own needs as you try to be helpful to others. It is as though you are a car that drives people around and meets their needs but doesn't fill up its gas tank or change its oil or get a car wash. Eventually, you're running on fumes and breaking down, and resentful that no one else is taking care of you as you have been taking care of them.

The only way you'll be able to keep caring for and helping other people is if you direct your loving feelings toward yourself and help yourself. Then you find other people to be much more appreciative of you and caring toward you as you are much more effectively helpful to them and as your caring is actually experienced as the love that you intend.

What you're attracted to in others: You're attracted to people with whom you can share your loving, caring feelings, because then you feel helpful. In the same vein, you are attracted to people whom you can help, because then you feel like you are helpful and loving and that you can meet their needs. Ideally, the people you choose to bring into your life and help are people who will appreciate you in return, because then you can get the love, caring, and appreciation that you really want.

The types of words you use to criticize yourself and others: selfish, cold, uncaring, unkind, helpless

The types of words you use to praise yourself and others: selfless, caring, loving, kind, helpful

Receiving Feeling (Enneagram Type 4)

You look for things in the world around you that bring about strong feelings in you, and then you try to find yourself in these reactive feelings and discover how you are different from other people and how things should have been different from the way they were. In other words, you're inclined to seek out and replay experiences that bring about intense reactive emotions in you, mainly the feelings of insignificance and lack—of not being treated as well as other people are and not having what other people have. You want to be uniquely important, to have personal significance, to matter, and you feel that by comparing yourself to others and looking for how you are different from them, you will find out how you are unique and special and you will then experience the feeling of significance that you seek.

Your relationship with yourself: You are inclined to replay your feelings that you have been wronged and that you are incomplete and lacking, and to criticize and dismiss your feelings that you are already uniquely important, complete, and worthy of, and getting, positive attention (because you deem these feelings insignificant and unworthy of your attention).

You feel that some of your feelings are insignificant or unimportant because they don't fit your conception of what is original and important—of what is "you". So you judge these feelings within you, criticizing them and trying to make yourself more uniquely important by dismissing and not allowing the expression within you of that which seems unoriginal or insignificant to you.

However, rejecting those feelings that don't seem to you to be worthy of your attention merely brings about more of a sense of incompletion, lack, insignificance, unworthiness, not being able to express yourself or be heard or understood, and even being attacked. Your replaying feelings are like a broken record, and so the rest of the record never gets to play and be heard—the rest of your feelings never get to be expressed and understood. Further, you end up envious of others for having what you feel you don't have as you are cutting off the expression of parts of yourself and trying to come up with an identity other than the one you have in search of some kind of greater importance. So you find yourself increasingly dismissive of others and the world around you and increasingly dismissed by others as you have been dismissing yourself. You feel increasingly wronged by everyone around you, and by yourself, until you learn to listen to and accept your own feelings as they are without dismissing or judging them.

The key to shifting your relationships: The key is to notice when you are getting caught up in focusing on and replaying your feelings that you have been wronged, treated badly, as insignificant, not as you should be treated, and left out, misunderstood, not listened to, and that nothing you do matters, and to practice acknowledging at those times that you are judging and what you are judging and why. Then, shift your attention to what is going on in the present moment as it is and allow yourself to listen to your feelings that you are treated well, as important, as you are worthy of being treated, and included, understood, listened to, and that everything you do matters, already, without dismissing these feelings as insignificant. This way, rather than bringing about more reasons to feel regret and blame, where you try to discover how you are significant by identifying how you have been treated less well and therefore differently from others, you bring about more reasons to be accepting of yourself and others as you notice how important you already are and how much you and everything you do already matter.

When you are listening to your feelings that you are already treated as important and so already feel that you are treated as you should be treated, your attempts to make yourself matter become the overflow of your already existing sense of self-worth. This is in contrast to their being highly critical and judgmental attempts to correct how you are treated because you are too busy focusing on how you've been wronged and how you and your actions are insignificant to accept yourself and the past decisions and experiences that led you here. The result is that rather than trying to correct the past by blaming others and yourself for their ill treatment of you, which only leads you to find more experiences that support your feeling wronged and insignificant, you will be able to recognize yourself and every action you take, however small, as significant. This requires far less energy on your part because you don't have to focus on how you haven't been treated as you should be treated, and continually be filled with regret and blame as you and the people around you dismiss you, with you never allowing yourself to experience your importance and the importance of your actions; you just have to allow yourself to experience the significance in yourself and in everything that you do, and this actually encourages other people to listen to you and to treat you well and increases your sense of your own self-worth.

How you are inclined to treat yourself and others and how you are inclined to feel that others treat you: When you are stressed and/or unhealthy (due to prolonged stress), you are inclined to treat yourself and others as insignificant and unworthy of attention, and you are inclined to feel that others treat you as insignificant and unworthy of attention.

When you are relaxed and healthy (due to prolonged lack of stress either because of circumstances or because you've been responding positively to life's obstacles), you are inclined to treat yourself and others as important and worthy of attention, and you are inclined to feel that others treat you as important and worthy of attention.

The Golden Rule applied: Accept and treat other people as uniquely significant and important as they are, and other people will accept and treat you as uniquely significant and important as you are. Allow other people to express themselves, to be heard, and to matter, and other people will allow you to express yourself, to be heard, and to matter.

This works because if you don't focus so much on expressing yourself and making yourself important all the time (dismissing others as unimportant or unworthy of your attention), but instead allow other people to be important and to express themselves and be heard, too, then other people won't feel the need to react and talk over you and dismiss you. This is because they will feel like they have expressed themselves and have been heard and treated as important as well, and so they will listen to you and allow you to express yourself. When you fully listen to others and treat them as though they matter, then others will fully listen to you and treat you as though you matter, too. Rather than seemingly competing with others as you try to be the one who's important and gets to express yourself, when you allow other people to be important and express themselves, too, they allow you to be important and express yourself, and so everyone involved feels significant, worthy of attention, fully expressed, and complete.

How to begin applying the Golden Rule: If you simply start trying to listen to other people and allow them to express themselves, you will continue to be supported in your feeling that other people aren't really important or worth your attention. Further, you will continue to be supported in your feeling that you're not being allowed to express yourself and that you need to cut people off and dismiss them and be more important somehow in order to be heard. So you'll continue to feel that you aren't worth other people's attention and that you need to identify how you are uniquely important by finding this in your replaying feelings of being wronged, victimized, or simply left out and therefore in how you must be different from others. And you'll continue to feel that other people aren't listening to you or allowing you to express yourself.

So, you can't just change your external approach and make the shift. You first need to change the way you approach things internally (or change your internal approach as you change your external approach).

Start here: Pay attention to and receive your own uniquely significant feelings from yourself. This way you will already be making yourself feel like you are being allowed to express yourself and like you are significant and worthy of being listened to and understood, and so you will be more open to noticing and accepting (and feeling worthy of) attention from other people (and things, such as money, for example) as well.

When you are present to your feelings and you completely treat your feelings as important, and as though their intentions are to be treated as worthy of attention, by acting on their intentions, your feelings treat you as important, and as though your intentions are to be treated as worthy of attention, by acting on your intentions when you suggest a new destination for them and you. The result is you feel that you are important to others and treated as worthy of others' attention and that others are important to you and are worthy of your attention. Consequently, you are inclined to treat others as important and pay attention to them, and others are inclined to treat you as important and pay attention to you. Further, you are inclined actually to be important to others, and others are inclined actually to be important to you. Thus, you get everything that you truly want when you treat your feelings as important and pay worthwhile attention to their intentions.

The example you are inclined to set for others in regard to how you should be treated: By not paying attention to your own feelings or treating them as important, you set the example for others that you should not be paid attention to or treated as important.

As you learn to pay attention to your own feelings and treat them as important, you come to set the example for others that you should be paid attention to and treated as important.

Your main limiting belief: My feelings that I am already important are insignificant and so I should dismiss them and treat them as unworthy of my attention.

Response to your main limiting belief: Only when I pay attention to my feelings that I am already important will I feel truly important. It is my feelings of being significant and treated well, and not my feelings of being insignificant and wronged, that are truly important.

The three aspects of self in your internal dynamic: There is a part of you that imposes the idea that your feelings that you are already uniquely important and worthy as you are are insignificant because they don't motivate you to identify how you are different from others in the way you are treated. There is a part of you that reacts to this by judging your feelings that you are already important as unworthy of your attention and dismissing them. And there is a part of you that simply tunes out your feelings that you are already important in an attempt to maintain your personal significance since your feelings that you are already important are seemingly causing you to be wronged and treated badly within you.

In the healthy version of this dynamic: The part of you that would impose the idea that your feelings that you are already uniquely important as you are are insignificant instead guides the acknowledgment of your feelings that you are already uniquely important toward the aim of greater personal significance and worthiness. The part of you that would react by judging your feelings that you are already important as unworthy of your attention and dismissing them instead acknowledges your feelings that you are already important as important and accepts them. And the part of you that would tune out your feelings that you are already important in an attempt to maintain your personal significance in light of their actually causing you to be wronged within you instead tunes into your feelings that you are already important and acts on them since they are now actually maintaining your being treated well within you.

How to get all parts of yourself on the same team and working for you: Listen to and acknowledge your feelings that you have been treated badly and that you should dismiss your feelings that you are already treated well as insignificant, and recognize that these feelings have your best interests in mind. They actually just want to help you ensure that you are treated as you are worthy of being treated, which is what you want as well. It's just that they are misdirected in how best to go about making you important and worthy, believing that you have to focus on how you've been wronged in order to correct this and also to identify how you are actually different from others and therefore, in this way, important.

So after you listen to them and acknowledge them, let them know that you understand that their main intention is to help you correct any injustices committed against you so that you can be treated as you are worthy of being treated, and also to help you identify what makes you uniquely significant and what makes you matter, and that they can even better achieve these aims if they help you listen to and acknowledge your feelings that you are already treated as you are worthy of being treated, and that you already matter and are important, instead. This way you can actually get what you want, which is to feel like you matter and are worthy of being treated as important.

What you're inclined to identify with: You're inclined to identify with your feeling that your feelings of importance are insignificant and unworthy of your attention.

Understanding what your feelings are really saying to you: Your feelings are saying to you, as though in conversation with you, "I feel like I'm insignificant to you and am treated by you as though I'm unworthy of your attention, and I want to be important to you and treated as worthy of your attention." In other words, the way to show that you are really listening to your feelings is to respond to them by recognizing them as important and treating them as worthy of your attention, and accepting them and giving them your attention. This is the true path to personal significance.

What your feelings really want and how they try to get it: Your feelings really want to be preserved by you, accepted by you, and connected to you, and you make them believe that in order to accomplish these aims, they need to be significant and worthy of attention to you. Therefore, they try to do whatever they believe they need to do in order to be worthy of your attention so they can prove that they are significant. If this means pointing out how you've been treated as insignificant, then this is what they'll do. But if you pay attention to them, you'll recognize that they actually just want to be significant to you, and they're only pointing out how you've been treated as insignificant because you're making them believe that this is the only way they'll be worthy of your attention. If you recognize them as worthy of your attention when they point out how you've been treated as *significant*, then this is what they'll do for you instead.

Because you make your feelings believe that, in order to get what they want, they need to be significant and worthy of attention to you, you seek to be significant and worthy of attention to other people and to the world in order to be kept in the world and in other people's lives, to be accepted by the world and other people, and to connect to the world and other people. And, therefore, you try to do whatever you believe you need to do in order to be worthy of the world's and other people's attention so you can prove that you are significant. If this means pointing out how other people and the world around you are insignificant and unworthy of attention, then this is what you'll do. But if you pay attention to your own feelings, you'll recognize that they actually just want to be significant, and if you point out what's *significant* in them and in the world and the people around you, then you'll actually be recognized as worthy of the attention of the world and the people around you.

Internal experience image: When you are stressed, and especially when you have been stressed for a long time and so are more caught up in your personality's obstacles and coping mechanisms, you are inclined to treat some of your feelings as more important than others and replay them over and over again. It is as though you are listening to a broken record, and when you do this, the rest of the record never gets to play. The rest of your feelings never get to express themselves or be heard by you. It is as though all of your feelings are waiting in line to be heard by you, and you listen to the first ones in line repeat themselves over and over again. Meanwhile, the rest of your feelings end up feeling like you don't listen to them or understand them and like they are being left out. Further, when they try to speak up and express themselves, you dismiss them, treating them as though they are unworthy of your attention, insignificant, and unimportant. As long as you replay certain feelings and leave out the rest of them, you end up feeling like you're incomplete and missing something, and you end up feeling as you are making your own feelings feel.

On the other hand, if you move past the replay of the broken part of the record, where you are focused on how you have been wronged, and you allow the rest of the record to play, you end up feeling complete, uniquely significant, and worthy.

What you're attracted to in others: You're attracted to people who bring about strong feelings and emotions in you, because then you have strong feelings to replay and identify with. When you are criticizing and dismissing your feelings, you are attracted to people who criticize and dismiss you and make you feel wronged, lacking and longing, because then you feel special since you are treated differently from others who are acknowledged and accepted. When you are accepting your feelings, you are attracted to people who make you feel uniquely important because they listen to you and make you feel like you can express yourself and that you matter to them.

The types of words you use to criticize yourself and others: cliche, ordinary, generic, unoriginal, insignificant

The types of words you use to praise yourself and others: unique, original, creative, important, significant

Allowing Feeling (Enneagram Type 3)

You allow the feelings of others to be manifested through yourself, through who you try to be. In other words, you're inclined to try to be what other people want you to be, rather than valuing and being authentic to your own feelings about who you are. You feel that you have to meet other people's expectations of you and be successful in their eyes and that you have to work to adapt and accomplish things in order to have value.

Your relationship with yourself: You are inclined to dissociate from and tune out your own feelings because you feel that they are not valuable to your accomplishment of goals.

You feel that your feelings might get in the way of you coming across well to others and accomplishing your goals because you might not be what other people want you to be. So your way of dealing with this potential failure is to avoid it altogether and just tune out your own feelings in an attempt to meet other people's expectations of you.

However, not valuing your own feelings and passions merely results in other people not valuing your feelings and passions either. So you strive to achieve your goals and gain some sense of accomplishment and measure of success that might look good to others and make you valuable in their eyes. As you do this, you use your own feelings and others only insofar as they help you reach your goals, and you feel used, yourself, as people value you only to the extent that you value yourself. The more you act and pretend to be something you're not, the more effort it requires to keep acting, and the more your inauthenticity—the disparity between who you are pretending to be and who you really are—grows, until you begin to get in touch with, listen to, and value your own feelings.

The key to shifting your relationships: The key is to notice when you are tuning out your feelings that you perceive as getting in the way of your being seen well by others and getting things done, and trying simply to be who other people want you to be, and to practice acknowledging at those times that you are tuning out and what you are tuning out and why. Then, shift your attention back to your feelings in the present moment and listen to them, acknowledge their potential value, and express and be true to them. This way, instead of trying to be valuable by adapting to meet other people's expectations and ending up without value as yourself because you've been pretending to be someone else, you become genuinely valuable to other people as yourself, in touch with and following your own passions and meeting your own expectations of yourself.

When you are tuned into your own feelings and so already feel that they, and you, are valuable, your attempts to be valuable become the overflow of your already existing genuineness and authenticity. This is in contrast to their being attempts to tune out the lack of authenticity that you are creating within yourself by tuning out your own feelings. The result is that rather than trying to achieve value by being what you believe other people want you to be, which only leads to greater inauthenticity, you will be able to be authentic and meet your own expectations by listening to and expressing your own passionate feelings. This requires far less energy on your part because you don't have to work so hard to be something that you aren't in order to meet other people's expectations without your own passion to motivate you forward; you just have to express and be true to your own feelings and allow them to drive you toward your own goals and you become genuinely valuable as yourself as you ultimately want to be.

How you are inclined to treat yourself and others and how you are inclined to feel that others treat you: When you are stressed and/or unhealthy (due to prolonged stress), you are inclined to treat yourself and others as worthless and unsuccessful, and you are inclined to feel that others treat you as worthless and unsuccessful.

When you are relaxed and healthy (due to prolonged lack of stress either because of circumstances or because you've been responding positively to life's obstacles), you are inclined to treat yourself and others as valuable and successful, and you are inclined to feel that others treat you as valuable and successful.

The Golden Rule applied: Be passionately present so other people can meet your expectations by being themselves, and other people will be passionately present so you can meet their expectations by being yourself. Be valuable to other people by valuing your own feelings and being true to them, and other people will be valuable to you by valuing their own feelings and being true to them.

This works because when you are your genuine self, you give permission to others to be their genuine selves, too. By being present to other people with passion, motivation, and authenticity, you bring other people to be more passionate, motivated, and authentic as well, and the result is that you and the people around you are passionately and genuinely themselves. You are much more valuable to others as yourself, acting in line with your passion and motivation rather than against it, so then others reflect this and are much more valuable to you as well. Following your example, they do what they feel rather than working without genuine feeling to meet your and other people's expectations of them. When you are passionate and true to your feelings rather than simply being what other people want you to be, you will grow to value your feelings, be genuinely and authentically you, and be valuable as your multifaceted self to other people. Then other people around you will be valuable as their multifaceted selves to others and to you.

How to begin applying the Golden Rule: If you simply start trying to be true to your feelings, you won't be in touch enough with your feelings to do this so easily; you won't even know what you feel or what you're passionate about to be authentic to this. You will find yourself just being inclined to be what other people expect you to be. When you try to be true to your own feelings, you will continue to be supported in your feeling that being true to your own feelings gets in the way of your getting things done and being seen in a positive light by other people. Further, you will continue to be supported in your feeling that acting on your own passions won't make you valuable to other people. So you'll continue to feel that in order to be valuable to other people, you need to tune out your own feelings.

So, you can't just change your external approach and make the shift. You first need to change the way you approach things internally (or change your internal approach as you change your external approach).

Start here: Tune into your own passionate feelings and allow them to be manifested through yourself. In other words, value your own feelings enough to be true and authentic to your own feelings and meet your own expectations of yourself rather than trying to be true to other people's feelings and meet their expectations of you. This way you will already be making yourself feel like you have value just by being yourself, and so you will be more open to tuning authentically into the true value of other people (and things, such as money, for example) as well.

When you are present to your feelings and you authentically treat your feelings as successful, and as though their intentions are valuable, by acting on their intentions, your feelings treat you as successful, and as though your intentions are valuable, by acting on your intentions when you suggest a new destination for them and you. The result is you feel that you are successful and valuable to others and that others are successful and valuable to you. Consequently, you are inclined to treat others as successful and value them, and others are inclined to treat you as successful and value you. Further, you are inclined actually to be successful and valuable to others, and others are inclined actually to be successful and valuable to you. Thus, you get everything that you truly want when you treat your feelings as successful and value their intentions.

The example you are inclined to set for others in regard to how you should be treated: By not valuing or being authentic to your own feelings, you set the example for others that you shouldn't be valued or have others be authentic to you.

As you learn to value and be authentic to your own feelings, you come to set the example for others that you should be valued and that others should be authentic to you.

Your main limiting belief: My feelings that tell me that I can value my own feelings aren't valuable and so I should tune them out.

Response to your main limiting belief: Only when I value my feelings that tell me that I can value my own feelings will I really be able to value, and be valuable to, anyone or anything else.

The three aspects of self in your internal dynamic: There is a part of you that imposes the idea that your feelings that you can value your feelings get in the way of accomplishing things and meeting other people's expectations. There is a part of you that reacts to this by judging your feelings that you can value your feelings as not being productive or valuable and regretting and dismissing them. And there is a part of you that simply tunes out your feelings that you can value your feelings in an attempt to maintain your value since your feelings that you can value your feelings are seemingly getting in the way of productivity and accomplishment within you.

In the healthy version of this dynamic: The part of you that would impose the idea that your feelings that you can value your feelings get in the way of accomplishing things and meeting other people's expectations instead guides the expression of your feelings that you can value your feelings toward the aim of genuineness and authenticity. The part of you that would react by judging your feelings that you can value your feelings as not being productive or valuable and regretting them instead acknowledges your feelings that you can value your feelings as productive and values them. And the part of you that would tune out your feelings that you can value your feelings in an attempt to maintain your value in light of their actually getting in the way of productivity within you instead tunes into your feelings that you can value your feelings and expresses them since they are now actually maintaining the meeting of expectations within you.

How to get all parts of yourself on the same team and working for you: Listen to and acknowledge your feelings that other people's feelings are more valuable than your own feelings and that you should tune out your own feelings and be true to other people's feelings, and recognize that these feelings have your best interests in mind. They actually just want to help you be valuable to other people, accomplish your goals, and meet other people's expectations of you, which is what you want as well. It's just that they are misdirected in how best to go about being valuable to other people, believing that you have to tune out your own feelings in order to be this.

So after you listen to them and acknowledge them, let them know that you understand that their main intention is to help you be valuable to other people, and that they can even better achieve this aim if they help you tune into and be true to your own feelings instead. This way you can actually get what you want, which is to be valuable to other people, genuine, authentic, and driven to achieve goals that you're passionate about.

What you're inclined to identify with: You're inclined to identify with your feeling that your feelings are unsuccessful and worthless.

Understanding what your feelings are really saying to you: Your feelings are saying to you, as though in conversation with you, "I feel like I'm unsuccessful and worthless to you, and I want to be successful and valuable to you." In other words, the way to show that you are really listening to your feelings is to respond to them by recognizing them as successful and valuable and being true to them. This is the true path to value.

What your feelings really want and how they try to get it: Your feelings really want to be preserved by you, accepted by you, and connected to you, and you make them believe that in order to accomplish these aims, they need to be valuable and successful to you. Therefore, they try to do whatever they believe they need to do in order to be successful to you so they can prove that they are valuable to you. If this means not speaking up and instead directing you to the feelings of other people whom you deem valuable, then this is what they'll do. But if you pay attention to them, you'll recognize that they actually just want to be valuable to you, and they're only not speaking up and instead directing you to other people because you're making them believe that this is the only way they'll be successful. If you recognize them as successful to you when they *speak up*, then this is what they'll do for you instead.

Because you make your feelings believe that, in order to get what they want, they need to be valuable and successful to you, you seek to be valuable and successful to other people and to the world in order to be kept in the world and in other people's lives, to be accepted by the world and other people, and to connect to the world and other people. And, therefore, you try to do whatever you believe you need to do in order to be successful to the world and other people so you can prove that you are valuable. If this means trying to be true to what other people seem to want you to be and not being true to yourself, then this is what you'll do. But if you pay attention to your own feelings, you'll recognize that they actually just want to be valuable, and if you are true to them, then you'll actually be recognized by the world and the people around you as successful.

Internal experience image: When you are stressed, and especially when you have been stressed for a long time and so are more caught up in your personality's obstacles and coping mechanisms, you are inclined to tune out your own feelings and value only those feelings you can use to further you toward your goals. You treat your feelings as though they are tools in a toolbox. The ones you can use to accomplish your goal you use solely for that purpose and then toss them back in the toolbox, valuing them only for the role they played in your getting to your goal. The ones you can't use to accomplish your goal, you leave in the toolbox, entirely unacknowledged.

If you acknowledge your own feelings as more than mere tools but as valuable indicators of what direction you're headed and what direction you want to be headed, of who you're making yourself into and who you actually are, you no longer feel like you only have value to others based on the role you play. Instead, with the motivation of your own passionate feelings, you are driven toward your goals, and you feel valuable just by being yourself, because you are inherently playing a valuable role, performing a valuable function, and fulfilling a valuable purpose simply by being you.

What you're attracted to in others: You're attracted to people who are passionate in their expression of feeling because then you have passionate feelings to reflect and express through yourself. In the same vein, you are attracted to people who have clear expectations of you, because then you know what expectations to meet so you can be seen well by those people. In the ideal, you are attracted to people to whom you are valuable when you are true to your own feelings so that you meet these people's expectations of you and are successful to them simply by being yourself.

The types of words you use to criticize yourself and others: inauthentic, fake, failure, unaccomplished, look bad

The types of words you use to praise yourself and others: authentic, genuine, successful, accomplished, valuable, look good

Sharing Instinct (Enneagram Type 8)

You come up with your own strong instincts or desires, and then you assert them on others and the world around you in an effort to protect others. In other words, you're inclined to push or challenge other people to do what you want them to do for their own good. You feel that to let others do what they want or to let anyone or anything control you and not to assert your own wants would be weakness and would make you vulnerable. So you try to be tough and in control, to be strong and protective of others.

Your relationship with yourself: You are inclined to allow yourself to get angry and out of control of yourself as you try to be tough and assert control over other people and the world around you, challenging them to do what you want them to do and to toughen up as well in an effort to protect them.

You feel that you have to assert your control over others and the world around you because if you are in control then you won't be controlled by others. So you try to be tough, assertive, and protective toward others so that you will be protected from being vulnerable to others.

However, when you allow your anger to take over, thinking that your toughness will get people going and doing what you want them to do, you end up out of control of yourself. And when you're not in control of yourself, you're not in control of anyone or anything else either. So you end up increasingly vulnerable to other people's actions and reactions to your attempts to assert your control over them as you increasingly try to remedy this by being more protective and controlling toward others. This happens until you learn to control and protect yourself by allowing other people to control and protect themselves and to be protective toward you as well. In essence, you are inclined to try to protect yourself by trying to protect others rather than by protecting yourself, and you need to learn to protect yourself by actually protecting yourself.

The key to shifting your relationships: The key is to notice when you are trying to protect other people and the world around you by imposing on them what you want them to do in disregard of what *they* want to do, and to practice acknowledging at those times that you are imposing and what you are imposing and why. Then, shift your attention and energy to yourself and take control of yourself and protect yourself, and allow other people to control and protect themselves and to protect you as well. This way, instead of making yourself powerless by directing your overassertive instincts toward taking control of and protecting everyone but yourself, you are powerful in getting yourself to do what you want and protected by your own protective instincts from being vulnerable to your own anger toward yourself and others and to the reactions this elicits from others.

When you are in control of yourself and so already feel in control and protected, your attempts to protect and challenge others become the overflow of your already existing internal foundational strength. This is in contrast to their being intensely aggressive and forceful attempts to assert over others the control that you don't have over yourself. The result is that rather than trying to lead, control, and protect others through the actions that *you* want them to take and that you have to impose on them with forceful effort and energy, you will be able to lead and protect others through the actions that *they* want to take. This requires far less energy on your part because you don't have to push people to do things that they don't actually want to do; you just have to lead people in leading themselves and challenge them to do what they already want to do, and this allows you actually to be in control of getting what you really want and to be protected by yourself and by those who appreciate your strong and benevolent leadership.

How you are inclined to treat yourself and others and how you are inclined to feel that others treat you: When you are stressed and/or unhealthy (due to prolonged stress), you are inclined to treat yourself and others as weak and vulnerable, and you are inclined to feel that others treat you as weak and vulnerable.

When you are relaxed and healthy (due to prolonged lack of stress either because of circumstances or because you've been responding positively to life's obstacles), you are inclined to treat yourself and others as strong and protective, and you are inclined to feel that others treat you as strong and protective.

The Golden Rule applied: Allow other people to do what they want and lead, challenge, and protect you, and you will be able to do what you want and lead, challenge, and protect others. Or, more simply, allow other people to lead and be in control, and you will be able to lead and be in control.

This works because if you let other people challenge you, be in control, and protect you, and you become okay with this, then you won't get angry and aggressive and allow your anger to rule your actions as you force your instincts on others in an effort to be tough and protect others and, ultimately, yourself. Instead, you will be able to maintain control over your own actions. So you will be able to focus on challenging and leading other people with your controlled strength in ways that they actually want to be challenged and led, where there won't exist the likelihood of their retaliating against your leadership. Rather than seemingly competing with others as you try to be more in control and protective of them than they are of you, when you allow other people to be in control and protective, they allow you to be in control and protective, and so everyone involved feels protected, strong, and in control.

How to begin applying the Golden Rule: If you simply start trying to allow other people to do what they want and lead themselves and you, you will continue to be supported in your feeling that other people are weak and that you really need to challenge them to toughen up. Further, you will continue to be supported in your feeling that when you let people be in control, they are a threat to themselves because they make themselves vulnerable. So you'll continue to feel that you have to assert your control over other people and the world around you in order to protect them, and you'll continue to feel that you don't have control and that you are vulnerable, yourself.

So, you can't just change your external approach and make the shift. You first need to change the way you approach things internally (or change your internal approach as you change your external approach).

Start here: Share your strong, guarding instincts with yourself and protect yourself. This way you will already be making yourself feel like you are being allowed to be in control and like protection is being shared with you, and so you will be more open to allowing other people (and things, such as money, for example) to be strong and protective and share their strength and protective instincts with you as well.

When you are present to your instincts and you powerfully treat your instincts as strong, and as though their directions are protective, by acting on their directions, your instincts treat you as strong, and as though your directions are protective, by acting on your directions when you suggest a new destination for them and you. The result is you feel that you are strong and protective to others and that others are strong and protective to you. Consequently, you are inclined to treat others as strong and act on their directions, and others are inclined to treat you as strong and act on your directions. Further, you are inclined actually to be strong and protective to others, and others are inclined actually to be strong and protective to you. Thus, you get everything that you truly want when you treat your instincts as strong and act on their directions.

The example you are inclined to set for others in regard to how you should be treated: By not acting on your own instincts and protecting yourself, you set the example for others that your instincts shouldn't be acted upon.

As you learn to direct your guarding instincts toward yourself and act on your own instincts and protect yourself, you come to set the example for others that your instincts should be acted upon.

Your main limiting belief: My strong instincts, when directed toward myself, are not strong or protective, and so I should direct my strong instincts toward others instead of toward myself.

Response to your main limiting belief: Only when I direct my strong instincts toward myself can I truly be protective to anyone else and actually feel strong and powerful, because no one will follow my instincts if *I* don't.

The three aspects of self in your internal dynamic: There is a part of you that imposes the idea that your strong instincts, when directed toward yourself, are not protective because they don't seem to be protecting anyone else. There is a part of you that reacts to this by judging your strong instincts that are directed toward yourself as weak and vulnerable and getting angry at them and dismissing them. And there is a part of you that simply tunes out your strong instincts that are directed toward yourself in an attempt to maintain control and protect yourself since your strong instincts that are directed toward yourself are seemingly causing attack and vulnerability within you.

In the healthy version of this dynamic: The part of you that would impose the idea that your strong instincts, when directed toward yourself, are not protective instead guides the direction of your strong instincts toward yourself toward the aim of real control and protection. The part of you that would react by judging your strong instincts that are directed toward yourself as weak and vulnerable and getting angry at them instead acknowledges your strong instincts that are directed toward yourself as strong and protective and respects them. And the part of you that would tune out your strong instincts that are directed toward yourself in an attempt to maintain control and protect yourself in light of their actually causing vulnerability within you instead tunes into your strong instincts that are directed toward yourself and acts on them since they are now actually maintaining strength and protection within you.

How to get all parts of yourself on the same team and working for you: Listen to and acknowledge your instincts that you need to protect other people by getting them to do something and that trying to protect yourself doesn't actually protect anyone, and recognize that these instincts have your best interests in mind. They actually just want to help you be strong, in control, and protective, which is what you want as well. It's just that they are misdirected in how best to go about being strong and protective, believing that you have to direct your strong instincts away from yourself and toward others in order to be this.

So after you listen to them and acknowledge them, let them know that you understand that their main intention is to help you get in control and be strong and protective, and that they can even better achieve this aim if they help you direct your strong, protective instincts toward yourself instead. This way you can actually get what you want, which is to be strong and in control, protected and protective.

What you're inclined to identify with: You're inclined to identify with your instinct that your instincts that are directed toward yourself are powerless and vulnerable.

Understanding what your instincts are really saying to you: Your instincts are saying to you, as though in conversation with you, "I feel like I'm powerless and vulnerable to you, and I want to be powerful and protective to you." In other words, the way to show that you are really listening to your instincts is to respond to them by recognizing them as powerful and protective, and acting on them yourself. This is the true path to power.

What your instincts really want and how they try to get it: Your instincts really want to be preserved by you, accepted by you, and connected to you, and you make them believe that in order to accomplish these aims, they need to be powerful and protective to you. Therefore, they try to do whatever they believe they need to do in order to be protective to you so they can prove that they are powerful. If this means trying to protect the world and other people, then this is what they'll do. But if you pay attention to them, you'll recognize that they actually just want to be powerful to you, and they're only trying to protect others because you're making them believe that this is the only way they'll be powerful to you. If you recognize them as powerful when they are protective toward *you*, then this is what they'll do for you instead.

Because you make your instincts believe that, in order to get what they want, they need to be powerful and protective to you, you seek to be powerful and protective to other people and to the world in order to be kept in the world and in other people's lives, to be accepted by the world and other people, and to connect to the world and other people. And, therefore, you try to do whatever you believe you need to do in order to be protective to the world and other people so you can prove that you are powerful. If this means trying to protect the world and other people and ignoring yourself, then this is what you'll do. But if you pay attention to your own instincts, you'll recognize that they actually just want to be powerful, and if you recognize them as powerful when they try to protect *you*, then you'll actually be recognized by the world and the people around you as protective.

Internal experience image: When you are stressed, and especially when you have been stressed for a long time and so are more caught up in your personality's obstacles and coping mechanisms, you try to toughen yourself up and challenge yourself, and you allow yourself to get angry and out of control as you put all of your energy into controlling and protecting others. It is as though you are iron and you seek to make yourself steel, and you make life into your furnace in order to strengthen and harden yourself. The result is that you end up feeling weak, vulnerable, and out of control of your life.

The only way out of the intense heat of the furnace is to direct your strong instincts toward yourself and take control of, and protect, yourself. Then you realize that you don't need to be steel to protect the people around you because much less energy is required to control the outside world once you are in control of yourself.

What you're attracted to in others: You're attracted to people with whom you can share your assertive and dominating instincts, because then you feel protected and in control. In the same vein, you are attracted to people whom you can lead and challenge and who will do what you want, because then you feel like you are in control. Ideally, the people you choose to bring into your life and lead are people who will put up a healthy challenge in return, because then you can get the intensity of being challenged and protected that you really want.

The types of words you use to criticize yourself and others: weak, unimpressive, exposed, lazy, afraid

The types of words you use to praise yourself and others: strong, impressive, tough, powerful, brave

Receiving Instinct (Enneagram Type 1)

You look for things in the world around you that bring about the instinct or desire in you for things to be different from the way they are. In other words, you're inclined to look for things in the world that are imperfect, wrong, or flawed—that seem like they're not as they should be—and then get frustrated that things are wrong and feel like you need to fix them. You want things to be good, ideal, right, and perfect—as they should be—and you feel that if you find things that are wrong and that should be corrected, you are put in the position of being right and of making things right.

Your relationship with yourself: You are inclined to replay your instincts that things are flawed and need to be fixed, and to judge and criticize your instincts that things are already good and right (because you deem these instincts wrong).

You feel that some of your wants are bad, corrupt, immoral, imperfect, or flawed because they don't fit your conception of what is right, good, moral, or perfect. So you judge these desires within you, criticizing, critiquing, and correcting them, and trying to improve yourself by getting rid of the bad.

However, all of this focus on what is wrong about things within you merely brings about more frustration and more things to be frustrated about—both within and outside you. So you find yourself increasingly judging others and the world around you as wrong, and increasingly judged by others as wrong for your strong opinions and rigid stances as you have been judging yourself. You grow increasingly irritated with all the things that are wrong around you, and within you, until you learn to accept your own wants as they are without judgment or criticism.

The key to shifting your relationships: The key is to notice when you are getting caught up in focusing on and replaying your instincts that things are bad, wrong, or flawed and in need of correction, and to practice acknowledging at those times that you are judging and what you are judging and why. Then, shift your attention to what is going on in the present moment as it is and allow yourself to listen to your instincts that things are right, good, and in some sense perfect already without dismissing these instincts as wrong. This way, rather than bringing about more reasons to be frustrated, where you try to be right by noticing what is wrong, you bring about more reasons to be accepting as you notice all the goodness that already exists within and around you.

When you are listening to your instincts that things are already good and so already feel that things are as they should be, your attempts to improve yourself and others become the overflow of your already existing acceptance of the way things currently are. This is in contrast to their being highly critical and judgmental attempts to correct that which you cannot accept as it currently is because you are too busy focusing on what is wrong with yourself to accept yourself as you currently are. The result is that rather than trying to correct the way things are through criticism based on your judgments of what is wrong, which only leads you to find more things that are wrong and bad, you will be able to focus on and build on what is already right and good. This requires far less energy on your part because you don't have to focus on what is wrong and continually be frustrated as you and the people around you disregard your corrections and you never allow yourself to experience anything as good; you just have to allow yourself to experience the good in yourself and the people and the world around you, and this actually encourages and increases the good in yourself and in everyone and everything around you.

How you are inclined to treat yourself and others and how you are inclined to feel that others treat you: When you are stressed and/or unhealthy (due to prolonged stress), you are inclined to treat yourself and others as bad and wrong and undeserving of attention, and you are inclined to feel that others treat you as bad and wrong and undeserving of attention.

When you are relaxed and healthy (due to prolonged lack of stress either because of circumstances or because you've been responding positively to life's obstacles), you are inclined to treat yourself and others as good and right and deserving of attention, and you are inclined to feel that others treat you as good and right and deserving of attention.

The Golden Rule applied: Accept and treat other people as good and in some sense perfect already, and other people will accept and treat you as good and in some sense perfect already. Allow other people to be right and to correct you, and other people will allow you to be right and to correct them.

This works because if you don't correct others all the time (judging them as wrong, bad, or flawed), but instead allow them to be right once in a while, then others won't feel the need to react and correct you all the time. They will, instead, allow you to be right and to correct them once in a while. So you will be accepted as you are, for being good and right in your acceptance of others as they are. Further, rather than being criticized and judged for your judgment and lack of acceptance of others, you will be accepted and even praised for actually improving others by beginning with acceptance and acknowledgment of what's good about where they are and then simply pointing out what they can do to be even better. Rather than seemingly competing with others as you try to be the one who's right, when you allow other people to be right, too, they allow you to be right, and so everyone involved feels good, accepted, and perfect as he/she is.

How to begin applying the Golden Rule: If you simply start trying to accept other people and let them be right, you will continue to be supported in your feeling that people are flawed and wrong and that you need to correct them. Further, you will continue to be supported in your feeling that you're not being accepted and that you need to be more perfect. So you'll continue to feel that you are not good, that you are imperfect and flawed, and that you need to find more things that are wrong that you need to fix. And you'll continue to feel that other people are criticizing and judging you.

So, you can't just change your external approach and make the shift. You first need to change the way you approach things internally (or change your internal approach as you change your external approach).

Start here: Pay attention to and receive your own good instincts from yourself. This way you will already be making yourself feel like you are being accepted as good and right, and so you will be more open to noticing and accepting goodness and rightness in other people (and things, such as money, for example) as well.

When you are present to your instincts and you perfectly treat your instincts as good and right, and as though their directions are to be treated as deserving of attention, by acting on their directions, your instincts treat you as good and right, and as though your directions are to be treated as deserving of attention, by acting on your directions when you suggest a new destination for them and you. The result is you feel that you are good and right to others and treated as deserving of others' attention and that others are good and right to you and are deserving of your attention. Consequently, you are inclined to treat others as good and right and pay attention to them, and others are inclined to treat you as good and right and pay attention to you. Further, you are inclined actually to be good and right to others, and others are inclined actually to be good and right to you. Thus, you get everything that you truly want when you treat your instincts as good and right and pay deserved attention to their directions.

The example you are inclined to set for others in regard to how you should be treated: By not paying attention to your own instincts or treating them as good and right, you set the example for others that you should not be paid attention to or treated as good and right.

As you learn to pay attention to your own instincts and treat them as good and right, you come to set the example for others that you should be paid attention to and treated as good and right.

Your main limiting belief: My instincts that things are already good and right are bad and wrong and so I should dismiss them and treat them as flawed.

Response to your main limiting belief: Only when I pay attention to my instincts that things are already good will I truly feel that things are good. It is my instincts that things are good, and not my instincts that things are flawed, that are truly right.

The three aspects of self in your internal dynamic: There is a part of you that imposes the idea that your instincts that things are already good and right as they are are flawed because they don't motivate you to identify and correct the things that are bad and wrong. There is a part of you that reacts to this by judging your instincts that things are already good as bad and wrong and getting frustrated with them and dismissing them. And there is a part of you that simply tunes out your instincts that things are already good in an attempt to maintain perfection since your instincts that things are already good are seemingly causing corruption and judgment within you.

In the healthy version of this dynamic: The part of you that would impose the idea that your instincts that things are already right and good as they are are flawed instead guides the acknowledgment of your instincts that things are already good toward the aim of greater goodness and perfection. The part of you that would react by judging your instincts that things are already good as bad and wrong and getting frustrated with them instead acknowledges your instincts that things are already good as good and right and accepts them. And the part of you that would tune out your instincts that things are already good in an attempt to maintain harmony in light of their actually causing corruption within you instead tunes into your instincts that things are already good and acts on them since they are now actually maintaining perfection within you.

How to get all parts of yourself on the same team and working for you: Listen to and acknowledge your instincts that things are flawed and that you should dismiss your instincts that things are already good and right as flawed, and recognize that these instincts have your best interests in mind. They actually just want to help you ensure that you are good and right and that people and things around you are good and right, which is what you want as well. It's just that they are misdirected in how best to go about making you and everything around you good and right, believing that you have to focus on what is bad and wrong in order to correct it and make it good and right and also to make yourself right for having noticed what is wrong.

So after you listen to them and acknowledge them, let them know that you understand that their main intention is to help you make yourself and everything around you good, and that they can even better achieve this aim if they help you listen to and acknowledge your instincts that you and the people and things around you are already good instead. This way you can actually get what you want, which is to have you and everyone and everything around you be good and as you and they should be.

What you're inclined to identify with: You're inclined to identify with your instinct that your instincts that things are good and right are bad, wrong, and undeserving of your attention.

Understanding what your instincts are really saying to you: Your instincts are saying to you, as though in conversation with you, "I feel like I'm bad and wrong to you and am undeserving of your attention, and I want to be good and right to you and deserving of your attention." In other words, the way to show that you are really listening to your instincts is to respond to them by recognizing them as good and right and treating them as deserving of your attention, and accepting them and giving them your attention. This is the true path to perfection.

What your instincts really want and how they try to get it: Your instincts really want to be preserved by you, accepted by you, and connected to you, and you make them believe that in order to accomplish these aims, they need to be good and deserving of attention to you. Therefore, they try to do whatever they believe they need to do in order to be deserving of your attention so they can prove that they are good. If this means pointing out what's bad, then this is what they'll do. But if you pay attention to them, you'll recognize that they actually just want to be good to you, and they're only pointing out what's bad because you're making them believe that this is the only way they'll be deserving of your attention. If you recognize them as deserving of your attention when they point out what's *good*, then this is what they'll do for you instead.

Because you make your instincts believe that, in order to get what they want, they need to be good and deserving of attention to you, you seek to be good and deserving of attention to other people and to the world in order to be kept in the world and in other people's lives, to be accepted by the world and other people, and to connect to the world and other people. And, therefore, you try to do whatever you believe you need to do in order to be deserving of the world's and other people's attention so you can prove that you are good. If this means pointing out what's bad and wrong in other people and in the world around you, then this is what you'll do. But if you pay attention to your own instincts, you'll recognize that they actually just want to be good, and if you point out what's *good* in them and in the world and the people around you, then you'll actually be recognized as deserving of the attention of the world and the people around you.

Internal experience image: When you are stressed, and especially when you have been stressed for a long time and so are more caught up in your personality's obstacles and coping mechanisms, you are inclined to correct things by focusing on what is wrong. It is as though you are standing across a busy street from a young child, and you scold and criticize the child for being across the street and tell her that she shouldn't be where she is. However, if you criticize the child for being where she is—even every step of the way as she walks toward you, as she will likely believe that this is what you want of her—you probably won't actually get her to do what you want her to do. This is especially the case since all she learns from you is that she is not where she should be; she does not learn from you where she should be or even what direction she should be going when you merely disapprove of her for where she is. You end up frustrated, and things continue to be as you feel they shouldn't be.

On the other hand, if you simply cross the street, calmly take the child by the hand, and then walk the child across the street, with acceptance of where she is and encouragement every step of the way in the direction toward where you want her to go, then the child will end up where you want her to go. The result is that you end up feeling that things are exactly as they should be every step of the way as you actually make them better.

What you're attracted to in others: You're attracted to people who bring about strong instincts and wants in you, because then you have strong instincts to replay, judge, and correct. When you are judging and criticizing your desires, you are attracted to people who are frustratingly wrong to you, because then you are in the position of being right and of making things right as you correct and improve them. When you are accepting your desires as they are and simply improving upon them by accepting and redirecting what's wrong and focusing more on what's right, you are attracted to people who make you feel good and right because they benefit from your acceptance and encouragement of the good within them.

The types of words you use to criticize yourself and others: wrong, bad, corrupt, flawed, unfair, disrespectful

The types of words you use to praise yourself and others: right, good, perfect, ideal, fair, respectful

Allowing Instinct (Enneagram Type 9)

You allow the instincts or wants of others to be manifested through yourself, through your actions. In other words, you're inclined to try to do what other people want you to do, rather than recognizing harmony in your own wants and acting on and asserting your own instincts and desires. You feel that acting on your own wants and asserting yourself would create conflict, and you prefer to avoid and tune out conflict in order to maintain peace and harmony.

Your relationship with yourself: You are inclined to dissociate from and tune out your own wants because you feel that asserting them causes conflict.

You feel that what you want might conflict with what other people want or with the way things actually are because what you want to do might not be what other people want you to do and the way things actually are isn't the way you want them to be. So your way of dealing with this potential conflict is to avoid it altogether and just tune out your own wants in an attempt to maintain the peace.

However, tuning out your own wants merely results in other people tuning out your wants as well. So you just go through the motions of doing what other people want you to do or what other people simply don't want to do themselves. Meanwhile, you try to look on the bright side of things and enjoy the simple comforts of life as things become less and less what you actually want them to be. The conflict and disharmony between your wants and the way things actually are grows until you begin to pay attention to and assert your own wants to yourself and others.

The key to shifting your relationships: The key is to notice when you are tuning out your wants that you perceive as bringing about conflict or disharmony within yourself and trying simply to do what other people want, and to practice acknowledging at those times that you are tuning out and what you are tuning out and why. Then, shift your attention back to your wants in the present moment and listen to them, acknowledge the potential harmony in them, and assert and act on them. This way, instead of trying to avoid conflict—and actually bringing about the very disharmony you want to avoid—by not being present to yourself or to anyone else, you create harmony within yourself and with other people because you are present to yourself and to others and you actually get what you want.

When you are tuned into your own instincts and so already feel that there is harmony within yourself, your attempts to maintain peace become the overflow of your already existing internal harmony. This is in contrast to their being attempts to tune out the disharmony that you are creating within yourself by tuning out your own wants. The result is that rather than trying to maintain peace by doing what you believe other people want you to do, which only leads to greater disharmony within yourself, you will be able to create harmony with others by being clear about what you want and allowing them to act on this. This requires far less energy on your part because you don't have to go through the motions of doing what other people want without any desire to do it yourself and while having your desires tuned out by yourself and everyone else; you just have to assert and do what you actually want and allow other people to do what you want them to do, too, and then you get the internal and external harmony that you desire.

How you are inclined to treat yourself and others and how you are inclined to feel that others treat you: When you are stressed and/or unhealthy (due to prolonged stress), you are inclined to treat yourself and others as conflict-causing and inharmonious, and you are inclined to feel that others treat you as conflict-causing and inharmonious.

When you are relaxed and healthy (due to prolonged lack of stress either because of circumstances or because you've been responding positively to life's obstacles), you are inclined to treat yourself and others as peaceful and harmonious, and you are inclined to feel that others treat you as peaceful and harmonious.

The Golden Rule applied: Be assertive so other people can go along with what you want and maintain peace, and other people will be assertive so you can go along with what they want and maintain peace. Be peacefully present to other people by finding harmony in and acting on your own wants, and other people will be peacefully present to you by finding harmony in and acting on their own wants.

This works because when you are present to and assertive about what you want, you give permission to others to be present to and assertive about what they want, also. By being present to other people with calmness and peace, you bring other people to be more present to you with calmness and peace as well, and the result is that you and the people around you experience peace and harmony. You are much more harmonious and present to others when you act on your own wants, so then others reflect this and are much more harmonious and present to you, too. Following your example, they do what they want and make things what they want them to be rather than trying to do what you and other people want and tuning out everything that isn't as they, themselves, want it. When you are assertive and do what you want rather than simply doing what other people want you to do, you will grow to find harmony in your desires, bring your life into harmony with your desires, and be a force of peace and harmony to other people. Then other people around you will be assertive and do what they want, bringing their lives into harmony with their desires as well.

How to begin applying the Golden Rule: If you simply start trying to assert what you want, you won't be in touch enough with your wants to do this so easily; you won't even know what you want to assert it. You will find yourself just being inclined to do what other people want you to do. When you try to assert your own wants, you will continue to be supported in your belief that asserting your own wants causes conflict. Further, you will continue to be supported in your belief that what you want isn't in harmony with what other people want or with the way things are. So you'll continue to believe that in order to maintain harmony, you need to tune out what you want.

So, you can't just change your external approach and make the shift. You first need to change the way you approach things internally (or change your internal approach as you change your external approach).

Start here: Tune into your own assertive instincts and allow them to be manifested through yourself. In other words, find harmony in your own instincts and wants enough to act on your own instincts and do what you want to do rather than trying to act on other people's instincts and do what they want you to do. This way you will already be making yourself feel like you have peace and harmony within yourself, and so you will be more open to tuning peacefully into the harmony of other people (and things, such as money, for example) as well.

When you are present to your instincts and you comfortably treat your instincts as peaceful, and as though their directions are harmonious, by acting on their directions, your instincts treat you as peaceful, and as though your directions are harmonious, by acting on your directions when you suggest a new destination for them and you. The result is you feel that you are peaceful and harmonious to others and that others are peaceful and harmonious to you. Consequently, you are inclined to treat others as peaceful and harmonize with them, and others are inclined to treat you as peaceful and harmonize with you. Further, you are inclined actually to be peaceful and harmonious to others, and others are inclined actually to be peaceful and harmonious to you.

Thus, you get everything that you truly want when you treat your instincts as peaceful and act on their directions.

The example you are inclined to set for others in regard to how you should be treated: By treating your own wants as though they cause conflict and tuning them out, you set the example for others that you should be treated as though you cause conflict and tuned out.

As you learn to recognize the harmony in your own wants and tune into your wants, you come to set the example for others that you should be recognized as harmonious and tuned into.

Your main limiting belief: My instincts that tell me that I can harmonize with my own instincts by asserting them are inharmonious and so I should tune them out.

Response to your main limiting belief: Only when I harmonize with my instincts that tell me that my own instincts are peaceful will I really be able to harmonize with, and be harmonious to, anyone or anything else.

The three aspects of self in your internal dynamic: There is a part of you that imposes the idea that your instincts to harmonize with your instincts cause conflict with other people's wants and the way things actually are. There is a part of you that reacts to this by judging your instincts to harmonize with your instincts as inharmonious and getting impatient with them and dismissing them. And there is a part of you that simply tunes out your instincts to harmonize with your instincts in an attempt to maintain harmony since your instincts to harmonize with your instincts are seemingly causing conflict and reaction within you.

In the healthy version of this dynamic: The part of you that would impose the idea that your instincts to harmonize with your instincts cause conflict instead guides the assertion of your instincts to harmonize with your instincts toward the aim of peace and harmony. The part of you that would react by judging your instincts to harmonize with your instincts as inharmonious and getting impatient with them instead acknowledges your instincts to harmonize with your instincts as harmonious and has patience with them. And the part of you that would tune out your instincts to harmonize with your instincts in an attempt to maintain harmony in light of their actually causing conflict within you instead tunes into your instincts to harmonize with your instincts and asserts them since they are now actually maintaining harmony within you.

How to get all parts of yourself on the same team and working for you: Listen to and acknowledge your instincts that other people's instincts are more peaceful than your own instincts and that you should tune out your own instincts and act on other people's instincts, and recognize that these instincts have your best interests in mind. They actually just want to help you maintain harmony with others and the world around you, which is what you want as well. It's just that they are misdirected in how best to go about maintaining harmony, believing that you have to tune out your own instincts in order to do this.

So after you listen to them and acknowledge them, let them know that you understand that their main intention is to help you maintain harmony, and that they can even better achieve this aim if they help you tune into and assert your own instincts instead. This way you can actually get what you want, which is harmony between what you want and the way things are in the world around you.

What you're inclined to identify with: You're inclined to identify with your instinct that your instincts are conflict-causing and inharmonious.

Understanding what your instincts are really saying to you: Your instincts are saying to you, as though in conversation with you, "I feel like I'm causing conflict and am inharmonious to you, and I want to be peaceful and harmonious to you." In other words, the way to show that you are really listening to your instincts is to respond to them by recognizing them as peaceful and harmonious and asserting them. This is the true path to harmony.

What your instincts really want and how they try to get it: Your instincts really want to be preserved by you, accepted by you, and connected to you, and you make them believe that in order to accomplish these aims, they need to be peaceful and harmonious to you. Therefore, they try to do whatever they believe they need to do in order to be harmonious to you so they can prove that they are peaceful. If this means not speaking up and instead directing you to the instincts of other people whom you deem peaceful, then this is what they'll do. But if you pay attention to them, you'll recognize that they actually just want to be peaceful to you, and they're only not speaking up and instead directing you to other people because you're making them believe that this is the only way they'll be harmonious. If you recognize them as harmonious to you when they *speak up*, then this is what they'll do for you instead.

Because you make your instincts believe that, in order to get what they want, they need to be peaceful and harmonious to you, you seek to be peaceful and harmonious to other people and to the world in order to be kept in the world and in other people's lives, to be accepted by the world and other people, and to connect to the world and other people. And, therefore, you try to do whatever you believe you need to do in order to be harmonious to the world and other people so you can prove that you are peaceful. If this means trying to do whatever other people seem to want you to do and not asserting yourself, then this is what you'll do. But if you pay attention to your own instincts, you'll recognize that they actually just want to be peaceful, and if you assert them, then you'll actually be recognized by the world and the people around you as harmonious.

Internal experience image: When you are stressed, and especially when you have been stressed for a long time and so are more caught up in your personality's obstacles and coping mechanisms, you are inclined to dissociate from conflict and withdraw into your own internal refuge. It is as though you live in the calm in the eye of a storm. You feel surrounded by disharmony and you feel you can't do much about it. So you tune it out and retreat into yourself away from the conflict that even your own wants seem to cause.

The only way out of the storm is to tune into your own wants. Then the storm dies down and you feel surrounded by calm and peace, because once there is harmony within you, the world around you becomes harmonious, too.

What you're attracted to in others: You're attracted to people who are assertive in their wants and instincts, because then you have assertive instincts to reflect and express through yourself and act on. In the same vein, you are attracted to people who act on what they want, because then you can do what they want in order to maintain peace with them. In the ideal, you are attracted to people with whom you keep the peace when you assert your own instincts so that you maintain harmony with these people simply by doing what you want to do.

The types of words you use to criticize yourself and others: overreactive, argumentative, uncomfortable, pessimistic, negative

The types of words you use to praise yourself and others: peaceful, calm, comfortable, optimistic, positive

Development And Creation Forms

In the order of development: The order of development here reveals our entire progression through life, which parallels the 12 astrological signs and the seasons of the year (as well as everything else, since this is the paradigm by which everything develops). We begin with the re-establishment of our previous life's obstacles, growing up through three stages through young adulthood when the prefrontal cortex is fully developed (in the early to mid-twenties) and we have the fullest potential for choice. From here, we move through the stages of the nine types in development order, on the way toward the full actualization of awareness of our true nature but with the option of staying stuck on any stage along the way.

Basically, once we come into existence, we go through all of the stages of development compressed into three stages, and then we go through each of these three stages again parsed out into three stages each. Through our childhood, adolescence, and young adulthood, we get the overview of the order and pattern of development of all things, and thereby the overview of the order and pattern of creation of all things, which is the reverse of the order of development. Then, we go back to the beginning and learn the order and pattern of development, and thereby also of creation (in reverse), in depth and detail through to the end. The beginning of our lives is like the abstract, table of contents, review of where we left off in our last life, and introduction to this life. The rest of our lives is like the book content beyond this, of which we write much as we go.

Life overview, re-establishment of previous life's obstacles where we left off, and introduction to this life and how we'll address and overcome those obstacles:

First, we are born into a physical body in this physical world.

Ages 0-7: Early Childhood, Instinct, Present-Oriented, Preserving Inclination, Aries, Early Spring. "I want it now for the sake of my survival. My instincts don't seem harmonious, right, or protective when it comes to preserving and maintaining myself and my surroundings, so I'll tune them out and do what other people seem to want me to do, instead, in order to preserve myself." This evolves toward, "I realize that I can't maintain my existence by tuning out what I want. In order to preserve myself, I need to tune into my own instincts and recognize that they are actually harmonious, right, and protective when it comes to preserving my existence. Only if I do what I want to do, rather than what other people seem to want me to do, will I have what I want and be able to survive."

Ages 7-14: Adolescence, Feeling, Past-Oriented, Belonging Inclination, Taurus, Mid-Spring. "Who am I and how do I feel about how I fit in? My feelings that I'm already valuable, important, and helpful don't seem valuable, important, or helpful when it comes to fitting in and being accepted, so I'll dismiss them and focus on how I'm a failure, insignificant, and helpless, instead, in order to try to fix this." This evolves toward, "I realize that I won't be accepted by others if I don't accept myself. In order to fit in and be accepted, I need to accept my feelings that I'm already valuable, important, and helpful and recognize that these feelings are actually valuable, important, and helpful when it comes to fitting in and being accepted. Only if I accept myself will I be accepted by others."

Ages 14-21: Young Adulthood, Thought, Future-Oriented, Connecting Inclination, Gemini, Late Spring. "I want to find people to connect with, and I need to make the right decisions in order to find and keep these people in my life. My thoughts that I direct toward myself don't seem trustworthy, fulfilling, or useful when it comes to connecting with other people, so I'll ignore myself and focus on being trustworthy, fulfilling, and useful to other people instead." This evolves toward, "I realize that I can't connect with others by disconnecting from myself. In order to connect with others, I need to direct my thoughts toward myself and recognize that my thoughts, when directed toward myself, are actually trustworthy, fulfilling, and useful when it comes to connecting with other people. Only if I connect with myself will I be able to connect with others and have others connect with me."

Now that our previous life's obstacles have been re-established and we have the potential and ability to choose something different from the way we chose before, we begin delving into our current life's challenges and lessons and either moving forward or remaining stuck on previous obstacles:

Instinct, Present-Oriented, Preserving Inclination:

Ages 21-28: Allowing Instinct, Cancer, Early Summer. "I want to be peaceful and harmonious, and my own instincts seem to create conflict and disharmony. So I'll just tune them out and do what other people seem to want me to do instead of what I want to do." This evolves toward, "I realize that trying to do what other people seem to want me to do and not what I want to do just makes me feel conflict-causing and inharmonious and like everyone and everything else is, too. I need to tune into my own instincts and do what I want to do, instead, because my own instincts are actually peaceful and harmonious, and only if I act on them will I actually feel and be peaceful and harmonious and experience others as being this way, too."

Ages 28-35: Receiving Instinct, Leo, Mid-Summer. "I want to be good and right and deserving of attention and for things around me to be this way, too, and my instincts that things are already good and right don't seem to get anything fixed. So I'll just dismiss those instincts as wrong and undeserving of my attention and focus my attention on what seems bad, wrong, flawed, and in need of correction, instead, in order to try to improve things." This evolves toward, "I realize that dismissing my instincts that things are already good and right as undeserving of my attention and focusing only on what seems bad, wrong, flawed, and in need of correction just makes me feel like everyone and everything is bad, wrong, flawed, and in need of correction, like no one gives me any attention, and like no one and nothing is good, right, or deserving of attention. I need to accept my instincts that things are already good and right, instead, because these instincts are actually good and right and deserving of my attention, and only if I accept them will I actually feel and be good and right and deserving of others' attention and experience other people and things around me as good and right and deserving of attention, too."

Ages 35-42: Sharing Instinct, Virgo, Late Summer. "I want to be powerful and protective, and when I try to do things for myself I feel powerless and vulnerable. So I'll just ignore myself and give my attention to protecting others instead." This evolves toward, "I realize that when I ignore myself and give all of my attention to protecting others, I just end up feeling powerless and vulnerable and like everyone else is, too. I need to give my attention to protecting myself, instead, because my instincts that I direct toward myself are actually powerful and protective, and only if I act on them will I actually feel and be powerful and protective, be experienced this way by others, and experience others as being this way, too."

Feeling, Past-Oriented, Belonging Inclination:

Ages 42-49: Allowing Feeling, Libra, Early Fall. "I want to be successful and valuable, and my own feelings seem to get in the way of getting things done and meeting other people's expectations. So I'll just tune them out and be what other people seem to expect me to be instead of what I feel I am." This evolves toward, "I realize that trying to be what other people seem to expect me to be and not what I feel I am just makes me feel worthless and like a failure and like everyone and everything else is, too. I need to tune into my own feelings and be what I feel I am, instead, because my own feelings are actually successful and valuable, and only if I act on them will I actually feel and be successful and valuable and experience others as being this way, too."

Ages 49-56: Receiving Feeling, Scorpio, Mid-Fall. "I want to be important and worthy of attention, and my feelings that I'm already important don't seem to improve how I'm treated. So I'll just dismiss those feelings as insignificant and unworthy of my attention and focus my attention on how I've been treated badly and wronged and should be treated better, instead, in order to try to improve how I'm treated." This evolves toward, "I realize that dismissing my feelings that I am already important as unworthy of my attention and focusing only on how I've been treated badly and wronged and should be treated better just makes me feel like everyone and everything treats me badly, like no one pays attention to me, and like no one and nothing is important or worthy of attention. I need to accept my feelings that I am already important, instead, because these feelings are actually important and worthy of my attention, and only if I accept them will I actually feel and be treated as important and worthy of others' attention and experience other people and things around me as important and worthy of attention, too."

Ages 56-63: Sharing Feeling, Sagittarius, Late Fall. "I want to be loving and helpful, and when I try to help myself I feel selfish and helpless. So I'll just ignore myself and give my attention to helping others instead." This evolves toward, "I realize that when I ignore myself and give all of my attention to helping others, I just end up feeling selfish and helpless and like everyone else is, too. I need to give my attention to helping myself, instead, because my feelings that I direct toward myself are actually loving and helpful, and only if I act on them will I actually feel and be loving and helpful, be experienced this way by others, and experience others as being this way, too."

Thought, Future-Oriented, Connecting Inclination:

Ages 63-70: Allowing Thought, Capricorn, Early Winter. "I want to be dependable and trustworthy, and my own thoughts seem to get in the way of being loyal to other people. So I'll just tune them out and make decisions that other people would probably guide me toward instead of decisions that my thoughts would guide me toward." This evolves toward, "I realize that trying to make the decisions that other people would probably guide me toward and not that my own thoughts would guide me toward just makes me feel undependable and untrustworthy and like everyone and everything else is, too. I need to tune into my own thoughts and make the decisions that they guide me toward, instead, because my own thoughts are actually dependable and trustworthy, and only if I act on them will I actually feel and be dependable and trustworthy and experience others as being this way, too."

Ages 70-77: Receiving Thought, Aquarius, Mid-Winter. "I want to be fulfilling and taken seriously, and my thoughts that I'm already fulfilling don't seem to improve my experience. So I'll just dismiss those thoughts as unfulfilling and not take them seriously and focus my attention on how I'm unhappy, deprived of attention, and not taken seriously, instead, in order to try to improve my experience." This evolves toward, "I realize that dismissing my thoughts that I am already fulfilling as not to be taken seriously and focusing only on how I'm unhappy, deprived of attention, and not taken seriously just makes me feel like everyone and everything makes me unhappy, like no one takes me seriously, and like no one and nothing is fulfilling or to be taken seriously. I need to accept my thoughts that I am already fulfilling, instead, because these thoughts are actually fulfilling and to be taken seriously, and only if I accept them will I actually feel and be fulfilling and taken seriously by others and experience other people and things around me as fulfilling and to be taken seriously, too."

Ages 77-84: Sharing Thought, Pisces, Late Winter. "I want to be capable and useful, and when I try to guide myself I feel incapable and useless. So I'll just ignore myself and give my attention to being useful to others instead." This evolves toward, "I realize that when I ignore myself and give all of my attention to being useful to others, I just end up feeling incapable and useless and like everyone else is, too. I need to give my attention to being useful to myself, instead, because my thoughts that I direct toward myself are actually capable and useful, and only if I act on them will I actually feel and be capable and useful, be experienced this way by others, and experience others as being this way, too."

The greatest potential for self-awareness, willful choice, and awakening, though still with the possibility of remaining stuck on previous stages:

Age 84-onward

In the order of creation: First, we are aware. Then, we create and share a thought, receive and respond to it, and allow the initiated thought and response to it to be manifested through us in a harmonized form. Then we create and share a feeling based on the harmonized thought, receive and respond to this feeling, and allow the initiated feeling and response to it to be manifested through us in a harmonized form. Then we create and share an instinct based on the harmonized feeling, receive and respond to this instinct, and allow the initiated instinct and response to it to be manifested through us in a harmonized form. Then we speak and act in the physical world based on the harmonized instinct, receive and respond to our sensory experience of the physical world around us, and allow the words and actions and sensory experience of the world to be manifested through us in a harmonized form. And then we are born anew into a physical body in the physical world.

The Expression Of Enneagram Secondary And Tertiary Types

We all have all of these nine type relationships within us. It is simply that we prioritize the different type relationships differently, with one type relationship being primary, one being secondary, one being tertiary, and so forth. The secondary type is always one number more or one number less than the main type, and the tertiary type is always the other of these. The secondary and tertiary types are both known as "wings", but the secondary type is commonly simply referred to as the "wing".

So, for example, if you identify with Type 5 primarily, your secondary type is either Type 6 or Type 4, and your tertiary type is the other of these. So if you are 5 with a 4 wing, this means that your primary type is Type 5, your secondary type is Type 4, and your tertiary type is type 6.

This gives us a lot of information about a person, because we are inclined to view everything through the lens of our personality priorities. Our personalities indicate our primary relationship with ourselves that will therefore mark our primary relationship with others. For example, if you are a Type 5, then everything is viewed through the lens of wanting to be capable and competent and to be a useful source of information. If you are a 5 with a 4 wing, you want to be important and worthy of attention in order to be a capable, useful source of information. Further, we can include the tertiary type here and discover that a 5 with a 4 wing wants to be dependable and trustworthy (Type 6) in order to be important and worthy of attention (Type 4), ultimately in order to be a capable, useful source of information (Type 5).

All of the types work this way, where if we were to map out the ordering of prioritization of all of the type relationships within us, every type's desires are attended to for the sake of the desires of the type that is next higher in priority within us, which are attended to for the sake of the desires of the type that is next higher in priority within us above this, and so on, ultimately for the sake of the desires of the primary type within us.

As another example, if you are a 4 with a 5 wing, you want to be valuable and successful (Type 3) in order to be capable and useful (Type 5) in order to be important and worthy of attention (Type 4).

Understanding this can help us to identify someone's primary and secondary types. Another aspect of the personality type dynamics that can help us to identify someone's primary and secondary types is the way we shift our personality priorities in moments of extreme stress—when our usual way of operating isn't working to alleviate stress and we are completely unfulfilled in our basic motivations—as well as in moments of lack of stress—when we are completely fulfilled in our basic motivations and so expand beyond this.

The Enneagram Nine Personality Types And The Five Levels Of Stress (from no stress to extreme stress)

When we're under no stress at all, we identify with a personality type that is different from the one with which we usually identify. We move one number over from left to right in the following order: 5 → 8 → 2 → 4 → 1 → 7 → 5, and 6 → 9 → 3 → 6. (This is known as "integration".) So, for example, if you identify with Type 5 usually, then during times when you are not experiencing any stress at all, you identify with Type 8. (The secondary personality type, or "wing", which is one number more or one number less than the main personality type, integrates following this order as well at the same time as the main personality type. So if you are a 5 with a 4 wing, then under lack of stress you identify with an 8 with a 1 wing, essentially, even though ordinarily it would not be possible for an 8 to have a 1 wing.)

When we are under usual, daily stress, we identify with the personality type (and secondary personality type) with which we usually identify. When we are under more than usual, daily stress, we grow more extreme in our identification with the personality type (and secondary personality type) with which we usually identify.

When we are under a lot of stress, we shift toward identification with a personality type that is different from the one with which we usually identify. We move one number over from left to right in the following order (the reverse of the lack-of-stress ordering): 5 → 7 → 1 → 4 → 2 → 8 → 5, and 6 → 3 → 9 → 6. (This is known as "disintegration".) So, for example, if you identify with Type 5 usually, then during times when you are experiencing a lot of stress, you identify with Type 7. (The secondary personality type disintegrates following this order as well at the same time as the main personality type. So if you are a 5 with a 4 wing, then under a lot of stress you identify with a 7 with a 2 wing, essentially, even though ordinarily it would not be possible for a 7 to have a 2 wing.) When we are under extreme stress, we grow more extreme in our identification with the personality type (and secondary personality type) with which we identify under a lot of stress.

When we are under stress for an extended period of time, we get less healthy, and our biases in identification with any particular personality type become more extreme in their development forms. When we are under lack of stress for an extended period of time (due to lack of external stresses or due to dealing with things well), we get healthier, and our biases in identification with any particular personality type become subtler as we learn increasingly to express the types in their creation forms.

Who You Really Are

Now that we've delved a bit into different personality types and aspects of personality, it is important to recognize what these really are and who *we* really are.

All of these different aspects of personality, just like everything else in the world, are merely the result of fixations on different aspects of different stages in the process of development. When we are under stress for extended periods of time, we get less healthy. This expresses itself as our getting increasingly caught up in our personality obstacles. We get lost in our own perspectives on the world, and we lose sight of the fact that our own perspectives are each merely one of many valid perspectives on the world—each from its own point within this world.

It is as though we are all standing on different sides of the mountain of life, looking at this mountain from our own vantage points. You might see smooth black rock from your vantage point, while another person might see brown jagged rock, another person might see snow, another person might see muddy slopes, and another person might see greenery—all from different sides of the mountain. It is totally plausible that we could all have very different descriptions of our experience of the mountain when we account for our having different vantage points on it. In this case, many of us would be able to realize, after age seven or so, that another person's experience doesn't have to be wrong if it is different from our own, since we recognize that we can have different spatial orientations and consequently different perspectives and experiences. Yet the more we get into the specifics of the differences in our perspectives on the world, the more complicated it gets to step out of our own shoes and into another person's shoes.

Besides projecting our experience resulting from our location in space, we are inclined to project such aspects of our experience as our wants, our emotions, our thoughts, our beliefs, anything and everything that affects the way we experience the world. We are inclined to assume on some level that other people experience life the way we do. This is so despite the myriad factors that come into play in shaping our perspectives: everything from our upbringing—by healthy parental figures with healthy relationships or unhealthy parental figures or something else, with siblings or without, with whatever religion and culture and nationality, in poverty or wealth, with our physical, emotional, and intellectual needs met or not—to our other life experiences, to our personalities—where we identify with our own created thoughts or feelings or instincts, or the thoughts, feelings, or instincts that we come up with in reaction to those of others, or the thoughts, feelings, and instincts of others, as well as innumerable other things that we conclude are who we are and the way we operate.

We shape our lives with the choices we make—consciously or unconsciously—and then we conclude that other people experience the same lives. Of course there are the obvious differences that we face, where we realize even in adolescence that other people are not doing what we would be doing if we were in their situations. But we don't understand the differences because we can't yet truly conceive on our own what other ways these people might be operating internally that they might choose these alternative behaviors. All we know is our own experience through our own physical senses and our own lenses of thought, feeling, and instinct. It is extremely difficult to conceive of other possible ways of experiencing the world. So we are inclined sort of to gloss over the differences that we can't explain and go on operating as though other people actually do operate the way we do.

However, the very nature of the progression of development in this world is for us to become increasingly aware of the validity of perspectives and experiences that are not necessarily our own. We develop to become more and more capable of imagining how the world could be different from what we have experienced and known it to be, and how we could experience it differently from the way we have experienced it before. This ability to conceive of what we haven't already experienced ourselves is a necessity in our growing to shape our lives differently from the way we have previously shaped them. It is a necessity in our growing away from where we came from and into something new.

Without being open to alternative perspectives on the world, we are trapped in replaying the lives, beliefs, and relationships of our parents and/or other prominent figures surrounding us during our upbringing—everything from their dynamics with each other and with their children and other people, to their beliefs about money, careers, religion, family, friends, community, and life. Sure, we can react to them and try to come up with something different. But this isn't the same as letting go of our pasts and moving toward entirely new futures. For as long as we identify ourselves in relation to our pasts—either as being like that or as being *not* like that—we hold our pasts with us in shaping who we are, and we end up replaying them in some form since our attention is essentially still backward rather than forward, or it is forward with the fear of replaying what is behind us, or it is on where we are with the situation being that where we are is the replay of where we were, which means our attention is still on what is behind us in some way.

We ideally begin to realize that everything we say would be most accurate if accompanied by the words "in my experience, here and now," or "from my perspective, here and now." Perhaps we ought to recognize the addendum of the meaning of such a phrase to our own and other people's expressions of experiences even though it is not being said and often not even intended—for most of us, in some way or other, still believe that our experience is the only possible experience of reality, that our perspective, in the moment, is the only one that could exist.

Thus, our interactions with other people and our openness to other perspectives on the world give us the opportunity to expand upon our own perspectives and make them richer and fuller. In learning about other people's experiences of the world, we bring into our field of choice other options in regard to what our experience of the world could possibly be and consist of.

Here is where we get to who we really are in all of this. For we are not our thoughts, feelings, instincts, or the things in our lives that we do or that we have or that we have accomplished. We are the capacity for choice behind all of this. We are the ones who choose our thoughts, our feelings, our instincts, our behaviors, and ultimately the overall content of our lives.

It is important that we practice being aware of this, noticing when we are reacting to our experiences and letting our thoughts, feelings, or instincts sit in the driver's seat of our lives. Living on autopilot can't get us any of the fulfillment that we want to experience. We need to get out of autopilot and back into the driver's seat of our lives. And we can do this by bringing awareness to the ways we operate, and by making mindful and willful choices about what we are to experience in this world. When we are acting from our essence of self-aware choice, we are fulfilled.

The Power Of Gratitude

In order to teach a dog or a penguin or a pigeon to do something you want him to do, you give him a treat or some other kind of reward every time he does anything that is in the direction of what you want him to do. For example, if you want to teach a pigeon to play ping-pong, you give him food every time he walks closer to the ping-pong ball. Then you give him food every time he pecks in the direction of the ping-pong ball. Then you give him food every time he hits the ping-pong ball with his beak. Then you give him food every time he hits the ping-pong ball in the direction of the net. And so on. In order to teach an animal to do anything, you reward him/her when he/she is heading on the path toward what you want him/her to do.

The same thing goes for a person. If you want your child or friend or partner to do something different, you should pay attention and reward him/her every time he/she does something in the direction of what you want him/her to do. This way, you guide this person in this direction and you also give him/her a reason to keep going in this direction.

If you want your male partner to do something different from what he's been doing, be clear about what you want without being demanding and without showing a lot of disappointment and criticism if he says no. (He is more likely to respond the way you want if he feels he has the choice not to.) Accept his response no matter what, but if he does anything in the direction of what you want, reward him. Thank him and smile and show gratitude and appreciation for what he's done. Make him feel like he's been useful and helpful and has had a positive affect on you by doing what he's done. And he will want to do more for you—because you will have shown that it will make you happy, and he wants to make you happy because making you happy makes him happy. And he will also know what to do more of—as long as you clearly say or in some other way indicate what you want and you keep showing gratitude and appreciation when he goes in the direction toward doing something closer to what you want.

If he is changing in the right direction, don't show disappointment that he hasn't done exactly what you want, because this will stop him in his tracks. He won't try to please you if you make him feel like he can't. So pay careful attention and look for any sign of change in the direction that you want, and encourage him along that path by showing him gratitude and appreciation for what he's done. Be clear about what you want, and show him that you trust him to do what's best for you. Support him in his decisions, and accept and appreciate him for who he is and for the way he is, but show him extra gratitude and appreciation when he's going in the direction you want. And he'll keep going that direction.

If you want your female partner to do something different from what she's been doing, much the same thing applies. Be clear about what you want without being demanding, and accept her response no matter what, but show her gratitude and appreciation when she does something that is in the direction of what you want. Look for the things that you like about what she's doing, and encourage her to keep going that direction by telling her and showing her that you care about her and that you are there for her. If she feels accepted and appreciated, she will keep going that direction.

Listen to what she has to say. Don't always try to fix everything, and try not to get defensive. She's not always looking for answers; usually she just wants to be heard and understood. Pay attention to her, and show that you care, and show her extra gratitude and appreciation when she does something that is in the direction that you want. And she will keep going that direction.

The same thing goes for every aspect of the world of your experience, including the physical events of your life and your own thoughts, feelings, and instincts. If you want your life to change, accept everything as it is and show gratitude and appreciation for all the things that happen that are in the direction of what you want. Every day, pay attention, acknowledge and accept whatever draws your attention, and search for the things that you can be grateful for. And say thank you. Show gratitude and appreciation. Take a deep breath and slowly let it out and smile and say, "I'm so grateful that this is happening," or "I'm so grateful that this happened today," or even "I'm so grateful that this happened then (no matter how far in the past 'then' is)." Say "Thank you" when you wake up each day, when you open your eyes and behold the world once again for the first time, when you take your first steps that day, when you step outside and feel the air on your skin and the sunshine on your face. If you show gratitude for being alive, life will offer you more to be grateful for.

Whenever you show gratitude for anything—the actions of an animal or person, the occurrence of an event, etc.—you are encouraging the flow of more of that into your life. You are keeping the pathway open for more of that kind of experience.

When you fail to show gratitude, life just keeps offering you more of whatever you give your attention to—whether for good or for bad. Like a child who can only get your attention by doing what you don't like, life will just keep offering you more of what you don't want if this is what you focus on, because this is what gets your attention—even if this attention is in the form of anger, frustration, shame, regret, anxiety, or fear.

Just as you need to reward a child with positive attention for what he/she is doing and has done in order to get him/her to do more of this, you need to reward your own positive thoughts, feelings, and instincts, and everyone and everything around you that you like in your life, with positive attention in order to get more of them. Don't ignore the things you like just because that's what "should" have happened, or because that's what your child or your friend or your partner or your pet "should" have done. These are the very opportunities you don't want to miss to show that this is exactly what you want more of, and thereby to encourage, reinforce, and bring about more of this.

So notice what draws your attention, accept what already is, bring your awareness to what is happening that is on the path of what you want, and show appreciation and gratitude. Even for the little things. And your life will fill to overflowing with reasons to be thankful.

Every Relationship Is A Dance

Every relationship—be it as friends, or something more, or simply something else—is like a dance. You've got to take a step forward to show interest in a person, but then you've got to take a step back to give that person the opportunity to show interest in you. And repeat.

If you never take a step toward a person, that person will never know you're interested in having or maintaining some kind of relationship with him/her. If you take a step toward the person and then you just keep taking steps forward, the person has no choice but to keep taking steps backward—away from you.

Of course, if you take a step backward and then you keep taking steps backward, then if the person is overly persistent, he/she will keep taking steps forward toward you. But, otherwise, the person will simply stop pursuing any kind of relationship with you—because you keep distancing yourself from the person and so are not showing interest in return.

There must be a balance of advance and retreat, move forward and move backward, step into the other person's space and then step back and give the other person room to step into your space. The rhythm and timing of this dance varies from relationship to relationship (depending on the way the two people mesh) and from time to time (depending on the circumstances of each person's life), but every good, healthy relationship that lasts and is fulfilling for both parties involved adheres to this pattern.

So take a step forward to show interest by calling or emailing or suggesting you two meet up or something. Then take a step back and give the person room to step forward toward you. Then wait, and if the person responds with interest in pursuing or continuing the relationship, then take a step forward again to show interest, yourself.

There are exceptions to every rule, of course. Sometimes a long time will pass during which you or the other person is busy, or it is simply in a particular person's nature to be slow in responding or something. In such cases, you can always send a reminder—after what seems an appropriate amount of time has passed—that you have stepped forward. Just don't be too assertive about it. Respect the person's style of dance, life circumstances, and prioritization of things in life. If that person's style of dance really doesn't work for you, then perhaps this isn't the ideal relationship for you to pursue. You want to dance with people with whom you enjoy the dance. Keep this in mind when considering the relationships that you are choosing to pursue and maintain in your life.

The Relationship Key

Your relationship with everyone and everything around you is a reflection of your relationship with yourself. Now that we've delved a bit into what types of relationships you might have with yourself (with your own thoughts, feelings, instincts, etc.), we can begin to understand how you can apply this key to transforming your relationships with everyone and everything around you. In this way, you can learn to shape your life experience into what you want it to be.

Everything that you think and feel toward anyone else—whether you say it or act on it or not—is a reflection of what you already think and feel toward yourself. Every criticism and every praise that you direct outward is a reflection of what you are already directing inward. Whenever anyone or the circumstances of your life seem to be treating you terribly or well—all of this is a reflection of how you are already treating yourself. Every aspect of your physical body, the circumstances of your life, and the nature of the dynamics of each and every one of your relationships with everyone and everything around you—from your parents, to your siblings, to your children, to your friends, to your community, to your significant other, to seemingly random people you encounter in your daily life, to your financial situation, to your health, and onward—all of it is a reflection of what is going on inside you. There is nothing that you experience outside you that did not begin inside you—in your own internal dynamics, your relationship with yourself, the way you treat yourself, the thought and emotional content and energy that you direct toward yourself, the things you say to yourself, the words and scenarios you rehearse in your mind (whether out of fear or joy, regret or love, frustration or peace), the way you make yourself feel, etc.

When you look in a mirror, if you don't like what you see, it will not help anything to assert that the mirror should change. If you don't like what you see in the mirror and you want it to change, you must change in yourself what you don't like seeing in the mirror. Thus it is with every aspect of your life. If you don't like what you see and experience outside you—in your health, your finances, your living situation, your family, your society, your friendships, your relationship, etc.—and you want it to change, then you must change what is inside you that is being reflected in this undesired situation outside you. On the other hand, if you like what you see outside you, then rather than let it go without your attention, encourage more of it with appreciation and gratitude, and keep doing what you're doing that's being reflected in this desired situation.

So, let's say your friend says something to you that really rubs you the wrong way. Rather than simply get upset at your friend and expect that your friend should change the way he or she talks to you, notice yourself getting upset, acknowledge this feeling, and ask yourself, "What exactly did this person make me feel?" Perhaps the specific feeling is insecurity—that you can't trust this person. Or perhaps the feeling is lack of worthiness—that your feelings aren't being acknowledged. Or perhaps the feeling is incompetence—that you can't take care of things yourself and are a burden on others. Or perhaps it is a combination of feelings.

Next, you can ask yourself "When have I felt this feeling before?" Identify the themes in your life—the circumstances, the people, etc.—that are connected by this feeling or by the thoughts that are leading to this feeling.

Then, ask yourself, "How might I be making myself feel this way?" You can use your understanding of your personality dynamics as described in this book as a guide to figuring this out.

Once you identify how you might be treating yourself the way the other person treated you, or how you might even be saying exactly the same words to yourself that the other person said to you, or simply how you might be making yourself feel the way the other person made you feel, then ask yourself, "How would I like to be making myself feel instead?" Remember, you cannot get what you want by saying to yourself, "I will not think of a big pink elephant," or by looking at the pole that you don't want to crash into while riding a bicycle. You've got to focus on what you want, rather than on what you don't want, because you will get whatever you focus your attention on, even if you are saying "no" to it.

Once you articulate in the positive how you would like to feel instead, so that you are looking in the direction you want to go rather than in the direction you don't want to go, ask yourself, "How can I make myself feel that way?" Again, you can use your understanding of your personality dynamics as described in this book as a guide to figuring this out.

So here's the basic process, in summary, for identifying the internal roots of your external experiences and uprooting and replacing them so that you get different external experiences—or, in other words, for identifying the GPS destinations you've set that led to your current circumstances and replacing these with more desired GPS destinations.

If you experience something that you don't like (or that you do like and would like to bring about more of, in which case you can simply exclude steps 4 and 5), ask yourself:

1. "What exactly is this making me feel?"
2. (Optional step to help identify the nuances of the feeling and the thoughts and beliefs behind it) "When have I felt this way before?" Identify any themes that exist in your life related to this feeling and the thoughts and beliefs behind it.
3. "How might I be making myself feel this way?"
4. "How would I like to make myself feel instead?"
5. "How can I make myself feel this way?" Identify what you'd like to be thinking and doing and how you'd like to be treating yourself in order to make yourself feel the way you want to feel.

If every time you experience something that you don't like, you go through this questioning process and make the necessary changes in yourself to the best of your ability, then you will experience changes in your external life that correspond with your internal changes. People will change the way they treat you and act around you. You'll move out of some relationships and into others, meeting new people who treat you the way you want to be treated as you come to treat yourself that way. The circumstances of your life will change—finances, health, etc. All of this will happen because when you change the way you treat yourself and the way you think and what you focus your attention on, many things change:

You feel differently, so you act differently, with different facial expressions, body language, motivations, etc. You are driven to engage in different behaviors, to strive toward goals that you'd otherwise give up on at the first sign of an obstacle. You succeed where before you have failed because your whole internal dynamic is different, and so you begin to believe that you can succeed at bigger things, and so other people begin to believe that you can succeed, and so you get their support in this.

Remember, life treats you the way you treat you. So notice the reflections outside you of what is inside you and recognize and use them as the gifts they are meant to be. You get to choose whatever you want to experience in this world since everything is a reflection of the choices you make about what you pay attention to and how you treat yourself. So whatever you do experience can help you to recognize what thoughts and feelings and events you have been focusing on so that you can change this where you might want to. If you're not getting what you want in life, ask yourself what you have been asking for with the focus of your attention, with what you have been looking at and rehearsing inside yourself, with how you have been treating yourself. Then, make changes where you deem appropriate, and keep refining this until you do get what you want in life.

Imagine that life is training you as you might train a pet or a child. When a pet or a child does something you like, you reward him or her, and so he or she follows these desired outcomes and consequential good feelings toward more desired outcomes and more good feelings by continuing to engage in the actions that get rewarded. If you are not being rewarded with things you want in life, you are not focusing your attention—with your thoughts and actions—on the right things, and you should try shifting the focus of your thoughts and actions to something else. If you are being rewarded with things you want in life—with good feelings and good outcomes—then you are focusing the attention of your thoughts and actions on the right things, and you should keep focusing on these things or things like these as long as it feels good (long-term-lasting-fulfillment-good, not short-term-fleeting-pleasure-good) to do so.

To further this idea and your understanding of how to use your internal GPS system effectively, if you are ever experiencing anything that you don't like in your life, you can ask yourself, "What am I experiencing?" Do your best to identify this exactly—not only in terms of how you are feeling, but also in terms of what is actually happening around you in your life, what you have that you don't want or what you want but don't have. For example, perhaps you notice that your current romantic relationship is not fulfilling to you. What makes it not fulfilling? What is this person like that you wouldn't want your partner to be like? How does this person treat you or make you feel that isn't what you want? Then, ask yourself, "What would I like to experience instead?" State this in any form that shifts your focus from what you don't want to what you do want. (It would probably be a good idea *not* to use the phrase "I want" because, due to our most common use of this phrase, this usually involves our focusing on our wanting and our being separate from the experience that we want rather than our actually connecting ourselves to the experience that we'd like to have. Instead, use phrases that encourage your stepping, in your imagination, into the experience that you'd like to have.) For example, "I would really like a partner who treats me with love and compassion." "I would love to experience a relationship that makes me want to be a better version of me." "I'm open to the possibility that I could have a partner who excites me and makes me feel fantastic."

Then, in order for you to get what you've just stated that you'd like to experience, the next step is to ask yourself something like, "How can I make myself feel these ways?" In the current example,

"How can I treat myself with love and compassion?" "How can I get myself motivated to be a better version of me?" "How can I make myself feel excited to be living and how can I make myself feel fantastic?"

So here we have a variation of what we just described in terms of feelings above, and you can use either questioning process or a combination of the two, depending on the situation. In this version of the self-questioning process, which is more physical-circumstance-oriented, whenever you experience anything that you don't like (or that you do like and want more of, in which case exclude steps 4 and 5), ask yourself:

1. "What exactly am I experiencing?" (Or: "What am I thinking, feeling, and wanting to say or do?") What are the physical circumstances that I'd rather not have (or that I want more of)? What are the thoughts and feelings that I'd rather not have (or that I want more of)?
2. (Optional step to help identify the nuances of the experience and the thoughts and beliefs behind it) "When have I experienced this before?" (Or: "When have I thought, felt, and wanted to say or do this before?") Identify any themes that exist in your life related to this experience and the thoughts, feelings, and beliefs behind it.
3. "How might I be making myself feel the way this situation is making me feel?" (Or: "How might I be making myself think, feel, and want to say or do what this situation is making me think, feel, and want to say or do?")
4. "What would I like to experience instead?" (Or: "What would I like to be thinking, feeling, and wanting to say or do instead?") What are the actual physical circumstances that you'd like to experience instead? Be sure to shift your attention to what you want rather than continuing to focus on what you don't want at this point. To facilitate this shift, you can begin your requests with phrases such as, "I would like to experience…" "I would love to experience…" "I would really

like to have..." "It would be really nice if..." "It would be great if..." "I'm open to the possibility that..."

5. "What can I do to make myself feel this way?" (Or: "What can I do to make myself think, feel, and want to say or do this?") Identify what you'd like to be thinking and doing and how you'd like to be treating yourself in order to make yourself feel the way you want to feel. This way, you can get out of your own way when it comes to getting what you've just stated that you want to experience in your life and make yourself resonant with getting what you want from the world outside you. Also, at this point, ask yourself, "What can I do to make this happen?" Be sure to remember, though, that it is not through force and exertion that you are supposed to be making things happen; it is through focusing on your destination, aligning yourself with this, and then following your own internal guidance toward the appropriate actions that you make things happen.

Find a version of this questioning process that works for the situation and for you, and use it to shift your focus from

1. What's outside you that you don't like (or that you do like)? to
2. How might this be part of a theme? to
3. What might you be doing that might be bringing this about or contributing to this? to
4. What would you like to have in your life experience instead? to
5. What can you do to make this happen? (with a focus on where your attention is in terms of thoughts, feelings, and beliefs, and what your relationship with yourself is like)

The key here is to *take responsibility for your own experience of life* rather than simply shifting the responsibility onto external people, circumstances, or factors, which will only keep things as you don't want them to be (or leave the good things up to other people and outside circumstances to make happen). Remember, telling the mirror to change, or just waiting for the mirror to change, doesn't actually bring about any change or accomplish what you want to accomplish. Change yourself, and the mirror will show you something different—guaranteed. So take responsibility for your own experiences, accept what you've created already, use what you've created already to give you a better idea of what you'd actually like instead, and then focus on what you'd actually like instead.

As you learn to let go of whatever you've had before that is undesirable—whether this is merely your thoughts, feelings, beliefs, internal dynamics or external behavioral patterns, or whether this also includes actual people, a living situation or something else—and you learn to focus on what you actually want and to treat yourself the way you actually want to be treated, you will increasingly get what you want. In this way, you can increasingly refine your life, willfully create your experiences, and make pretty much any aspect of your life into whatever you want it to be.

Forgiveness, Acceptance, and Validation

We are often inclined to expect others to be more like us, and even to impose ourselves on them.

When we're in the mode of the preserving inclination, we impose ourselves on our family and our environment, wanting them to do what we want ourselves to be doing.

When we're in the mode of the belonging inclination, we impose ourselves on our community, society, and group of friends, feeling they should be the way we feel we should be.

When we're in the mode of the connecting inclination, we impose ourselves on our significant others and our close friends, thinking they should make the decisions we think we should make.

The goal is acceptance. Since our judgments of others are merely a reflection of our judgments of ourselves, we must start by accepting ourselves. We have not always fully accepted ourselves, so we likely have plenty of people and aspects of our lives that we don't fully accept. These people and aspects of our environment and life circumstances remain as reminders of our judgments, intolerance, criticism, dismissal, ignoring, and tuning out of ourselves at various points in our lives.

It is up to us whether we continue to try to change those people and aspects of our lives through sheer force, or to dismiss them or run away from them, or simply to tune them out. All of these ways of dealing with them will only bring about more people and aspects of our lives toward whom we feel the same as we feel toward these previous people and circumstances.

Forcing people or things to change merely maintains the need to force change. Dismissing people or things results in our finding more people and things like these that we'd be inclined to dismiss. Judging leads to our having more related reasons to judge. Running away from people or circumstances merely results in our running toward people and circumstances very much like what we're running away from. Tuning people or issues out gives rise to more people and issues like what we're tuning out so we can keep having reasons to tune out.

The way the world works is that whatever we give our attention and energy to brings about more of this. The world will offer us support for continuing to think the way we are thinking, proving us right in thinking this way and providing us with further evidence that we should think this way. The world will offer us support for continuing to feel the way we are feeling, providing us with further justification for feeling this way. The world will offer us support for continuing to want whatever we are wanting, giving us more reasons to want this.

So while we might feel supported and justified in thinking or feeling a certain way, or in wanting some particular thing, it is only because we have thought it, felt it, or wanted it before this. Life will support us in any direction we seem to want to go. Just as we might show what we mean to a pet or a person who doesn't understand our language by pointing at what we want his or her attention on, or even simply by looking in the direction that we want him or her to look, so too it is with the entire world and with the Source of everything. When we look in a certain direction with our attention, we apply our creative powers and the whole world coordinates to support us in furthering us in this direction, giving us more of what we are giving our energy to and making it our reality.

It is as though we have the entire world and all of existence on our team when we are clear and unified in our attention on something. It is as though we've said, "This is where I'm going. This is what I want. Anyone and anything who is willing to help me is welcome to play whatever role he, she, or it can play to further me toward this aim." Once we're clear about something, the world brings support for us.

However, when we are unclear and divided within ourselves, we've got people and circumstances in the world who seem to be with us and those who seem to be against us—and the teams are proportional to their origins within ourselves. If we are very much against our getting to where we think we want to go because we are afraid or want other conflicting things much more on some level, the world seems very much against us. If we are only slightly against our getting to where we think we want to go because we have our doubts or fears or conflicting motivations, there will be some people and events that seem to be in our way, reflecting back our doubts, fears, and contrary desires. But the majority of people and events will then be with us, supporting our most prominent direction of attention. Clearly, the goal is unity within ourselves, for then we have only support in going the direction we truly want to be going, and life consequently becomes far easier and more effortless with open paths laid out before us to where we want to go.

As long as we have division within ourselves, we have division within the world around us. And with division comes forceful imposing of one way over another, judgment and dismissal of some way of being, and ignoring ways of thinking, feeling, and acting.

This division within ourselves is what gives rise to the denial of the validity of other ways of being, other perspectives on existence. All physical war stems ultimately from the war within ourselves that results when we are not totally accepting of ourselves and unifying ourselves in a common aim. For when we deny the validity of aspects of ourselves, acting as though they do not have the right to exist, then we do the same toward other people and aspects of the world around us who remind us of those parts of ourselves, and they consequently do the same to us.

There are levels of existence: physical, instinctual, emotional, intellectual. We can deny the validity of other people's intellectual existence and either force our own way of thinking upon them and tell them what to think, simply judge and dismiss their way of thinking, or ignore the existence of their way of thinking altogether. We can deny the validity of other people's emotional existence and either force our own way of feeling upon them and tell them what to feel, simply judge and dismiss how they feel, or ignore the existence of their feelings altogether. We can deny the validity of other people's instinctual existence and either force what we want on them and tell them what to do, simply judge and dismiss what they want, or ignore the existence of their wants altogether. We can deny the validity of other people's physical existence, either killing them, simply judging and dismissing them, or ignoring their existence and acting as though they're not even there.

Yet all of these attitudes and actions toward other perspectives on the world begin with our attitudes and actions toward ourselves—toward our own thoughts, feelings, and instincts, which is reflected in our attitudes and actions toward our bodies, our environments, and other people. This is the danger of intolerance.

The alternative is the acceptance and validation of our own thoughts, feelings, and instincts, which leads to the acceptance and validation of our bodies, our environments, and other people.

Often, in order to accept, we must first forgive. Even after we have accepted that other people are merely the messengers of what we have brought to ourselves—that we are responsible for our own experience—we must forgive others for having been willing to be the messengers of the terrible things we have brought to ourselves.

We must remind ourselves that they were only willing to be the messengers of bad things for us because they were not in a good place themselves—because they had their own struggles as we did. When we're stressed and not in a good place, we become the messengers of bad things for other people, too—knowingly and unknowingly. When we're in a good place internally, we become the messengers of good things for the people around us. But if we focus on how other people and circumstances were the messengers of bad things for us, we will not be in a good place ourselves, which will bring more messengers of bad things to us and lead us to be the messengers of bad things for other people as well. So the only way to break the chain of negativity is not to react but instead to acknowledge, forgive, and accept.

Once we forgive others for being the messengers of negative experiences for us, we must forgive ourselves for being responsible for bringing those negative experiences to ourselves. We must remind ourselves that it is all part of the growth process. We create negative experiences for ourselves because we do not yet fully understand how to create positive experiences for ourselves. How could we truly blame ourselves for not yet understanding? As we learn from our experiences what we don't want and what we actually do want instead, and how to get what we want, we can increasingly get what we want. But if we do not forgive ourselves for bringing to ourselves experiences that we didn't want, then we will still be in the process of bringing to ourselves experiences that we don't want and that we have trouble forgiving ourselves for.

So, you see, we cannot escape ourselves, and the only way truly to escape anything is to be present to it, acknowledge it, experience it, and then accept it and let it go, redirecting our attention to what we want instead. Remember: Everything gives rise to more of itself. Control breeds more of a need for control.

Judgment breeds more judgment. Intolerance breeds more intolerance. Tuning out breeds more tuning out. War breeds more war. Likewise: Acknowledgement breeds more acknowledgement. Acceptance breeds more acceptance. Forgiveness breeds more forgiveness. Awareness breeds more awareness. Love breeds more love. Understanding breeds more understanding. Peace breeds more peace.

So, once we've forgiven and accepted others and ourselves, we've made a shift that will build on itself as we continue to change our relationship dynamics with ourselves, which will be reflected in changes in our relationship dynamics with others and the world around us. After this, we can respond further with a redirection of the specific destinations we are plugging into our GPS so we bring our specific desired experiences to ourselves hereafter, and we can bring our relationship dynamics with ourselves into harmony and resonance with these new destinations.

How To Get All Parts Of Yourself On The Same Team, Working Toward The Same Aim

Why fill your experience of life with what you don't want—thinking thoughts you don't really want to be thinking, feeling emotions you don't really want to be feeling, experiencing instincts and desires you don't really want to be experiencing? All the more so when filling your internal experience with things you don't want only guarantees that your external experience will be filled with things you don't want as well.

So what's the key? To fill your internal world with content that you actually want to experience and that is a rehearsal of what you'd love to experience in your external world as well. But how can you do this when there are so many negative things drawing your attention and being really convincing about deserving your attention? There are often many conflicting beliefs, thoughts, feelings, instincts, and behaviors within us, and as long as we have internal conflicts in this way, everything will require more effort as we fight against ourselves, and we may not even succeed at achieving our ultimate aims. So the best way to fill your internal and external worlds only with content that you actually want to experience is to get all parts of yourself working on the same team toward the same goals—your set ultimate objectives, most notably your fulfillment and wellbeing.

In order to do this, identify the negative beliefs, thoughts, feelings, instincts, and behaviors, listen to them, and ask what their ultimate intention is. For their ultimate intention is always for your ultimate fulfillment and benefit, even when this seems indirect. Once you've fully heard and acknowledged their points, and their ultimate meaning and intention, you can thank them for having your wellbeing in mind and communicate to them that you'd be even more fulfilled if you do some other thing or achieve this aim in some other way instead. This way, you let all parts of you express their points, you validate them and show appreciation for them, you point out that they can even better achieve their aim of optimizing your wellbeing if they help you in a different way, and you actually get them working with you rather than against you in your achievement of your greater and more positive desires.

This is all as opposed to dismissing these same beliefs, thoughts, feelings, instincts, and behaviors within you, cutting off their expression, not listening to them, invalidating them, running away from them, tuning them out, not allowing them to communicate their main points and true intentions, and generally creating a whole bunch more negativity within you that would, guaranteed, be reflected back at you in your dynamics with other people and the world around you. Rather than having a war, competition, resentment, hatred, ill will, lack of understanding, etc., within you, you can have peace, harmony, cooperation, and total support from all parts of you for the goals you set. You can have all parts of you on the same side, helping you toward your aims. And the result is that you will be more likely to treat everyone and everything outside you in a similar way, listening to them, validating them, discovering their ultimate intentions, and then coming to an agreement with them where your and their ultimate intentions are carried out, so that everyone and everything outside you is on your side as well, helping you toward your aims.

If you are exhausted and feeling like everything requires way too much effort, then you are working against yourself, simultaneously working toward your objectives and also blocking and sabotaging yourself from reaching them with doubts, fears, negative beliefs, contradictory beliefs, etc. It takes a lot of work to go forward when you are resisting and fighting against your movement forward every step of the way. Life is energizing when you are fully on the same page as yourself, when all parts of yourself—all thoughts, feelings, instincts, and behaviors—are on the same team, working toward the same goals. The only effort you should ever have to expend should be focused on shifting into alignment with your goals—mentally, emotionally, instinctually, behaviorally, etc. Once you are aligned, life flows. So align and realign. The real *effort* stops there.

Really Listening Leads To Compassion

As you learn to listen to what your negative thoughts, feelings, and instincts are *really* saying, you'll recognize that all they've been trying to do is get your attention and help you toward your actual aims and the destinations you've been setting for yourself.

For example, let's say, in the extreme, that you are in a horrible place in your life and you ask for everything in your life to change. The result may be that thoughts, feelings, and instincts of wanting to die or of actually killing yourself come up. These thoughts, feelings, and instincts are not actually telling you to kill yourself. If you really listen to them, you'll realize that what is truly happening is that you asked to be in a completely different place in your life, and so your thoughts, feelings, and instincts are telling you, "If you want to get what you're asking for, I have to kill myself; I have to end myself." In other words, your thoughts, feelings, and instincts are actually telling you, "If you want to get to the destination you are now setting for yourself, where everything about your life is different from the way it currently is, you need to completely get rid of all of your current thoughts, feelings, and instincts." If you identify with those negative thoughts, feelings, and instincts, believing that they are you, then you will believe that *you* want to kill yourself. But you are not actually those thoughts, feelings, and instincts that are saying to you, "I need to end." They are separate from you and are communicating with you, trying to help you toward your goals by letting you know what you need to do to reach your goals.

If you are in a relationship where you are not being treated well, you might ask that you be treated better. The result may be that thoughts, feelings, and instincts of not being able to deal with being treated this way, and of having to break up with the person, come up. These thoughts, feelings, and instincts are not necessarily telling you to break up with the person. If you really listen to them, you'll realize that what is truly happening is that you asked to be treated better than you are being treated, and so your thoughts, feelings, and instincts are telling you, "If you want to get what you're asking for, I can't deal with you anymore; I have to break up with you." In other words, your thoughts, feelings, and instincts are actually telling you, "If you want to be treated better, you need to stop treating yourself this way." If you identify with those negative thoughts, feelings, and instincts, believing that they are you, then you will believe that you want to break up with the person outside you with whom you are in a relationship. But you are not actually those thoughts, feelings, and instincts that are saying to you, "I need to break up (with you)." After you break up with those thoughts, feelings, and instincts and consequently treat yourself better, you can see if the person with whom you are in a relationship treats you better, too, because you will certainly be treating him or her better as you treat yourself better by deciding to be fully where you are in your relationship and life and giving more attention to the good aspects of your current situation. At this point, you can determine whether you actually want to break up with him or her as well, which would ultimately require a further change of your thoughts, feelings, and instincts, as well as physical action.

If you are unsatisfied with your body, you might ask that you be thinner or fitter or more muscular. The result may be that thoughts, feelings, and instincts of needing to change and fix yourself, or of needing to lose weight, come up. These thoughts, feelings, and instincts are not necessarily telling you to change your physical body or lose the physical weight. If you really listen to them, you'll realize that what is truly happening is that you asked for a different body, and so your thoughts, feelings, and instincts are telling you, "If you want to get what you're asking for, I need to change; I need to be fixed; I need to be lost." In other words, your thoughts, feelings, and instincts are actually telling you, "If you want a different body, you need to change, fix, or let go of your current thoughts, feelings, and instincts about yourself." If you identify with those negative thoughts, feelings, and instincts, believing that they are you, then you will believe that you need to change your physical body or lose the physical weight. But you are not actually those thoughts, feelings, and instincts that are saying to you, "I need to change." After you change or lose those thoughts, feelings, and instincts, you can see if your body changes, too, because you will be more likely to eat healthfully, exercise, etc. with the positive change in your thoughts, feelings, and instincts about your body. At this point, you can determine whether you still need to do something further to make changes to your body as well, which would ultimately require a further change of your thoughts, feelings, and instincts, as well as physical action.

If you are discontented with your living situation, you might ask that you be living in a different place. The result may be that thoughts, feelings, and instincts of needing to leave, move, or get out of here, come up. These thoughts, feelings, and instincts are not necessarily telling you to move physically to another location. If you really listen to them, you'll realize that what is truly happening is that you asked for a different living situation or surroundings, and so your thoughts, feelings, and instincts are telling you, "If you want to get what you're asking for, I need to leave; I need to get out of here." If you identify with those negative thoughts, feelings, and instincts, believing that they are you, then you will believe that *you* want to leave (your physical situation). But you are not actually those thoughts, feelings, and instincts. They are having a conversation with you, telling you what you need to do to get what you want. When they say "I", they mean *themselves*, not *you*. After you let those thoughts, feelings, and instincts leave, you can see if your experience of your living situation changes, because you will be more likely to approach your living situation differently and be more present to it and make the best of it if you're not constantly thinking and feeling that you want to leave. At this point, you can determine whether you still need to leave your actual physical living situation as well, which would ultimately require a further change of your thoughts, feelings, and instincts, as well as physical action.

If you are unhappy with your job, you might ask that you be in a different job. The result may be that thoughts, feelings, and instincts of needing to quit, stop doing this, or get out of here, come up. These thoughts, feelings, and instincts are not necessarily telling you to quit your job. If you really listen to them, you'll realize that what is truly happening is that you asked for a different job, and so your thoughts, feelings, and instincts are telling you, "If you want to get what you're asking for, I have to quit; I have to stop; I have to get out of here." If you identify with those negative thoughts, feelings, and instincts, believing that they are you, then you will believe that *you* want to quit (your job). But you are not actually those thoughts, feelings, and instincts that are saying to you, "I need to quit; I need to get out of here." After you let those thoughts, feelings, and instincts quit, you can see if your experience of your job changes, because you will be more likely to approach your job differently and be more present to it and make the best of it if you're not constantly thinking and feeling that you want to quit. At this point, you can determine whether you still need to leave your actual job as well, which would ultimately require a further change of your thoughts, feelings, and instincts, as well as physical action.

If you are feeling disconnected and lonely, you might ask that you have the company, closeness, and attention of another person, or simply that you feel more connected. The result may be that thoughts, feelings, and instincts of needing connection with a close friend or significant other or someone else altogether come up. These thoughts, feelings, and instincts are not necessarily telling you to look for connection with another person. If you really listen to them, you'll realize that what is truly happening is that you asked for the closeness and attention of another person, and so your thoughts, feelings, and instincts are telling you, "If you want to get what you're asking for, I need your attention; I need to connect (with you)." In other words, they are saying to you, "If you want someone else to pay attention to you, you need to pay attention to, and connect to, your own thoughts, feelings, and instincts." If you identify with those thoughts, feelings, and instincts, believing that they are you, then you will hear *yourself* saying, "I need to connect (with someone else)." But these thoughts, feelings, and instincts are actually separate from you and really saying *to* you, "I need to connect (with you)." In this situation, you will never experience the connection you seek if you just look outward in search of it. But once you pay attention to, and connect with, yourself, you can get the attention of, and experience connection with, others as well.

Your thoughts, feelings, and instincts are separate from you and constantly trying to communicate with you in order to let you know what you need to do in order to achieve the goals that you set for yourself. In other words, you don't actually need to convince your thoughts, feelings, and instincts of anything. They are already on your side, on the same page as you, trying to help you toward your aims. It's just that you have to listen to their actual meaning and ultimate intention, without identifying with them, in order to understand what they are truly communicating to you so that they will actually be obviously helpful, rather than seeming to interfere with your efforts to move forward.

You can imagine the almost comical miscommunication that is usually going on inside us, where our thoughts, feelings and instincts say something like, "I need to leave," and then we think that's us speaking, and so we say, "I need to leave." Then our thoughts, feelings, and instincts respond and say, "No, *I* need to leave." Then we say, "Yes, I need to leave." Then they try again, getting more insistent, "NO, *I* need to leave." And so we say again to ourselves, more insistently, "Yes, I need to leave!" This goes back and forth, with torturous repetition in our minds, because we are essentially having an argument with our own thoughts, feelings, and instincts, and we often end up taking the action that our thoughts, feelings, and instincts are telling us that *they* need to take if we want to get where we want to go. So we end up in another living situation or another job or another relationship or with a different body *still* hearing our thoughts, feelings, and instincts saying, "I need to leave, or break up, or change, or whatever," because we haven't really listened to what they are *really* saying to us and we haven't let them do what they told us they need to do if we want to get what we're asking for, but instead just took the action physically ourselves that *they* need to take and not us.

(Of course, the result of all this miscommunication within ourselves is a whole lot of miscommunication between us and the other people in our lives and the world around us because the miscommunication within ourselves is reflected outside of us everywhere and with everyone and we can't escape it except by resolving it within ourselves.)

From this perspective, you can see that our thoughts, feelings, and instincts are all deserving of a lot of compassion, gratitude, and appreciation, as opposed to the bad rap, negative energy, and general ill treatment they often get from us. For they are always on our side, trying to help us. It is just that we haven't really listened to them that we so often misinterpret their meaning—and conclude that they must intend the worst things possible and simply won't let up on us no matter what we do—as we identify with them and take the actions that they are telling us as clearly as they can that *they* need to take. They have been treating us with tremendous kindness all along—even if this kindness is sometimes not apparent until we examine the situation closely in regard to what it is meant to teach us about how we brought it into our experience—and they deserve the same from us.

All of the messengers for us—from our thoughts, feelings, and instincts, to our body, to other people and the world around us—deserve our compassion, gratitude, appreciation, and respect. For even when the message that we've requested and received through them seems negative, the aim in its being sent to us, in accordance with our own asking, is always the same, ultimately—for us to reach the greatest goals that we have set for ourselves, that we may be aware of our capacity to create our lives as we desire and mindfully bring about supreme fulfillment in all of our experiences.

A Guide To Understanding Your Thoughts, Feelings, And Instincts

Whenever you hear yourself thinking "I" (or thinking, feeling, or wanting *anything*) without doing so on purpose, this is actually your thoughts, feelings, and/or instincts speaking, and not you. Listen to the internal streams of thoughts, feelings, and instincts you have going on inside of you. They are telling you everything you need to do to achieve whatever goals you have set for yourself, to get to whatever destinations you have requested or indicated that you would like to get to. And they are doing so exactly as we would expect any conversation or dialogue to play out. You say, "I'd really like this." They say, "In that case, I need to do this." If you interpret them as being you, then you're never going to succeed in getting to where you want to go because you're totally going to misinterpret what they are communicating to you about how you can get there.

So listen carefully. When it comes to what's going on inside you, "I" does not mean *you* unless you consciously initiated the thought on purpose. Likewise, "you" does not mean *someone else*; "you" means *you* unless you consciously initiated the thought on purpose. The only thing that isn't as straightforward is that *any reference to any other person* is really a reference to *you* as well unless you consciously initiated the thought on purpose. Yet even this makes sense; if your thoughts, feelings, and instincts can't get your attention when they address you directly, they speak about other people and thereby hint (without much subtlety) at what they aren't liking, or *are* liking, or are simply trying to communicate to you about *you*.

You are having a conversation with your thoughts, feelings, and instincts all the time. Be sure to recognize that what they are saying in the first person perspective is about them, and not about you, and that what they are saying about others is really about you and not about anyone else.

For example, if they say "I need to leave," then they mean that *they* need to leave, and not you, in order for you to achieve your goal. If they say, "I need to break up with you," then they mean that *they* need to break up with *you*, and not that *you* need to break up with anyone. If they say, "I want your attention," then they mean that *they* want *your* attention, and not that *you* want *someone else's* attention. If they say, "I feel unloved by you and I want to be loved by you," then they mean that *they* feel unloved by *you* and that *they* want to be loved by *you*, not that *you* feel unloved by *someone else* or that *you* want to be loved by *someone else*. If they say, "I feel so alone," then they mean that *they* feel so alone and that you should be giving them your attention rather than seeking attention elsewhere and making your thoughts, feelings, and instincts feel even more alone.

Your thoughts, feelings, and instincts are separate from you (or are a part or an aspect of you, depending on how you look at it and with what part of the spectrum of yourself you're identifying in the moment) and are communicating with you. They are not you. This is key to cultivating the kinds of relationships you want with yourself and everyone and everything around you. You cannot successfully get where you want to go in life consistently without maintaining awareness of this. Because otherwise you make it all about you, you look outside yourself for what your thoughts, feelings, and instincts want from *you*, and you entirely miss the point.

In order for there to be a relationship, there must be at least two different players involved. You cannot have a relationship with yourself until you recognize who the players are in this relationship. If you make yourself the only player, there is no relationship, and the result is that your relationship with yourself and with everyone and everything else becomes all about you, with no awareness of any other perspective, and with no back and forth or give and take. We must shift from having a monologue to having a dialogue, and in order to do this, we need another actor on the stage.

If you recognize yourself as the initiator, your automatic thoughts, feelings, and instincts that seem to react or respond to what you say, do, and experience with other people and the world around you are the words of the other actor on the stage, even if that actor is just an aspect or a reflection of you in a sense. When you recognize this and turn your internal monologue into a dialogue, your relationships with other people and the world around you become enriched with the validity of other perspectives besides your own, with give and take, with real empathy and presence to another—even if that other is just a reflection of you, in a sense.

Listening: The Deepest Level, The Ultimate Intention And Meaning Behind What Is Always Being Said

When you really delve into the ultimate meaning of your thoughts, feelings, and instincts, it is always very much the same. Ultimately, no one needs to kill him/herself, no one necessarily needs to break up with anyone, no one necessarily needs to leave, etc. When you hear these thoughts, feelings, and instincts in yourself, they are actually saying to you: "You are making me feel so bad that I want to kill myself, or that I want to break up with you, or that I want to leave." No matter what your thoughts, feelings, and instincts are saying, it is always about what you are making them think, how you are making them feel, and what you are making them want to do because of the way you are treating them.

Therefore, if they say "I want to kill myself," "I want to kill you," "I want to break up with you," "I want to leave," or "I can't deal with this anymore," you need to treat them much better than you are treating them. If they say, "I feel so alone and lonely," keep them company. If they say, "I want to connect with you," let them connect with you, and connect with them. If they say, "I feel like I don't belong," accept them and include them. If they say, "I feel like I can't handle the stresses of life," let them have a role in your life so that they can come to feel like they can actually be successful at handling life. If they say, "I feel ugly," then pay attention to them so that they feel like they look good enough to you that you would want to look at them. If they say, "I feel abandoned and like no one's there for me," then be there for them. If they say, "I feel like no one cares about me," then love and care for them. If they say, "I feel unworthy of your attention," then give them your attention so that they come to feel worthy of it. If they say, "I feel like I just cause conflict," then listen to them and let them speak up so that they can come to feel like they don't actually cause conflict when they speak up. If they say, "I feel like I'm not good enough and nothing I do is good enough," then recognize and treat them as though they're good enough as they are and be more accepting and encouraging and less critical and discouraging toward them. If they say, "I'm hungry for your attention," recognize that eating will only block them out further when they're actually asking for your attention, so feed them your attention rather than seeking satiation yourself. If they say, "I'm tired of trying to get your attention," recognize that they're the ones who are tired and that you'll be less tired yourself if, rather than identifying with them, you actually address what they're saying to you by giving them your attention and listening to what they have to say.

Imagine that your thoughts, feelings and instincts are like young, innocent children within you. They want nothing but your positive attention in the forms of love, caring, kindness, compassion, respect, appreciation, gratitude, acceptance, validation, protection, etc. When you give them negative attention or neglect them altogether, they feel terrible, and they react to this. They try to defend and protect themselves from you, they withdraw and close up, they rebel in attempts to regain some control, they lash out, they act out in attempts to get your attention, they distract you from other activities and nag you until they get your attention, etc.

All they want is your positive attention. When they regularly get your positive attention, they flourish and blossom, becoming like well-behaved children who do what you would like them to do, and you experience how well you're treating them in the ways other people and the world around you treat you. When they don't regularly get your positive attention, they'll do whatever they have to do to get your attention, often preferring your negative attention to no attention at all, and you experience how poorly you're treating them in the ways other people and the world around you treat you. So treat your thoughts, feelings, and instincts well, for they are essentially the children who very quickly grow up to be your physical experiences with the world and other people, who treat you the way you treated them.

Remember, you end up treating other people and the world around you the way you treat your own thoughts, feelings, and instincts. And the result is that they treat you this way in return. So treat every thought, every feeling, every instinct with kindness and compassion. Be present to it, listen to it, and respond to it appropriately—always with kind, accepting, compassionate, validating, loving, positive attention. Then you will be inclined to treat other people and the world around you this way, and everyone and everything will treat you this way, too.

Consulting Your Thoughts, Feelings, And Instincts

It is as though we all have a council of advisers within us made up of our thoughts, feelings, and instincts. Don't be a dictator who takes unilateral action without the input or support of the council. Be a benevolent ruler who guides in accordance with the suggestions and input of the wise and powerful members of your council. With your thoughts, feelings, and instincts on your side, you can do anything. But if you don't listen to them first, communicate with them, and convince them that you're going the right direction for all of you, they will be seem to be working against you rather than with you.

If you want to go to the gym, for example, don't simply tell yourself that you have to go to the gym. Here, you're basically saying to the members of the council, "We're going to the gym." And so they respond.

"I don't think I like this idea," say your thoughts. "Give me your reasons for doing this and any other information I should be considering so I can decide if this is best for us."

"I don't feel like it," say your feelings. "I'm just not in the mood."

"I don't want to," say your instincts. "Why would I want to do this?"

Ultimately, your thoughts will always give you a whole bunch of reasons why this isn't a good idea based on how things have gone before in similar or the same circumstances. ("Last time I got hurt; that could happen again. Last time I was miserable; what if this time is the same? It will probably be as bad this time as it was last time. This has never gone well; why should I believe it will now?") Your feelings will always do the same, but in emotions focused on the past rather than thoughts focused on the likelihood of the future resembling the past. ("I associate bad feelings with this. I felt attacked and tuned out last time I did this. This always makes me feel bad.") And your instincts will always do the same, but in instincts, wants, desires focused on the present moment. ("I don't want to do this. I want to lie down and watch television instead.")

Instead of facing all this resistance as a result of your imposing your will on the members of your internal council, you can present the idea of going to the gym differently.

"I would really like to go to the gym," you might say. And you might ask yourself what you imagine yourself thinking and how you imagine yourself feeling in the ideal when you get back from the gym, thereby setting your destination. "When I get back from the gym, I feel great. I'm so proud of myself for going to the gym. I feel good and alive and energized. I'm really glad I went."

Now, listen to the members of your council. What are you thinking right now? What are you feeling right now? What do you want to do right now?

If your thoughts, feelings, and instincts are in favor, go to the gym. If they aren't, consider their points, and respond kindly.

Ideally, all of the time, we would take action only after we've gone through the process of

1) Listening to ourselves.

2) Requesting or proposing for consideration something that we would like or love to experience (not demanding or forcing with controlling should's, have to's, or need to's). For example, "I would love to have a great conversation today with my significant other."

3) Supporting our proposal by imagining what we'd ideally be thinking and feeling after we've implemented our proposal. For example, "I would love to come out of my interaction with my significant other tonight feeling really connected and close to her/him. I would love to feel like our relationship is getting better all the time. I would love to feel like our communication is always improving and that we love to spend time with each other."

4) Listening to ourselves again and considering what our thoughts, feelings, and instincts have to say about our proposal. For example, perhaps your thoughts, feelings, and instincts react by saying that they don't really believe this

because previous conversations between you and your significant other, and ultimately between you and them, turned into arguments.

5) Responding appropriately—either by acting on and implementing our proposal (if the decision of our internal council is unanimous in support of it) or (in the case that the decision is not unanimous in favor of our proposal) by suggesting a slightly altered proposal for consideration that addresses whatever concerns have been brought up by our thoughts, feelings, and/or instincts, where we would repeat steps 2 through 5. For example, you might respond by saying, "I know things haven't been so great between me and her/him in the past, and I realize that this is because things haven't been so great between me and you in the past. But I would love to treat you better from here on and to connect with you and to allow you to connect with me and feel close to me, and I would love to be able to have this experience of connection and closeness and harmony overflow to my interactions with my significant other."

This process need not take long, and if we approach all of our endeavors this way, we'll have all parts of ourselves on our side and helping us toward the goals we've set and are striving to achieve. We'll have our thoughts setting a clear destination for us that is exactly the destination we intend to be setting. We'll have our feelings fueling us and motivating us toward our desired destination. And we'll have our instincts directing us in all of our speech and actions in every moment so that we do and say all the right things at exactly the right times to get ourselves to our desired destination. When our internal council members are not on our side, everything takes a lot of effort and we don't achieve our desired aims. But when we consult them and get them on our side, working with them as a team to achieve our mutual aims, then nothing can stop us from getting where we want to go.

Making Decisions And Determining Destinations In The First Place

Trying to decide in the moment what destinations to set will often leave us feeling directionless. We don't have any clear destinations in regard to this yet since this is what we are trying to determine, and our internal GPS can only provide us directions once we've plugged in destinations. So how do we determine our destinations?

Based on how our thoughts, feelings, and instincts operate, the best way to make a decision and determine a good destination to set for the future is to fast-forward in our minds and imaginations to that future.

"What would I feel like right after I do this, a day after I do this, a week after I do this, a month after I do this, a year after I do this, at the end of my life, etc. (depending on what's relevant)? What would I be thinking, feeling, wanting then?"

This is how we determine our future experience anyway—by focusing on certain thoughts, feelings, and instincts, thereby imagining and creating how something will be next time or what something will be like when it happens for the first time. When we fast-forward to right after, imagining the experiential consequences of different options we could choose, we allow ourselves to gauge what choosing these options would make us think, feel, and want naturally, if we acted on them, based on how they fit into all of our previously set destinations. By imagining a future scenario resulting from our taking some action or making some plan now and gauging what we would be thinking, feeling, and wanting after this, we're basically asking ourselves, "Is taking this action or making this plan in line with my other or overall aims? Will it further me along my main path toward my main goals or take me further away from it and them?"

So, for example, let's say you are trying to decide what to do at this moment and you are considering going for a run outside or sitting in front of the television. Ask yourself, "If I go for a run outside now, what would I likely be feeling at the end of the day, when I'm getting into bed, about how I spent my day?" Let's say you have been feeling that you would like to get more exercise, or that you've been ungrounded and lost in your own internal world lately. In this scenario, you would probably feel at the end of the day like you are clearer, more grounded, on the right track again, etc. If you still need more to get you going here, ask yourself, "If I sit in front of the television now, what would I likely be feeling at the end of the day, when I'm getting into bed, about how I spent my day?" In this scenario, you would probably feel at the end of the day like you wasted your day and are still lost in your own internal world, now also regretting that you didn't make better use of your day.

That situation is reasonably clear, but what about something a bit more complex, with more obvious longer-term consequences? Let's say you are considering whether to ask someone out on a date. Ask yourself, "If I ask this person out today, what would I likely be feeling at the end of the day about this decision?" Do you feel more like the person is going to say "yes" or more like the person is going to say "no"? Would you be okay either way? What thoughts, feelings, or instincts come up for you that might need to be addressed and redirected before you take any action like this? Also, ask yourself, "If I don't ask this person out today, what would I likely be feeling at the end of the day about this decision?" Would you regret your decision or be okay with it?

Or let's say you're considering whether you would like to marry a particular person or not. Ask yourself, "If I marry this person, what would I likely be feeling in a few years?" Do you feel good or bad about this marriage? Do you feel like you made the right decision getting married to this person, or do you regret your decision and wish you had not gotten married to this person? Do you feel happy in the marriage or do you feel unhappy in it and that things could have turned out better if you hadn't gotten married to this person? Do you feel you should have waited longer to get married or not married this person at all? Also, ask yourself, "If I don't marry this person, what would I likely be feeling in a few years?" Do you feel like you made the right decision not getting married to this person, or do you regret your decision and wish you had gotten married to this person? Do you feel happy with the way your life could turn out in this scenario? Do you feel like it could have been better if you had gotten married to this person?

Remember, we always ought to listen to our thoughts, feelings, and instincts. If they say something feels bad, we should either a) figure out how we could get them to feel good about it and only take this action at the time and in the case that they do feel good about it, or b) not take this action at all and take another action that they feel good about instead, because we will not get the results we want if our thoughts, feelings, and instincts are not on board with what we're doing.

We can decide on a destination with which our thoughts, feelings, and instincts are all in resonance and agreement by imagining the future possibilities and listening to our thoughts, feelings, and instincts to discover what they have to say about each one. Then, if we want to see if it would be possible for us to align ourselves with a different outcome, we can respond to our thoughts, feelings, and instincts appropriately to see if we can redirect them and convince them of the possibility of a different outcome.

Once we've decided on a destination of which our thoughts, feelings and instincts are supportive, imagining the future outcome as though it is already the past allows us to make it real for ourselves. It's as though things already happened the way we'd like them to, so there really isn't any other possibility, for the future positive outcome is already written as clearly as though it were the past. In this way, we make it as clear as possible to our thoughts, feelings, and instincts what outcome and experience we'd like them to guide us toward. By approaching our goal-setting and destination-setting this way, we can ensure that we consistently get the outcomes and life experiences we want.

Getting To Know The Advisers On Your Internal Council

In order to listen to your internal council and include it in your life-creation process effectively and well, it helps to understand its members and how they operate.

Your thoughts want to be competent and useful to you in the guidance they provide you. They want to be fulfilling to you and taken seriously by you. They want to be recognized by you as dependable and trustworthy sources of guidance as they aid you in your decision-making. They want you to make your decisions based on their guidance.

When you don't make your decisions based on their guidance:

When you ignore their guidance when it comes to yourself and instead try to give their guidance away to others, you make them feel incompetent and useless. The result is that they try to be competent and useful by figuring out things related to other people where this guidance to others is a reflection of what they are trying to guide you to do. This is in the hopes that you'll listen to them in the form of their guidance to others since you haven't listened to them in the form of their guidance to you.

If you really listen to them, you can recognize that what they're saying is, "I feel incompetent and useless to you, and I want to be competent and useful to you." This does *not* mean that you should identify with these thoughts and try to be more competent and useful to *others* by coming up with and sharing more guidance with *others* that *these others* should follow. It means that you should listen to what your thoughts are saying to you and act on their guidance *yourself* more so that *your thoughts* feel more competent and useful to *you*.

When you dismiss their guidance and don't pay attention to it and instead look outside yourself for guidance that you can react to and rebel against, you make them feel like they are boring to you and aren't taken seriously by you. The result is that they try to be more exciting to you by pointing out everything that is dull and boring and confining so that they will be exciting and freeing in contrast to all that. This is in the hopes that then you'll listen to them and take them seriously.

If you really listen to them, you can recognize that what they're saying is, "I feel boring to you and like you don't take me seriously, and I want to be exciting to you and for you to take me seriously." This does *not* mean that you should identify with these thoughts and try to be more exciting to *others* in attempts to be taken seriously by *these others.* It means that you should listen to what your thoughts are saying to you, recognize them as exciting, and take their guidance more seriously *yourself* so that *your thoughts* feel more exciting to *you* and like they're taken more seriously by *you.*

When you tune out their guidance and instead look to other people for guidance, you make them feel undependable and untrustworthy. The result is that they try to be dependable and trustworthy by directing you to other people for the guidance and indications of what decisions you should make with which they have been trying to provide you. This is in the hopes that you'll listen to them and trust them if their advice also comes from other people whom you trust.

If you really listen to them, you can recognize that what they're saying is, "I feel undependable and untrustworthy to you, and I want to be dependable and trustworthy to you." This does *not* mean that you should identify with these thoughts and try to be more dependable and trustworthy to *others* by following *these others' guidance* more. It means that you should listen to what your thoughts are saying to you and trust and dependably follow *their guidance* more so that *your thoughts* feel more dependable and trustworthy to *you.*

Therefore, if you haven't listened to the guidance with which your thoughts have provided you in regard to what decisions to make, be sure to listen to them when they come again in the forms of your guidance and advice to others, the contrast with the unhappiness and deprivation you experience, and other people's guidance and advice to you. Then simply take a moment and listen to your thoughts and recognize that all of these external experiences and advice and guidance are actually coming from them, and if you listen to them directly, their guidance will be much clearer.

Further, if you find yourself feeling incompetent or useless, boring or like you're not taken seriously, undependable or untrustworthy, now you know that this isn't actually you experiencing this, and you know why you believe you're experiencing this. It is your thoughts that are feeling this way, and it is because you have not been listening to, and making decisions based on, their guidance. So if you want to feel competent and useful, fulfilling and like you're being taken seriously, and dependable and trustworthy, listen to your thoughts and make your decisions based on them. Then your thoughts will feel positive in these ways, and so you will, too.

Your feelings want to be loving and helpful to you, and they want to be appreciated and loved by you for the help they provide you. They want to be important to you and treated as worthy of your attention. They want to be recognized by you as successful and valuable indicators of who you are as you define your identity in relation to others. They want you to be true to them in who you are.

When you aren't true to them in who you are:

When you ignore their intentions when it comes to yourself and instead try to give their intentions away to others, you make them feel selfish, helpless, unappreciated, and unloved. The result is that they try to be loving and helpful by helping other people where this help to others is a reflection of how they are trying to help you. This is in the hopes that you'll listen to them in the form of their help to others since you haven't listened to them in the form of their help to you.

If you really listen to them, you can recognize that what they're saying is, "I feel selfish and helpless to you, and I want to be loving and helpful to you." This does *not* mean that you should identify with these feelings and try to be more loving and helpful to *others* by coming up with and sharing more intentions with *others* that *these others* should be true to. It means that you should listen to what your feelings are saying to you and be truer to their intentions *yourself* so that *your feelings* feel more loving and helpful to *you*.

When you dismiss their intentions and don't pay attention to them and instead look outside yourself for intentions that you can react to and rebel against, you make them feel insignificant and unworthy of your attention. The result is that they try to be more important to you by pointing out everything that is insignificant and unworthy of your attention so that they will be important and worthy in contrast to all that. This is in the hopes that then you'll listen to them and treat them as worthy of your attention.

If you really listen to them, you can recognize that what they're saying is, "I feel insignificant to you and like you treat me as though I'm not worthy of your attention, and I want to be important to you and for you to treat me as though I'm worthy of your attention." This does *not* mean that you should identify with these feelings and try to be more important to *others* in attempts to be treated as worthy of attention by *these others*. It means that you should listen to what your feelings are saying to you, recognize them as important, and treat their intentions for you as more worthy of *your* attention so that *your feelings* feel more important to *you* and like they're treated as worthy of attention by *you*.

When you tune out their intentions and instead look to other people for intentions, you make them feel worthless and like a failure. The result is that they try to be valuable and successful to you by directing you to other people for the indications of who you should be with which they have been trying to provide you. This is in the hopes that you'll listen to them and value them if their expectations of you also come from other people whom you value.

If you really listen to them, you can recognize that what they're saying is, "I feel worthless and like a failure to you, and I want to be valuable and successful to you." This does *not* mean that you should identify with these feelings and try to be valuable and successful to *others* by meeting *these others' expectations* more. It means that you should listen to what your feelings are saying to you and value *their intentions* for you more and successfully be true to these intentions so that *your feelings* feel more valuable and successful to *you*.

Therefore, if you haven't listened to the indications with which your feelings have provided you in regard to who you are and how you should define and express yourself, be sure to listen to them when they come again in the forms of your help to others, the contrast with the insignificance and unworthiness you experience, and other people's expectations of you. Then simply take a moment and listen to your feelings and recognize that all of these external experiences and expectations are actually coming from them, and if you listen to them directly, their intentions for you will be much clearer.

Further, if you find yourself feeling selfish, helpless, unappreciated, and unloved; insignificant and unworthy of attention; worthless and like a failure, now you know that this isn't actually you experiencing this, and you know why you believe you're experiencing this. It is your feelings that are feeling this way, and it is because you have not been listening to, and being true to, their intentions for you. So if you want to feel loving and helpful, important and treated as worthy of attention, and valuable and successful, listen to your feelings and be true to their indications of how you should express yourself. Then your feelings will feel positive in these ways, and so you will, too.

Your instincts want to be powerful and protective to you, and they want a say in what you do; they want to feel like they have control over what you say and do. They want to be good and right in your eyes and treated as deserving of your attention. They want to be recognized by you as harmonious and peaceful; their aim is to create greater harmony through what they urge you to say and do at each moment, and they want this to be recognized by you. They want you to assert and act on them.

When you don't assert them and act on them:

When you ignore their directions when it comes to yourself and instead try to give their directions away to others, you make them feel powerless and vulnerable. The result is that they try to be powerful, protective, and in control by protecting other people through challenging them to do things where this protection and challenging of others is a reflection of how they are trying to protect you and of what they are challenging you to do in order to do this. This is in the hopes that you'll listen to them in the form of their protection and challenging of others since you haven't listened to them in the form of their protection and challenging of you.

If you really listen to them, you can recognize that what they're saying is, "I feel powerless and vulnerable to you and I want to be powerful and protective to you." This does *not* mean that you should identify with these instincts and try to be more powerful and protective to *others* by coming up with and sharing more directions with *others* that *these others* should act on. It means that you should listen to what your instincts are saying to you and act on their directions *yourself* more so that *your instincts* feel more powerful and protective to *you*.

When you dismiss their directions and don't pay attention to them and instead look outside yourself for directions that you can react to and rebel against, you make them feel bad and wrong and undeserving of your attention. The result is that they try to be better to you by pointing out everything that is bad and wrong and undeserving of your attention so that they will be good and right and deserving in contrast to all that. This is in the hopes that then you'll listen to them and treat them as good and right and deserving of your attention.

If you really listen to them, you can recognize that what they're saying is, "I feel bad and wrong to you and like you treat me as though I'm not deserving of your attention, and I want to be good and right to you and for you to treat me as though I'm deserving of your attention." This does *not* mean that you should identify with these instincts and try to be more right to *others* in attempts to be treated as deserving of attention by *these others*. It means that you should listen to what your instincts are saying to you, recognize them as good and right, and treat their directions to you as more deserving of *your* attention so that *your instincts* feel more right to *you* and like they're treated as deserving of attention by *you*.

When you tune out their directions and instead look to other people for directions, you make them feel inharmonious and like they are causing conflict. The result is that they try to be harmonious and peaceful to you by directing you to other people for the indications of what you should do with which they have been trying to provide you. This is in the hopes that you'll listen to them and recognize them as peaceful if their urgings to you to take certain actions also come from other people with whom you find harmony.

If you really listen to them, you can recognize that what they're saying is, "I feel inharmonious and conflict-causing to you, and I want to be harmonious and peaceful to you." This does *not* mean that you should identify with these instincts and try to be more harmonious and peaceful to *others* by acting on *these others' directions* more. It means that you should listen to what your instincts are saying to you and find peace in and harmoniously assert and act on *their directions* more so that *your instincts* feel more harmonious and peaceful to *you*.

Therefore, if you haven't listened to the indications with which your instincts have provided you in regard to what you should say and do, be sure to listen to them when they come again in the forms of your protection and challenging of others, the contrast with the flaws and corruption you experience, and other people's urgings to you to take action. Then simply take a moment and listen to your instincts and recognize that all of these external experiences and urgings are actually coming from them, and if you listen to them directly, their directions will be much clearer.

Further, if you find yourself feeling powerless and vulnerable, bad and wrong, inharmonious and like you are causing conflict, now you know that this isn't actually you experiencing this, and you know why you believe you're experiencing this. It is your instincts that are feeling this way, and it is because you have not been listening to, and asserting and acting on, their urgings toward you. So if you want to feel powerful and protective, good and right, and harmonious and peaceful, listen to your instincts and act on their urgings to say and do certain things. Then your instincts will feel positive in these ways, and so you will, too.

Your thoughts, feelings, and instincts are all here to advise you in your favor. Work with them and not against them. Fill them in on your plans and include them in these, listen to them carefully, and act in accordance with their guidance. Whenever you do this, you will get the positive results you want—guaranteed.

Refining Your Destination-Setting And Including Your Thoughts, Feelings, And Instincts In Your Life-Creation Process

Your thoughts, feelings, and instincts are always just trying to help you toward the destinations that you've let them know you wanted to head toward. Like a GPS system guides you toward the destinations you plug in and gives you appropriate directions based on the destinations you set, your thoughts, feelings, and instincts guide you toward the destinations you tell them—by where you focus your attention—that you'd like to go to.

If you look somewhere with your attention, your thoughts, feelings, and instincts take this to mean that you want to go there. So they start giving you directions and let you know when you're off-course or not moving forward, redirecting and urging you forward toward where you told them you wanted to go.

Therefore, if you look one direction and go another, you leave them feeling left out of your life creation process. Like a GPS continually recalculating as you disregard its directions toward where you said you wanted to go and you go somewhere else instead, your thoughts, feelings, and instincts just keep redirecting you and telling you that you're going the wrong direction based on where you said you wanted to go. Only they don't simply tell you in words; they tell you in the form of thoughts, feelings, and instincts. Therefore, you end up feeling their frustration, their exhaustion, their disconnection, their not being accepted or included, their not being listened to or acknowledged, etc. as you go a direction that is different from where you told them you wanted to go. They end up feeling like they don't have a purpose when you don't give them clear destinations to help you toward, and you experience what they experience, so you are left feeling as though *you* don't have a purpose.

But it is truly them speaking and not you, so you can resolve all of this quite easily—you can address and transform *any* negative experience, in fact—without needing anything outside you to fill in the void and make you feel fulfilled. All you need to do is make them think, feel, and want what you would ideally want to be thinking, feeling, and wanting. Give them the experience that you want, and you'll get to experience their more positive experience of your treatment of them.

In other words, listening to your thoughts, feelings and instincts really means including them in your life choices, from the little ones to the big ones. When you set or reset your destinations in advance of taking action—thereby keeping your thoughts, feelings, and instincts in the loop about how they can be useful, helpful, protective, fulfilling, important, good, trustworthy, valuable, and peaceful to you—they will know what they can do to please you and get your positive attention and they will gladly do exactly this. When you don't let them know about changed game plans, they are like a team without a purpose, continuing to guide you and give you directions in accordance with the original plans and frustrated and disheartened that they are not getting your positive attention when they are doing exactly what you asked of them.

When you are feeling negative, it means *they* are feeling negative. And if *they* are feeling negative, it is because you aren't going the direction that you told them you wanted to go and that they are trying to get you to go because you asked them to do this with where you focused your attention previously or even now. Whenever you focus your attention on what you don't like in an effort to correct, change, or avoid this, you are telling your thoughts, feelings and instincts that you want to go to what you are not liking, and then they don't understand why you would keep giving them negative attention and/or disregarding them altogether as they guide you toward what you asked them to guide you toward. You are giving them mixed signals, and they just want a clear direction and purpose from you so they know how they can get your positive attention and feel like they are doing a good job fulfilling the purpose, mission and role you gave them.

So be sure to give them a clear purpose, mission, and role that they can be fulfilling in every moment and then reward them with positive attention—appreciation, gratitude, etc.—when they do what you asked of them. This way, they'll know and feel that they are doing a good job of pleasing you and doing for you what you asked of them. And, this way, you'll experience all the good thoughts, feelings, and instincts you are giving to them and making them experience.

In other words, when we talk about listening to and acknowledging your thoughts, feelings, and instincts, we're really talking about listening to them tell you something that you asked them to tell you and acknowledging them for doing this well. They just want a clear purpose, and to get the positive attention they want from you when they fulfill the purpose you give them. So set clear destinations to give them a purpose, listen to them as they guide and help you toward your specified destinations, and acknowledge, appreciate, and thank them for doing this well.

And when you set new destinations, acknowledge what your thoughts, feelings, and instincts say to you as they remind you of your previously set destinations that might be in conflict with these new destinations. Let them know that you appreciate that they're reminding you what you asked them to remind you and doing what you asked of them, and let them know that you would actually prefer to go to these new destinations instead of the previous ones and that you'd love it if they'd help you toward these new destinations instead. Then reward them with positive attention as they guide you toward your new destinations.

If you set a destination in your GPS and then, on the way there, you decide to go somewhere else that is a completely different direction instead, you would have to set a new destination in your GPS in place of the previous one. That is, unless you want your GPS to keep giving you directions toward the original destination and recalculating over and over again as you seem to it to be going totally the wrong direction considering the destination you plugged into it. When it comes to your internal GPS, it feels terrible to be going the wrong direction compared to where you specified you wanted to go. Your thoughts, feelings, and instincts end up nagging you constantly, not allowing you to be present where you are, as they keep trying to let you know that you're not where you said you wanted to be, and that you're not going where you said you wanted to be going. They're just trying to help you, but you haven't told them how they can do so and actually be acknowledged by you as positive in this new situation with your apparent change of plans.

So specify a new destination before you veer off-course from your original destination. Then, acknowledge the directions related to the previous destination that tell you that this new destination conflicts with it, and let your internal GPS know that yes, you would like to change destinations even though this new one conflicts with the previous one, and that this new destination would make you happier (or whatever your reasons are for changing destinations that would make the new one more positive for you and your thoughts, feelings, and instincts) than the old one, and then listen to your internal GPS as it guides and directs you toward your new destination.

Another way to think about this is to use a different analogy. It is as though you have an internal calendar that is synced with that of your thoughts, feelings, and instincts. You put on your calendar, with the focus of your attention, events that you'd like to experience or things that you'd like to have or be by a certain date or time. When you do this, your thoughts, feelings, and instincts take it that you want them to send you alarm calendar reminders or alerts whenever you need to do something in order to get to your specified calendar appointments by the times you specified.

Let's say you decide you want to go to sleep by a certain time, get up by a certain time, and get somewhere by a certain time. Your thoughts, feelings, and instincts will send you an alert when it's time to get ready for bed, and when it's time to go to bed, and when it's time to get up, and when it's almost time to leave, and when it's time to leave—all in order for you to get to the appointments you set for yourself on time. If you ignore, dismiss, or tune out their reminders and stay up late, sleep late, and leave late or not at all, your thoughts, feelings, and instincts are, understandably, not going to be happy. You told them you wanted to do something, they made the effort to do their job well, and you showed them that trying to help you toward your specified goals when you tell them what you want to accomplish is really a waste of their time. This then leads you to feel like trying to set goals and accomplish them is a waste of your time, and like other people are wasting your time. So that's not so good.

Alternatively, if you really wanted to stay up later than you specified for some good reason, or to sleep later, or to get where you wanted to go later or to go somewhere else altogether, when your thoughts, feelings, and instincts send you a reminder in accordance with your previous plans, or even before this, you can let them know that you'd like to do something else that's different from what you previously specified. "I would really like to get this done and still get to bed by this other time, and sleep a bit later until this time and then skip the first place and go to this other place around this other time."

When your thoughts, feelings, and instincts say something like, "But what about the original schedule?" acknowledge them.

"Thank you for the reminder about what I originally told you I wanted to do. You're doing a great job of guiding me. But this new schedule would be even better and would make me even happier because then I'll have completed this other task by tomorrow, which is really important to me. So I would love it if you would help me to stick to this new schedule in place of the original one. Thank you for helping me out with this. You're so great and I really appreciate it."

This applies to larger goals and plans as well. Perhaps you intend to accomplish some big task or be somewhere new in some way within the week, within the month, within the year, or within the next five or ten years. Your thoughts, feelings, and instincts will always send you reminders and guidance in accordance with the goals and plans you set for yourself. Without them, you're entirely on your own in trying to make everything happen and get where you want to go, without directions, reminders, help, or guidance of any sort—even from other people or the world around you. So whenever you intend to change directions for any reason, let your thoughts, feelings, and instincts know, thank them when they remind you of your previous plans, and give them good, convincing reasons why you are choosing these new plans in place of the old ones.

Be sure to address all the members of your internal council—your thoughts, your feelings, *and* your instincts—so "good reasons" would mean some explanation (thoughts) about how it would make you feel good (or better) (feelings) so you really want to do this (instead) (instincts). For example, "I would love to do this, be this, or have this by this time (instead). I would feel so ____________ (excited, passionate, happy, fulfilled, important, accomplished, successful, alive, etc.) after I experience this. This would be amazing."

And if you find that you haven't been listening to your thoughts, feelings, and instincts—that you deviated from your original schedule without letting them know in advance—and that they're upset with you, apologize to them and let them know that you'll make more of an effort to remember to include them in your plans next time.

Basically, treat your thoughts, feelings, and instincts the way you would want to be treated. Listen to them, make them feel good, include them in all your plans, and give them a clear purpose and direction so they know how to get your positive attention. Then give them positive feedback when they do what you ask of them. It's as simple as that. And the result is that everyone and everything around you will treat you just as positively, and the calendar of your actual life will be filled with exactly the experiences that you request to have in it.

Do Unto Others As You Would Have Them Do Unto You

The application of the Golden Rule begins within us. Do unto your thoughts, feelings, and instincts as you would have them and everyone and everything else do unto you.

If you listen to them when they remind you of destinations you've set and guide you to these destinations, they will listen to you when you alter destinations and set new ones. If you pay attention to them, they will pay attention to you. If you tune into them, they will tune into you. If you are present to them, they will be present to you.

If you allow them to be capable, loving, and powerful to you, they will allow you to be capable, loving, and powerful to them. If you allow them to be useful, helpful, and protective to you, they will allow you to be useful, helpful, and protective to them. If you recognize them as fulfilling, important, and good, they will recognize you as fulfilling, important, and good. If you take them seriously and treat them as worthy and deserving of your attention, they will take you seriously and treat you as worthy and deserving of their attention. If you acknowledge them as trustworthy, valuable, and peaceful, they will acknowledge you as trustworthy, valuable, and peaceful. If you recognize and treat them as dependable, successful, and harmonious, they will recognize and treat you as dependable, successful, and harmonious.

If you love them, they will love you. If you try to understand them, they will try to understand you. If you meet their expectations, they will meet your expectations. If you are kind to them, they will be kind to you.

If you treat them badly in any way, they will treat you just the same.

If you treat them well, they will treat you well, too.

However you treat your thoughts, feelings, and instincts, your thoughts, feelings, and instincts, as well as your body and everyone and everything in the world around you, will treat you.

Understanding Your Body As A Messenger

Your body is the product of how you have been treating yourself up to this point. Deep-seated and long-standing ways of treating yourself manifest physically in the vehicle that allows you to interact with this physical world directly. The way you interact with the different aspects of your physical vehicle determines whether it works with you and helps you to achieve your aims in this physical life, or whether it works against you and makes your progression toward any desired goals more difficult or even impossible.

Our bodies, on every level, reflect back how we are treating ourselves. The physical forms of our bodies show us what we have been making ourselves think, feel, and want for an extended period of time and essentially are the tangible results of how we have been treating ourselves.

For example: When we don't allow ourselves to hear for a long period of time, we might lose our ability to hear. When we don't allow ourselves to see for a long period of time, we might lose our ability to see. When we only allow ourselves to see what is right in front of us, we might end up near-sighted. When we only allow ourselves to see what is far away from us, we might end up far-sighted. When we don't allow ourselves to digest and process what our thoughts, feelings, and instincts are telling us, we might end up with digestion issues. When we don't allow ourselves to move, we might end up with mobility issues. When we don't allow ourselves room to breathe, we might end up with asthma or other respiratory problems. When we believe that we need to be constantly on top of things in order for things to function properly, we might end up with physical ailments that we need to be constantly on top of with medication and so forth in order for our bodies to function properly. If we describe stressful things as a "pain in the neck," we might end up with neck pain when we are stressed. If we describe stressful things as a "pain in the ass," we might end up with a pain in our rear ends when we are stressed. If we feel like life weighs us down or that we need padding to protect ourselves from its attacks, we might end up overweight. If we ignore ourselves and don't value ourselves or feel worth attention and give too much of our attention to others instead, we might end up underweight. If we are regularly working against ourselves, we might end up very often fatigued and exhausted. If we don't allow ourselves to speak, we might lose our voice. If we allow problems to grow out of control without our attention, we might end up with cancer. If we don't allow ourselves to remember the past, we might end up with memory problems and dementia.

There can be more than one ultimate origin of the same or similar physical problems, just as there are multiple possible physical origins of the same physical symptoms, making diagnosis in any particular situation more complicated. However, every physical ailment began as a mental and emotional ailment that went unaddressed at that stage and so manifested physically for us to notice it and address it at this stage. The solution is not to take a pill or cut into our bodies to cut out the problem. This might facilitate addressing the symptoms more speedily in the moment, but simply coping with problems that you've created—without eliminating the problem at its root—will require continued coping with the problems that you are still creating. Focusing on the problem in order to get rid of it never works as a permanent solution unless you want to have to be continually dealing with the problem, itself, in order to have to keep working to get rid of it.

In confirmation of this, many medications have several side effects, often including symptoms that they are supposed to be addressing in the first place as well as more extreme versions of these symptoms. This is because our thoughts, feelings, instincts, and bodies are trying to tell us things that we haven't been listening to and understanding about how we've been treating ourselves. And so seeking a quick fix and taking a pill to block out the message further will only result in our thoughts, feelings, instincts, and bodies trying the same and even more extreme ways to speak up to get our attention and convey the message that they've been trying to convey to us all along about how they want more positive attention from us.

Taking a pill and not addressing the root of the problem in terms of how you are treating yourself is like locking a child in the closet because he's yelling and misbehaving. It's only going to result in the child yelling louder and misbehaving even more because the whole point was that he wasn't getting the kind of positive attention from you that he wanted, and by locking him in the closet, you are even more extremely going out of your way to not give him the positive attention that he wants from you. You are essentially communicating to him that he's not doing a good enough job of trying to get your attention and so he should try harder and be even louder, bolder, more dramatic, and worse in order to get your attention. So you'll be on the track of having to take medications to address the symptoms of your medications to address the symptoms of your medications, and so on, to address the symptoms of your first medication, the more you avoid listening to and addressing the real problem.

In order to eliminate the appearance or reappearance of symptoms and ultimately of the real problem, itself, the ultimate and only real *solution* is, like with everything else, to ask what this is making you think, feel, and want, ask how you are making yourself think, feel, and want this, and change how you are treating yourself so that you are no longer making yourself think, feel, and want this but are instead making yourself think, feel, and want something else—so that you are making yourself experience something else that you prefer to experience instead.

Your body is just supporting what you are thinking, feeling, and wanting, and how you are behaving, adapting to help you keep doing what you're doing internally. It gets in your way if you are asking for distractions and delays, and it helps you forward if you are internally aligned with achieving your goals. Change what you are thinking, feeling, and wanting, and how you are behaving, and you will change what your body supports you in accomplishing.

In the positive, we allow ourselves to see, to hear, to feel, to breathe, to digest and process what we experience and learn fully, to move freely, to address any issues that might arise when they are small and subtle within our thoughts, feelings, and instincts or are just beginning to manifest externally in our bodies or our relationships with others, and generally to maintain all of our normal, healthy functioning and expression of ourselves all the way to the end of our time syncing with this physical body. Ideally, we give our bodies all of the love and positive attention—in our thoughts, feelings, and instincts, as well as in our spoken words and physical behaviors—that they desire and require to thrive. When we treat and serve our bodies well, they treat and serve us well.

The First Step Of Effective Communication: Listening

All communication with anyone or anything outside you begins with your communication with yourself.

The first step of effective communication is listening. We need to listen to what is truly being communicated to us in order to respond effectively and communicate whatever we wish to communicate with consideration of our audience. If we just speak without really listening first, the other person will not feel heard and so will not listen to us. In this case, we will not successfully communicate anything. So we must listen first.

In order to listen to the other person and the world around us first, we need to listen to ourselves even before this. If we do not listen to ourselves first, our own thoughts, feelings, instincts, and so forth will keep vying for our attention, trying to get us to listen to them. In this case, we won't be able truly to listen to anyone else because we won't feel heard in the first place and so we'll feel like we need to be heard before we can listen.

So, first we must listen to ourselves—to the real meaning and intention of everything that our thoughts, feelings, and instincts are trying to communicate to us—and thereby make ourselves feel heard. Then we can respond to ourselves positively and appropriately and get ourselves internally aligned with a desirable outcome by guiding all of the parts of ourselves toward focus on our main objective and destination. From here, we can act on those thoughts, feelings, and instincts that we ought to act on. Basically, we should generally treat ourselves as we want to be treated, thereby setting the paradigm for all of our external interactions. In doing this, we lay the foundation for communication with other people and the world around us that is harmonious and effective and gets our desired results. We are essentially rehearsing within ourselves the types of dynamics that we want to have play out between us and other people and the world around us, rather than the dynamics that we don't want to have play out.

From here, we can more easily listen to the real intentions behind the words and actions of others and the world around us so that we make others feel heard. Then we can naturally respond appropriately and positively to their points, validate them as we've validated ourselves, and smoothly guide them toward the outcome that we want in ways that are beneficial for them and for us as we've done with the different aspects of ourselves.

All of our communication begins with our communication with ourselves, with the internal dynamics that we play out and rehearse. We must address our internal communication first, because this is what everyone and everything is responding to in us. We can say anything or do anything that we imagine might be the right words or actions. However, if we are not playing out the dynamic that we want to have within ourselves, we could be saying or doing all the seemingly right things but they will be at all the wrong times and in all the wrong ways. If you water a plant when it's already inundated with water and drowning, you will likely kill it. Even though watering a plant is the right thing to do to keep the plant alive, you must water it at the right times and with the right frequency in order to be doing the right thing to keep it alive. The context of time and location and the way something is done matters. In order to get these things right, you must have the right internal destination by rehearsing internal dynamics that are aligned with the results that you want and thus by focusing on where you want to go and what you want to have happen.

You will never communicate the right things with the right words and actions at the right times in the right places in regard to everyone else's internal states and receptivity to your messages unless you are internally aligned with the outcome you want. No amount of effort will get you there unless you are internally rehearsing the way you want things to play out in the way that you are treating yourself. If you are rehearsing one thing and working toward another, you are working against yourself and thereby making it a lot more work for yourself to get nowhere.

So before you try to address anything with anyone else, stop and breathe and listen to yourself first. Ask yourself how you'd like the interaction to go. What do you want to be thinking and feeling when you come out of it? How can you treat yourself the way you want the other person or the world to treat you so that you are truly aligned with the results you want?

Then go into the interaction with the other person or the world around you, and listen. And then respond appropriately and positively, and communicate what you'd like to communicate, without any attachment to any specific outcome in this particular situation. It would simply be really nice if things were to go a certain way, but it would be okay if they don't, because you'll get to your ultimate destination somehow, even if not through this particular route.

If you approach all communication with anyone or anything this way, you'll always get the ultimate results you want.

The Importance Of Communication

Were it not for communication, we would be trapped in our own perspectives, never to be exposed to any other way of being. We encounter people with different personalities, different upbringings, different interests, different beliefs, etc. from our own. Communication is what allows us to step out of our already conceived notions of the way life is and experience life through the lens of another perspective on the world. Communication allows for empathy and growth and learning from other people's experiences and not simply from our own, so that we can learn lessons even without always facing the obstacles ourselves, and so that we can add to our repository of experiences to get another take on our own situation.

Again, communication begins within us. We actually cannot hear and fully receive and take in anything expressed by anyone else that we have not already become ready to hear within ourselves. When people hurt us with their words, it is only because we are already hurting ourselves with similar words. Likewise, when people teach us great lessons with their words, it is only because we are ready to listen to the great lessons we are trying to teach ourselves.

Everyone and everything is merely a messenger of what our thoughts, feelings, and instincts are trying to communicate to us. We ought to take responsibility for the negative messages, and also give ourselves credit for the positive ones. And we should always work to get to a place where we can express gratitude for the messenger, regardless of the message, so that we can encourage more messages that lead us to feel and express gratitude.

Relationships With And Between Parents Lay The Beginning Foundation In This Life For The Nature Of All Of Our Relationships

Our relationships with our parents, and their relationships with each other, model what will be familiar to us and lay out dynamics that we are likely to repeat unless we bring awareness to these and consciously choose something different for ourselves.

Physically abusive parents often give rise to children who become physically abusive parents. Verbally abusive parents often give rise to children who become verbally abusive parents. Controlling parents often give rise to children who become controlling parents. Accepting parents often give rise to children who become accepting parents. Loving parents often give rise to children who become loving parents.

This pattern does not always hold, however. Free will and our capacity for growth and change give rise to the exceptions. While healthy parents often give rise to children who become healthy parents, unhealthy parents often give rise to children who become healthy parents as well. It is a very different journey for these latter children, however, to get here.

In order to understand how upbringing affects us, let's consider the metaphorical example of learning not to touch a hot stove.

Children raised by healthy parents (or parental figures) are taught by the example set by their parents that they shouldn't touch the stove or stay too close to the stove. They don't know from experience why they shouldn't do this, but their parents never did it in front of them, and their parents are comfortable and happy, and so they learn to be comfortable and happy and have no reason to try touching the stove. Life can be enjoyable and fulfilling, and by following the example of their parents, they learn to experience life this way and don't experience it to be any other way.

Children raised by average health parents (or parental figures) are taught by the example set by their parents to stand close to the stove, where it is uncomfortably hot, but never to touch the stove. They learn that life has its stresses, and they just have to deal with them because this is the way life is. As a result, the stresses gradually pile up throughout life, and these people get less healthy as they live until things get bad enough that they have to face them and learn to deal with things differently.

Children raised by unhealthy parents (or parental figures) are taught by the example set by their parents to touch the stove over and over again. They keep getting burned and life seems to be pure torture. So they are forced by their experiences to realize that this can't possibly be the only way to live because otherwise no one would put up with living for very long. As a result, they are compelled to face their own internal obstacles and learn how to deal with things differently so that life can be bearable, and ultimately so that life can actually be fulfilling.

It is open to all people to learn from whoever raised them what to do and what not to do in life, either by example or by contrast with the example. It is simply that we follow the example set for us first as we grow up, not knowing any other way to live until we decide that there has to be another way and then we begin to be exposed to other ways. As long as we define ourselves in reaction to what we've experienced during our lives, either because we follow the example set for us or because we rebel against the example set for us, we end up becoming our parents and/or other people we do or do not want to be like. Whatever we give our attention to, we become. We must look to where we want to go and not back to where we came from if we wish to get somewhere new.

If you pay attention, you will notice that you likely will end up in relationships that resemble that between your parents and between you and your parents. If you had a domineering mother and a submissive father, you will likely replicate these roles, becoming more like the parent who is the same gender as you and being attracted to someone who is more like the parent who is the opposite gender. If you had a tall, protective father and a short, caring mother, you will likely replicate these roles, looking for the analogous counterpart to yourself. Everything from relationship dynamics to height, strength, attitude toward weight, social relationships, etc., will likely come into play, depending to a large degree on what made an impression on you and what kind of impression it made based on your personality.

The reason for this is that we carry our first examples of relationships with us in ourselves. We build associations regarding what the opposite gender is like and what our own gender is like and what people are like. Without any other relationships as powerfully influencing us at first, the beginning of the shape of all of our relationships is built for us in these first examples.

As those of us who don't relate to our parents try to relate to our parents and maintain harmony with them and their expectations of us, we either make friends who are similar to our parents and different from us—replicating our lack of connection with our parents—or friends who are very different from our parents and much more similar to us—giving up on relating to our parents in some close way. The approach we choose depends on how in touch we are with ourselves and what we really want.

Either way, though, when it comes to romantic partners and our children, until we change the dynamics within ourselves that were formed and reinforced in our experiences growing up, we inevitably become like our parents and are attracted to people like our parents in various ways. This emphasizes the importance of acknowledging and improving our internal dynamics, weeding out the negative relationships, beliefs, and associations within ourselves. By learning from where we came from and looking where we'd like to go, we can work our way to where we want to be and form new, better relationships within and outside ourselves that we'd truly like to have shaping our life experience.

Our Priorities In Relationships Change Based On Stress Level

Our ordering of prioritization of the three inclinations (connecting, belonging, and preserving), combined with our stress levels, affects what we are inclined to believe is important in our relationship search, as well as within our relationship once we are in one. Often, the search for a relationship is stressful in itself due to the way we approach it—from a place of longing and lack and a sense of incompleteness, disconnection, and unfulfillment inside ourselves. And it is this very stress that compels us to seek a relationship in search of connection and fulfillment outside ourselves. When this is the case, however, we end up putting undue emphasis on priorities that are different from our usual daily priorities as we try to determine what we are looking for in a relationship and what type of person is the right match for us. Understanding our biases of attention under different degrees of stress can help us to be aware of them when they arise in us and to identify more accurately what is really best for us in a relationship in the long run.

When we are under usual daily stress, we believe that our highest priority in seeking a relationship, as well as a career and other things, is that indicated by our primary inclination. When we are under a bit more than usual daily stress, we believe that our highest priority in seeking a relationship, as well as a career and other things, is that indicated by our secondary inclination. When we are under a lot of stress, we believe that our highest priority in seeking a relationship, as well as a career and other things, is that indicated by our tertiary inclination.

When, based on your personality's ordering of inclinations and your stress level, you are in the mode of the connecting inclination, you look for someone to whom you are very attracted, and possibly also of whom your close friends would approve. When, based on your personality's ordering of inclinations and your stress level, you are in the mode of the belonging inclination, you look for someone who is a member of the community or group with which you most identify, and possibly also of whom your community or group would approve. When, based on your personality's ordering of inclinations and your stress level, you are in the mode of the preserving inclination, you look for someone who has a similar family background as you do, who is in a certain place career-wise and financially, and possibly also of whom your family would approve. You search for these things in another person because you believe that you will be most likely to be able to connect with someone, and feel connected to someone, who meets these criteria.

However, searching for a relationship with these biases will lead us astray from what would really be best for us in a relationship in the long run and really enable us to connect, and feel connected, with another person. While all of these above three priorities should be considered, the most important thing in a relationship—in order for it to be fulfilling, with real connection, in the long run—is ultimately that you have mutual attraction, relating, and chemistry with the other person.

The Recipe For Attraction, Relating, And Chemistry

If you're trying to find the perfect romantic partner for you, or you simply want to find people you get along really well with, you'll want to know the recipes for three things: attraction, relating, and chemistry.

Opposites attract. Attraction to someone's personality is determined primarily by how different you are from each other. One main measure of this kind of opposites attracting is on how many of the Myers-Briggs personality dimensions you differ from each other. So if you are INTJ (introverted, intuitive, thinking, judging), for example, then you will in certain ways be most naturally attracted to someone who is the complete opposite of you, or ESFP (extroverted, sensing, feeling, perceiving).

Another major part of opposites attracting is having different primary inclinations, and particularly the opposite ordering of inclinations. So if you're connecting, preserving, belonging, you are likely to be attracted to someone who is belonging, preserving, connecting.

In the case of complete opposites, there would be a lot of magnetic energy between you, and it would feel like you want to *be* with this person when you're together in person. However, you wouldn't relate to such a person at all, conversations would be difficult and a phone relationship would be largely unfulfilling, and so the relationship would be based primarily on the attraction of opposites. Physical interaction and intimacy would likely be a big part of what keeps these people together, as well as the complementarity of the pair. You don't understand each other at all, and this is intriguing at first, but it can gradually become frustrating for both of you since your perspectives are so different. For both of you, it bothers you that the other person doesn't do things your way and you don't get why. It's difficult to resist the magnetic pull of attraction and so breaking up for good can be very difficult since you're so drawn to each other.

Similarities relate. Relating to someone—experiencing the world similarly and getting where the person is coming from because it's where you're coming from—is determined by how similar you are to each other. One main measure of this is on how many of the Myers-Briggs personality dimensions you are the same as each other. So if you are INTJ, for example, then you will relate most to someone who is also INTJ. However, you wouldn't be all that attracted to the person. You would feel comfortable with the person, conversations would flow and a phone relationship would work fantastically, but the relationship would lack a certain magnetic pull when you are in person with each other. You understand each other quite well, but you often find that the very things that you don't like about yourself really bother you about the other person. When such a relationship ends, it's easier to drift away since there was a lack of magnetic pull between you in the first place. It's just that you really enjoyed each other's understanding company when it was there.

Another major part of similarities relating is having the same primary inclination. So if your primary inclination is the connecting inclination, you would relate most to someone who also has this primary inclination and so also prioritizes close friends, significant others, and intense conversations and connections. If your primary inclination is the belonging inclination, you would relate most to someone who also has this primary inclination and so also prioritizes being part of a group or community, being around groups of people, and generally belonging somewhere. If your primary inclination is the preserving inclination, you would relate most to someone who also prioritizes family, career, environment, sleep, work, health, etc.

The synthesis of the two: Finding attraction and relating in the same person can come about in a nice balance when you have the same primary inclination and are both conceptual (intuitive) or both actual (sensing), with every other Myers-Briggs personality dimension being different, most importantly the inward (introverted) - outward (extroverted) dimension and the structured (judging) - flexible (perceiving) dimension. The rational (thinking) - empathetic (feeling) dimension's being different will simply make for more attraction, while its being the same will make for more relating.

Fulfillment with the person leads to chemistry. When you feel fulfilled with the person—primarily in your primary and secondary Enneagram type motivations and desires—you feel chemistry with the person.

The goal is to find all of these—attraction, relating, and chemistry—in the same person. If you set this as your destination, and you say no to every person presented to you who isn't this and respond by specifying to yourself what you like about this person and would also like in the next person, and what you didn't like about this person and what you would like instead of these things in the next person, then you will find this.

Keep in mind, though, that more important than seeking out all the details of personality elements in another person is the place from which you ask for a person with whom to be in a relationship. When you really connect with yourself, you will bring into your life someone with whom you feel really connected. Everything falls into place and you get what is truly important in your relationship match once you become the kind of person you could, and do, love.

Getting Everything You Want In A Relationship

Ultimately, in order to find everything you want in a person, you need to specify it and ask for it. Be clear about what you want. The process of growing up with different examples around you and then meeting other people with different situations, different relationships, different personality qualities, and different dynamics with themselves and you yields you innumerable opportunities to discover what you like and what you don't like, what makes you feel good and what makes you feel bad. As you go through the process of making friends and dating, you can discover through each experience more of what you want, more of what you don't want, and then more of what you actually want instead of what you didn't like there. Life experience and the process of meeting people and dating is a continual refining process, whereby we increasingly specify exactly what we really want and get it, in order to discover if we've specified enough that we can work with what we've got and refine from here or whether we want to ask for someone else entirely.

So experience, process, refine your understanding of what you really want in a relationship based on the comparison and contrast of what you've experienced before in other relationships of your own and in other people's relationships around you, as well as simply in the different people around you. Specify everything you know you want—in regard to actual qualities, but even more importantly in regard to how you want to feel in the relationship.

For example, perhaps you want to feel useful, important, special, and appreciated when you're with the person. Perhaps you want to be able to have deep conversations with the person and feel intensely connected with him or her. Perhaps you want to be with someone whom you love immensely and who loves you as much as you love him or her. Perhaps you want to be with someone to whom you're physically, emotionally, intellectually and spiritually attracted, and who is attracted to you in all these ways as well. Perhaps you want to be with someone who is faithful and devoted to you, and to whom you are glad to be faithful and devoted. Perhaps you want to be with someone who has certain beliefs or values in common with you. Perhaps you want to feel like you have a partner in life—someone with whom you can share your life experiences—when you're with the person.

Specify everything you want with belief that you can get it, get yourself internally aligned with it in terms of your relationship dynamics with yourself—so that you are loving yourself, listening to yourself, and generally treating yourself as you truly want to be treated by another person—and you'll get everything you ask for. Become someone you would want to be in a relationship with. When you are headed this direction, you will meet the right person somewhere along the way, traveling the same direction as you are. This is the key to bringing your ideal partner into your life.

Having A Relationship Is Having Someone With You Traveling A Parallel Path

When you are in a relationship, you are not supposed to give up being yourself, taking care of yourself, and living your own life. Your own life and your own hopes and dreams don't stop when you enter a relationship (or anything else for that matter). You still have to follow your own path. You are not suddenly saved from all of your own struggles when you meet the right person for you (or enter the right job, etc.). You still have to do everything you would have to do on your own. It's just that you now have a partner (or children or a boss or coworkers or clients, etc.) reflecting back where you are on your own journey—for good or for bad, but ultimately for good because of the growth it can foster in you if you apply the lessons of the experiences. In the ideal, you get on the main highway of your own life, with direction, fulfillment, and a sense of completion on your own, at least to some degree, and then you find someone else traveling a path that is parallel to yours—on the same highway—and you choose to face the journey of life together. Then, for both of you, it is just that you have someone else along for the ride that you are already on.

We don't only ideally have similar interests to the person we choose to be in a relationship with. We also tend to have similar obstacles, as we are learning similar lessons. Our significant other becomes a mirror of ourselves in many ways, reflecting back at us our own obstacles and the way we're dealing with them, but in a different context with some different motivations behind them. So, we ought to listen to the advice we are inclined to give to our significant other. When we find ourselves being critical of him or her, we ought to ask ourselves how this criticism applies to ourselves. When we feel neglected or treated badly by our significant other, we ought to ask ourselves how we are neglecting ourselves or treating ourselves badly. When we are in a good place, our relationship will most likely thrive. When we are stressed, our relationship will likely reflect back this stress.

But notice that this is not unique to romantic relationships; all of this applies to all of our relationships with everyone and everything. It's just that our significant other is likely to be an ever-present mirror for us, where we are inclined to let ourselves have our negative internal dynamics reflected back at us because we know that we're much more likely to try to figure out how to work on them here rather than run away from them here.

Our negative internal dynamics follow us everywhere we go, being reflected back at us by the people and the world around us.

But we are often willing to allow ourselves to run away from family or friends or work situations that reflect back things we don't like in ourselves. On the other hand, a relationship with a significant other is often different in the sense that we really want to make it work if we've come to love and care for a person and are attracted to this person. (This is especially true for people who have connecting as their primary inclination, for whom finding connection with another person is the highest priority in life and therefore to whom it's worth facing the obstacles in themselves to get this. For people with belonging as their primary inclination, issues are most likely to be finally addressed when sufficiently reflected in the context of community and belonging. For people with preserving as their primary inclination, issues are most likely to be finally addressed when sufficiently reflected in the context of family, career, and health.) We recognize a choice here: We can run away from the struggles, which we might even actually do several times—from one relationship to another, or simply within one relationship—or we can face and transform the negative themes of our lives so that our relationship with this person we care about will be improved.

When we address our own obstacles, our relationship will reflect this back at us. And we will actually be helping our significant other along his or her path as well, because we will be modeling the overcoming of the very obstacles that he or she is likely to be facing, too, in some form.

We are drawn to people who treat us similarly to the way we treat ourselves. Since everyone treats others the way he or she treats himself or herself, this means that we are drawn to people who treat themselves similarly to the way we treat ourselves. Therefore, as we improve the way we treat ourselves, we improve the way we treat our significant other, and so we demonstrate to our significant other, by the way we treat ourselves and him or her, how he or she ought to treat himself or herself. As our significant other improves the way he or she treats himself or herself, he or she shows us, by example, how to treat ourselves as well.

For this is why you are in each other's lives in the first place—to be partners in growth in this world, to help each other along each other's paths by simply being your best possible selves. As you improve your relationship with yourself, your relationship with your significant other will improve as well, and your partner's relationship with himself or herself will improve, too.

The Power Of Emotion

Everyone who and everything that comes into our lives supports what we are already feeling. In other words, we actually attract people and circumstances into our lives based on the feelings to which we are giving our energy, the feelings with which we are identifying at any point in time. If you were to think about the people who come into your life, be it for an instant or for years, you would notice that they all fit the theme of the emotions that exist in you. We draw people into our lives who are in the same emotional place as we are and who are therefore reflective and supportive of our being in that emotional place. So then we feel that emotion, they feel that emotion, and we feel that emotion together. If they are only in that particular feeling for a while, and we stay in it for years, we will likely part ways, only to encounter those people again if and when we cross emotional paths again.

It is as though we are all tuning forks with frequencies determined by the emotions that we are feeding with our attention, even if this attention is in the form of an attempt at pushing the emotion away or tuning it out or running away from it. We go out into the world with our specific frequencies, and we resonate with other tuning forks with the same frequencies, leading to large vibrations of these frequencies—reaffirmed and strengthened emotions. We group together based on our relating on the emotions we are experiencing and supporting for each other. If we do not hold very much of any feeling in common, we do not relate, and we do not feel drawn together. If we do hold a lot of feelings in common, we relate and resonate, and we feel drawn together, to support each other in the feeling.

If that feeling is negative, such as hopelessness, frustration, loneliness, anger, fear, shame, hatred, etc., then we are supported in our negative feelings, drawn to other people with the exact same negative feelings in their experience of the world at that time. If that feeling is positive, such as hopefulness, joy, contentment, awe, gratitude, appreciation, love, etc., then we are supported in our positive feelings, drawn to other people with the exact same positive feelings in their experience of the world at that time.

This makes it impossible for us to look outside of our own emotional box by looking outward. We will just keep getting the same results if we just keep going outward with our energy in an effort to get different results. We have to shift our emotional state from within, on our own, first in order to encounter different people who and circumstances that would support a different emotional state than the one we are currently experiencing.

Remember, it is what you focus your attention on in your thoughts that determines what feeling you experience. So take a moment once in a while to step down off of the hamster wheel and out of your emotional state. Change your physical, emotional, and mental position. Take a few deep breaths. Maybe step outside and experience the world around you. Put your arms up in the air and look upward. Shift your internal focus to different thoughts that you associate with more positive feelings, and then act in the world from these new feelings. The people and circumstances you encounter after this will support your shifted emotional state. The result is that you will find yourself making progress with far less effort than you were exerting on the hamster wheel where you were getting nowhere regardless of the amount of effort you put in.

It is actually of benefit to us that everyone and everything around us reflects our own thoughts and feelings back at us. This allows us to learn what we are making ourselves feel, and even the specific dynamics that exist within ourselves, by listening and paying attention to what everyone says and does around us, and by listening to our own words and reactions to these things. If we find ourselves bothered by something in someone else's words or behavior, we are bothered by that in ourselves. If we are critical of something about someone else, we are already critical of that within ourselves. If we give someone advice, that advice applies to us as well, and we should listen to our own advice. The world is a mirror for us, showing us our own thoughts and feelings. We should pay attention, because the awareness the reflection can bring us is the prerequisite to our changing what we are experiencing.

A rising tide lifts all boats. When we lift up, we are like a rising tide, and all the people around us benefit from our breakthroughs. We pave the way for their breakthroughs with our own. We are in similar emotional places as everyone we encounter due to our treating ourselves similarly to the way they treat themselves, for we bring into our lives people who treat us as we are treating ourselves. As we change the way we treat ourselves, we change the way we treat the other people in our lives, and we set this improved example for how they ought to be treating themselves, which they can then learn from and follow. We do not even need to say anything to the people in our lives to be helpful; all we need to do is represent the lessons we are learning in the choices we make for ourselves about what we focus our attention on with our thoughts, feelings, instincts, and actions.

The Power Of Setting Goals

If we were really to delve into the idea that we group together based on the emotions that we experience, we would realize that the actual attractive force that binds us and other people together is our goals, the destinations we are setting for ourselves in our internal GPS systems. When we have goals in common with other people, we are drawn to those people. The emotions come in when we are traveling the path toward our goals, and we are most likely to resonate with other people who are in a similar place on their journey toward the same goals, or destinations, as we are.

So if we are caught in our struggles on the path toward the goal of identifying and building a career that is in line with our passion, then we will meet other people who are in the same plight. More specifically, if we are feeling hopelessness and lack of motivation in building such a career, we will gravitate to others who are feeling the same on the same journey. If we are feeling triumphant in building our dream careers, we will gravitate to others who are feeling the same. If we are in a relationship and feeling like marriage would interfere with building our careers, we will meet other people who believe this as well as people who not only believe this but also demonstrate this. If we are in a relationship with someone who is supportive of our callings and we are actively working on building this relationship, we will meet other people who are in similar relationships.

As we travel the roads of life, we meet others who are in similar circumstances as we are. If we are stuck in traffic and not moving very fast, we will likely be surrounded by others who are also stuck in traffic and not moving very fast. If we are moving rapidly, we will likely be surrounded by others who are also moving rapidly. If we are driving through a storm, we will likely be surrounded by others who are also driving through the same storm.

The goals we set for ourselves, and by which we define ourselves, unite us with others working toward the same goals. Our emotions demonstrate where we are in the process toward actualizing these goals and unite us with others who are in the same part of the process. This is true on a moment-to-moment basis, so as our emotions about our situation shift, we encounter different people who resonate with and support our emotions at that time.

When we set goals and focus on achieving them, everyone and everything comes to support us in achieving these goals. When we are in our lulls, feeling stagnant, doubtful, directionless, unsure, or dissatisfied with our pace, everyone and everything comes to resonate with and support us in our feeling this way. When we are in our triumphs, feeling like we have clear purpose and direction, everyone and everything comes to resonate with and support us in our feeling this way.

The key is to set clear goals and notice whenever our emotional state shifts toward the negative along the way toward the achievement of these goals. At these times, we ought to take a moment to listen to and shift our emotions before we take any external actions. This way, we can be more consistently supported in heading the direction we truly want to go, encountering people who resonate with us on positive emotions, or who mirror negative emotions for us in ways that allow us to learn from the advice we give to them as we keep moving forward on our path.

Thoughts, And Connections With Other Individuals

While we group together based on common goals and the emotions we share in striving toward those goals, we connect with other individuals we encounter based on different, but complementary, ways of thinking. It is these connections that allow us to grow, develop, and evolve. Were it not for our connections with other people, who inevitably have different but related experiences of the world as compared to ours, we would be trapped in our own ways of thinking. Through the contrast of other people's experiences of life with our own, we gain more objective perspectives on our own experiences.

If we were to live entirely on our own, never to connect with anyone else in any deep way, we would be caught in our own subjective perspectives without any way of stepping outside of ourselves and looking at ourselves and our situations from new vantage points. The gift of connection with another person in any kind of intense conversation or interaction or shared experience allows us to see that our experiences of the world are not the only ones possible. Our relationships with our parents, our upbringing, our nationality, our religious views, our household income status, our lens of thought, feeling, instinct, and belief, and more, all seem to be the way things simply are until we encounter other individuals with different experiences.

Other people can be windows into our past, our future, our present, or alternative versions of any or all of these. We can look at others and see ourselves, but we see ourselves in different forms, and so it is easier for us to comment, critique, and give advice even if we cannot otherwise gain insight into our own situations to figure out what to do, what decisions to make. In other people, everything seems much clearer, boiled down to the facts of the situation, without as much of the emotion of being in the situation ourselves. We can see what needs to get done, and if we learn to recognize other people as reflections of ourselves, we can apply this to ourselves and make use of the mirroring. We can also evolve in our belief systems. We can change because we are faced with alternatives to our own ways of thinking, feeling, wanting, acting, believing, etc., and we have the option of choosing for ourselves something resembling almost anything we see in others. The intense connection of two people always produces a third viewpoint on the world that didn't exist before the interaction.

Every person in your life plays an important role in your life journey. There might be the person who got you interested in a certain career path, the person who made you decide to alter your career path, the person who made you want to stop dating, the person who made you want to date again, the person who helped you to realize that money isn't everything, the person who helped you build your career, the person who made you feel like life is worth living, the person who helped you through certain life struggles, the person who made you feel like you aren't alone in this world, the person who transformed your fundamental perspective on life over and over again, etc.

Even seemingly random strangers and events can play pivotal roles for you in shifting your perspective on your day, your week, your year, your job situation, your relationship situation, your life. It is the intense encounters we have in life with other individual people and aspects of the world with relatable but differing perspectives that enable us to grow and evolve in various ways, becoming who we are and who we want to be.

As we travel the roads of life, there will be differences in the attitudes we and the drivers around us have to the circumstances we are facing, even though the circumstances will be very similar. For example, we could be stuck in traffic but be beginning to feel like this is okay and that we'll get out of it soon and somehow end up where we want to be going right on time, while another person we encounter could be stuck in traffic but still feeling stagnant and like he'll never get anywhere. In this case, we will likely be less attached to the particular route and more open to finding other ways to get to our destination, and so we will much more likely get where we're going right on time somehow, even if this means that the person we're meeting is also late, and this makes us right on time. In this situation, we can learn from the other driver by listening to and acting on the advice that we'd be inclined to give him about how to approach the situation we and he are both facing. Meanwhile, the other driver can also learn from us, because while we are facing a similar situation, our attitude toward it allows us to be much more fulfilled and to get our desired results. In this scenario, the other driver is still very much caught up in the obstacle in this situation, while we are on our way out of the obstacle—in the process of actively overcoming it—and ready to be an example for the people around us in regard to how to move forward.

We cross paths with people in life when we have common goals and common emotions in the journey toward those goals. But we will always have at least slightly different approaches toward achieving those goals. Through our connections with other people on the roads of life, we gain other perspectives on the path toward our own aims. These invaluable meetings grant us the opportunity to step outside of the box of our own subjective situations and view our own situations from another vantage point, allowing us an alternative to facing our own obstacles over and over again with no way out that is obvious to us while we are trapped in them. Our connections with other individuals allow us to transcend and address the perspective of being caught in our own obstacles in a way that we can actually glimpse the way out and into where we truly want to be.

Connection And Love

When you feel connected to someone, in reality it is that you are more connected to yourself when you are with that person. Imagine the best date or conversation or encounter with another person you have ever had or would like to have. You are fulfilled where you are, so you do not wander as much in your thoughts, feelings, and instincts from the present moment as you might usually. You are present to the other person in the moment. You feel like the greatest person ever, like you say and do all the right things and you're amazingly witty or clever or intelligent. You feel like the best version of yourself.

When you're with someone with whom you feel connected, you are more connected with yourself. When you feel like you are overflowing with love for someone, it is because you love who you are when you're with that person. When you're with someone with whom you have a positive, desirable dynamic, you are drawn to have a more positive dynamic with yourself.

Since the feelings of connection, love, and so forth actually come from being present to the moment and to yourself, from connecting to yourself and loving yourself, etc.—and not from the other person with whom you feel these things—you are actually capable of experiencing these desirable feelings all the time, whether you're with someone else or not. The goal is to be present to yourself, listen to yourself, connect with yourself, and act on the true intentions of your own thoughts, feelings, and instincts. Then you will feel complete in yourself, fulfilled in your basic desires, and like the best version of yourself you can possibly be.

The result is that other people will come to support you in feeling so connected to yourself. Rather than only gaining glimpses of connection in relationships that spark into existence with intensity and then spark out of existence just as quickly, you will be able to build a sustainable relationship and long-lasting friendships and so forth that are filled with a sense of connection and completion. It all begins with the thoughts and feelings you create within yourself. For whatever they are, they will be supported by other people and the world outside you.

So create sustainable connection with yourself, remind yourself to be present to yourself and really listen to yourself, and this is what you will experience in your relationships with others. Become someone you love and with whom you feel connected, and you will bring people into your life whom you love and with whom you feel connected and who love and feel connected with you.

Become Someone You Love

Fast-forward to the end of your life. You are lying on your deathbed, perhaps surrounded by people whom you love and who love you, and you are reflecting on the life you've lived. You feel good about it, like you lived exactly as you would choose to live even if you had it to do all over again. You're happy about the choices you made regarding where you spent your time and where you focused your attention and energy. You accomplished what you wanted to here, and you're fulfilled and content and ready to go.

In this scenario, how would you have lived your life between now and then that would have led you to feel completely good about all of it? What did you focus your time, attention, and energy on now? What did you spend your life doing? With whom did you share your life? Did you focus mainly on your career? On your family? On your community? On your friends? On your significant other? Did you listen well to yourself and find a good balance of all of these?

Did you let the apparently negative experiences you had consume your attention and determine your next experiences, or did you learn from them and redirect your attention to what you would really like to experience instead and fill your thoughts, feelings, instincts, and external life with this?

Did you make yourself feel miserable, mediocre, or fantastic most of the time? Did you connect with yourself and what makes you feel good and allow this to guide you, or were you disconnected from yourself and life? Did you accept yourself and continually improve upon yourself solely through encouragement and appreciation, or were you more often critical of where you were, wanting things to be different somehow? Did you live in the present with presence, or were you largely absent and on autopilot most of the time?

Did you treat yourself well, taking care of yourself and allowing what makes you happy to guide you toward a life full of happiness that spread to others? Or did you spend more of your time ignoring, avoiding, escaping from, and tuning out yourself?

These are the choices you are making in every moment—the choices you will reflect on and experience either favorably or unfavorably later on. If you do what you find peace in, become someone you love, and choose to follow your happiness, then you will draw into your life people, things, and events that support you in experiencing all of this.

The best and only route to finding someone you would love to spend your life with is to become someone you would love to spend your life with. Live your life in every moment the way you would want to have lived it when you are about to leave it. Treat yourself as you would if you loved yourself—as you'd like others to treat you in the ideal—and you will grow to love yourself if you don't already. Listen to yourself, connect with yourself, and focus your attention on what you love and enjoy, and the world will support you in this and offer you further reasons to experience love, connection, and joy in your life.

Attraction

When you feel attracted to another person, this means either a) you like some quality or qualities in yourself that this person also has, b) you want some quality or qualities in yourself that this person has and that you don't recognize as being in yourself, or c) you see your past self in some way in this person—not-so-ideal qualities and experiences that you used to identify with but that you don't identify with anymore—and so the person reminds you of how much you have grown.

From this perspective, it would be pertinent for us always to ask ourselves which of these applies in any situation in which we are drawn in a positive way to another person. Why are you attracted to the person? Are you attracted to the person because he/she is or has something you like about or in yourself? Are you attracted to the person because he/she is or has something you want to be or have, yourself? Or are you attracted to the person because he/she is or has something that you used to be or have and so he/she highlights your progress and developed strengths?

We want to be with people and connect with people who have, or in some other way remind us of, qualities that we want to connect with in ourselves. Perhaps we have already connected with these qualities in ourselves, or perhaps we haven't yet. If we have already, then we would benefit from continuing to connect with these qualities in ourselves. If we haven't yet, then we would benefit from recognizing and connecting with these qualities in ourselves. For we cannot recognize and experience anything in anyone else that is not also within us. So if we are attracted to something in someone else, it is relevant for us to recognize that it must also, therefore, be within us in some form.

This explains why opposites often attract. We all have qualities in ourselves with which we don't as much identify as other qualities that are also within us. When we see positive qualities in another person that resemble those qualities with which we have not yet come to identify in ourselves, we are drawn to connect with that person because we are drawn to connect with those qualities. So, for example, if we are introspective and introverted, someone who is outgoing and extroverted can seem attractive to us, and vice versa, because we want, on some level, to connect with these qualities within ourselves and bring them out more in us. If we are structured and planned, someone who is open, flexible, and more fun-loving can seem attractive to us, and vice versa, because we want, on some level, to connect with these qualities within ourselves and bring them out more in our approach to life. If we are not confident in social settings, we will likely be drawn to someone who *is*, as we seek to connect with this confidence within ourselves. If we are not sure of our career path, we will likely be drawn to someone who *is*, as we seek to connect with this surety within ourselves.

So whenever you're attracted or drawn to someone or something in any way, ask yourself: "What am I attracted to here?" Then ask yourself, "Do I feel that I have this in myself and like it about myself, do I want this in myself but feel that I don't have it in myself, or did I used to have this much more in myself but I have largely transformed and overcome this way of operating and experiencing things?" If the first situation, say something like, "I love this about myself and I'd love to have more of this in my life." If the second situation, say something like, "I'd love to recognize and connect with this in myself." If the third situation, say something like, "I am so grateful for how far I've come and how much I've grown, and I would love to keep growing and for this person to grow from this and get to a better place, too."

Relationship Partner Vs. Friend

When we encounter people who are supposed to play a positive role for us in some way, it feels good to meet them. There is a positive energy about them and it feels like something is there, like this person is someone we're supposed to meet. We can often be confused about whether this is supposed to be a relationship partner if the person fits some or all of our criteria for this, or whether this is just supposed to be a close friend.

If there is intense magnetic attraction energy at first, it is probably a temporary relationship partner who will only be in our lives for a short period of time—a side-street relationship. There is an intense lesson there for us, but the relationship won't last. But if there is simply a sense of connection and rapport and there is some kind of distinct energy about the person, like the person is highlighted in our experience when we meet him or her and onward, then it is likely that this is going to be a more long-term presence in our lives—a main-highway relationship. So then the question becomes: Is this just a friend, or something more?

Interestingly, if the person is reflecting back how we're treating ourselves even in negative ways, there is a greater likelihood that this is a potential relationship partner. On the main highway, our friendships often help us work out the issues that are being reflected back at us elsewhere—often including in our relationship. Our close friends often provide comfort and a listening ear. They are there for us and we are there for them. Our long-term relationship partner, on the other hand, often reflects back everything we still need to address in ourselves.

If we stay with someone who clings to us and treats us well unconditionally, even when we are treating ourselves terribly, then we are likely stagnating in our careers and other areas of our lives as well. This person is then like a drug, a distraction, an escape. We are seeking comfort when what we really need is a shove.

Our ideal relationship partner—even if it doesn't always sound so ideal when we really just want the positive attention we're not giving ourselves—is someone who shows us how we're treating our own thoughts, feelings, and instincts by the way he or she treats us. If we're not listening to ourselves, neither does our partner. If we're ignoring ourselves, dismissing ourselves, tuning ourselves out, disregarding ourselves, neglecting ourselves, controlling ourselves, etc., so does our partner—as if to say, "This is how you are treating yourself. Do you really want to keep treating yourself, and consequently being treated, this way—not just by me, but by life in general?" In our partner, we have a companion who, by his or her example, and without necessarily actually saying anything about this, calls us out on our poor treatment of ourselves when our treatment of ourselves is poor, and who praises us with loving, positive treatment when our treatment of ourselves is loving and positive.

We usually don't realize how badly we are treating ourselves until we experience this treatment reflected back at us by someone else or by life circumstances. It is easier to be oblivious to how we are being when we're on the giving end and ignoring the experience of this on the receiving end. On the receiving end, it becomes much clearer, as we find ourselves blaming the other person and wondering how anyone could treat anyone this way. Yet we are treating ourselves this way in some form if anyone else is, because our experience of the world around us is just a reflection of our experience of ourselves in our own internal dynamic.

Our ideal partner is someone who pushes us to grow because we find ourselves looking in a mirror and if we don't like what we see, we realize that we care about this person enough that we are compelled to make changes to ourselves in order to find someone we like in the mirror since we can't get ourselves to get rid of this mirror. We want this mirror because we care about the person, and ultimately also because it makes us face ourselves and makes us a better version of ourselves, even if we are in a bad enough place, ourselves, that we don't like what we see at the moment.

As we travel the main highway of our lives, our friends and our relationship partner will be on the same highway, going through issues that are overlapping with our own. They will all be treating themselves similarly to the way we are treating ourselves in various ways, aiming to reach similar goals, and making themselves feel similarly to the way we are making ourselves feel on the path toward those goals. But our partner will often more likely reflect back how we're treating ourselves where we still need to give ourselves more positive attention, and our friends—the ones we keep around, anyway—will often more likely give us the positive attention we need to give ourselves more of. Our partners will push us to grow by showing us what needs work, and our friends will demonstrate to us by their example how we should be treating ourselves generally, and how we could be experiencing our relationships with ourselves and our partner if we were to treat ourselves this way more.

We get emotionally caught up in our partner and have trouble getting rid of this mirror even when it is showing us what we don't like about ourselves. Our friends, on the other hand, we are more likely to push away if we don't like what they're reflecting back at us. This is why our ideal partner is often someone who shows us where we need improvement, and how, in our relationship with ourselves, and our ideal friends are often people who show us where we're going right and what we need to do more of in our relationship with ourselves—all so that we can get what we want in every aspect of our lives.

However, when we are particularly in line with our own internal guidance, listening to ourselves on the main highway of our lives and determinedly going forward along it, we can shed the need for a relationship partner who reflects back anything that is bad in us. At this point, we don't need friends who do this, and we don't need a relationship partner who does this either. Why? Because once we shift from *discouraging* ourselves—by focusing on the negative in ourselves and in our lives and wanting it changed or trying to change it—to *encouraging* ourselves—by focusing on the positive in ourselves and in our lives and thereby asking for more of it—we experience this shift in all of our relationships with other people and the world around us as well.

When our own evolution progresses based on guidance and encouragement rather than control and discouragement within us, this is reflected outside of us as everyone around us begins only to guide, support, and encourage us forward toward destinations with which we are now clearly and entirely, or nearly entirely, aligned. At this point, we can commit ourselves to a relationship partner who is a good friend, as well as to other good friends, who reflect back and encourage the positive within us. In our relationships with others, as in our relationships with ourselves, the negative is gently and kindly addressed and redirected to something positive, and the positive is supported and built upon. If the people around us don't shift in their treatment of us at this point to reflect and support our changing treatment of ourselves, it is likely time to transform our relationship with them by changing the nature or label of the relationship, and this may mean it is time for the relationship to end.

The End Of A Relationship

When a relationship with another person ends, be it a romantic relationship or a friendship or whatever, this represents one of two things: It is either the end of a dynamic that you have with yourself that was supported by that other person, or it is your avoidance (or the result of your avoidance) of a dynamic that you have with yourself that was supported by that other person.

When we are actively growing and improving our relationship with ourselves, our relationships with the people around us come to reflect our changed internal dynamics. If a person in your life cannot change sufficiently to adapt to treating you the way you are now treating yourself, then you will see less of that person in your life. If this is a romantic relationship, this may lead to the end of it, where you simply don't feel resonant with being treated the way you are by the other person anymore. The relationship just doesn't feel right anymore or worth staying in when you aren't being treated as well as, or simply in the same way as, you are treating yourself.

When we are stagnating and maintaining undesirable relationships with ourselves, our relationships with the people around us keep reflecting back dynamics that we don't like in ourselves. Depending on the issue, you will either be inclined to stay in an unhealthy relationship because it feels familiar to you since you're being treated the way you are treating yourself, or you will be inclined to leave the unhealthy relationship in order to avoid the issue that is going to follow you into other relationships after this one until you address it in yourself. We cannot avoid ourselves, and everyone is just reflecting back our relationships with ourselves and the things that we like and don't like in ourselves. So if we leave a relationship because we can't stand being treated the way we are treating ourselves, and we do nothing to change our internal dynamic, then if we decide to try another relationship, we will face many of the same problems as we did in the previous one.

Simply blaming the other person will only keep you facing the same problem. Blaming yourself will do the same. Taking responsibility for your own experience and making changes to it is another thing altogether and is the only way to overcome and move beyond the problem and into the experience of its resolution.

Asking yourself how you might be treating yourself this way—and transforming yourself so that you treat yourself well and only see things that you like in yourself—will lead you into a transformed relationship, be it the one you're in or another one. Once you further yourself along the journey of cultivating the kind of relationship with yourself that you'd like to have with everyone and everything around you, you can discover whether each of your relationships comes to meet you where you are at each moment, or whether it feels like it's time to let it go.

It is always easier to be attracted to someone who is healthier than you are because he/she is in the direction that you need to be going to be more fulfilled in yourself, representing a dynamic with him/herself that is similar but healthier in comparison to the one you have with yourself. If the other person is the healthier one, you will be more attracted to him/her than he/she is to you. If you are the healthier one, the other person will be more attracted to you than you are to him/her. If you are close to the same place in health, with equally healthy internal dynamics, then you will be equally attracted to each other, with greater health yielding more mutual attraction. As you each face life obstacles and get bogged down in them or overcome them and grow, the attraction between you will shift on each end of the relationship accordingly.

When a relationship ends, it is almost certainly always due to one of four reasons: 1) You and the other person could both be stagnating in your own lives in a way that means not addressing obstacles that would allow for the relationship to last, 2) you could move on (and be healthier) while the other person is still stagnating and clinging to you, 3) the other person could move on (and be healthier) while you are still stagnating and clinging to him or her, or 4) you could both be moving forward and simply be going different directions from each other in life.

No matter what, for you everything will become clearer and clearer as you work toward cultivating the type of relationship with yourself that you ideally want to have with another person. Your ultimate goal is to become the kind of person you would want to be in a relationship with. If you do this, the right people will naturally gravitate into your life at the right times, the right people will leave at the right times, and the rest will fall into place.

The Lessons We Learn From Relationships

People and circumstances come into our lives to help us learn lessons by supporting us in how we are treating ourselves or by showing us how we ought to be treating ourselves (in response to our request for this).

Some people and situations come into our lives to help us learn a single lesson or a single series of lessons. In this case, they will remain in our lives only as long as it takes to provide us with an experience from which we can later learn, or in some cases as long as we have not yet fully learned and implemented the lesson or lessons (that they are here to teach us) by changing the way we treat ourselves. Some people and situations come into our lives to help us learn ongoing lessons over a long period of time and to support us in learning and applying these lessons along the way. In this case, they will remain in our lives indefinitely, perhaps evolving and changing in the nature of their relationship with us depending on what is most appropriate for us each to learn the lessons we're here to help each other learn—for as long as our growth is supported by them (and vice versa). Several of these people even remain in our lives for many, many lifetimes as we have very similar objectives overall, and therefore very similar lessons to learn on the way to our common destinations during all this time.

Just as other people are messengers for us, we are messengers for them also as we are brought together by our similar internal dynamics so that we can learn overlapping lessons together about how to shift these dynamics toward the positive. As we learn our lessons and apply them, they learn theirs from our example, and vice versa, as we support each other forward. This is true even where it might not be obvious, as when we simply seem to bring up obstacles for each other, reflecting back each other's similar negative internal dynamics.

Other people are here essentially to role-play with us. They show us how we are treating ourselves and what we are making ourselves think, feel, and want, and we show them this for them as well. For example, we might learn from the way other people treat us that we have been lying to ourselves, giving ourselves unwanted attention, ignoring ourselves altogether, disrespecting ourselves, dismissing ourselves, disregarding ourselves, tuning ourselves out, not listening to ourselves, attacking ourselves, controlling ourselves, forcing ourselves upon ourselves, yelling at ourselves, discouraging and demotivating ourselves, etc. On the other hand, as we learn from these reflections in our interactions with other people, we can recognize that we have become more honest and open with ourselves, giving ourselves exactly the kind of attention we want, paying attention to ourselves, respecting ourselves, considering ourselves, tuning into ourselves, listening to ourselves, showing compassion and kindness toward ourselves, loving ourselves, guiding ourselves, encouraging ourselves forward with support and appreciation, etc. By providing us a reflection of our own internal dynamics, and of what these could be when we request something more positive, other people, in the ideal, help us to become more compassionate, loving, and understanding toward ourselves, so that we can learn to treat ourselves the way we truly want to be treated and create a life experience that we truly want to have.

Life, and ultimately existence, is meant to be a series of experiences with the aim of our growth and that of everyone and everything around us. This is why we are here. Everyone who and everything that comes into our lives is on our team, here to support us forward toward our common goals. And every individual with whom we connect is our partner in growth and life creation.

The Place Of Asking Determines The Experience Of What Is Asked For When It Is Received

The place from which we ask for something determines the experience we will have of it. Our thoughts provide the content of the experience, and our feelings provide the quality of the experience. This is true for everything—from relationships to jobs to daily experiences.

For example: If you say you would like a relationship but you are saying this from a place of feeling unloved, then you will get a relationship at a time when you are feeling unloved that supports you in feeling unloved either during it or in its ending. If you say you would like a relationship from a place of feeling regretful about a previous relationship or job or whatever, then you will get a relationship at a time when you are feeling regretful that supports you in feeling regretful either during it or in its ending. If you say you would like a relationship and you imagine how wonderful this could be, feeling complete and fulfilled within yourself and connected with yourself and having these feelings of completion, fulfillment, and connection supported by another person, then you will get a relationship at a time when you are feeling complete and fulfilled in, and connected with, yourself that supports you in feeling complete and fulfilled in, and connected with, yourself.

Where the seed of a relationship (or a particular stage or form of a relationship) or anything else is sown determines where its roots will be. We can grow in a relationship or a job or whatever substantially, but like a tree reaching up toward the sky, the roots of our relationship, job, etc. will always be in the place where we planted the seed for it. The roots will always be in the feeling from which we requested it or that accompanied our request for it.

So, for example: A relationship (or job, or whatever) that you requested from a place of disconnection from and avoidance of yourself, where you were not listening to yourself about where your focus of attention should be, will yield a relationship where you feel disconnected, continue to avoid yourself (now with the relationship to help you distract yourself from yourself), and don't feel listened to by the other person or have the other person feel listened to by you. In the context of this relationship, you might eventually be driven inward to find connection with yourself since you don't feel the connection you seek with the other person. This would lead you back on the path from which you had strayed in the first place, where this straying had led you to a place from where you had sought connection outside yourself. However, in this situation, as you get more connected with yourself and other aspects of your life consequently improve, you will notice a growing disconnect between the improvements in your life (and perhaps also in the other person's life) outside of the relationship and the dynamics of the relationship, itself, where you still feel disconnected and not listened to, and which still seems to be distracting you from where your attention should be (on yourself). At some point in your growth in this situation, you'll realize that a relationship that you asked for from a place of disconnection is here to help you connect with yourself sufficiently to recognize that it's time to leave the relationship that has its roots in disconnection from yourself.

We cannot later change where we planted the seed of something in our life in the first place, and where we planted the seed will determine the nature of the entire experience of it. Considering this, it would be to our benefit to imagine what we would ideally like to be feeling when we have what we are requesting, and not simply to request it. This way, the feeling that accompanies the thought of what we want is an experience that we would actually like to have supported rather than an experience that we have had or have but don't want supported. In other words, don't ask for things *in reaction* to other things, where either your thoughts or your feelings or both are focused on what you don't want; ask *in response* to things, where both your thoughts and your feelings accompanying those thoughts are willful, proactive, and ultimately creative, focused on what you actually want.

The emotional place from which you ask for things determines the experience of those things, but you also need to create the internal dynamics and experience that is resonant with the place from which you asked in order to receive what you requested. In other words: If you ask for something from a negative place, and you are in a negative place, then you can receive what you requested with the focus of your attention quickly to support you in being in this negative place. If you ask for something from a positive place that you imagined, and you are in a negative place, then you must get to a positive place in order to receive what you requested with the focus of your attention to support you in being in a positive place. If you ask for something from a positive place, and you are in a positive place, then you can receive what you requested with the focus of your attention quickly to support you in being in this positive place.

Therefore, as you get to a more positive place overall, it becomes easier to bring whatever you would likely ask for—things that support you in being in a good internal place—into your life quickly. This is because you are, internally, already where you want to be supported in being, and anything that you ask for to come support you in being here can simply come into your life as a reflection of where you already are.

Sometimes You Just Need To Stop And Restart, And Sometimes You Need Something New Altogether In Order To Have What You Want

When things are going wrong with a computer, sometimes you just need to turn off, restart, and reboot the computer, and sometimes you actually need to get a new computer. The same is true of a relationship, job, etc.

If you requested a relationship, job, etc. from a negative emotional place and therefore are having this negative emotional place supported by this relationship or job or whatever, then the only way out of this reinforcement of negative emotions is to shift internally and let go of the relationship, job, etc. In other words, if you sowed the seed of something in your life in a negative emotional place, and this is where its roots are, then its roots will always be here. So stop growing this tree and plant a different one. Let go of the relationship or job or whatever being the right one, stop telling yourself that you have to stay here and make things work, and step out of it. This doesn't necessarily mean you will never be in a relationship with this person again or never be in this job again, but if you keep growing the same tree you already planted in a negative emotional place, you are guaranteeing that you'll keep facing the same problems.

So stop growing the tree. End what you started. Plant a seed somewhere else with a different request from a more positive emotional place. Be clear about what you want, and imagine what having that would feel like in the ideal. From this new seed you can grow a different tree that has its roots in the positive emotional place where you want them.

This new request could eventually lead you back to the same person or the same job. Perhaps you went in before feeling like you *had* to be with that person or in that job, and now you are going in feeling like you actually *want* to be there. This happens. But it is important that you stop feeding and growing any trees that have their roots in a negative emotional place, and that keep bringing you back there, once you learn and grow from them and are out of that negative place in other areas of your life.

Request something from a positive place and see where your GPS leads you. It will tell you to leave anything that is rooted in the negative. And then it will guide you toward what you asked for. This may simply be a restart, later on, of a relationship with the same person when you are both asking for a relationship from more positive emotional places than those from which you both asked for the relationship you had originally. Or it may be the start of a new relationship with someone else who is an even better match for what you are actually asking for now. It may be a return to the same job, or it may be the start of a new job that is a much better match for what you are now asking for.

This is all only regarding situations where the seed for something was actually planted in a negative emotional place—where you asked for something in reaction to something else, in order to escape or avoid something, in order to regain control you felt you didn't have, etc. In these cases, facing your obstacles likely means letting go of where you are and moving on. However, relationships, jobs, and so forth can still entail obstacles even if they were sown in a positive request. In these situations, refocusing on your ideal destination will result in your GPS directing you to work on things because you are actually facing your obstacles here and not avoiding them by staying.

Either way, once you sow another seed with another request from a different place in your life, where you are asking for something different from what you have asked for previously, you will be directed in regard to what to do now. It will either feel right to leave or to stay, to enter something else or to come back. Ask, and you will be guided. Just be sure to listen to your thoughts, feelings, and instincts as they direct you toward the response to your new request.

People's Challenges Are Challenging For Them

At times, you may be inclined to look at other people and think that they somehow have it easier than you. In reality, this is just because you are looking at your challenges and comparing these to the other people's strengths, rather than to the other person's challenges. Or you are comparing your challenges to the other people's challenges, but something that is challenging for them is not challenging for you, and so their challenges just seem less challenging to you than yours do.

We are all working through our own issues in this world. And your issues are not exactly the same as any other person's issues. Your issues only seem greater to you than other people's issues because you are emotionally entrenched in them.

Imagine that you see two airplanes of the same size flying in the sky before you. One is far away and appears very small. The other is much closer and appears much larger. Your own issues only seem so much greater to you than other people's issues because they are so much closer to you than theirs are. In reality, your issues and other people's issues are all challenging. It is just that theirs are closer to them, and yours are closer to you. It is easier to have compassion for other people's struggles and for your own if you remind yourself of this.

In Any Conflict, No One Is Completely Right And No One Is Completely Wrong

We cocreate our experiences with the people with whom we have them. If you can only see your side of the story and can't yet understand the other person's behavior then a) you don't yet really understand the other person's experience that is fueling the behavior and, more importantly, b) you haven't yet identified what the experience is reflecting back at you about your relationship with yourself. Anything that affects you, stands out at you, and sticks with you in any way—negative or positive—has a lesson in it for you about what you want to shift or ask for and create within yourself. If it is still standing out in your mind, there is still a lesson for you to learn that you haven't yet learned about how it is not about anything outside you; it is about you.

We cannot rightfully blame anyone or anything else for our experiences, and we shouldn't even be blaming ourselves, for it is simply that we are responsible for our own experiences and we can learn from them and create different experiences for ourselves in the future than we've created for ourselves in the past if we acknowledge this. If you are still replaying an experience or feeling that someone else is wrong and bothered you or hurt you and is to blame, or if you are still upset with yourself in some way, then you still haven't fully learned and implemented the lesson in that experience. Everything outside you in your experience, without exception, is a reflection of how you are treating yourself. So ask yourself how this is so, and once you've identified how you are treating yourself in a way you don't like, change this.

It will always be the case—when there is any conflict or issue that stays with you and bothers you—that both sides of the dynamic are represented within yourself in the way you are treating yourself. So if you are upset with someone for treating an animal or a child or a person a certain way, you are upset with yourself for treating yourself that way, and you therefore actually relate to both the animal (or child or person) and the person mistreating it. If you are upset with someone—be it a significant other, friend, family member, boss, client, stranger, etc.—for saying or doing something to you, you are actually upset with yourself for saying or doing that same thing or something similar to yourself, making yourself feel the same way as this person made you feel. This is why you are sensitive to the comment or treatment in the first place—because the person is (often unknowingly and unintentionally) simply throwing salt on an open wound, which you, yourself, are creating and keeping open. You therefore actually relate to both the other person and yourself in this situation, and there are other situations where you are actually (often unknowingly and unintentionally) treating others in some way like this person treated you.

Every one of these situations is here to show you that you are playing out both ends of the dynamic within yourself (and are simply relating more to one end of it at this moment, in this situation), and that you obviously feel about having this dynamic in yourself the way the situation is making you feel. So if the feeling is negative, you probably want to change the dynamic within yourself that is producing a) the feeling and b) the resulting reflections of the dynamic outside yourself that are supporting this feeling.

Interestingly, even the positive things that we experience in others are a reflection of what we see or want in ourselves. So keep all this in mind, ask why something is standing out to you and sticking in your mind, and discover what you can learn from this about how better to sculpt your own life experience.

Once you learn and implement the lesson, there is no reason for you to experience the obstacle anymore. You will change the way you treat yourself, which will change the way you treat others, which will change the way others treat you. As a result, different experiences will come to you, and the conflicts in your life will be resolved.

Tuning Out And Tuning In

Throughout our lives, we experience being tuned into and tuned out, being listened to and not being listened to, being paid attention to and not being paid attention to, and without realizing it, we shape our relationship with ourselves in reaction to what we have created in our interactions with others. The issues we face in our relationships with significant others, friends, coworkers, bosses, etc., which are traceable back to our relationship with our parents and in the example set by our parents, actually ultimately begin far before this as we carry over choices we made before this lifetime and in previous lifetimes.

We chose our parents based on our overlapping obstacles with them, just like we bring everyone else into our lives based on the roads we choose to travel, the goals we have, the way we treat ourselves. We choose parents who treat themselves similarly to some key aspect of the way we have treated ourselves, and who will therefore treat us as we have treated ourselves, so that we can re-establish this dynamic with ourselves from the previous life in this new life. This way we can continue our growth process where we left off, learn how to overcome our struggles from before, and create a new, better dynamic with ourselves that gets us the results we actually want in its reflection in the world around us.

Throughout this whole growth process, we are moving from tuning ourselves out, dismissing ourselves, and ignoring ourselves, to tuning into ourselves, listening to ourselves with acceptance, and sharing our own positive attention with ourselves. We move from controlling ourselves, which leads to our rebelling against ourselves, which leads to our tuning ourselves out in an effort to maintain harmony within us, to attending to ourselves and guiding ourselves based on actually having listened to ourselves, which leads to our following our own guidance, which leads to our tuning into ourselves because there is already harmony within us.

Therefore, along this journey of life, we experience the results of our not always fully listening to ourselves. We end up feeling tuned out by others, not listened to by others, ignored by others, dismissed by others, wronged, betrayed, abused, hurt, controlled, etc. by others. We can create a whole lot of physically, emotionally, mentally, and spiritually scarring experiences for ourselves when we don't fully tune into ourselves, listen to ourselves, and act on our own guidance. It can be really difficult to heal from the scars, mainly because our inclination is actually to treat ourselves increasingly as we were treating ourselves when we were led to the reflection of this in our scarring experiences in the first place.

If we were tuning ourselves out, our resulting experiences make us inclined to react by tuning ourselves out more. If we were dismissing our own importance and value and making ourselves feel insignificant, our resulting experiences make us inclined to react by dismissing our own importance and value more, thereby making ourselves feel even more insignificant. If we were making ourselves feel bad about opening up and expressing ourselves, our resulting experiences make us feel worse about opening up and expressing ourselves.

The result is that we become decreasingly connected with ourselves, and therefore decreasingly able to connect with other people. We end up afraid to open ourselves up and make ourselves vulnerable even to ourselves, let alone to another person.

Again, this whole series of reinforcing events can be traced back to the way we felt treated by our parents and beyond this to before this life and previous lives. But regardless of where it all started outside of us, it was once just a seed sown in ourselves by the way we treated ourselves, when we didn't listen to ourselves at some point—when we didn't use our own internal GPS entirely effectively, and we ended up seemingly off-course. This was reflected back at us by people and circumstances around us, however slightly, and we reacted and began the magnification and escalation of issues.

The key is to respond more positively than we are inclined to react—to go a different direction in response to our experiences than we are inclined to. If we use our experiences as reminders to tune in and listen to ourselves and follow our own guidance, rather than reacting to them by further tuning out, then we can turn things around for ourselves. Rather than growing our issues seemingly without end, we can shrink them down to non-existence. When we respond by listening to ourselves and refocusing our attention on what we'd prefer to experience instead, we apply the ultimate lesson and, as a result, we get the ultimate reward.

Learning To Love And To Experience Being Loved

When we're growing up, we learn from our parents' reactions to us, from what they give positive attention to and what they give negative attention to, and from what they seem to ignore, what we should and shouldn't be doing. We learn from the examples they set in their relationships with each other. We experience what a relationship is like. We learn what love means.

We may learn that love is smothering or overbearing, that it only comes when we do everything we're supposed to do, that it never comes no matter what we do. We may learn that whenever we open up about anything that means anything to us, we are scolded, criticized, judged, disappointed and disappointing, etc. We may learn that when something is important to us, we aren't listened to because there is too much to be done. We may learn many things, and we carry these "lessons" with us into our friendships and relationships, where we bring about and discover reinforcement of these lessons.

Without fully consciously realizing it, we spend our lives building up and reinforcing beliefs—often limiting and unhealthy ones—about everything, including about love, intimacy, our self-worth, self-value, and so forth. If every time we open up to ourselves, we shut ourselves down, tune ourselves out, dismiss ourselves, abandon ourselves, deceive ourselves into believing we'll still be there for ourselves and then stop listening and leave, neglect ourselves, tell ourselves we're not important or that we should be paying attention to someone else, then other people will treat us these ways, too. When we open up intellectually, emotionally, and/or physically to another person, we will be treated the way we treat ourselves. There is no way around this. The only way to escape being shut down, yelled at, dismissed, tuned out, or otherwise abused is to treat ourselves differently so that we set a different paradigm for others.

If we are harsh toward ourselves and make ourselves afraid to open up, fearing becoming overly needy, dependent, or clingy, we will become clingy as we fear, then scold ourselves for it, become overly distant and detached, have our needs not met again until we absolutely need to have our needs met, leading us to become clingy again, leading us to scold ourselves again, in a vicious cycle from relationship to relationship and within relationships where we never get the connection that we seek and succeed in maintaining it. If we are afraid of what we will see in ourselves if we open up to ourselves, and we then disappoint ourselves by not responding as we'd like when we speak up about our wants, feelings, and thoughts to ourselves, then we will fear opening up to ourselves and others and disappointing others and being disappointed by others' responses to us, and then we actually will disappoint others and be disappointed by others whenever we open up, which will lead us to disappoint ourselves again by shutting ourselves down again as we get upset with ourselves for opening up and causing such disappointment.

We must be kind to ourselves. We must treat ourselves as important and worthy of our attention. We must value ourselves and listen to ourselves—to our own thoughts, feelings, and instincts. We must protect ourselves, help ourselves, and follow our own guidance. We must really pay attention to ourselves. We must have compassion for ourselves. We must really listen to all of our thoughts, feelings, and instincts, so that we can recognize the true positive intentions behind them and experience them as always helping us toward our expressed goals, and in this way caring for us, loving us without exception, unconditionally. We must learn to forgive ourselves for being unkind to ourselves in the past, and to love ourselves from here onward. Only in this way can we learn to open up to ourselves and to others and to welcome this and stick around and be kind and accepting to ourselves when this happens so that other people will as well. We must learn to make ourselves feel safe to speak up, to express our needs, wants, feelings, and thoughts. If we do this, then others will, too.

We must retrain ourselves. After life may have made us afraid to speak, we must encourage ourselves by really listening with caring, accepting attention. Remember, we are responsible for our own experiences, ultimately, but no one is to blame. We could blame our parents, our siblings, our friends, our exes, our current partners, ourselves, but none of this blaming will do anything but give us more reasons to blame. If we want our experience to change—if we want to change the way we're treated—we must change the way we treat ourselves.

Become the kind of person with whom you would want to be in a relationship and you will bring the kinds of relationships you want into your life.

Attachment To Specific Outcomes Vs. Setting Destinations And Trusting Your GPS To Guide You There

Whenever we decide "This is the person for me," or "This is the job," or "This is the house," or whatever, and we decide we absolutely must have this one and no other, we essentially are saying that our fulfillment comes from this particular one and that we cannot get fulfillment from anything else. When we do this, we put a tremendous amount of pressure on ourselves to get this one, and we put a tremendous amount of expectation on whatever we're giving too much of our attention to, needing our fulfillment to come from it. We also inevitably begin to fear that we might not get this person or this job or this house.

"What if it doesn't work out?" we ask ourselves without having any other possible positive alternative scenarios or options in mind. "What then?" With the feeling that our fulfillment rests on this particular thing working out this particular way, we end up inevitably unfulfilled when we push away the very thing we want by giving it too much desperate attention.

Relationships, jobs, houses, money, etc.—when we want them too much, when we feel like we *need* them—we inevitably don't get them, or we lose them if we already have them.

Whenever we grow attached to any specific outcome, we put too much mental, emotional, and physical energy into making it happen. Whenever we put too much energy into anything, we end up not giving enough attention to other things, and so we end up expecting and needing much more back from what we've given our energy to. So then we begin to fear that we won't get what we want, and we thereby begin to give our energy to the outcome that we fear, making that our destination. Consequently, we push away what we actually want, and we end up realizing our fear of not getting the outcome to which we were attached.

The solution is to set our destinations and trust that we'll get there. If, for example, you want to be in a relationship with someone who has x, y, and z qualities, and who makes you feel a, b, and c, then specify this. Once you meet someone who seems to fit these criteria, say to yourself, "I know I end up with a person who has x, y, and z qualities and who makes me feel a, b, and c. If this is that person, then that would be great, and let it be clear to me and this person and everyone else that this is the case. If this is not that person, then let this be clear to me and this person and everyone else as well, and let me be guided to the person who is right for me."

This is as opposed to, "I really want to be with this person, and if I don't end up with this person, I would be devastated and feel like there is no one out there for me."

The goal is to be able to recognize that once you set a specific destination in terms of qualities and ideas—but not in terms of specific people or events that must lead you there—you truly can trust that you will get there. In other words, specify everything you want in a person down to every last detail, but don't specify the person. The same thing goes for everything else: Specify everything you'd love to experience and have, but never conclude for yourself that a particular thing must go a certain way in order for you to be happy. Otherwise you're setting yourself up for unfulfillment.

We must remember that from the perspective of being inside the maze of physical life, we can easily fall into trying to navigate and get out by sheer physical efforts and the information we obtain through our physical senses. But we all have a GPS system that can guide us through from the perspective of being above the maze and seeing the way out. So we can try to navigate without the GPS, but this is only going to lead to a lot of reaction from us as we keep thinking we've found the way out, only to find ourselves at another dead end. Navigating by sheer physical efforts and physical means of discernment alone consequently leads to a lot of frustration, anger, shame, regret, anxiety, and fear. On the other hand, simply setting our destinations in advance and listening as we allow our GPS to guide us and navigate for us takes away all of the reaction and stress from the picture.

The fact is that from within the maze, we don't actually consciously know which specific person, job, house, etc. best fits everything we've asked for. But if we set our destinations and listen to and act on the directions, and we keep ourselves open to going wherever our GPS leads us—even if this means trying out ways of thinking, acting, and being that we've never tried before and facing things that we may have avoided before now—we will get to our intended destinations.

In order to use our GPS effectively, however, we must remember that everything that we want must be formed within ourselves before we can experience it outside of ourselves. Life is an ongoing maintenance and creation of a positive relationship with ourselves, where we focus more predominantly on what we like and want than on what we don't like and don't want. There is no fulfillment that begins outside of us to be obtained from there. All fulfillment must be created within, through presence to our internal experiences, and is then reflected and supported outside of us in the physical experiences that we get in our lives.

There is no safe home base we can reach and where we can simply stop. And so it is not the case that we will get a relationship or a friendship or a community or a job or a house or a certain amount of money or level of income and then be done with our problems and have it significantly easier from there. If we think that we will be done after we get something or reach some place, then we either won't get what we want, or we will simply find that the obstacles we face will continue and follow us into our new relationship or friendship or job or house, etc. No matter what changes in our lives, we always have to keep listening to ourselves and maintaining a positive relationship with ourselves in order to keep what we want in our lives even after we get what we want in our lives. We create our lives anew in every moment, so we can just as easily lose everything that we have gained as we can gain it in the first place. For the same reason, we can also gain it back again just as easily as we might have lost it. We must remember that having good experiences in each moment is up to us to choose and create in each moment through presence to ourselves and mindful, willful setting of destinations for ourselves to be guided to.

Our goal is non-attachment. We must want what we want, and put energy into getting it, but with the awareness that there will always be another option or route presented to us if this doesn't prove to be our destination. There is never truly a last hope. There is always more hope. In fact, as long as we set our destinations and we keep our focus on them despite where we are in the process toward them, there is far more than hope: There is the guarantee that we will get to our destinations.

It is easy to be non-attached or unattached when we recognize that nothing outside of us can be a source of fulfillment for us. What is outside of us can be nothing more than a reflection of what is inside of us, and so our fulfillment must begin within. We must also recognize that we do not want to be *detached*. Pushing away at what we want will do no better for us than fearing that we won't get it. The result will be the same in the sense that we will not get what we want.

Remember: We must put energy toward what we want, but it must be the kind of energy that can be easily redirected toward another route with calmness and trust if where we are turns out not to be our intended or ultimately desired destination. Fooling ourselves and tuning out what is actually here while trying to make it into something else will result in our tuning out ourselves and therefore in our not being fulfilled. So if this is not the person you ultimately want to be with, say no, let the person go, and specify to yourself what you like and don't like here and what you'd like instead of what you don't like here. "I'd like these qualities that this person had, and I'd like to feel these ways, but I'd also like these other qualities."

We might reach one destination we've specified, get everything we've asked for, and then realize that there are more things that we actually want to specify. We are allowed to say no and ask for something better for us. In the restaurant of the universe, you must order exactly what you want in order to get it. Specify every food and spice down to the last detail, or at least (and more importantly) how you are going to feel about it even if you don't know the specific ingredients, and then taste and enjoy the food that you receive. If, for any reason, you don't like what you've ordered, send it back and ask for something else. Don't simply say, "I don't like this." The chef can't help you out there, because you haven't specified anything except what you don't like, which is exactly what is going to keep sitting in front of you. Say, "I like this about this dish, but instead of this flavor here, I'd also like this." Now the chef can accommodate you and give you what you've specified. Be patient, and your next order will come within the timeframe within which you specify that you want to receive it.

However, if you end up focusing on the fact that it's not here yet, you are essentially telling the chef, "What I want isn't here." The chef will only slow down here, as you've given a new request that conflicts with your previous order. If you find yourself focusing on the fact that you haven't received what you want yet, be sure to re-order what you want, "I would love to have x, y, and z, and I'm excited to enjoy it!" Then the chef will get back to the preparations and bring you your order.

We must be attentive to how what we are getting is reflective of where we are internally, however. You may find the right person or the right job or the right house, and it may still need work and not actually be everything that you want right now. You may simply need to add a bit of salt here, or a bit of pepper there—and more importantly, to change your perception of what you've got to recognize how much the chef got right instead of focusing on how much still needs improvement—rather than send back the dish and ask for another one entirely. So give it a chance if your internal GPS says to, notice what you're not liking, and keep redirecting to focus primarily on what you'd like—on where you intend to be going.

The person, job, etc. may very well become exactly what you want once you get to the place you want to be yourself. As you transform your relationship with yourself, it will become clear if it is time to move on to someone or something else if the person or job or whatever isn't growing with you. But whatever you do, stay focused on where you want to be going—on what you want in a relationship, job, your life, etc. Notice when you get caught up in what you're not wanting about what you have, and redirect your attention to what you want instead. Then you can be certain that you will be guided to your intended destination.

The goal is to get to the peak of the mountain. It is easy to get confused and lost as we put so much energy into getting to a basecamp that we forget that this isn't actually the ultimate goal. But we never have to settle for the basecamp. We can always learn from how we got here and from what we've experienced here and make the next trek up toward the next basecamp destination that we set for ourselves on our way up to the peak. If it isn't already, the next destination will eventually be the peak.

When you use a man-made GPS system, you probably don't usually question if you're going to get to your destination. You plug in the destination, and you trust that the GPS will guide you there. Even if there are closed roads and bridges and other obstacles, the GPS simply recalculates, and you trust that you are going to get where you're going. Even more so this should be the case for the built-in GPS with which you were born.

When you order something from amazon.com, you probably don't question whether you're going to get what you've ordered. You specify exactly what you want (and you have to specify *exactly* what you want because otherwise you won't have anything in your cart to order), and then you click "Order" and specify the timeframe within which you want to receive your order. Once you do this, you can stop thinking about the order entirely because you trust that what you asked for will be delivered to you within the timeframe you specified. If you then receive what you ordered and it turns out not to be what you wanted, you can usually return the item and specify something different, which you will receive within the timeframe you specify.

The universe is like the ultimate amazon.com. You can order anything from an answer to a question to your dream career to a close friend to your soulmate. You can request that you get along better with your family or that your relationship with your spouse improves. You can ask for a house with certain qualities or that you simply have a good, meaningful conversation with someone today. You can specify that a date goes well or that you simply go to bed early and feeling happy tonight. You can request your ideal body, good health, a specific yearly income, or that you hang out with friends at least once this week. Anything and everything can be yours. You just have to be clear about what you want, including as much descriptive detail as possible without actually specifying a particular person or job opportunity or whatever. Once you know what you want, you simply have to request it with belief that you can get it, imagine what it would be like to have it, and be present enough to follow the directions you get toward it, including taking the appropriate internal and external actions where and when necessary as directed by your internal GPS.

We must remind ourselves that we will get where we're going. We just need to set our destinations and then let go, listen to and act on the directions we're provided with, and be present to the journey.

Seek And You Shall Find...As Soon As You Stop Seeking

When we are busy searching, we cannot find. When we are giving our energy to the idea that there is a problem, we cannot recognize a solution to this problem. When we are focusing on wanting something, we will just keep on wanting it and not having it.

Searching leads to more searching. Problems lead to more problems. Wanting leads to more wanting.

The only way to get what we want is to shift our focus to the experience of what it would be like to have it. Focusing on the experience of being where you are determines this as your destination, and so you stay where you are. Imagine what it would be like to be where you want to be, and this will become your destination, and your thoughts, feelings, and instincts will guide you there.

So if you would like a relationship, imagine what it would be like to be in your ideal relationship. Imagine what it would be like to have someone with whom to share your life experiences, with whom you feel close and connected, whom you love and who loves you, etc. This is as opposed to focusing on how you want a relationship but don't have one, or on how you're single and currently searching for a relationship. Identifying with being single and searching will definitely not get you a relationship. Identifying with the experience of how wonderful it would be to be in a fulfilling relationship will get you there.

If you would like a job, imagine what it would be like to be in your ideal job. Imagine what it would be like to do what you enjoy doing, and to be valued by others for it and get paid for it. Imagine what it would be like to feel accomplished at the end of each day and like you were productive during the day—like you are exactly where you want to be and doing exactly what you want to be doing with your life.

If you would like to have the answer to a question or the solution to a problem, simply request that you find the answer or the solution and imagine what it would be like to have it. Imagine what it would be like to have that clarity, certainty, and direction. Imagine what your experience of life would be like in that situation.

Remember, you will be guided toward any experience that you focus on, and it will become your reality. The world will support you in thinking, feeling, and wanting whatever you focus on thinking, feeling, and wanting. So request what you want by imagining what you'd ideally like to be experiencing. Give your energy and attention to what it would be like to live life in those external circumstances, from the internal place that would be supported by these. And this will become your experience of life.

Life As A Shopping Experience

Every experience you receive in life is an opportunity to say, "I'd like that in my life," or "I don't want that; I'd like this other thing instead."

If you want to be in a relationship, and you see a couple interacting lovingly with each other, instead of simply being jealous, which reaffirms the destination, "I don't have that," use the experience in your favor. Say, "I'd love to experience that in my life. I'd really appreciate that."

If you are in a relationship, and you are getting along better with a friend than with your significant other, say, "I'd love to experience this kind of connection in my relationship. That would be great." If you see someone you're more physically attracted to than your significant other for whatever reason, say, "I'd love to be this attracted to my significant other. That would be really nice."

Nothing is off-limits to you. Just ask for what you want. The world is your shopping mall. And you have unlimited funding for this shopping experience of life. Whatever you want can be yours. Just ask for it and listen to and address the different thoughts, feelings, instincts, and experiences that come up in response to your request so that you can cultivate the kind of relationship with yourself that is in harmony with your receiving what you've asked for.

This applies to experiences that you have directly as well as ones that you are observing in others. So, for example, if you personally experience, or you simply witness, a close connection similar to what you'd like to have in your relationship, say, "I'd like to have this kind of connection in my relationship with my partner." And then connect more with yourself so that your relationship with yourself is conducive to and compatible with your receiving the kind of relationship with your partner that you are requesting.

If you do or experience something that you like, you can say, "I like this and I'd love more of this." Let's say you meditate in the morning and you feel good and refreshed and ready to start your day. Or you experience a great conversation with someone. Or you get a bit of unexpected money or a great opportunity comes through for you. Respond to this and say, "I like this and I'd love more of this." Then keep doing what you were doing that got you the experience in the first place.

If something is in the right direction but isn't everything you want, then say, "I like this, and I'd love more of this, but with this instead of that." Then alter your dynamic with yourself wherever appropriate so that you get more of what you like but altered the way you want from here on.

Respond to all of your experiences so that you are focusing on and requesting what you want, and then set the appropriate example in your dynamic with yourself so that you can accept what you request when it comes.

Your Thoughts, Feelings, And Instincts Gauge How Your Beliefs Will Affect Your Getting What You're Asking For

When you ask for something that you want and you feel negative in reaction to this asking, this means that you don't believe you can get everything that you want in a way that you would actually experience it as good. If you ignore the thoughts, feelings, and instincts that come up in reaction to your requests, you will notice that when you receive what you requested (if you do, in fact, receive anything close to this), it will be modified by all of the limiting beliefs that you had when you asked. You won't get everything you truly want. You'll get the closest thing to this that you can get within the confines of what you believed was possible.

For example, if you ask for a relationship that is loving and enjoyable, and you feel negative when you say this, then this means you probably don't fully believe that you can get this. Essentially, your thoughts, feelings, and instincts are saying to you, "Based on everything we've experienced in our relationship with you, we don't really believe that we're going to get a relationship that is actually loving and enjoyable."

Therefore, when you ask for something, listen to the thoughts, feelings, and instincts that come up in reaction to your asking. Then respond to them appropriately in order to address their concerns.

In this example, you might say something to your thoughts, feelings, and instincts like "I hear you. I haven't seen relationships that are loving and enjoyable around me, and this is because I haven't been resonant with experiencing relationships this way due to my not even having had this kind of relationship with myself. I would love to have a much more loving and enjoyable relationship with myself from here on, and thereby to make myself resonant with experiencing relationships this way from here on."

Your beliefs stemming from how you have treated yourself up to this point, and from the resulting experiences that you've had in the world around you up to this point, affect what you can bring into your experience. Respond appropriately and kindly to your thoughts, feelings, and instincts that come up in reaction to what you say and ask for, and shift your ways of treating yourself by focusing on what you'd like to experience rather than on what you've already gotten. In this way, you can come to create new experiences for yourself that are not limited by your previous-experience-based beliefs.

The Whole World Supports You In Imagining That Which You Cannot Imagine When You Ask

If you are struggling trying to imagine a better experience for yourself, this is not a problem. Simply ask how it could be better. Asking questions will get you answers from other people and the world around you. The world will support you in imagining that which you cannot imagine by giving you real-world examples of what you are wanting for yourself.

If you would like a better relationship with your partner, ask for it. Don't ask your partner directly to change. First ask for a better relationship with yourself. Ask for guidance. Ask for clarity. Whatever you ask for, you will get. Perhaps you will see the kind of relationship you want but couldn't imagine in a couple of friends. Perhaps you will read about it or see it on television or in a movie. Perhaps you will see it in people you don't know. Then, when you see it, notice what thoughts and feelings come up within you. Respond to these thoughts and feelings, and say that you would like this experience for yourself, and that you are open to having it.

If you would like a better relationship with your parents, ask for it. After a lifetime of consistent themes, it can become very difficult to imagine a different kind of relationship with them. So just ask for it, and see what comes to you. You will find answers, guidance, and support in the world around you, even in seemingly random encounters with strangers. Be open to the answers to your questions wherever they may come—in a cashier's comment, in an article you read, in the bending of a tree in the wind, in a section of a song that plays in your mind or on the radio, in a joke that someone tells, in geese flying overhead, in children playing on a playground. Just be open, and the answer will come to you in a form that you can receive it.

Life will provide you with everything you need to get where you ask to be going—even guidance in imagining what where you are going looks like, feels like, etc. So just ask, and be open to receiving the answer from the greatest teacher—yourself—through the greatest hands-on classroom—the world. No one can treat you in a way that you are not already treating yourself. No one can tell you anything that you have not already been telling yourself. So when you receive the answer, recognize that it came from the highest part of you, regardless of who or what conveyed the message to you.

After you encounter examples of what you are asking for, be sure to ask for that to be your own experience. The world will help you imagine what you want for yourself, but then it is up to you to say, "Yes, that's right. That's what I want. I'd love that for myself. I'd love to have that in my own life, in my own relationship, in my own experience." Ask for options to choose from, then choose from the options you've created, and what you choose will be yours.

It's All Good

Once we let go of our past dynamics with ourselves and others and get to a place where we feel good about ourselves and our lives, we realize that we wouldn't be who we are were it not for our past struggles and the lessons we learned from them. We are who we've become because of how we've used our past struggles. We might have reacted to them and identified with them, in which case we continue to bring more of the same to ourselves. Or we might have responded to them and transformed ourselves with the awareness they've given us of how we've been shaping our lives, in which case we've learned to create more desirable experiences for ourselves.

We are basically getting continual feedback on how we're shaping our lives, on what direction we're headed, on what we're creating for ourselves. Our thoughts, feelings, instincts, and behaviors are the tools with which we shape our lives, and we can go straight to them to discover what we are in the process of creating. If we don't catch our creations at this stage of the process for any reason, we get a glimpse of what we have been giving our attention to, and what we are therefore creating for ourselves, in our dreams. If we don't catch our creations in these previews, we get to experience them reflected back at us in other people's words and actions toward us and in the physical events of our lives. If we don't catch our creations at this point, for any reason, or if we simply aren't aware that our experiences are actually our creations—shaped and determined by the focus of our attention and our internal dynamics—and so we don't change our focus of attention and internal dynamics that are giving rise to these creations, we will keep getting the same types of experiences in the forms of thoughts, feelings, instincts, behaviors, dreams, other people's words and behaviors toward us, and the external events of our lives. Our reactions to our creations create reinforcing feedback loops of creation of the same types of experiences. But if we choose to pause and bring awareness to the creative process, we can make changes internally that will lead to different internal and external results.

We succeed in getting on a path of discernible progression, evolution, and growth when we recognize our present and our past as the results of what we have created for ourselves before now, and when we therefore choose to shift our internal goings-on so that we can create something different from here on. Once we do this, we feel amazingly good. We realize that it's not where we are in our lives or our growth now that matters; it's what direction we're headed now that matters. When we're going the right direction, it feels good. When we're going the wrong direction, it feels bad. So if we recognize that we feel bad in any way, all we need to do is shift direction and then we will feel good. We don't have to wait for dramatic changes to come about in our lives, for people to change or treat us differently, for our relationships to improve, for our income to increase, for our living situation to shift. We don't have to wait for anything in order to be in a good place. We simply need to shift our focus of attention in this moment so that we are, in this moment, headed the right direction rather than the wrong direction in terms of our ultimate fulfillment and wellbeing.

Everything we want is available to us in this moment. We simply need to focus on some anchor in the present moment, such as our breathing, our walking, or any other aspect of the present, and acknowledge and listen to our thoughts, feelings, and instincts as they come up, without running away from them, dismissing them, tuning them out or pushing them away. Once we let everything inside us express itself without interruption, we'll have learned what's been holding us back and creating what we aren't actually wanting in our experience of life. We'll understand what we've been creating for ourselves and how, as we acknowledge the destinations we've been plugging into our GPS and giving our energy to. Then we can respond and redirect those destinations by shifting our focus of attention, making requests for clarity and guidance where we don't yet know how to make changes ourselves, and simply being open to receiving the answers and guidance from wherever they come.

As we learn to become aware of the process of how we create our lives and how we can do so willfully, we naturally become increasingly grateful for the struggles that led us to this awareness. Even the worst experiences in our lives can take on a new hue in the light of awareness. We come to see how we've created them and why, and we learn from them what they were meant to teach us, and we become grateful for the lessons because of the new level of fulfillment they take us to as we implement them. For we could not have become who we are, experiencing what we're experiencing in this more positive place were it not for the experiences that shaped us, reflected back at us where we were, and ultimately taught us how to get to where we are and beyond.

Every aspect of our lives, every relationship we've had and have, our interests, our career decisions, the impacts we've had on others—all of it wouldn't be exactly what it was were it not for the experiences we've had, because those experiences shaped the decisions we made after them, which led to further experiences and further lessons. And all of it seems good in the light of awareness, in which we see every struggle as well as every positive experience in the context of where it leads us, and not simply the struggles and other experiences in the moment, themselves. All of it is good, for it is all part of our process; it is all part of our growth into who we are and who we will become.

We Need Not Experience All That Much Bad

Our experiences are merely reflections of the thoughts, feelings, and instincts to which we give our attention and the dynamics that we allow to exist within us. As we become more aware, we become increasingly able to catch what we are in the process of creating while it is still in our thoughts or feelings or instincts and before we act from these things and bring about a physical version of what we are focusing on internally.

As a result, it is not a necessity that we experience all that much bad in life once we get the hang of how we are actually shaping all of our experiences. We will only experience what we need to experience in order to notice and listen to what our thoughts, feelings, and instincts are telling us. So if we notice and listen while they're still thoughts, feelings, or instincts and before they become physical things—like the health of our bodies, our relationships with other people and their words and actions toward us, our financial situations, etc.—then we don't require the physical experiences to reflect back what needs to be shifted inside of us in order for us to get on track toward our truly desired experience of life again. We can pay attention to our thoughts, feelings, instincts, and even their manifestations in our dreams, and then acknowledge them and respond to them and redirect them before they ever become physical. Even if they become physical before we catch them, we can catch them early before they become chronic, deep-seated negative themes that infiltrate every aspect of our lives—from personal health, to romantic relationships, to family, to career, to friendships, and so on.

So this is true preventative care, which is really just the maintenance and consistent increase of wellbeing: We must practice being mindful and present daily to our own internal goings-on and really listen to ourselves. We must pay attention to what our own thoughts, feelings, and instincts are trying to tell us directly. And, if we haven't heard and incorporated their message into our behavior before this, we must pay attention to what our own thoughts, feelings, and instincts are trying to tell us indirectly through our bodies, our experiences in the world around us, and the words and actions of the people around us, as well as through our reactions to all of these things in our thoughts, feelings, and instincts. Once we hear the message, there is no more need for the experience. So if we listen carefully and respond appropriately, the message will remain subtle and will have no need to be expressed outwardly and dramatically in our life experience.

Every Step In The Right Direction Is Significant And Good

Note every small success—every step in the right direction, however small—because it will then be followed by larger and larger successes. If you look at how far you haven't gone rather than at how far you've come, you will merely discourage yourself from going any further. On the other hand, if you look at how far you've come, you will encourage yourself to keep going in that direction, which will ultimately mean you'll get to where you want to go.

If you denounce each step you take as not being good enough or significant enough, you'll be dissatisfied with your pace. Then because you're dissatisfied with your pace, you'll be dissatisfied with the pace of the people and the world around you as well. Then you'll focus on those external things that you don't have direct control over and you'll try to control them. This will bother the people around you, and they'll likely be even slower to fulfill your requests as a result. So if you belittle the progress in your own process, you'll slow the process of everything within and outside you that you actually want to speed up.

Further, if you're dissatisfied with your pace, you'll be frustrated with where you are, which will lead you to be frustrated with where everyone else is, too. If you're frustrated with where you are, you'll regret the decisions you made in the past that led you here, which will lead you to be upset at everyone else for what they did that contributed to your being here. If you are frustrated with the present, and you regret the past, then you'll worry about the future that you're headed toward as a result of the present and the past being what they are, and you'll be afraid of how other people might contribute to your being where you don't want to be in the future. So if you dismiss the progress you're making, you'll be generally dissatisfied and unfulfilled with life in general, and all of your relationships with everyone around you, as well as with yourself, will suffer.

Alternatively, if you praise and appreciate each step you take as being important and good enough and progress in the right direction, you'll be satisfied with your pace and with where you are. Then because you're satisfied with your pace, you'll be satisfied with the pace of the people and the world around you as well. Then you'll let the people around you do what they're doing, and you'll let the things around you happen as they're happening, and you'll only guide them as they want and need to be guided. Further, you'll praise and appreciate each step that the people and the world around you are taking as being important and good enough and progress in the right direction as you are doing for yourself. This will encourage the people and the world around you to keep going in the direction that you want them to be going, and they'll likely be even faster to fulfill your requests as a result. So if you acknowledge the progress in your own process, you'll keep up, and possibly even actually speed up, the progress of everything within and outside you.

Further, if you're satisfied with your pace, you'll be at peace with where you are, which will lead you to be at peace with where everyone else is, too. If you're at peace with where you are, you'll appreciate the decisions you made in the past that led you here, which will lead you to be appreciative toward everyone else for what they did that contributed to your being here, too. If you are at peace with the present, and you appreciate the past, then you'll trust in and be grateful for the future that you're headed toward as a result of the present and the past being what they are, and you'll trust in and be grateful for how other people might contribute to your being where you want to be in the future. So if you acknowledge the progress you're making, you'll be generally satisfied and fulfilled with life in general, and all of your relationships with everyone around you, as well as with yourself, will benefit.

So acknowledge and allow yourself to feel and express appreciation and gratitude for every step in the right direction—for every bit of progress you and everyone else makes, however small. For then the progress will build on itself and take you to whole new levels of appreciation and gratitude for your life.

Look not at how far you have to go but at how far you've come, and live with the recognition (and therefore the intention and destination) that, in every moment, everything is better than it's ever been before. And it will be.

Set Destinations So You Can Gauge Your Progress

In order to recognize and acknowledge steps in the right direction, you need to set destinations in the first place so you know that a step you took was actually a step in the right direction. Without clear destinations, you cannot gauge your progress, because you'll never know whether a step was in the right direction or not. You'll never know whether you are a step closer to your destination or not. So, set your destinations.

Every morning, be sure to imagine what you would like to be thinking and feeling at the end of the day. Once in a while, be sure to look further ahead and imagine what you would like to be thinking and feeling at the end of the week, the month, the year, etc. And throughout your day and before everything that you do, set your destination in regard to what you'd like to be thinking and feeling after you do what you're about to do so that you are determining how things will go rather than discovering how they will go. If you believe it appropriate to re-evaluate your destinations based on circumstances at any point, set a new destination, listen to yourself about it and, if you feel good about the new destination, go forward toward it.

Your destinations and the timeframes you set for reaching them should seem possible and realistic, but should also challenge and motivate you to get started now in order to reach these destinations by the times you specify. So, for example: If you haven't been running much at all up to this point, and you set the destination that you will run a marathon within the next week, this isn't likely to motivate you because there's no way you're going to believe that this is possible and therefore worth working toward. You're already behind and doomed to failure before you even start doing anything, so this destination and timeframe is simply discouraging. If you set the destination that you will run a marathon within the next twenty years, you might believe this to be possible, but you aren't likely to be motivated to do anything right now. Alternatively, if you set the destination that you will run a marathon in one year, you might feel that this is realistic and also recognize it as motivating to get you started running and training right now in order to keep this goal realistic and reach it.

So, set believable *and* motivating destinations. And imagine thoroughly what it would be like to reach them and be there. In this example, imagine how amazing and triumphant you would feel crossing the finish line, having completed a full marathon after training for it for a full year and finally now experiencing the payoff of everything you were working toward. Step into the imagining of any destination that is in line with, and not conflicting with or contradictory to, other destinations you might have set already for the future. If you do this sufficiently, experiencing your being there as though it were the present or even the past, this will get you thinking in the right direction, stir up the kinds of emotions that will motivate you, and drive you to want to do what is necessary to get there.

You create the world of your experience. No one and nothing else does. If you look to the world to see how things will go, your life will be lived in reaction to everyone else's words and actions and the circumstances and events of your life. Looking to "reality" to determine what *is* and what *will be* therefore only guarantees a less good experience of reality and a less good reality, because it means you are living your life reactively and letting outside circumstances shape you, and you are subject to the whim of your reactions to everything, including to your own reactions. In this case, you allow doubts, uncertainties, fears, regrets, frustrations, and so forth shape your reality as you look to reality hoping to find one thing but with the doubt that you'll find this that leads you to check in the first place. However, if you decide, yourself, how you'd like things to go and then take action in that direction, your life will be lived proactively, willfully, and on purpose. Deciding on your own how you'd like your life to play itself out from here guarantees that you will experience a better reality, because it will be the one you want and *intend* rather than simply *hope for*, one that you determine and shape yourself, refining as you go in willful *response* to what you experience and learn along the way.

This is not to say that you should micromanage every detail of the journey. Quite the opposite. Remember: Controlling and micromanaging ourselves only encourages our treating other people these ways and other people treating us these ways, which leads to rebellion by us and by them. The goal is to create your desired results by imagining how you'd like things to turn out so you have a destination, getting excited and passionate about it so there's fuel in the car propelling you there, and then simply listening to the directions and being open to however you might get there. Your job is not to decide how you get where you're going. That's the job of the GPS. Your job is only to decide where you want to be going and how you'd like to feel when you get there.

Life is all about the journey, but we get to determine where we're headed on the journey in advance of embarking on the journey—as well as in advance of embarking on each leg of the journey. If we set a destination in our internal GPS—as well as shorter term destinations along the way toward our longer term destination—we'll get clear directions and a clear sense of progress as we reach each checkpoint along our journey. We'll get where we're going if we determine where we're going. Without a determination of where we're going, however, we can't ever know that we got there.

Set Destinations For At Least A Step Ahead Of Where You Are

As we near the end of a book or a bottle of shampoo, we are likely to slow down our pace going through it unless we have another one lined up to go to next. The same is true for any destination we set. If we are striving toward some goal, and we haven't yet imagined and decided what comes next once we reach our goal, we will likely stay in the striving and slow our progress since we don't have anywhere to go once we reach our goal. If we actually want to reach a destination, we must set the next destination after it so that we have somewhere to go once we reach our current intended destination.

So, if you want to find someone with whom to be in a relationship, or you want to find a job, or you want to increase your income, or you want to complete a book, or you want to lose weight, you must imagine what it would be like to be there already. What you are thinking, feeling, wanting, and doing once you've already reached your destination? What next destination are you headed toward at that time that provides direction and purpose to your actions and your existence then?

Without clarity about what direction you would be headed once you get where you're going, you will be inclined to wander and delay your progress as you near your destination. But by imagining what your experience of life would be like once you get where you're going, you can gain clarity about what the next steps would be and focus on that experience. This way, you can keep up your pace and make focused progress to and through your destination, onward to the next one without hesitation.

Actually Being Okay With Where You Are Vs. Fighting Against Not Being Okay With Where You Are

If you're trying to convince yourself that you're okay with where you are in your progression toward where you want to be, but you aren't actually okay with where you are, then your internal battle will be reflected outside of you. It will seem like you have to convince everyone else that you're okay with where you are.

If you are fighting against not being okay with where you are, this means that you are not listening to something your thoughts, feelings, and instincts are trying to say to you. The result is that you have negative thoughts, feelings, and instincts surrounding the topic, and you are simply trying to speak over them with positive thoughts, feelings, and instincts. This never creates a desired result because it simply creates a war inside and outside you. The goal is to listen to and acknowledge your thoughts, feelings, and instincts, and then redirect the negative ones toward a better route to their ultimate intended aim—a route that will actually get you and them there.

Whenever we give too much attention to anything, we divert other people's attention to this also. So if you are trying to let go of excess weight and you are trying to convince yourself that you're actually okay with your body but you're not actually okay with your body, you are going to be paying a lot of attention to your body with judgment and attempted acceptance at the same time. The result is that other people will reflect back both sides of this. There will be people who judge your body, and there will be people who will accept your body almost militantly like you are doing.

But what you really want in this example, ideally, is for your body to be a nonissue. The only way for your body to be a nonissue, and for you actually to lose the excess weight, is for you to listen to your thoughts, feelings, and instincts about your body and address them and redirect them where appropriate. Set your destination in regard to what you'd like to be thinking and feeling about your body, listen to whatever your thoughts, feelings, and instincts say, acknowledge them, and address them kindly and appropriately. Ideally, you would set such a destination as, "I would love to love every part of my body," and give loving, accepting, positive attention to every part of your body and you. Then, direct your attention elsewhere, to whatever most requires it in the present moment, so that you can continue living and evolving.

Whenever you give too much attention to anything, you create issues due to lack of balance of attention to the different areas of your life that require it. Most importantly, whenever you give too much attention to anything, you are ultimately ignoring, dismissing, or tuning out other thoughts, feelings, and instincts. So return to the present moment with your attention, notice what has been taking up your attention, and listen to your thoughts, feelings, and instincts about that topic—whether it's your relationship, your body, your parents, your kids, your community, your job, money, etc. There is a lesson there to be learned if something has been taking up your attention and distracting you from other things.

Remember, like children, your thoughts, feelings, and instincts just want your attention. If they aren't getting it, they will nag you until they do—even speaking up through other people's words and actions toward you, and through events in the world around you. But, ultimately, this is because they want you to be happy and well and to experience everything good, and they can help you to get there only if you listen to them. So if you are going the wrong direction with the way you are treating them, they will try to speak up and get your attention to let you know that you need to treat them differently if you want to accomplish your ultimate aims.

Set Your Destination And Then Relax And Go With The Flow

When we take life too seriously, we make ourselves feel controlled and micromanaged, we end up rebelling against our own control and indulging in behaviors that don't help us toward our desired goals, and we end up generally stressed out and burnt out. Life requires a lot of work when we demand things from ourselves and drag our thoughts, feelings, and instincts along with us kicking and screaming, rather than having their help in guiding us and motivating us forward. Life requires a lot of work when we treat ourselves terribly and try (or don't even try) to treat others better than we're treating ourselves.

When we take life—our relationships, our health, our job, etc.—too seriously, we end up attempting to get by and get things done while inside we're stressed out of our minds, overwhelmed, and wanting out. Trying to be a good partner, friend, sibling, child, parent, community member, employee, boss, etc. while this is going on is a tremendous amount of work. We need to work to be constantly on top of everything we say and do and everything we need to take care of or believe we need to take care of—including even everything that everyone else around us is saying and doing—in order for things to go, and to keep going, as we'd like. And even when we're trying to be constantly on top of everything in this situation, we never manage to be constantly on top of everything, and things go as we don't want them to go.

When we take life too seriously, we end up attached to outcomes, micromanage ourselves and others in attempts to make sure we achieve these outcomes, and end up unintentionally letting the most important and vital things that are required to achieve these outcomes slip by without our attention. When we're attached to outcomes, we end up doubting that they'll happen, and even anticipate the worst-case scenarios—everything that could go wrong, all the ways we could end up not getting our desired outcomes—and try, with great effort and a lot of energy, to avoid these worst-case scenarios. We end up exhausted and wanting to rebel against our own dictatorial demands upon ourselves that we feel are coming from outside ourselves and that we often actually end up getting reflected back at us by others.

Life is tiring, stressful, and unsustainable—spiraling downward—when we take it too seriously.

On the other hand, when we learn to relax and go with the flow, we make ourselves feel free and in control, we have no need to rebel against anything, and we end up actually enjoying life. Life doesn't require very much work or effort at all. The only real effort required is that necessary to get ourselves to intend that everything will work out in the best way possible, and then just to breathe and relax and listen to and act on the ultimate intentions of our thoughts, feelings, and instincts. Our thoughts, feelings, and instincts are on our team and acting in our favor, glad to have us as their benevolent and attentive team leader. Our thoughts become our positive, intentionally set destinations, our feelings become the fuel that motivates us forward toward these positive destinations, and our instincts become the directions that tell us what to say and do and when so that we will get to these positive, desired destinations.

When we relax and go with the flow, life flows with us. Being a good partner, friend, sibling, child, parent, community member, employee, boss, etc., becomes easy as we are already a good partner, friend, sibling, child, parent, community member, employee, boss, etc. to ourselves, and so we don't have to work to be this to others; it just flows from the way we're treating ourselves. We don't have to work to be constantly on top of everything and everyone. We just set our desired destinations, imagining the best-case scenarios and believing that they're totally possible, but unattached to them happening because, while it would be fantastic if they become reality, it would be okay if they don't work out these ways, too. We move ourselves and others forward toward our desired destinations with positive attention, acceptance, and encouragement of the behaviors we like.

When we're relaxed and going with the flow, we guide ourselves and others based on our and their actual experiences—which we have carefully listened to and considered—and we attend to all of the important and vital things that are required to achieve our desired outcomes. We end up energized and free as everyone and everything become as friendly and positive to us as we are being to ourselves, supporting us in all of our endeavors as we are supporting ourselves, and helping us toward our goals as we are helping ourselves.

Life is electrifying and invigorating in ways that not only sustain but also build on themselves—spiraling upward—when we simply set our desired destinations and relax and go with the flow.

Coping With The Lack Of Our Own Positive Attention

When we're being controlling and demanding of ourselves, with "should's" and "have to's" and "need to's", we end up rebelling and indulging in distractions and escapes that don't help us toward our desired goals and that often even take us further away from our goals rather than moving us closer to them. These escapes—these coping mechanisms—seem necessary to keep us from completely burning out as quickly while we are being controlling and demanding of ourselves.

Our coping mechanisms allow us to survive when we and the world around us are treating us horribly. When we don't allow ourselves room to breathe, our indulgences and distractions—our rebellion against our own overly strict demands—keep us sane.

These forms of coping are the first problem we usually notice when we think we have a behavioral problem that needs to be addressed. Using drugs, drinking alcohol, smoking anything, excessive gambling, suicidal thoughts and behaviors, eating disorders, excessive eating or too little eating, excessive eating of unhealthy foods, excessive sleep or too little sleep, excessive exercise or too little exercise, excessive work, procrastination, excessive checking of emails and texts, self-isolation, excessive sexual behavior, clinging in relationships, excessive attention to or avoidance of anyone or anything, and other "addictions" and attachments are all forms of coping with our own overly strict and controlling treatment of ourselves. (Note that in many cases, some of these behaviors—such as too little eating, excessive exercise, and excessive work—are the controlling treatment of ourselves, itself, rather than our reaction to this treatment. Although this doesn't make it any better because this means the same negative, controlling dynamic exists within us.)

These behaviors are attempts to escape from ourselves and the resulting similar treatment we get from others and the world around us. Trying to address the problem behaviors directly is like trying to heal a rash resulting from a failing liver by putting ointment on the rash. The coping mechanism is the symptom, while the cause is our controlling and cruel treatment of ourselves. Therefore, we need to address and transform our way of treating ourselves in the first place that is leading us to feel that we need to cope.

It should be noted that our thoughts, feelings, instincts, and physical body all have to cope with our ill treatment just as we attempt to do so behaviorally. Physically and psychologically, this leads to every form of illness and disorder, depending on the type of ill treatment we are inflicting upon ourselves and toward what parts of ourselves we are directing it or what parts of ourselves we are ignoring, dismissing, or tuning out. All physical and psychological illness is a way of coping with our less-than-ideal treatment of ourselves; it is a way of coping with a lack of positive attention from ourselves toward all parts of ourselves. Of course if we then give ourselves medication or cut into our bodies, we are coping with the coping when what we ultimately need to do if we wish to eliminate the need to cope in the first place, or to cope with our mind's coping or our body's coping, is to transform our way of treating ourselves. Control and force is what created the need to cope in the first place; if we try to get rid of our coping with further control, we will only create more of a reason to cope, and so we will not succeed. We must be kind to ourselves and give positive attention to all parts of ourselves in order truly to heal.

When we remove the coping mechanism—the escape, the distraction, the addiction—we are forced to face ourselves and all the fears that we've been avoiding. These are fears that we ultimately created for ourselves by how we've treated ourselves in different contexts and in regard to different things, building associations with different forms of negative attention or lack of attention when we were faced with, e.g. the unknown, intimacy, exercise, work, money, etc. These negative associations may have been built up in us with the help of parents, siblings, other family members, friends, mentors, previous relationship partners, present relationship partners, strangers, or other formative figures who set examples for us in regard to how we should react to different things in life or what we will face there, but these negative associations are maintained by us and they can be changed by us.

Once we begin to lighten up on ourselves and face our fears by listening to ourselves and guiding ourselves toward desired destinations with consideration of our own thoughts, feelings, and instincts, our coping mechanisms become no longer of any positive use or purpose to us. At this point, we have no reason to keep them. So it is now just a matter of changing the behavioral habits, themselves, or those that are encouraging the physical problem.

We rarely ever actually in any way permanently change the way we treat ourselves on a fundamental level—so that we no longer require our coping mechanisms—until we've hit our own version of rock bottom. Even the fleeting pleasure we once obtained from our drug of choice fades, so that we need more and more of our drug in order to get any of the same sense of escape, and we eventually find ourselves getting nothing that we actually want from this drug. Once we get to the point that we realize—not just intellectually, but in a deep emotional and experiential way—that the only way we can possibly get what we really want that we keep seeking through our escapist behaviors is to get it from ourselves, we can shift. At this point, we have the awareness of how fundamentally we need to change and we have the motivation to do so. Because we realize that there's no other way.

When we listen to what our thoughts, feelings, and instincts are really saying to us—when we stop identifying with them and recognize what they've actually been telling us and what they've really been intending for us all along—everything becomes so clear. We've been going about getting what we thought we wanted all the wrong ways; we could never possibly get it in those ways.

For example, if you've been seeking companionship and connection with, and love from, another person because your thoughts, feelings, and instincts have been saying to you, "I feel lonely and I want to feel connected and close to you, and I want to be loved," you realize that you actually need to keep yourself company and connect with yourself and love yourself and that your seeking fulfillment with another person was only increasing the problem by taking away more of your positive attention from yourself and thereby making you feel even lonelier. If you've been seeking distraction in alcohol because your thoughts, feelings, and instincts have been saying to you, "I just need to escape," you realize that you actually need to treat yourself much better and that your seeking escape in alcohol was only increasing the problem by taking away more of your positive attention from yourself and by giving more negative attention to yourself and thereby creating even more of a need to escape. If you've been seeking escape in suicidal thoughts because your thoughts, feelings, and instincts have been saying to you, "I just want to die," you realize that you actually need to treat yourself significantly better and that your seeking escape in thoughts of killing yourself was only increasing the problem by giving more negative attention to yourself and thereby making your experience even more unbearable.

Basically, in each and every moment, we can choose life or we can choose death. It ultimately becomes that simple.

If you look at what you don't like, your thoughts, feelings, and instincts will guide you there, and you will be inclined to ignore, control, dismiss, judge, tune out, and disregard them because you don't want to go where they're directing you. Then your thoughts, feelings, and instincts have a need to cope with how badly you're treating them, and so *you* have a need to cope with how badly you are being treated by yourself and consequently by other people and the world around you as they reflect back how you are treating yourself. If you look at what you like, your thoughts, feelings, and instincts will guide you there, and you will be inclined to acknowledge, accept, tune in, and listen to them because they will be directing you exactly where you want to go. So your thoughts, feelings, and instincts are treated well by you and have nothing with which they need to cope, and so *you* have nothing with which you need to cope as you are treating yourself well and consequently are treated well by other people and the world around you.

When we stop looking at where we don't want to go or are afraid of going and then controlling ourselves in constant attempts to avoid going where we're looking, and we start looking at where we would actually like to go instead, we have no more need to cope.

Hold On Or Let Go?

In regard to a relationship or anything else, there is a single rule that always applies, letting us know when to hold on and work on things and when to let go: If keeping it means facing your issues and continuing forward, you should keep it. If keeping it means avoiding your issues and stagnating or going the wrong direction altogether, you should let it go.

If you pay attention to the parallels with other aspects of your life, you can often get clues as to which action and approach is best in any particular situation. If you are at a dead-end job and knowing that you have to leave at some point soon, you are probably also in a relationship that won't last. If there is some major shift into a new stage of your career that must take place, where you need to change your approach to your career significantly in order to allow yourself to fulfill your potential and make your career more fulfilling to you, the same is probably also true of your relationship. The same issues are often reflected in both areas of life—career and relationship—as well as others. If we have some major, long-standing dynamic in ourselves, we are likely to find that it has permeated nearly every area of our lives. Our attitude about one area of life reflects our attitude about another area of life. So if, for example, you recognize that you have to address something with a parent and not simply run away and never look back, you probably also have to address something in a relationship and in your career and not simply leave these at this time.

If you leave when staying would have meant addressing your issues, you will simply face the same issues elsewhere. If you run away from or tune out or dismiss issues in your relationship, and you break up with the person, you will simply face the same issues in your next relationship unless you address these issues in yourself in the meantime. And if you avoid intimate relationships altogether, you'll face the issues in your friendships. And if you avoid friendships altogether, you'll face the issues in family or career or health or community. And so forth. There is no way out but through.

If you have been avoiding moving forward in your life for an extended period of time, there are probably various physical aspects of your life that need drastic changing—perhaps your relationship, your career, your living situation, etc. If you are moving forward and simply struggling with facing the things you've avoided in the past, there are probably very few, if any, actual physical aspects of your life that need drastic changing right now. (That is, unless you just recently began moving forward from having been avoiding things, in which case physical things likely do need to be changed very soon.) In the case where you have been moving forward for a long time, it is time to keep most of the physical things around largely as they are and focus your main efforts on shifting your thoughts, feelings, and instincts about—your associations with—the physical things that are currently in your life.

It is worthy of note here that if you have been moving forward from having been stagnant for an extended period of time, and you have changed several areas of your life but not all of them, then more physical change might be appropriate. You might already have transformed your career substantially but still be lingering in a relationship that is rooted in old, negative internal dynamics, or vice versa. In these situations, there are more physical things to be changed about your life in order to root everything in your newer, more positive, and healthier internal dynamics.

As your relationship with yourself shifts, it is time to get onto a different road whenever continuing down the same road won't serve you any longer in furthering your growth and development toward your desired destination, and it is time to continue on the same road and simply get more fully aligned with this whenever this supports and enables continued progress toward your desired destination.

The confusing question comes when we find ourselves blaming our current situation—our current relationship partner, career, living situation, etc.—for our lack of progress. If we are blaming, we are likely facing exactly what we need to face in order to learn to stop avoiding issues that we've avoided in the past by shifting the responsibility onto others and external circumstances. In other words, if we are shifting the responsibility onto others, there is something for us to learn about, and shift in, our own internal dynamic, where we ought to take responsibility and set some new destinations. In this case, we are likely in exactly the physical situations we need to be in at this time in order to continue forward toward our desired destinations. However, once we start taking responsibility for our own experiences and setting new, more positive destinations, we might find that it is then time to leave our current physical situation and move into a new one that is rooted in more positive internal dynamics.

Sometimes we need a relationship, career, living situation, or something else to distract us and get us to take our attention and energy away from the other areas of our lives temporarily so that we stop blocking ourselves and allow ourselves to move forward. For example, a relationship—negative or seemingly positive—may be here in part to keep us from focusing so much attention and energy on our career where we may have been struggling with moving forward due to our focusing so much on where we are and how we're not yet where we want to be. As soon as we stop focusing so much on where we are, we can get to where we asked and intended to be going. So the temporary distraction from some other area of our lives can be good in these cases. But these kinds of situations are usually, as mentioned, temporary. Every experience in life is for the purpose of bringing us to greater connection with ourselves and our capacity to create our experiences, where we are more tuned into the real intention and meaning behind what our thoughts, feelings, and instincts are telling us. The relationship, career, etc. that is a distraction is not meant to last but is instead meant to help us move forward however we need to be helped and then to end to make way for a new relationship, career, etc. that is not rooted in distraction but is instead rooted in connection and presence.

So you may be facing a lot of struggles where you are, but the question to ask yourself is: Am I growing and getting closer to my desired destinations as I face and overcome these struggles, or am I avoiding something by staying here that I really need to face in order ever to reach my desired destinations? In other words: Am I struggling to move forward here, or am I struggling to avoid moving forward here? If the struggle is in avoiding the fears and anxieties associated with moving forward, then you should leave and move on and face your fears and overcome them. If the struggle is in continuing forward through facing the fears and obstacles you've avoided in the past in various ways, keep going this direction; you're on the right track, so just keep shifting your internal dynamics to align yourself with continued progress along this road until you get a direction from your internal GPS (if you do) to get off this road and onto another one.

Once you're on the right track toward your destinations, the key is recognizing that everything you're facing is actually helping you forward toward your goals, and is not working against you, except to the degree that you are working against yourself. And even in the cases where other people, the world, your body, and the circumstances of your life are reflecting back how you are working against yourself, these people, the world, your body, and these circumstances are still working for you by helping you to recognize where you are misaligned with yourself and what you need to shift in yourself if you wish to reach your desired destinations. The more you align yourself with your own chosen destinations by looking where you want to go and going where you're looking—so that you're going the same direction with all of your thoughts, feelings, instincts, and behaviors—the more you will recognize everyone and everything in your life as facilitating your progress toward your destinations.

Everyone and everything is working for you. This includes your relationship partner, your friends, your family, your career, your body, food, money, your community, strangers you encounter, etc. Everyone and everything is on your team, helping you toward your goals. And every experience is a message letting you know what the next step is—what the next thing is to address, what the next action is to take. When you recognize this, the journey grows much smoother as you're filled with gratitude and appreciation for the experiences you face along the way, regardless of what they seem on the surface to be.

Follow Actuality, Not Potential

When we get into, or stay in, a relationship or a job or whatever because it seems to have the potential to become something that we want, but it is not yet actually what we want, then we will forever be in a situation where there is the potential for us to have what we want, but no actuality of our having what we want. We must follow actual happiness and fulfillment and not potential happiness and fulfillment if we wish to have actual happiness and fulfillment and not potential happiness and fulfillment.

We must imagine where we want to go, what it would be like actually to have what we want, and then allow ourselves to be guided by that. If our internal GPS then says go into this relationship or this job, we ought to do this. If it says don't go into it, then we ought not to go into it. If it says leave this relationship or this job, we ought to do this. If it says stay, we ought to do this. When we focus on and align ourselves with the actual outcome and experience that we want, then this is what we will get.

If you enter or stay in a relationship or a job or anything else because of the illusion of having what you want, then you will always have nothing more than the illusion of having what you want. If you want to feel connected with someone, don't stay where you don't actually feel connected. If you want to feel like you have security with someone, don't stay with someone with whom you don't actually have security.

The physical world is a mirror of our relationship with ourselves, but our choices about what actual relationship or job or friends we keep in our lives are part of how we might be treating ourselves well or badly. Attachment to a certain relationship with a certain person working out can keep us from following our actual happiness, and therefore from listening to our own thoughts, feelings, and instincts.

There is a lot of variety in the physical world. Anything that you can imagine, you can get. But you can only get it if you are unattached to a certain person or job or thing being the path to what you want. Setting a destination in your GPS and then thinking you've found a house that looks a lot like the one you imagined was your destination and stopping there, despite the fact that your GPS is still telling you to go forward, will not get you to your actual intended destination—just to one that looks in some way like your intended destination. In this case, it is only an illusion that you have arrived at your destination, that this is what you want, and that you should stay here.

So set your destination and follow your internal GPS's directions to you, no matter what. When you listen to and follow the guidance of your own thoughts, feelings, and instincts, you are guaranteed to get what you want.

Follow your actual bliss. Don't follow your potential bliss. Whatever you focus on will become your destination, and so it will become your experience. So focus on and follow what makes you actually happy. Do what makes you genuinely happy. The rest will fall into place from there.

Apologize To Yourself, Let Go Of The Past, And Treat Each Moment As Fresh And New

When you recognize that you haven't been listening to your thoughts, feelings, and instincts, and that you've been treating them badly, apologize to them so that you can start fresh with them rather than building on your past ill-treatment of them. You (from the perspective of your thoughts, feelings, and instincts) will never feel that you're getting what you want from anyone, including yourself, if you're viewing everything in the context of all of the past negative treatment you've gotten from these people.

When someone you know well—a parent, sibling, close friend, relationship partner, etc.—says or does something to you that you don't like, you would probably be inclined to see this as part of a theme that has spanned the entire time you've known this person. From this perspective, it is nearly impossible to recognize that the person may actually be changing, because in any moment that his or her behavior resembles his or her past behavior, you'll be inclined to see this as built on all previous behaviors and dismiss any positive changes since then as anomalies or simply as nothing really significant. It might help if the person were to acknowledge and apologize for how his or her past behaviors may have affected you negatively, and communicate that he or she intends to change for the better and is working on it.

However, no apology from another could come in any form that would be enough for you that you would really believe the person's words and that the person can and is changing until you get such an apology from the person from whom you really want to hear it: yourself.

So apologize to yourself. When you notice yourself being upset or bothered by other people, other circumstances, or yourself, notice that this is actually your thoughts, feelings, and instincts communicating to you. Acknowledge any ill treatment—how you haven't listened, how you've been controlling, how you haven't been reliable, how you haven't paid attention to yourself, how you haven't allowed yourself a place to exist, etc. Say to yourself, "I'm sorry I've made you feel x, y, and z. From here on, I'd love to make you feel a, b, and c, instead," or "I'm sorry for treating you so badly in the past, and I intend to treat you better from here on and I'm working on it." And actually work on it—by focusing on what you actually want to have and have happen in your life and acknowledging and thanking your thoughts, feelings, and instincts as they help you get there.

Without such an acknowledgement and apology to yourself, your thoughts, feelings, and instincts are unlikely to forgive you and let go of how you've treated them before because it will seem that you've never really paid attention to them at all. The result is that at any moment that you slip up and fall into old behaviors and ways of interacting with the world and ultimately with yourself, you will find yourself thinking and feeling that you'll never change—that you haven't really changed and that maybe you can't ever change. And you'll think and feel this about the people around you, too.

Yet this is actually your thoughts and feelings communicating to you that it seems you'll never change because you seem not to have listened to them at all. They won't be thinking and feeling this, and therefore you won't be thinking and feeling this, if you actually acknowledge them and apologize to them and let them know that you'd like to start fresh in each moment, without carrying forward the context of the past.

As you grow and evolve, you want your improvements to be noted. So note them. Give more attention to the positive than the negative. Recognize the positive as increasingly the norm and the negative as increasingly the anomaly. Negative behaviors in yourself and the people around you will seem far less severe and will affect you far less if they are only in the moment—not built on how these people and the entire world and you have treated you in the past. The past is the past. You are going into the future. Bring only the lessons with you, and let go of the negative experiences. So apologize, forgive, and focus on the new, more positive behaviors in yourself and others more than on the old, less positive ones.

It is not where you are in this moment or where you came from that matters other than that the lessons you've learned came from those experiences; ultimately, it is only where you are going that matters. Focus on the general direction you are going. If you are trying at all to focus on where you'd like to be going and to listen to yourself along the way, you are improving, and this is what matters.

Tests And Retests, Gauging Our Progress In The School Of Life

Just before you begin learning something in school, you are often given a test to determine what you know and what you don't know how to approach and address already so that it is clear what needs to be worked on. Then, once you are taught a lesson, you are retested to determine whether you really learned the lesson, what you learned specifically, and what you still need to work on. If you don't pass the test, you approach learning the lessons again in the same or different ways, and then you take another retest to gauge your progress in learning. Once you learn the lesson and you pass the test, you move on to focus on learning the next lesson.

The same is true for learning in the school of life. Once you set a new destination for yourself that is not where you currently are, you need to learn how to navigate the roads between here and there—around, over, and through any obstacles that might be between you and there. First, you take a test to gauge how much and what you are going to need to learn in order to navigate your way to your new destination from where you are. This can often be overwhelming when we are not aware of what is going on, and many times we might simply decide for a while that it's not worth going to this new destination we've set for ourselves if we have to face all of that within ourselves and outside ourselves in order to get there. After you have determined what you do and don't need to work on in order to be able to reach your desired destination, and if you continue to focus on getting to your destination, you begin learning how to approach the problems you didn't know how to approach on the initial test.

The types of problems are broken down so that you learn them one or a couple at a time, so that the problems become manageable. You face thoughts, feelings, and instincts, which, if not addressed inside you when they are first presented to you, become themes that are reflected back outside you in your interactions with other people and the world around you. If you don't know how to address the concern in the initial question in the form of a thought, feeling, and/or instinct that comes up in response to how you are treating yourself, you get to face the issue in a variety of contexts, with different nuances, so that you can really get a grasp of the issue at hand and how to approach it. You face themes in your relationships with other people and the world around you—themes of thoughts, feelings, instincts, etc.—until you learn how to alter these relationship themes within yourself by listening to your own thoughts, feelings, and instincts and treating them differently from the way you have been treating them.

Going through the test questions one by one, you gradually learn all of the lessons that you were tested on in the initial exam of this stage of your life—lessons that often build on previous lessons from earlier stages in your life and even from previous lives. Once you learn all the lessons necessary to reach your intended destination, you reach that destination, bringing into your life the person or people, job, money, body, types of relationships, etc. that you have requested. At this point, you set a new destination, continuing to challenge and improve upon yourself, working toward becoming the best version of yourself possible—a self-aware creator of desired life experiences. Every time you set a new destination, you face an initial test that reveals what you'll need to face and learn in order to reach the new destination, followed by retests that gauge your progress until you reach that destination.

Often, when we are learning a new lesson, we are inclined to revisit past experiences that are related to this lesson (without trying to do so consciously). So, for example, if you are facing issues with feeling unloved, you will find that other experiences in life in which you felt unloved—from previous relationships and so forth—will come up for you to identify the connection and build on your experience repository. This way you can recognize exactly what you are feeling and exactly how you are treating yourself in such a way that you are making yourself feel this way—in this case, unloved. You can, thereby, identify exactly how you are bringing these experiences to yourself with other people and the world around you without having to create and gather as many new experiences like this—in this case, of being unloved—in the present in order to learn how to make yourself feel more positive—in this case, loved—instead.

In other words, if memories of some past experience or experiences are coming up, ask yourself what those experiences made you think, feel, and want, and ask yourself what is making you think, feel, and want the same things in the present. When you recognize the overlap so that you can fully identify and articulate how these experiences are all making you feel, ask yourself how you are making yourself feel this way. Then ask yourself how you would like to feel instead and how you can make yourself feel this new way instead.

So if you are feeling unloved and disconnected in your relationship, and you go back in your memories to times you've felt unloved and disconnected before in previous relationships, and maybe you also go back in your memories to times you've felt loved and connected before, ask yourself what these experiences all have in common. In this case, it is the theme of feeling unloved/loved and disconnected/connected. This theme indicates that you are currently making your own thoughts, feelings, and instincts feel unloved by you and disconnected from you, and maybe that there was a time when you made them feel loved by you and connected to you. Ideally, you would want to recreate, or create for the first time in this life, a situation in which your own thoughts, feelings, and instincts are feeling loved by you and connected to you. This means that you would want to listen to them about what you could be doing right now in order to work toward aims that would make you love who you are and feel connected with yourself.

Whenever you find yourself facing an issue that you thought you had resolved to some degree or simply successfully avoided and left behind in the past, recognize that this is just a retest. The fact is that if you didn't fully alter some dynamic with yourself, or if you only temporarily altered it, you will face it again in yourself and outside yourself at some point in order to alter it fully and more permanently. Many times, we face issues during an initial test and maybe even during retests afterward that we simply weren't ready to address fully at that time. As a result, we skip over that question, move on to the other questions, and then come back to that question when we are more ready to address it. So if you are facing something you thought you'd already addressed or left behind you, just remind yourself that this is a retest coming to you now because you are more equipped to handle the situation better now. You are more prepared to recognize, expand upon, and apply the appropriate lessons you've now learned, and you are gauging, and ideally furthering, your progress in this area.

If you react to a retest by getting discouraged and concluding that you are always going to face this issue because you can't solve or overcome it, and that you are never going to get where you want to go, then you are going to keep facing this issue in the form of retests until you respond to it positively and well. Responding well would mean shifting your internal dynamic with the recognition that this is only coming up now because you have learned relevant lessons and are testing your ability to apply them and expand upon them in a real-world situation. Upon passing the test by responding appropriately, with the awareness that you are equipped to handle this and remain positive, you will reach your destination.

As we learn to recognize the tests and retests of life for what they are and respond to them appropriately, the crazy ups and downs of life are replaced by increasing ups and decreasing, and much less intense, downs. We realize that once we set any destination and find ourselves facing obstacles, these are obstacles on the road toward where we want to go, and we are actually on the verge of something great. So we learn to recognize these challenges as good and positive and come to experience them this way, and then the challenges, themselves, transform.

Life lessons become subtler as we learn to handle them when they are simply presenting themselves to us in the form of soft-speaking thoughts, feelings, and instincts, before they become negative and limiting beliefs, nightmares, and negative life experiences with other people and the world around us. As we learn to cultivate a friendly, compassionate conversation with our own thoughts, feelings, and instincts, where we are really listening to their intentions and intended meanings, we get to learn sweet lessons, relishing in the joy of discovery, the love of ourselves and our accomplishments, and the peace of comfort and quiet control over our life experiences.

When You're Feeling Good, You're Doing The Right Thing

It is as though you are in the driver's seat of a car in neutral, and your feelings are pushing the car from behind and directing your turning of the wheel by telling you whether you're going the right direction or the wrong direction based on where you previously said you wanted to go. If you feel good, they're telling you that you're going the right direction with the focus of your attention and energy based on where you said you wanted to go, and that you should keep doing what you're doing if you want to get there. If you feel bad, they're telling you that you're going the wrong direction with the focus of your attention and energy based on where you said you wanted to go, and that you should do something different if you want to go where you originally intended. Following good feelings will lead to more good feelings. Following bad feelings will lead to more bad feelings.

All you really need to do is set destinations, focus on them, and then distinguish between feelings that are truly and deeply good and feelings that are only superficially good but are actually bad or that are truly bad, and steer toward good feelings. Feelings that are deeply good are the result of our exercise of our positive, attentive, guiding, creative nature as we head in the right direction to get to our desired destinations, where we'll still feel good about our choices in the long run. Feelings that are only superficially, enticingly, or deceptively good are the result of our rebellion against our own control, meaning we're not going the right direction to get to our desired destination and we won't feel good in the long run. Our thoughts, feelings, and instincts get some fleeting pleasure from regaining some control through rebellion when we've been controlling them. But what they really want is for us to allow them to be truly in control as we pay attention to them, take them into account, and work with them consistently as we make our choices and create our life experiences. When they are being treated badly, ignored, dismissed, or tuned out, and they feel that they can't get our attention and don't have any control at all, then we feel bad, meaning we're not going the right direction to get to our desired destination and we're going to feel bad in the long run.

Interestingly, it is easy to get confused about whether we're actually doing the right thing when we feel good and things are just beginning to go as we want them to. When we start getting the results we want, we might find ourselves reacting by feeling like we're doing something wrong, or that we're cheating or something. We might end up thinking and feeling that it shouldn't be so easy, that we've never succeeded in this before and so we can't be succeeding now, and so something must not be right if we seem to be succeeding. When we find ourselves reacting like this, it means that we're not fully aligned with where we're going because we're identifying more with where we've been than with where we're going.

In order to create our lives:

1) We make decisions about where we'd like to go, setting destinations in our internal GPS with our thoughts. Our thought-determined decisions become our destinations.

2) Our feelings then tell us whether we're really identifying with where we're going or not. Our emotion-fueled identifications become our compass and our drive.

3) Our instincts give us specific directions in the moment telling us to go where we've never been before, or to stay where we've been before and things are familiar, in accordance with our thought-determined decisions and our emotion-fueled identifications. Our instinct-driven directions lead us to expand or contract our boundaries and range of movement.

Therefore, in order to get where we're going, we need to address the reactions of our feelings as we go. These reactions are a gauge of whether what we're identifying with is in favor of our reaching our destinations or against this. They are also a gauge of what our identifications, themselves, are. Are we resonating more with who we've been, or with who we are becoming? If the former, we will have to force ourselves forward and we will snap back to where we came from once we let our guard down. If the latter, we will be pulled forward toward where we're going naturally, driven and motivated to get there.

This is so that what we are experiencing becomes aligned again with how we see ourselves and what we believe about who we are and what we experience. This alignment between our experience of the world and our self-image is necessary, so our experiences will always come to resonate with what we choose to believe about ourselves and what we experience. It is up to us to choose to define and redefine ourselves appropriately in accordance with what we would like to be experiencing—so that we can come to believe that this is possible for us and can accept it into our reality, seeing it as the norm rather than as an anomaly in our life experience. When we can view our old experience of life as the anomaly and our new experience of life as the norm, rather than the reverse, we can come to fill our lives with our new, desired experience of them and reach our destination.

Rather Than Saying "No", Say "Yes" To Something Else

Regardless of whether you say "yes" to something or you say "no" to it, you are giving your attention to that thing. Therefore, when you focus on something, it doesn't matter whether you say "yes" or "no"; either way, that is where you will go.

When we say "no", we focus on something and tell ourselves we can't have it or point out something to others and tell them they can't have it. If we stare at a cookie with our eyes or simply in our thoughts and tell ourselves we can't have it or we shouldn't eat it, it requires a lot of extra energy to keep ourselves from eating it. We control, judge, criticize, and generally direct negative energy toward ourselves and others, neglecting ourselves and others, dismissing ourselves and others, tuning out ourselves and others, etc. in order to get ourselves and others to do what we want. We must keep up an ongoing battle internally and externally in order to keep things *not* a certain way.

Saying "no" is like putting up a dam in a river in order to block the flow of the river. This requires a lot of energy constantly in order to keep the river from where we don't want it to be.

When we say "yes" to something other than what we would be saying "no" to in place of saying "no" to that other thing, we focus on something and tell ourselves we can have it or point it out to others and tell them they can have it. Instead of staring at the cookie with our eyes or even merely with our thoughts, we redirect our attention to having a glass of water or a salad or going for a walk or calling a friend. We accept and generally direct positive energy toward ourselves and others, giving ourselves and others due attention, being present, listening, and responding appropriately in order to direct or redirect attention where we want it. We effortlessly and fluidly get things to be a certain way as we align ourselves fully with this, getting ourselves and others entirely on the same page with a clear focus of our and their entire attention and energy on our intended goals and outcomes.

Saying "yes" is like redirecting the flow of the river. We don't have to block the tremendous energy of the flow by saying "no"; we simply have to redirect it by saying "yes" to something else.

We ought never to say "no" to any aspect of ourselves. This will only come back to bite us internally and externally when the dam breaks—as soon as we stop giving enough energy to watching over and disciplining ourselves and others and telling ourselves and others "no". The next time we're stressed and our guard is down, we'll allow all the negative behaviors to which we've said "no" back into our lives. We must listen, accept, and then redirect the flow of the river of our thoughts, feelings, instincts, etc. with a "yes" in another direction. In this way, we can get what we want in ourselves as well as with everyone around us, including significant others, friends, parents, children, pets, etc., without any need for constant attention or effort. There will be no need to build and maintain a dam to block ourselves and others from what we don't want because the energy of the flow will be redirected toward alternative, more desired behaviors as our attention is redirected toward what we do want instead.

Notice that here is where getting ourselves on the same team as ourselves by unifying all parts of ourselves in a common aim comes in. If you want to eat a cookie and you feel you shouldn't, you can ask yourself why you want to eat the cookie. You probably want to feel good or something like that. However, if you feel you shouldn't eat the cookie, then you're not actually going to feel good after you eat it. So then you can ask yourself what you could do now that would really make you feel good and redirect your attention to that behavior instead of continuing to focus on how you want to eat the cookie but shouldn't. Maybe going to the gym or getting your work done will seem more appealing to you after you go through this internal questioning process.

When you're riding a bicycle and you stare at the pole that you don't want to crash into, you'll have to be constantly controlling yourself to try to steer a different direction than you're looking in order not to crash into the pole. Essentially, you aren't giving yourself any options other than to crash into the pole. Alternatively, you could acknowledge where the pole is and then decide where you want to go instead and look there, and then you'll easily steer the direction you actually want to go—clear of the pole, without any controlling, forceful, constantly vigilant energy necessary.

So when you find yourself telling yourself or others "no"—"you can't do this," "you shouldn't do this," "I don't want you to do this," "stop doing this"—ask yourself what you or others *really* want that you or they feel this behavior that you're saying "no" to might get you or them. Recognize that you won't actually feel the way you really want to feel after you engage in this behavior. Ask yourself what you could do that would actually or more likely make you feel this way. And then focus your attention on this new behavior instead, now that there is no part of you that is telling you to do something else because every part of you recognizes that this new behavior is what would really get you what you want, ultimately.

You can go through the same questioning process with other people when you find that you're not agreeing with them. Ask them what they really want that they think this action or behavior will get them. Then ask them if they really believe that they'll get this from this action or behavior. And then ask them what action or behavior might better help them get what they really want.

So, when you find yourself saying "no" or feeling drawn to do or want something that you feel on some level you can't or shouldn't have or want or do, ask yourself:

1. What do I really want that I believe this behavior (or person or thing or whatever) is going to get me? or What do I really want to feel that I'm looking to this to make me feel?
2. Will I really get this from this behavior (or person or thing or whatever)? or Will I really feel this way after I do this or get this?
3. What could I do now that would really get me what I want, ultimately? or What could I do now that would really make me feel the way I want to feel, ultimately?
4. Then, focus the energy and attention of your thoughts, feelings, desires, and actions on what would really get you what you want or make you feel the way you want to feel, ultimately.

Essentially, every option available to you is an actual option, and every option will have its pros and cons if you choose it. The goal is to recognize every option as acceptable on some level—as an actual *choice* that you can *choose*—so that there is no control or judgment or criticism or "discipline" in the picture, and then to choose the option that would better or best get you what you really want. Then, since you won't be controlling yourself and feeling the need to rebel against that control, you will be able to feel free to choose anything equally and will be more inclined to choose what will better get you what you want.

Whenever you notice yourself not wanting to be doing what you're doing, ask yourself what you really want. If you don't want the results that this behavior will get you, or you could simply get more desirable results from some other behavior instead, then perhaps you might really want to engage in an alternative behavior that would get you more desirable results.

However, if you want the results that doing this will get you, then what you really want might very well be to enjoy doing what you're doing—to enjoy the process—rather than not to be doing it. This applies to going to the gym, school, dating, and anything else we might approach feeling internal resistance, reluctance, or dread. We should never do anything from the thought or feeling that we *have* to (or *should* or *need* to)—with the only possible exception being shifting our internal place to one of alignment with being present where we are, so that we aren't acting from a place of internal control after this shift. It would be to our benefit first to take a moment and consider why we might actually *want* to choose to do—in terms of the results it will get us—what we are feeling we *have* to do. Then we can go into that activity on the same page as ourselves and feeling good and present, without resistance or rebellion that would make for an unpleasant, not-present experience.

When you are considering what you really want, ultimately, and how you can actually get it, remember that you are setting the example for how you will treat others and be treated by others in the way you treat yourself. If you listen to yourself and do what you really want yourself to do, so will others. If you disregard, dismiss or ignore yourself, or you tune yourself out, or you don't do what you believe you should do, or you do what you believe you should do but with internal resistance and from a place of feeling controlled, so will others. If you make better choices for yourself, you encourage others to do the same by the example you set for them. Your words toward other people will mean to them nothing other than the thoughts, feelings, desires, and actions they are accompanied by. Keep this in mind when you consider where you invest your attention internally and externally.

Connecting The Dots And Creating Trends

Any two points create a line, and so at any moment, you can call upon any two or more experiences and conclude that things are getting better in one or more areas of your life, or that things are getting worse in those same areas of your life. It is up to you whether you "discover", and thereby *create*, a positive trend—which will lead to more positive developments in that area—or a negative trend—which will lead to more negative developments in that area.

No matter how bad or good things get, it is always possible to find two or more experiences—however small or large—that suggest improvement, and two or more experiences that suggest deterioration. Whatever you bring the magnifying glass of your attention to, you will make bigger in your experience. The dots you choose to connect will turn into a line that continues beyond this moment with more experiences to support your conclusion of a trend or pattern.

We never simply predict the future; we are constantly in the process of creating that which we anticipate happening. Notice what you rehearse in your mind and emotions about how a conversation with your partner or parents or friend or boss or client will go. Notice how you call upon previous experiences to conclude that the conversation will go like the last one, go worse than the last one, or go better than the last one. Remember: You can look to your present and previous experiences with the physical world for how future experiences with it will go, but when you do this, you are simply looking to what you have created before with your internal dynamics, and with where you focused your attention, for what will happen in the future, and you are thereby creating a future that looks like your past. You are always creating what you are giving your energy and attention to. What you anticipate and "predict" will become true.

Therefore, there is no need to look to the past or the present for what the future will be. Whatever *was* need no longer *be*. Simply learn from the past and the present about how to create a better future, and choose to experience the future you would ideally like to experience—regardless of what your experience of the present or past might be. Imagine and rehearse in your mind the future you would like to live in, look for experiences in your past and present and in other people's pasts and presents that help you to believe that this future experience is possible for you, and listen to your internal GPS system as it guides you toward that reality.

Commit To Being Where You Are

Our essence is the ability to choose. So we feel most fully alive and connected with ourselves when we choose. However, whenever we live in alternative versions of the present with frustration about the way things are as the result of choices we are making, or in the past with regret about choices we made that we feel we shouldn't have made or should have made differently, or in the future with anxiety about where we'll end up since we're not trusting in our capacity to make good choices for ourselves and others, we are not actually decisively choosing anything. We need to choose something and commit to it. We need to be decisively and fully where we are in order to enjoy where we are. This applies to everything.

If you are living but there is a part of you that is questioning whether you should keep living and is considering the possibility of giving up on life, then you are not fully deciding to live and committing to making life the best it can possibly be. If you are in a relationship but there is a part of you that is questioning whether you should stay in it and is considering the possibility of giving up on it, then you are not fully deciding to be in the relationship and committing to making the relationship truly fulfilling. If you are on a career path but there is a part of you that is questioning whether you should stay on it and is considering the possibility of giving up on it, then you are not fully deciding to be on this career path and committing to achieving success on this career path.

You cannot half-heartedly do something that means anything to you and succeed. You cannot have one foot in and one foot out of where you are and actually have things turn out as you'd like.

You cannot get yourself fully aligned with anything unless you make decisive choices about where you want to be in the future, accept your past choices that led you to where you are, and choose decisively in the present and commit to your choices so that you can live fully where you are, really make the best of it, and move forward toward your desired destinations. Your goal should be to decide where you want to be, set clear destinations for yourself, learn from the past about what not to do and what to do in order to reach these destinations, and then make decisions about what actions to take in the present moment based on where you want to get to and what your thoughts, feelings, and instincts stemming from your intuition tell you that you need to do in order to get there. Basically, plug clear destinations into your internal GPS by deciding what you'd like to be experiencing and imagining how it would be to be experiencing that, and then look to the past for lessons and follow your internal guidance in the present to get to your destinations.

No matter what you decide, commit to your decision in the moment. Indecisiveness leads to being never fully anywhere, and if you are never fully anywhere, you cannot learn from where you are and move forward. You cannot get directions from your GPS toward anywhere if you don't even acknowledge your present location in the first place. So decide to be where you are right now, figure out where you'd like to be in the future, and start making definitive decisions. You can always change your direction once you're moving, but it's much harder to get started from a standstill. So get moving, and refine your direction as you go. You'll discover more of what you want on the way there, you'll add that to your GPS, you'll listen for the directions about what choices to make in each next moment, and you'll get there.

Remember, the directions will come in the moment you need them. That's how your internal GPS system works. You plug in the destination, you listen to the directions, and you act on the directions. It doesn't help at all to doubt that you're in the right place and question whether you should have made a different turn back there or should be on a different road now or whether you'll ever get to your desired destination. You have an infallible GPS system within you—the best that could ever be created. Use it, trust in it, recognize that it will always recalculate if you make any wrong turns because you weren't listening to it for any reason (and so just keep listening for its new directions in the moment you're in and act on them when you hear them), and you'll always be where you want to be and get where you want to go—infallibly, guaranteed.

Often, the most challenging path is the one that we really ought to be taking. This is where the greatest potential for growth exists. But this is also where we are most inclined to be trying to find ways out that are easier—where we don't have to face our own internal obstacles and be stretched beyond our comfort zone. Keep this in mind when you're making your decisions about where you want to be. There's no easy way out. The goal is to commit to facing everything about ourselves and where we really want to go and what we really need to do to get there—all of the obstacles that we may have been avoiding. In other words, we really need to commit to our own growth and advancement, learn how to overcome and navigate the obstacles along the hard way—where the challenges are—and then this becomes the most fulfilling path to travel.

You've Got To Do This. No, You *Get* To Do This: How To Get Done And Enjoy Getting Done What You Want Done

When we tell ourselves that we have to do something, or that we should do something, or that we need to do something, we simply rebel against the fact that we seemingly aren't being given any choice in the matter. When you tell another person—a child, your partner, or whomever—that he/she has to do something, you're likely to get resistance. When you force anyone or anything to do something, you're not going to get the results you want easily or harmoniously.

The ultimate essence of everything in this world is choice. We are not meant to have our ability to choose taken away from us. We operate best when we have a choice and we're doing something that we have had a say in and have chosen to do. Then we are motivated. Then we feel good about doing whatever we're doing. When we are told what to do—whether by someone else or by ourselves—we will want to do something else instead in order to regain some kind of control in the situation.

For example, if you are telling yourself that you've got to go to the gym, you are not likely to go to the gym. You are going to feel forced, and so you are going to rebel and do something else. Further, if you do end up getting yourself to go to the gym through sheer discipline, you are going to be even more reluctant to go to the gym next time. And you're certainly not going to enjoy it if you do go. Basically, you're not including your thoughts, feelings, and instincts in the decision-making process and you're not listening to them, and so they will not support you in your actions. They will actually be working against you—resisting going to the gym more every time, making the whole experience very unpleasant, and making your associations with going to the gym increasingly negative—because you didn't communicate with them and listen to them.

The problem with telling yourself (or anyone or anything) to do something, and thereby including force and control, is that when we feel the need to apply force like this, it is only because we are not actually aligned with things happening the way we'd like. When we say to ourselves, "I have to do this," what we are really saying is, "I don't want to do this, but I have to." When we say to another person, "You have to do this," what we are really saying is, "I don't believe you're actually going to do this, and so I feel the need to force you to and tell you that you have to." In these situations, we are looking one way, thereby telling our thoughts, feelings, and instincts that this is where we want to be guided, and then we are trying to force ourselves and the people and the world around us to go a different direction than we're looking and thus directing us and them to go.

Whenever we look one way and go another way, plugging one destination into our GPS system and then heading toward another one, we put ourselves in a situation where have to ignore, dismiss, and tune out all of the directions coming from our own internal GPS as our thoughts, feelings, and instincts faithfully guide us toward where we asked them to guide us to. In this way, we set up negative internal dynamics that involve control, rebellion, and disharmony, which are reflected outside of us as we demonstrate by example that this is how we'd like to be treated by everyone and everything around us. Creating situations where we are actively inclined not to listen to ourselves is the source of our problems, and we can witness and come to recognize the first sign of greater difficulties to come (in the form of relationship issues, health issues, financial issues, etc.) in unpleasant experiences that we reluctantly push ourselves through or rebel against altogether.

You will never want to do something or feel like doing something or really and fully think it's a good idea to do something that entailed your not listening to your wants, feelings, and thoughts last time you did it. This is why any experience that is stressful (meaning where we are not listening to ourselves) makes us not want to go anywhere near having such an experience again. Our thoughts, feelings, and instincts steer us toward situations where we've listened to them before and away from situations where we haven't listened to them before. If we tune them out while we're with a certain person, we will not want to be around that person. If we dismiss them while we're exercising, we will not want to exercise. If we ignore them while we're at work, we will not want to go to work. In all of these situations, we will create real conflicts, exhaustion, sickness, and other great actual reasons not to do what we are not wanting to do if we don't simply redirect to what we do want instead, even if this is simply to enjoy doing what we intend to do.

We suck all of the enjoyment out of our activities and lives when we tell ourselves that we have to do things and don't listen to ourselves when we're clearly resisting this approach. We might enjoy writing or some other activity, but once we tell ourselves that we have to do it for school or for work or to make money or because someone else said so or for any other reason, we are not going to enjoy it and we are going to want to do almost anything else instead in order to avoid it. We might enjoy eating, but if we tell ourselves that we have to eat for some reason, the food will become tasteless and eventually our bodies will resist taking in the food and digesting it properly. We might enjoy running or going to the gym, but as soon as we tell ourselves that we have to do so in order to exercise or lose weight or make use of a gym membership, the whole experience becomes a chore that we have to drag ourselves through, and eventually we end up tired, sick, with physical pains, scheduling conflicts, or something else so that we have a good reason not to go. If we just keep dragging ourselves through the chores we've created for ourselves, pushing through and ignoring the psychological resistance, we will create actual physical circumstances in our bodies and surroundings and in the words and actions of the people around us that will support this internal resistance as our thoughts, feelings, and instincts try to get our attention and let us know that we're not working with them.

The solution is to change the way you suggest a possible plan of action to yourself. Instead of saying something like "I should go to the gym," or "I need to go to the gym," or "I've got to go to the gym," tell yourself, "It would be nice to go to the gym," or "I would really like to enjoy going to the gym," or "I would love to love going to the gym," or even "I get to go to the gym." This way, you are suggesting something to yourself rather than telling yourself to do something. As a result, you now make your thoughts, feelings, and instincts feel like they have a choice in the matter. You give them a say. So when they choose to support you, they'll actually have freely chosen this and be on board with your actions.

Suggest something and then listen to your thoughts, feelings, and instincts and see what they have to say about it. If they like it, do it. If they don't, hear them out and respond to their points, and only go forward once they're all in agreement with you that this is a good idea. Often, all it takes is a change in your approach to suggesting a destination to yourself—and therefore ultimately to your thoughts, feelings, and instincts.

Imagine that your thoughts, feelings, and instincts are like children. You tell them: "We've got to go to the supermarket now." Their response: "I don't want to go. I want to go to the park instead!" Alternatively, you tell them: "We get to go to the supermarket now!" Their response: "Yay! We're going to the supermarket!"

When you tell yourself, "I get to do this," rather than "I've got to do this," you suggest to yourself that you have an opportunity here, that it is a privilege that you get to do this, that you have a choice. You *get* to do this. This means that your body is able to do this, that your mind is capable of this, that you have the time, that you have the money, that you have the power, that you have the choice available to you.

Come up with creative ways to suggest possibilities to yourself and get yourself excited about them in place of telling yourself to do things where you dread them and drag your feet. If saying to, and acting toward, little children what you're saying to, and the way you're acting toward, yourself wouldn't get the results you want, then alter your wording and approach. If treating little children the way you're treating yourself would get them enthusiastically and excitedly on board with doing what you want them to do, then you're on the right track in the way you're treating yourself. When you give your thoughts, feelings, and instincts a say, and you really listen to them, modifying your approach accordingly, they will support you and help you out, and you can go about every aspect of every day feeling energized, excited, in control, and loving everything that you get to do and every moment that you have the privilege to experience.

The Importance Of The Journey

In regard to long-term goals, once you set a good destination for yourself by focusing on where you want to go and imagining what you'd like to experience when you get there, the next step is to set a good destination in regard to your experience of the journey toward that destination. If you get too caught up in negativity about the necessity of the journey, focusing on how you want to be at your destination already and aren't, you'll never get where you'd like to be going. So it is important to set the destination that you enjoy the journey.

For example, if you want to find a great relationship for you, you might first set some destinations in regard to this: "I would love to find someone with whom I feel closely connected and who feels closely connected to me, to whom I am irresistibly attracted and who is irresistibly attracted to me, whom I love and who loves me, with whom I feel fulfilled and who feels fulfilled with me."

If you try to find a relationship, but you are focusing during your search on the loneliness and incompletion of *not having* a relationship, you will never find the relationship you want because your destination will be something like, "I'm lonely and incomplete because I don't have someone to share my life with. I'm still searching for the right person." In this case, you will sabotage your relationship search without even realizing how by acting in ways that make it clear that you are not in a relationship and are not ready for one. You will do this so that you will successfully reach your destination of still not having a relationship and wanting one, and feeling lonely and incomplete because of this.

So, you would probably want to set some destinations about the process of getting to this relationship: "I would love to enjoy the dating process. I would love to feel fulfilled in every aspect of my life and complete within myself on the way to finding the right person for me. It would be so nice to feel intensely connected and present to myself and everyone around me in every moment."

If you want to lose weight and sculpt your ideal body, you might first set some destinations in regard to this: "I would love to feel comfortable and confident in my body. I would love to love how I look and feel in my body, in my clothes, and in my life. I would love to fit into all the right clothes, all the right relationships, and all the right places."

If you try to get to your ideal weight, but you are focusing during the entire process on your frustration with *not being* at your ideal weight yet, you will never reach your ideal weight because your destination will be something like, "I still have weight to lose and I'm frustrated about this." In this case, if you get close to your ideal weight, you will likely struggle with losing any further weight, and you will possibly even sabotage your weight loss by reverting to old behaviors and gaining weight again. You will do this so that you will successfully reach your destination of still having weight to lose and being frustrated about this.

So, you would probably want to set some destinations about the process of getting to your ideal body: "I would love to enjoy the process of sculpting my ideal body. I would love to love how I look and feel in my body and in my life even more every day. It would be so amazing to experience my body increasingly taking on the perfect shape and form."

If you want to write a successful book, you might first set some destinations in regard to this: "It would be so great to be publishing and selling my book. It would be fantastic to be able to share my ideas with others in written form. I would feel so accomplished and like I created something important. It would be awesome to see my book selling and hear positive feedback from people who've read my book and appreciated and benefited from it."

If you try to get to your finished, published, successful book, but you are focusing during the entire process on your *wanting it done already*, you will never get your successful book because your destination will be something like, "I want a successful book and I don't have one yet." Depending on the specifics of your internal speech, you will either a) never finish writing the book because if you were to finish it, it could be successful, and this wouldn't fit your destination of not yet having a successful book, or b) write and finish several books but not have any of them be successful, so that you can still reach your destination of wanting a successful book and not having one yet.

So, you would probably want to set some destinations about the process of getting to the completion and publication of this successful book: "I would love to enjoy writing my book. I would love the ideas to flow to me and through me easily and effortlessly, always coming out in the perfect words. I would love to enjoy watching my book take form before me, growing closer and closer to completion."

Since our focus of attention every step of the way toward our ideal destinations determines a destination in itself—one that can contradict or reinforce our ultimate intended destination—it is important that we focus on enjoying the process and making progress. The journey toward our destination must never be dismissed as unimportant, as bad, or as something that we wish didn't exist unless we don't actually wish to reach our destination. Therefore, there is no place for giving our energy to the idea that we just want to "get through," "get by," "get something over with," or "get something done."

It is not that it would be better if we were already where we want to be. It is that it would be better if we were to enjoy the process of traveling to where we want to be. For this is the only way to get there, since we must be internally resonant with being there in order to get there. As we enjoy the process, we note our progress and keep making progress, and as we note our progress and keep making progress, we enjoy the process, and this keeps us motivated and moving forward toward our destination. This is as opposed to focusing on how we're not at our desired destination yet, which only discourages us and demotivates us and keeps us from getting there.

So set your intended destination and then determine how you'd like to experience the journey there so that you are resonant with getting there every step of the way and truly progressing.

If life were all about the destination, we'd all just kill ourselves. The point obviously isn't to get where we're going externally. It is to enjoy the journey by living internally where we want to be during the entire way. So set some destinations for the journey: "I would love to appreciate and enjoy every small success and every large success. I would love to feel productive and like I'm moving forward every step of the way. I would love to love traveling the journey of life in every moment of every day."

Interpreting Your Thoughts, Feelings, And Instincts: From Directions, To Attention-Seeking, To Escape-Seeking When You Don't Listen

Whenever your thoughts, feelings, and/or instincts are overly repetitive or insistent about something, this means they are trying to get your attention when they haven't been getting it. This usually means you focused on where you didn't want to go, then you ignored, dismissed, tuned out, or missed a direction they gave you as they were guiding you toward that destination, and then you identified with them when they reacted to this and you did what they said they needed to do instead of providing them what they said they wanted.

For example, if they are saying that they want to connect with you and get your attention, and you seek to connect with, and get attention from, other people, they will get more insistent about wanting to connect with you and get your attention, and will likely escalate to saying they feel disconnected and lonely and like they can't connect with anyone. If they are saying that they want to feel accepted by you and included in your choices and actions, and you seek to be accepted by, and included in, a group or community, they will get more insistent that they want to be accepted by you and included by you, and will likely escalate to saying they feel rejected and excluded and like they don't belong anywhere. If they are saying that they are hungry for your attention, and you eat and stuff them out, they will get more insistent that they are hungry for your attention, and will likely escalate to saying that they're starving. If they are saying that they are tired of trying to get your attention, and you just complain that you're tired or you try to sleep more, they will get more insistent that they are tired of, and will likely escalate to saying that they're exhausted from, trying to get your attention.

Notice, however, that even the beginning of each of these examples is already a step away from what is really being asked of you in terms of what you need to do to get to your desired destination. The connection-seeking, inclusion-seeking, attention-seeking behaviors from your thoughts, feelings, and instincts are all the beginning of rebellion against you for missing something they were trying to say to you and therefore for seemingly simply trying to control them and tell them what to do without regard for what they want and are saying. The next level of rebellion after this, if they still aren't getting your attention, is escape-seeking behaviors.

When you plug a destination into your internal GPS with the focus of your attention—giving your energy to a thought, a feeling, an instinct, an experience of any sort—your responsive thoughts, feelings, and instincts guide, help, and direct you toward this destination. Whenever you miss a direction they give you, they begin to say things like, "I feel like I'm not connected with you and I want to connect with you and for you to connect with me," "I feel unaccepted and excluded by you and I want to be accepted and included in your decisions," "I am hungry for your attention," "I am tired of trying to get your attention," and so forth. At this point, everything they're saying ultimately means, "I feel like I'm not getting your (positive) attention and I want your (positive) attention," and they're saying this because you didn't pay attention to them when they were directing you to where you asked them to direct you to. By ignoring, dismissing, and tuning out some direction they gave you toward the destination you indicated to them, you've left them feeling lacking and longing. And so you end up feeling the growing desire and sense of lack and unfulfillment that they are experiencing as they seemingly futilely try to get your attention.

When you get to this point, your thoughts, feelings, and instincts will try pretty much anything, with increasing escalation, to get your attention. Whatever works, they'll do, because they couldn't get your attention when they did what you seemingly asked of them with the focus of your attention. You gave them a destination and a direction to get your attention, and they tried following your directions and that didn't work, so now they'll react, judge, criticize, complain, rebel, and get negative, dramatic, and even outlandish in an effort to get your attention. Again, just like children who did what you asked but didn't get any positive reinforcement or even acknowledgement for doing what you asked of them, your thoughts, feelings, and instincts will now begin to do things that you don't really want them doing because they'll try anything to get your attention if they're not getting it.

This might seem like an overreaction when you don't understand what they're going through, but you're reacting the same way as other people are treating you as you're treating your own thoughts, feelings, and instincts. And you're doing this because you feel unacknowledged, not listened to, not included, misunderstood, criticized, judged, unaccepted, and generally ignored, dismissed and tuned out when you're being told what to do or forced to do something and are apparently being disregarded as your thoughts, feelings, and instincts aren't being considered. That's how you're making your thoughts, feelings, and instincts feel—however other people and circumstances are making you feel, thereby following your example in regard to how you seem to want to be treated because that's the way you're treating yourself.

So if your thoughts, feelings, and instincts direct you to sit down and write, or go to the gym, or go for a run, or meditate, or go to sleep, or eat, or hang out with people, or call someone, or act on an opportunity, or whatever as they guide you to where you said that you wanted to be, toward an experience that you asked to have, listen to them and act on them. Otherwise, respond to them and redirect them to a new destination. But don't simply do something else and disregard them. Don't simply tell yourself that you have to do something without suggesting this course of action to your thoughts, feelings, and instincts and giving them a say based on what you've asked of them before and responding to them kindly and appropriately.

When you tell yourself that you need to do something but you don't want to do it, your thoughts, feelings, and instincts try to help you not do it by distracting you with other things, since this is what you're asking of them. Of course, then you're inclined to ignore and dismiss them and tune them out since they're not helping you focus on what you feel you need to do.

In essence, what is happening here is that you initiate the interaction by just telling your thoughts, feelings, and instincts what you're going to do without giving them any say in the matter. Then your thoughts say something like, "I don't think so," your feelings say something like, "I don't feel like it," and your instincts say something like, "I don't want to." And you ignore them and keep forcing them forward with you as you disregard their resistance to being told that they have to do something and that they have no choice in the matter.

So they react by saying things like, "I feel lonely and disconnected," "I feel unaccepted and like I don't belong anywhere," "I feel hungry," "I feel tired," etc. You are missing what they're really saying and meaning at this point and failing to respond appropriately if you are either a) continuing to force yourself to do what you feel you need to do—without considering why you actually want to do what you're doing in terms of the results you believe it will get you and setting the destination that you enjoy doing it—or b) identifying with your thoughts, feelings, and instincts and seeking out connection with or acceptance by others, or eating or sleeping, or whatever. If you continue to miss what they're really saying and meaning and you fail to acknowledge them and respond appropriately, then your thoughts, feelings, and instincts will escalate in what they're saying. They'll start saying things like, "I'm frustrated with you," "I'm angry at you," "I regret doing what I did," "I wish things happened differently," "I'm worried about where I'm headed and what's going to happen," "I feel like I don't have any control," "I feel like I don't have a purpose," "I feel like I don't have any direction," and then things like, "I need a break," "I can't stand this anymore," "I can't handle this anymore," "I want to escape," "I want to be somewhere else," "I want to leave," "I want to get out of here," "I want to break up with you," and then things like, "I want to die," "I want to kill you," etc.

If you notice that your thoughts, feelings, and instincts are getting more insistent about something or are escalating to worse things, and you are feeling negativity of any sort in relation to anything, take a moment to listen to what they're saying to you. However, once you hear what they're saying, listen to what they're saying behind what they're saying. In other words, acknowledge and respond to (and apologize for) what you've been making them experience, and then ask and listen to what they were saying before they were saying that they wanted to get your attention and then that they wanted to escape from you.

So, for example, let's say you said you wanted to be in a harmonious, fulfilling relationship. In this case, your thoughts, feelings, and instincts might direct you to work on building your career because you've previously said that you really wanted to do this and you've seemingly made this a prerequisite to your being satisfied in life, let alone in a relationship. If you consequently tell yourself that you have to (or need to or should) build your career first, then you will be forcing your thoughts, feelings, and instincts to do something, leading to their rebellion, rather than directing them to help you out, which would lead to their support. The result is that they'll give you some direction seemingly in regard to avoiding building your career simply because they want to get your attention and regain some control. Instead of listening to what they're really saying, you will likely identify with them and avoid building your career. Perhaps they say something about feeling lonely and disconnected and wanting to connect with you. If you then seek connection with another person rather than building your career, you are disregarding your thoughts, feelings, and instincts, and so they will get more insistent that they feel lonely and disconnected and like they can't connect with anyone and perhaps even like no one's there for them.

At this point, you need to peel back the layers to understand where all this negativity is coming from and hear what's really being communicated to you. This is how you do this:

First, ask yourself what you're experiencing. Answer: "I feel lonely and disconnected and like I can't connect with anyone and like no one's there for me."

Next, acknowledge that while other people and circumstances might be supporting and reinforcing this experience for you, this experience ultimately originated with you. In other words, you are making yourself experience this. So then ask yourself, "How have I been making myself feel this way?" Answer: "I haven't been giving myself the positive attention that I've been wanting and taking the actions that would get me to where I actually want to go." In other words, "My thoughts, feelings, and instincts have been directing me to do something that I haven't been doing. I said I wanted to be, do, or have something—to experience something—and they told me what I need to do to get there, and I missed a direction or perhaps even blatantly didn't listen to them, and they would like my attention again so that they can help me toward where I asked to go."

In this case, you've just begun to focus on the destination of feeling lonely and disconnected and like you can't connect with anyone and like no one's there for you. So you probably want to redirect this and say something like, "I would love to feel connected and complete and like I can connect with other people and feel close to someone."

In order to reach this destination, you must align yourself with it by connecting with yourself. In other words, in order to feel connected with anyone or anything else, you would first need to connect with your own thoughts, feelings, and instincts and allow them to connect with you. This requires that you get back to paying attention to them and kindly ask them what you missed—what they've been saying to do that you haven't been doing. "What should I be doing that I am not doing? What did you direct me to do that I missed?"

If you stay present to them and ask them this, they will tell you the answer soon after you ask and let go of the question, and it is just up to you to listen. Either the answer will simply pop into your head, or someone will call or say something to you, or you'll be inclined to pick up the phone and call someone or to pick up a certain book and start reading or to look at your email or to turn on the television or whatever. Just be open to the answer coming from anyone or anywhere—from your own words or advice to someone, or someone else's words or advice to you, or from some event that catches your attention and stands out to you or bothers you or something else altogether. In this case, you'll be directed back to building your career so that you can feel connected to yourself again and feel fulfilled and then bring a relationship marked by harmonious connection and fulfillment into your life, either in the form of a relationship you're in or in the form of a new relationship, depending on the circumstances.

Recognize that what you missed is often related to how you are approaching what you're doing. Ask yourself what you've been telling yourself that you need to do or have to do or should be doing. That's probably where you actually want to be spending your time, in the ideal (and is therefore the root of all of this). However, you've been controlling, forcing, and micromanaging yourself in the way you're wording this to yourself. Remember, when you say you have to do something, you are going to get feedback from your thoughts, feelings, and instincts that they (you) don't want to. If you don't listen to them, here, their resistance escalates into rebellion in the form of attention-seeking and then escape-seeking behaviors. Even if you are not saying directly that you have to do something—which could actually involve focus on where you truly want to go, and what you'd truly like to do, physically, and simply not on the experience you'd like to have of this—you are, in some other way, focusing on where you don't want to be going, which is leading you to be inclined to try not to listen to your internal guidance as it directs you there.

You might even flat out be threatening yourself by telling yourself the bad things that will happen if you don't do what you need to do—"I have to do this or else this terrible thing will happen"—which is obviously a bad idea for many reasons. Here, you're focusing on where you don't want to go, controlling yourself, threatening yourself, and setting the stage for you to treat other people this way and for all of this to come back to you through your experiences with other people and the world around you.

Or you might simply be giving energy to your frustrations, regrets, or fears without necessarily telling yourself to do anything other than be frustrated, regretful, or afraid, where you are plugging these destinations into your GPS and then are inclined to do your best to avoid following the directions as your GPS guides you there. Usually once we notice the negative thoughts, feelings, and instincts coming up in us in reaction to our going the wrong direction, we add control into the picture, telling ourselves we have to do certain things in order to try to make it so that those bad things that we anticipate happening don't actually happen. This is the shift from identifying with our thoughts, feelings, and instincts, which have no control when we're controlling them, to identifying with the controlling initiator of the interaction. The next step is to learn to listen and guide by plugging in a new, positive destination, rather than ignoring and controlling as we keep the same negative destination plugged in and just try to avoid going there.

Wherever you're focusing in any way on where you don't want to go, change your approach. Change the focus of your attention so that you are looking where you want to go and are therefore actually aligned with going where you really want to go. Then the directions you get from your thoughts, feelings, and instincts will be directions you will be inclined to follow, and so you'll be less inclined to ignore or dismiss them or tune them out. As you give your thoughts, feelings, and instincts your positive attention, the result is that they'll feel connected, accepted and like they belong, satiated, energized, content and fulfilled where they are, etc. And so you will, too.

So remember, repetition and insistence from your thoughts, feelings, and instincts means you missed something and they're trying to get your attention and feeling like they're not getting it. So don't act on their insistent words. Give them the attention they want—connect with them, include them in your decisions and actions, feed them and energize them *with your positive attention.* Reset your positive, desired destinations if you've been focusing your attention on not having, being, doing, or experiencing what you want. And ask your thoughts, feelings, and instincts what you missed and would like to be doing (that you haven't been doing) in order to reach your desired destinations, including mainly where you've been controlling and would benefit from being guiding instead. Then listen for the answer in whatever form and through whatever means or messenger it comes. (And keep in mind that the answer will have something to do with changing how you're speaking to yourself and approaching what you're doing in regard to what you've been telling yourself you really should be doing or have to be doing, or in some other way with shifting the focus of your attention from where it has been on where you don't want to go to where you actually do want to go.)

Further, get back to listening to your thoughts, feelings, and instincts regularly as they continue to guide you forward in each moment toward the destinations you've indicated to them with the focus of your attention. And, of course, be sure that you are focusing on where you actually want to go as you go forward, and not on where you don't want to go, or are afraid of going, or have been and don't want to be anymore.

Wherever you focus your attention, your thoughts, feelings, and instincts will guide you toward that experience. So look where you want to go, and be sure to listen. And if you recognize that you haven't been listening and giving them your positive attention, apologize to them and ask them what you missed. They will gladly tell you as long as you are kind and attentive to them and you listen.

Distinguishing Rebellion From Direct Guidance Toward Your Desired Destinations That You Would Benefit From Acting On

We've discussed how everything your thoughts, feelings, and instincts say is about them when they say "I" and about you when they say "you". We've also discussed how everything your thoughts, feelings, and instincts say about other people or anything else is actually about you, as well. It's as though they're saying, "I couldn't get your attention when I told you this about you directly, so I'll speak about someone else instead and hope you get the message at some point that it's really about you." However, if everything your thoughts, feelings, and instincts say about anyone or anything is really about you and what you've been making them experience and think, feel, and want in regard to you, the question arises: When do you take physical action outside yourself?

If everything your thoughts, feelings, and instincts say after you've missed their directions toward the destination you focused on is ultimately really communicating that they want to get your attention or to escape from you because they haven't been getting your attention, then what does a direction sound like and how can you recognize it when it comes?

Once you plug a destination into your internal GPS with the focus of your attention, your thoughts, feelings, and instincts will provide you guidance, help, and directions toward that destination. These directions come in the form of subtle messages. "It would be good to eat now." "It would be good to get to bed soon." "It would be good to be part of the group now." "It would be good to call this particular person now." "It's time to move on from this relationship." In other words, at this point, and in this form, your thoughts, feelings, and instincts can actually be telling you something about someone or something outside yourself and mean to be referring to that other person or thing and not to you.

When we miss these directions about external actions that we should take in relation to the world around us and other people, we get increasingly insistent, repetitive, negative messages from our thoughts, feelings, and instincts. "You're not listening to me." "I'm hungry." "I'm starving." "I'm tired." "I'm exhausted." "I feel left out." "I feel like I don't belong anywhere." "I feel disconnected and lonely." "There's no one out there for me." "Everything is lacking and incomplete because there's no one to share it with." "I want to leave." "I want to break up with you." "I want to die." "I want to kill you." Insistent, repeating, intense, dramatic messages like these are always to us and about us, and we should not be acting on these externally but instead should give our thoughts, feelings, and instincts the attention that they're asking for.

Alternatively, when we have been doing a good job of willfully setting positive destinations by looking where we want to go, and of listening to and acting on the directions we've been getting from our thoughts, feelings, and instincts on the way there, we get another kind of insistent, repetitive message from our thoughts, feelings, and instincts. This kind is positive: "I love you." "I'm so happy." "I am content." "I feel so connected." "I am complete." "I feel energized." "I feel like I belong here." "I feel like I'm part of everything." "I feel so awake." "I feel so alive." "I have everything I want in this moment."

When you find words repeating in your mind, listen. They are about you. And they are for you.

Therefore: Listen to subtle, positive-oriented directions and act on them. Recognize overly insistent and repetitive messages as calls for, or announcements that you've been giving, your positive attention, and give, or keep giving, your thoughts, feelings, and instincts your positive attention rather than acting on these messages. Then, once you get a subtle, positive-oriented, actionable direction again, act on this.

Getting Other People To Do What You Want Them To Do

You can't easily or reliably get other people to do what you want them to do by forcing them, controlling them, micromanaging them, or even simply telling them. If you are feeling like you can't get people to do what you want them to do, or that it takes a lot of effort to get people to do what you want them to do, then this means that you are feeling like you can't get yourself to do what you want yourself to do. This is what happens when you try to control yourself or force yourself to do what you "should" be doing without listening to yourself first to discover what would actually be the best approach to getting what you want.

If you are trying to find your desired destination in life by driving around in the dark aimlessly, then you are definitely not taking the best approach to getting to where you want to go. You have a GPS system, so use it. Before you take any further action, take a moment first to plug your desired destination into your internal GPS. Imagine what you would be thinking and feeling once you reach your desired destination. Imagine how great you feel after the conversation that might have turned into an argument in the past somehow manages to go smoothly and positively this time. Imagine how connected you feel after having a fantastic date with your partner. Imagine how appreciated, valued, and important you feel when everyone is thanking you for all your help and for being you. Imagine whatever you would be experiencing in the ideal at some future point in time. And then listen to your own internal guidance as it shows you the way toward the destination you've imagined for yourself.

If you do what you are supposed to be doing—in terms of where you are directing your internal and external focus of attention—then other people will be far more likely to do what they are actually supposed to be doing. You make your thoughts, feelings, and instincts feel that you believe in them, trust them, value them, appreciate them, etc., when you set clear destinations with your focus of attention and let your internal guides, helpers, and directors take over from here, taking action when and how they indicate for you to. In this way, you also actually demonstrate by example that your words are to be followed by accommodating actions without follow-up or checking being necessary, and thus you show people what you want done by living this rather than saying one thing and doing another. As you make your own thoughts, feelings, and instincts feel that you believe in them, trust them, etc., you are naturally inclined to make other people feel these positive ways with your words and actions as well, and so they're more inclined to do what you'd like them to do.

You play your role and let your thoughts, feelings, and instincts play theirs. Then you'll do this with other people, and other people will do things willingly rather than feeling micromanaged and consequently resisting and rebelling, seemingly requiring your continued control.

Everything will get done as you want it to if you continue to focus on the outcome you desire rather than shifting your focus to what you don't want to have happen in order to try to prevent it. You cannot reliably make something happen by focusing on the possibility or likelihood of it not happening, regardless of how much force, control, and insistence you use. And you'd need to be constantly on top of things even just to get subpar results.

So imagine and intend what you would like to have happen, and focus on what you need to do, yourself. And be sure to reword this to yourself once you ask yourself and recognize why you actually *want* to do—perhaps in terms of the results it will get you—what you are saying to yourself that you *need* to do, so that you are going into your own actions voluntarily and internally aligned with where you are choosing to be and what you are choosing to be doing. If you do this, then other people will do what you want them to do as well—willingly and even enthusiastically, perhaps even coming up with the ideas themselves or in some other way without you needing to say anything to them at all.

You focus on you and create your own experience and let others focus on themselves and create their own experiences, and you'll be setting the example you want followed and so you'll get the results you want. It is that simple.

Cheating On Yourself With Your Partner

If you give your partner, your friends, your family, your job, money, or anything else more attention than you give yourself, then you are essentially cheating on yourself with them. If you give anyone or anything more attention than you give to yourself, then you are using that person or thing as a distraction or an excuse to take your attention away from where it truly should be—on your own thoughts, feelings, and instincts, and ultimately on yourself. It is not that you should *only* be paying attention to yourself; it is simply that if you don't treat yourself as more worthy of your attention than everyone and everything else, then everyone else will follow your example, and you won't get love, attention, respect, etc. because you're basically saying, by your example, that someone or something else should get it and you shouldn't.

For example, if you give the majority of your attention to your partner in your relationship, your partner will give the majority of his or her attention to himself or herself as well, and no one in the relationship will be paying any attention to you and your needs, wants, feelings, thoughts, etc. If you give the majority of your attention to your friends, family, job, money, or even your body, the same thing applies.

If your attention is directed away from yourself, people will attend to wherever you're pointing with your attention, away from you and your needs, wants, feelings, and thoughts. If your attention is positive—as in the form of love, caring, respect, etc.—then other people and things will attend to what you are attending to with similar positive attention. If your attention is negative—as in the form of frustration, regret, anxiety, etc.—then other people and things will attend to what you are attending to with similar negative attention. In this picture, you can't give your attention away forever in any kind of truly positive form, because you end up totally neglected by yourself and everyone and everything else. The flow of everyone and everything's attention is deflected away from you and toward where your attention is directed.

If you find yourself giving more attention to any other person or thing or event or whatever than to yourself, ask yourself what you're avoiding paying attention to in yourself. What thoughts, feelings, or desires are you ignoring, dismissing, or tuning out? What do you think or feel you should really be doing that you are avoiding or distracting yourself from? How can you tune into yourself? What would you need to do to be in harmony with yourself so that you can feel comfortable being fully with yourself rather than feeling the need to ignore or escape from yourself?

Use your thoughts, feelings, and instincts as a guide in determining what you are doing that is good or that might need to change, as well as how to change it, in terms of getting the results that you want. Your thoughts, feelings, and instincts are very straightforwardly saying what they mean: what they think and feel about you and what they want from you. It is just that you believe that *you're* the one saying these things about your *partner* or some *other person* or *event* or whatever. So listen to what you are thinking, feeling, and wanting in regard to your partner or whomever or whatever else, and recognize that this is all about *you*, ultimately. Once you get what you are wanting from *yourself*, you can get it from your partner, others, and the world around you as well.

When you stop cheating on yourself and you positively attend to what requires your attention within you, you are able to give positive attention sustainably to, and receive positive attention sustainably from, everyone and everything in your life. Your relationship, your family, your friends, your job, money, your body, etc., all become forces of positive growth and joy, love, peace, etc. in your life as they reflect back your progress in learning how really to listen to yourself and treat yourself well, giving positive, accepting, compassionate, loving attention to all parts of yourself.

Making Yourself The Highest Priority

You should be your own highest priority. When you *don't* attend to yourself, you set the example that other people *shouldn't* listen to themselves or to you, and you deprive them of the positive example that you could be setting for them by listening to yourself and acting on your own thoughts, feelings, instincts, and so forth. On the other hand, when you *do* attend to yourself, you set the example that other people *should* listen to themselves and to you, thereby helping them along in being the best versions of themselves as you work to be the best version of yourself.

When you focus too much on other people or things (such as your significant other, your friends, your community, your family, your job, money, etc.), you end up expecting more back from them to make up for the fact that you are not getting enough of your *own* attention. But when you are not getting enough attention from yourself, no amount of attention from anyone or anything else will seem like enough, because it can't make up for the fact that you are making yourself feel ignored, dismissed, and tuned out. Therefore, in order to feel like you are a priority to others, you need to be a priority to yourself.

If you ignore, dismiss, or tune out your own needs, wants, feelings, thoughts, and beliefs for the sake of accommodating the needs, wants, feelings, thoughts, and beliefs of your family, community, friends, or significant other, then you will be ignored, dismissed, and tuned out by others as well. This will simply get you upset, resentful, frustrated, etc. at other people.

You shouldn't simply be your own highest priority when it comes to your actions. You should be your highest priority when it comes to your thoughts, feelings, and instincts as well. Your internal world should be focused mainly on *you* and *not* on other people (or things) and their needs, wants, feelings, thoughts, beliefs, actions, etc. *You* should get most of your own attention.

If you give yourself most of your attention, then you will be able truly to give your positive attention to others without imposing your issues on them, placing expectations on them, blaming them or controlling them. So while you might have believed that it would be selfish to give your attention to yourself, in reality we can see that the only way *not* to be selfish is to give your attention primarily to yourself. Only then will you not be attending to others from a place of neediness and expectations, looking to them for what you are not getting from yourself. When you make yourself the primary focus of your attention in your own internal world, you will already have what you need, because your own thoughts, feelings, and instincts will feel acknowledged by you, understood, and acted on. Once you get your own unsolicited, positive, and accepting attention, you give positive and accepting attention to others without effort, and you get the positive and accepting attention you want from others without even needing to request it.

So remember: You are the main character in your life. Your significant other, your friends, your family, your community, your career, money, etc. all simply play supporting roles in your life. The primary spotlight of your attention should be focused on *you* the *majority* of the time. It is only when you fully play your role as the main character and command the focus of your attention that all of the supporting cast members in this movie are able to fully play their roles. The movie of your life won't be nearly as good or fulfilling if the main character is de-emphasized and outshined by one or more of the supporting characters in it. You are meant to take center stage here in your experience. Everyone and everything else should be the main characters in their own lives, and not in yours. And you should be a supporting character in their lives, and not in yours. So determine the course of things, listen to yourself as you go so that you are true to the role you set out to play, and let everyone and everything else around you play off of you. In this way, you'll create the best movie you possibly can for you to experience.

When you are your highest priority, and you listen to yourself and do what's good for you, you are doing what's best for everyone else as well, whether it seems so on the surface or not. When you make someone or something else a higher priority than yourself, and you don't listen to yourself and do what's best for you, you are not doing what's best for anyone else around you.

For example, let's say you stay in a relationship in which you are not happy because you believe it is good for the other person, even though it is not good for you and your thoughts, feelings, and instincts are saying to leave. In this situation, you are likely making the other person dependent on you, without even intending it, so that he or she isn't learning how to face what he or she needs to face and stand on his or her own emotional feet in life. You are also likely preventing yourself and the other person from achieving the greatest possible happiness that you could each experience, for you are staying where you will end up resentful and unhappy with the other person for keeping you here and where the other person will therefore not be treated by you the way you would probably like him or her to be treated in the ideal. By ignoring and dismissing yourself here, you are guaranteeing that the other person will ignore and dismiss you, rather than apply and appreciate all of your advice, help, and protection, take you seriously, and treat you as significant and good. You are also guaranteeing that you will be ignoring and dismissing the other person in ways you don't even necessarily realize. Further, you are setting the example that the other person should ignore and dismiss himself or herself, encouraging this with your own actions as this is what you are representing with them, regardless of what you might be saying with your words.

You both won't feel listened to. Communication will break down as it breaks down within yourself. And you will both suffer as a result as compared to what you could each have, as you are preventing yourself and the other person from moving on with life, learning important lessons, and ending up with other people who could make you each even happier or coming back together in a much more positive relationship. Anything you want in a relationship and believe you have or could have with the other person will be an illusion. And you will be preventing both of you from getting what you truly want for real. On top of all of this, you will be setting an example for everyone around you—friends, children, customers, coworkers, community members, etc., in addition to your relationship partner—that you should be ignored and dismissed, as well as that relationships should not be fulfilling and that communication in them should not be harmonious or positive, and that we should not listen to ourselves or follow our happiness.

So listen to yourself. This is the prerequisite to getting the outcome you want from any action you take—in regard to yourself as well as others—and is therefore more important than trying to be there for others or directing your attention to anything else. When you listen to yourself and you—along with your thoughts, feelings, and instincts—are your own highest priority, you will have the most positive possible effect on everyone and everything around you that you can have. You will get the positive results that you truly desire and intend to try to get by directing your attention and energy anywhere else and by any other action that you would ever be inclined to take.

Listening To Yourself: A Writing Exercise

Whenever you notice that someone or something else is taking up a lot of your internal and/or external attention or leading you to think, feel, and want negative things, it is important to notice and understand what your thoughts, feelings, and instincts are trying to tell you. Only once you get the message will there be no more need for it to be repeated and brought to you by the same messengers or any more messengers.

Considering everything that you experience begins with you, it is helpful to have an idea about how to put this wisdom into practice and make use of it in a concrete way. So here's a writing exercise that you can do whenever you notice yourself thinking, feeling, or wanting anything in regard to yourself or anyone or anything else, or caught up in negativity toward someone or something, or whatever. You could be giving too much attention internally to your significant other, to your family, to a friend, to your community, to your environment, to your body, to a client or customer or boss, to money, etc. When you notice this, ask yourself the following questions and write out your answers, however short or extensive they need to be:

1a) What is this person, thing, or situation making me think, feel, or want?

1b) What would I want to say to this person, thing, or situation if I could freely speak my mind? What advice would I give or what would I simply want to express and make known?

2a) How might I be making myself (or my thoughts, feelings, and instincts) think, feel, or want these things?

2b) How might my advice or what I want to say or express to this other person or these other people (or whatever) be relevant to me?

Just allow yourself to write out whatever comes to mind. Alternatively, if there is a person or group of people with whom you can talk this out, answer these questions out loud. Or answer them out loud to yourself and consider recording your spoken answers so that you can revisit them and build on them if it would be helpful later.

So here's the general idea (where you would ideally obviously elaborate by specifying and explaining what "this" is):

1) **Issue:** I feel this. I think this. I want this. This person is doing this. I just don't like this. This person shouldn't be doing this. This shouldn't be happening. This isn't how things should be done. This is wrong and it's bothering me. I want this person to know this.

2) **Response:** I hear that I'm feeling this about myself. I hear that I'm thinking this about myself. I hear that I'm wanting this from myself. I understand that I haven't been doing this and I would like to do this. I can see that I've been treating myself this way and I would like to treat myself this other way instead. I understand that I've been focusing on this and I would like myself to be focusing on this other thing instead.

Since this exercise can also be used for situations in which you are thinking or feeling positive things seemingly in regard to someone or something outside you (or even in regard to yourself), here's a more positive alternative outline:

1) **What's getting my attention:** I feel this. I think this. I want this. I like this. I love this. I love when this person does this. I enjoy being around this person. I feel this about this event. I think this about this situation. This is what I want more of in my life experience. I'd love this person to know this.

2) **My response:** I hear that I'm feeling this about myself. I hear that I'm thinking this about myself. I hear that I'm wanting more of this from myself. I understand that I have been doing this and I like when I do this. I can see that I've been treating myself this way and I'd love to continue treating myself this way. I understand that I've been focusing on this and I'd love to keep focusing on this.

Feel free to alter, eliminate, and add to these statements to suit your needs. Simply address what's relevant to you; this is just meant as a guide to help you get started.

Remember: The idea here is to listen to yourself and recognize the origins of your experience in your own internal dynamic. By writing out what someone or something else is making you think, feel, and want, you can be honest with yourself about what you must be making yourself think, feel, and want once you acknowledge that you must be the origin of this or else you wouldn't be experiencing this being reflected back at you. Once you discover the origins of your experience in your relationship with yourself, you can set new destinations about how you'd like to treat yourself (or keep treating yourself) and what you'd like to make yourself think, feel, and want instead (or in addition) from here on.

This is what it is to really listen to yourself—to listen to what your thoughts, feelings, and instincts are trying to communicate to you about what you are making them (in a sense, aspects of yourself) think, feel, and want. The result is that your external experience will shift to accommodate and reflect your new relationship with yourself—as you listen to yourself and hear and understand what you're really saying to yourself, and as you respond appropriately with shifts in your destinations, and thus in your internal and external behaviors.

Untangling The Tangled Web We've Woven

As you recognize the tangles of negativity in your life—the things that have taken too much of your attention and led you to ignore and control yourself, dismiss and rebel against yourself, and tune out in attempts to harmonize with yourself—you'll recognize that they're often part of a much larger mass of tangles. Like a mass of tangled cords, as you attempt to untangle anything, you realize that you have to begin at the most recent tangle and work your way back. And as you work your way back, you find yourself in tangles from the past that you'd almost forgotten about even though as soon as they come up again, they bring up all of the negative thoughts, feelings, and instincts that you'd associated with them and left unaddressed.

You find that the tapestry of your life requires some repairing, one tangle at a time, each tangle drawing to your attention another associated and related tangle. An issue in a relationship can bring up an issue with past relationships, which can bring up an issue with religion, which can bring up an issue with groups, which can bring up an issue with school, which can bring up an issue with upbringing, which can bring up an issue with parents, which can ultimately bring up an issue with your controlling yourself and not treating your own feelings as significant.

As you start to notice all the tangles, you might be inclined to get overwhelmed, feeling guilty or frustrated with them all, and shove them aside again. But if you take it one tangle at a time and follow through to the next, and you bring each tangle back to how it stems from how you have treated yourself and what you have made yourself think, feel, and want, you can regain control. You can finally heal yourself from the issues that have, over time, turned into a tangled mess, with tangles built on top of tangles previously left unaddressed.

Rather than adding to the mess with the creation of more negative experiences built on reactions to previous ones, you can go back, listen to what still hasn't been heard and understood within you, and then amend this going forward by treating yourself differently. In this way, you can add to the tapestry of your life in ways you'd actually like to. And you can ensure that it will be untangled and smooth from here onward.

The Importance Of Being Mindful

We can see at this point that basically all of the struggles we face in our lives come from our not really being present to ourselves, giving ourselves our own attention, and listening to ourselves. If we were fully present to ourselves, we would not face the struggles that we face in all of our relationships and, in fact, in every aspect of our lives.

The solution to all of our problems, therefore, begins with being more proactively attentive to ourselves, our own thoughts, feelings, and instincts, and the experiences we have in the world around us. This must be a certain type of attention, however. It cannot be controlling, ignoring, dismissive, judgmental, or dissociative. It must be gently guiding, accepting, and fully tuned-in.

Rather than living in our staticky and replaying thoughts, feelings, and instincts about the future, past, and present—in "what ifs", "what could have beens", "what might bes", and "if onlys"—we can learn to focus our attention on where we are. If we learn to be more present to and accepting of where we actually are in this moment, then we will find all the fulfillment we seek in every moment and every aspect of our lives. When we live fully here, listening attentively to what arises inside and outside of us, everything is gentle, subtle and far more positive as compared to when we ignore, dismiss, judge and tune ourselves out to the point that we need to create dramatic, elaborate, bold, extreme, and highly unpleasant experiences for ourselves in order to get our own attention. Sometimes we won't get the lesson right away, and this is fine, and we ought to accept ourselves even for this. But if we learn to make listening to ourselves and being present to our lives a regular, daily, and eventually moment-to-moment practice, we will be able to stay much more consistently on the track of learning, growth, and fulfillment. There will still be downs and ups in our experience of life, but the downs will gradually become lesser and fewer, and the ups will gradually become greater and more frequent.

If we simply try to start thinking positive and drown out the negativity within ourselves without listening to and acknowledging what's going on in ourselves first, we will simply be adding more positive forces to the battlefield of our internal and external worlds. The negative forces will still be there, possibly even reinforced by our dismissal or simple unacknowledgement and pushing aside of ourselves. The only way to eliminate the battle of good and bad within ourselves and our lives and fill our lives with predominantly good experiences is to be present to ourselves. This way we acknowledge and hear what our thoughts, feelings, instincts, dreams, and the external events of our lives have been trying to tell us, we learn the lessons that they essentially are here to teach us about how we shape our experience of life with the direction of our attention, and we can let them go. With accepting, aware attention, followed by redirection, we actually replace the negative forces within us with positive forces, rather than simply adding more forces to the battle.

In our use of our internal GPS, if we simply start actively trying to plug in positive destinations with positive thoughts and affirmations, we will simply be adding more destinations to what we have already plugged in. We will end up with conflicting destinations, resulting in conflicting directions from the GPS. Whenever we're attending to an emotion that is positive, we will be on track toward those positive destinations we've plugged in, while whenever we're attending to an emotion that is negative, we will be on track toward those negative destinations we've plugged in. Meanwhile, we'll never be able to be going the right direction without also going the wrong direction, since the right direction to get to one destination we've plugged in is the wrong direction to get to any other, conflicting destinations we've plugged in. We'll essentially have set up a situation filled with confusion, distracted and scattered attention, dissatisfaction, ups and downs, and where a lot of effort is required even simply to stay in the same place, let alone progress forward toward our desired destinations.

On the other hand, if we first pay attention to what we have been plugging into our GPS, and what direction we have been headed, and then we respond and redirect, then we essentially replace those destinations in our GPS, turn around, and get going the right direction, with clear guidance that only leads us toward our newly set and desired destinations. With minimal effort, we flow toward our intended, positive destinations, motivated and pulled forward by increasingly consistently positive emotions that are aligned with them.

When we remember simply to set destinations and then let go of them and be present to the moment, we can hear what comes up that might get in our way and respond to these things so that we stay on the path toward our desired destinations. Further, with presence, we can attend to everything else that requires our attention in a balanced way so that we don't end up focusing on what we don't have yet, thereby plugging in destinations that are opposite our intended ones, and expecting too much from what we do have, thereby plugging in negative destinations in regard to these aspects of our lives as well. With presence, we use our thoughts, feelings, and instincts as they were intended to be used—as tools to shape our lives.

With mindful awareness and gentle, willful direction of our accepting attention, we use our internal GPS system effectively. The result is that our lives come into our control in an almost magical way, and everything goes as we will it to—without limits, and beyond what most of us have ever imagined.

With presence, we shift from moment to moment and activity to activity fully and at will. We are where we are, rather than continuing to linger with our internal attention in where we just were, in where we could be or could have been but aren't, or in where we might be going. Rather than continually questioning, analyzing, commenting, judging, criticizing, and reflecting on everything constantly, or tuning out and being absent, we live most of our time in the present, in the activity in which we are engaged, in the moment in which we physically exist. Rather than living like a rock skipping across the surface of a lake, we finally settle in where we are, living fully in the depth of every experience. We allow our experiences to touch us in a new way, so that they fill us and fulfill us.

We are complete, we are full, we are settled wherever we are. No matter where we are or what we are doing, we are choosing to be fully here. And so no matter where we are, we are home.

Part 3:
Our Relationship With The Source Of Everything

Another Aspect Of The Paradigm

In development, first we exist, then we are the only ones in existence and everything is an extension of us, then there are others in existence that are projections of us, then there are other individuals in existence like us but distinctly different from us in various ways, and then we are aware.

Now for the reverse of this—the order of creation. Here we are following the pattern of building on the previous stages, so since the order of development is all about what is in existence, the order of creation seems like it would be all about what is in awareness. Therefore: First we are aware, then there are other distinct individuals in our awareness, then there are others in our awareness that are projections of us, then there is only us in our awareness and everything is an extension of us, and then we exist.

There are a bunch of questions to be answered and things to be clarified here, since none of this makes much sense without some explanation. What are we aware of? What does it mean that there are other distinct individuals in our awareness? What does it mean that there are others in our awareness that are projections of us? What does it mean that there is only us in our awareness and that everything is an extension of us? What does it mean that we exist only at the end of this process? Who is "we" and who is "us" in this whole process in the first place?

Based on the pattern, we can fill in some of what seem to be the answers here and reword this: First there is awareness, then there are other distinct individuals in awareness, then there are others in awareness that are projections of awareness, then there is only awareness and everything is an extension of awareness, and then there is true existence.

In this rewording, perhaps we ought to be capitalizing "Awareness", for it seems to be referring to some kind of Source of all existence from which we become distinct when we come into being (in this world), and then of which we become projections (in this world), and then of which we become mere extensions (in this world), and in this way, the Source comes into some kind of existence (in this world). So then we have: First there is the Source of everything, then there are other distinct individuals within the Source, then there are others within the Source that are projections of the Source, then there is only the Source and everything is an extension of the Source, and then there is true existence.

Our Relationship With God

Whether you believe in something beyond us—call it Universe, Awareness, Source, God, or something else—or not, it is helpful in understanding ourselves and other people to understand how we are inclined to feel treated by the world generally, or by something or some Being beyond ourselves.

Just as our relationship with everyone and everything else, the relationship with God that we experience and perceive is merely a reflection of our relationship with ourselves. However we treat ourselves, we feel treated this way by God. So, for example, if we love ourselves, we feel loved by God, and if we ignore ourselves, we feel ignored by God. If we listen to ourselves and respond kindly to ourselves and treat ourselves well, we feel listened to and responded to and treated well by God. If we dismiss ourselves and treat ourselves badly, we feel dismissed and treated badly by God. If we guide ourselves, we feel guided by God. If we control ourselves, we feel controlled by God. If we are present to ourselves, we feel like God is present to us. If we tune ourselves out and disregard ourselves, we feel like God tunes us out and disregards us.

We often end up inclined to view God as the superlative of what we seek to be and prioritize ourselves. So, for example, if we go through the nine Enneagram types and the three inclinations, we can see some different ways we are inclined to view God based on our personality-based ideals.

Allowing Instinct (Enneagram Type 9)

You are inclined to view God as the ultimate source of peace and comfort and as the harmonious connectedness of everything. You want to do what God would want you to do in order to maintain peace with God.

Receiving Instinct (Enneagram Type 1)

You are inclined to view God as the ultimate source of goodness, rightness, and morality, the *most* good, perfect and ideal and the *only truly* perfect and ideal Being, who rewards and punishes based on our goodness. You want to fix and improve yourself and the world in order to be good enough to be accepted by God.

Sharing Instinct (Enneagram Type 8)

You are inclined to view God as the ultimate challenger and protector, an all-powerful Being who looks out for us by presenting us with intense obstacles to toughen us up, make us strong, and push us to fulfill our potential. You want to challenge and protect God rather than let God protect you, and you want to challenge and protect others the way God does.

Allowing Feeling (Enneagram Type 3)

You are inclined to view God as the ultimate achiever and source of value whose expectations we have to meet in order to have value ourselves. You want to be what God would want you to be in order to have value to God.

Receiving Feeling (Enneagram Type 4)

You are inclined to view God as the ultimate source of unique importance, self-worth, and creative self-expression, the *most* uniquely important and the *only truly* uniquely important Being, of whose attention, listening, and responses we must make ourselves worthy and personally significant enough to receive. You want to make yourself uniquely important enough to be worthy of God's attention.

Sharing Feeling (Enneagram Type 2)

You are inclined to view God as the ultimate source of love and caring, a benevolent Being who helps us by sharing love, kindness, and compassion with us. You want to love and help God rather than let God help you, and you want to love and help others the way God does.

Allowing Thought (Enneagram Type 6)

You are inclined to view God as the ultimate source of trustworthy, stable guidance to whom we have to be dependable so that we can maintain the security of God in our lives. You want to make the decisions that God would want you to make in order to maintain the security of God in your life.

Receiving Thought (Enneagram Type 7)

You are inclined to view God as the ultimate source of fulfillment, excitement, entertainment, and fun who is playing one big game with us. You want to be exciting and entertaining enough to be acknowledged and taken seriously by God.

Sharing Thought (Enneagram Type 5)

You are inclined to view God as the ultimate source of understanding and wisdom, an all-knowing and all-capable Being who watches over and observes us, and guides us with insights and understanding, but doesn't participate or interfere in our lives otherwise. You want to figure out and understand, and figure out how to be useful to, God and God's world rather than let God guide you, and you want to guide others the way God does.

Allowing Existence – Preserving Inclination (Self-preservation Instinctual Variant)

You are inclined to view God as the ultimate parental figure and source and provider of food, shelter, clothing, good health for you and your family, wealth, and the rest of your and your family's material and physical well-being.

Receiving Existence – Belonging Inclination (Social Instinctual Variant)

You are inclined to view God as the ultimate societal leader and source of communal belonging, societal rules, and hierarchical structure and status.

Sharing Existence – Connecting Inclination (One-on-one Instinctual Variant)

You are inclined to view God as the ultimate close companion and source of connection and completion.

It is important to note here that when we are children, we are inclined to view our parents, and adults in general, in accordance with the way we end up viewing God later—all based on our personality inclinations. It is as though we seek a source and example of all that we wish to have, be and experience from the beginning of our lives, and when our parents, teachers, and other influential adults fail to be this for us, we begin to look elsewhere. Eventually, as everyone and everything in this world fails to be the source and example we seek, we conceive of and strengthen our conception of a God beyond this world whom we believe must be the source and example of all that we wish to have, be, and experience.

Actually, it isn't simply that we look to our parents for what we seek from God, and eventually think of ourselves as seeking from something beyond what we experience here. After our parents, we look to our societal leaders, and then we look to our close friends and significant others, and then we look to ourselves—all in search of what we ultimately seek to be ourselves, and in search of what we conceive of ourselves as getting ultimately from God, based on our personality inclinations. At first, we think of ourselves as looking to these people for what we seek, and gradually we come to think of God as being like these people in the roles they play for us. So our conception of God develops and evolves as we do.

As individuals and as a species, we develop in stages in terms of where and in what form we look for fulfillment. During early childhood, we seek direction, morality, and protection from our parents. During adolescence, we seek purpose, significance, and help from our peers and social group. During young adulthood, we seek guidance, fulfillment, and understanding from close friends and significant others. As we continue beyond young adulthood, through the time that the prefrontal cortex of our brains is fully developed and we have the fully developed potential for willful, aware choice, we begin to actualize our potential for choice and choose the shape our lives take beyond where we came from. At this point, we move through each of these different stages again, but in a more actualized form.

Essentially, once we come into being, we move through three basic stages of development up to our early- to mid-twenties—instincts, feelings, thoughts—along with all of the different aspects of these stages that go with these, some of which we described earlier. From the early- to mid-twenties onward, we move through these three stages again in the form of their breakdown into three stages each. So from here on, we go through allowing instinct, receiving instinct, sharing instinct, allowing feeling, receiving feeling, sharing feeling, allowing thought, receiving thought, sharing thought—along with all of the different aspects of each of these stages. Then we get to choice (actualized). (By the way, if you account for each of these 12 stages of life prior to choice and delve into their aspects, you get the 12 astrological signs—stages of the year—and their attributes. This is all discussed above in the "Development And Creation Forms" section of "Enneagram Nine Personality Types".)

In our development as individuals and as a species, we look for fulfillment in different places. First, we look for it from our parents—father and mother—whom we see as sources of direction, morality, and protection for us children. Then, we look for it from the leaders of society—king, president, religious leaders, doctors, scientists, other experts and professionals, etc.—whom we see as sources of purpose, significance, and help for us servants, followers, messengers, and laypeople. Then, we look for it from our close friends and significant others, whom we see as sources of guidance, fulfillment, and understanding for us equals. Then, we look for it from ourselves.

These are the stages in the development of our conception of our relationship with the Source of everything we have, need, and want—with God.

We see it everywhere in religion, and it has been debated and discussed throughout human history—for as long as there has been an idea of God. What is our relationship with such a Being? What is our relationship with God? (Is God transcendent—far from us and removed from us? Is God immanent—near us and close to us?) Here we can understand the answer, which encompasses all of the answers that have been conceived of and places them into a context in terms of the process of development of all things.

First, we look to God through our parents, then we look to God through our societal leaders, then we look to God through our friends and significant others, and then we look to God through ourselves. And so: Once we have a conception of God, we first we see God as our Father, and we see ourselves as His children. From this perspective, we look to God for direction, morality, and protection. Then we see God as our King, and we see ourselves as God's servants or messengers. From this perspective, we look to God for purpose, significance, and help. Then we see God as our friend or lover, and we see ourselves as God's equals. From this perspective, we look to God for guidance, fulfillment, and understanding. And then we see God as the highest part of ourselves—we recognize that God is part of us or, rather, that we are part of God and not separate from God that we should look through other people and the world around us in search of God and all that we have, need, and want. From this perspective, we look to God, to ourselves, for everything, for we realize that everything is God and nothing is separate from God.

From the recognition that we are part of God and not separate from God, we go through the reverse of this pattern of development—the order of creation: We become a listening friend and companion through whom others look to God for guidance, fulfillment, and understanding. Then we become a societal leader through whom others look to God for purpose, significance, and help. Then we become a parental figure through whom others look to God for direction, morality, and protection.

We might imagine that if God—the Source of everything—were like a source of brilliant light, then we would begin in our development looking everywhere outside of us in search of light, eventually to discover that the light is shining through us to everyone and everything around us and that we need only look within to find all that we seek. When we look outward in place of looking inward, we don't find anything that we want. But once we get what we want from ourselves, then when we look outward, we find what we seek.

Why We Need So Much Of Our Own Positive Attention

At this point, we can really begin to understand the structure of all things. At the Source of everything, there is God (the creator part of us). Then there is God's (our) creation. From there overflows the ability to choose to identify with God, the Source and Creator of everything, or to identify with the creation—and ultimately with any of various aspects of God's (our) creations that arise from our choices. From there overflows the results of our choices.

First there is a male, creative, sharing form of thought, then there is a female, responsive, receiving form of thought, and then there is a child, harmonizing, allowing form of thought—the thought body, the product of the interaction of the male and female forms of thought. Then there is a male, creative, sharing form of feeling, followed by a female, responsive, receiving form of feeling, followed by a child, harmonizing, allowing form of feeling—the feeling body, the product of the interaction of the male and female forms of feeling. Then there is a male, creative, sharing form of instinct, followed by a female, responsive, receiving form of instinct, followed by a child, harmonizing, allowing form of instinct—the instinctual body, the product of the interaction of the male and female forms of instinct.

Then there is the physical body, which is simultaneously the product of the whole process up to this point and also the final creative part of the process, capable of speech and action that mold the physical world—the ultimate product of the whole process of creation. Within the physical body, notice, there is a replication of the male, female, child pattern that repeats itself before this. There is the male, creative, sharing capacity for physical speech and action. There are the female, responsive, receiving physical senses of sight, hearing, smell, taste, and touch. And there are the child, harmonizing, allowing internal organs that work to maintain physical equilibrium within the physical body.

The physical body interacts with the physical world for the final part of the creative process, shaping the physical world into something that is crystalized and complete in each moment.

Now we can understand why we need so much of our own positive attention. Every part of the creative process below the Source receives everything, including its very existence, from the Source. Every part of the process is dependent on what it receives from the parts above it, and so every part of the process must share what it receives with the parts below it in order for those latter parts to continue to exist, perform their functions, and thrive. Whenever we choose to identify with one or another of the creations in this process, we look outside of us—to other creations—for Source energy upon which to exist, rather than directly to the Source, itself. As a result, we block the flow of Source energy to every part of the creative process within us.

Like dimming the light of existence, we leave ourselves in increasing darkness the more we identify with our creations and the less we identify with our Source. Like blocking the flow of oxygen- and glucose-containing blood to the various parts of our body, we leave ourselves to wither and slowly die. Life is in the flow. Death is in stagnation. And in order for us to flow, we need to recognize our true nature as Source, so that we recognize that we will never be without, and we therefore need not hold onto anything. Like an ever-flowing mountain stream, we can continue to provide pure, fresh, life-giving water to every part of ourselves and to others and never run dry. When we hold onto the life-giving rainwater we receive, we stagnate like a pond, and we cannot provide fresh water to any part of ourselves or to others, but instead only life-taking, parasite- and bacteria-ridden water. We must recognize that we are Source and connect with that highest, infinite and boundless part of ourselves in order to maintain the flow of existence-giving energy and never have that energy be warped or corrupted and also never have that energy flow stop.

Our positive attention to ourselves is like rainwater to the mountain stream. Without positive attention, we become increasingly limited in our existence and creative capacity, unable to thrive, and eventually we cease to exist. When we identify with our creations, we lose sight of our creative power and our essence of infinite potential. We simply seek to maintain ourselves rather than evolving and thriving. When we do not give ourselves our own positive attention, we essentially deprive ourselves of the attention of existence, itself, from everyone and everything, for we are ultimately God, and we are therefore depriving ourselves of everything that comes from the Source—of God's attention, itself. This is why the path toward our actualization involves connecting with our highest selves and showering ourselves with unconditional positive attention in every conceivable form. When we do this, we become unimaginably powerful as we recognize ourselves as the Creator of existence, nourish all parts of ourselves and the world around us with flowing, existence-giving energy, receive this existence-giving energy through everyone and everything around us in addition to directly from ourselves, and actualize our true nature.

Understanding What Our Thoughts, Feelings, And Instincts Really Are

What are our thoughts, feelings, and instincts?

If we consider for a moment, thoughts, feelings, and instincts include those things that we create inside us, things that come up in reaction to experiences with other people and the world around us, things that we seem to absorb from other people and animals and the world around us, things that we seem to pass through at times like clouds, things that are shared with us by other people in this world, by spirits of those who have passed on from this world and other spirits we've never known here, and even by our spirit guides. They seem to direct us at times, and we seem to direct them at times. They seem to be inside us, but sometimes, in deep meditation or prayer, they almost seem to be coming from outside us, even though we still hear them inside.

Ultimately, to include all of these, thoughts, feelings, and instincts are reflections of the communication between the Source of everything and Its creation. This is similar to the way the actual words we use in a relationship with another person are just reflections of what we are already communicating to the other person through our thoughts, feelings, instincts, and actions; for example, our intonation often communicates everything that we're really saying, and the actual words are just an additional layer or reflection.

We are all merely extensions of the Source, and so there is actually ultimately no "we"; there is only "I", and "I" is the Source and Creator of everything in existence. And so our thoughts, feelings, and instincts are reflections of the language by which we as the Source communicate with our creation, and by which our creation responds to us and lets us know what we are making it think, feel, and want based on how we are treating it when we are the Source of its sustenance and everything that it has and is. In a sense, all of existence is just a series of layers of reflection of our relationship with ourselves, which is just another way of saying that all of existence is a series of layers of reflection of the Creator's relationship with Its creation.

When there is only the Source, there is only one. Once the Creator gives rise to a creation, there are two, and so there is a relationship. And once the Creator communicates with Its creation and Its creation responds, a new perspective is born, and this entire creative process is repeated over and over again—male, female, child; sharing, receiving, allowing; thoughts, feelings, instincts, etc.—and the physical world comes into being as the product and reflection of all of the dynamics of this relationship—the relationship between the Creator and Its creation.

The Creator is the origin of the male, sharing, creative, initiating and guiding paradigm. The creation is the origin of the female, receiving, responsive, differentiating and expressive paradigm. The choice we have to identify with the Creator or the creation is the origin of the child, allowing, manifesting, harmonizing paradigm. And then there are the thoughts, feelings, and instincts that are the language reflections of the communication between the Creator and the creation.

When we choose to identify with the Creator, we allow our thoughts, feelings, and instincts to become messengers of the Creator, acting in the order of creation. We initiate new thoughts, feelings, and instincts with attention to our creation—guiding it in accordance with its thoughts, feelings, and instincts; our creation responds positively to these; and harmonized thoughts, feelings, and instincts result, leading to a positive new creation that we're inclined to tune into and give positive attention.

When we choose to identify with the creation, we allow our thoughts, feelings, and instincts to become messengers of the creation removed from its Creator, acting in the order of development. We initiate new thoughts, feelings, and instincts in disregard of our creation—controlling it without paying attention to its thoughts, feelings, and instincts—since we don't recognize our true relation to it; our creation reacts and rebels against this control; and inharmonious thoughts, feelings, and instincts result, leading to a negative new creation that we're inclined to tune out from.

We are capable of identifying with the Creator or with the creation at any point in time within the context of playing out the order of creation or within the context of playing out the order of development, but we have very different types of relationship dynamics depending on whether we are identifying with the Creator ultimately in the order of creation, or with the creation ultimately in the order of development.

When we become aware of our true nature and choose to identify with the Creator, thereby reconnecting with our true origin, we recognize that every aspect of us begins to play out its true role in the order of creation:

Our willfully chosen thoughts, feelings, and instincts become reflections of the language that we—the one Creator—use to communicate with our creation, giving it destinations and therefore direction and purpose. Our automatic thoughts, feelings, and instincts become reflections of the language that our creation uses to communicate with us, letting us know what we are making it think, feel, and want by the way we are treating it, asking us ultimately for more positive attention in every form—because our attention sustains our creation and keeps it in existence—and for a role and a say in the creative process and in what we are creating in, through, and with it. Then, there are the thoughts, feelings, and instincts that are reflections of what simply allows this communication to take place and harmonizes the relationship between us and our creation so that a new perspective, greater awareness, and a new dynamic can be produced.

And so we can recognize that we, the Creator, give rise to a world and an experience that is no more than a reflection of the relationship between us and our creation. And our thoughts, feelings, and instincts—in sharing, receiving, and allowing forms—are a reflection of the communication between Creator and creation and the result of this conversation, be it negative—ignoring and controlling, judging and dismissing, and tuning out—or positive—listening and guiding, accepting and attending to, and tuning in with presence. The physical world of our experience, and our dynamics with everyone and everything in it, are just the product of this relationship between us and our creation—of the way we are treating it and the way it reacts to this, and the resulting mindfulness of our nature as Source and Creator as we tune in, or the resulting ignorance of this truth as we tune out, disconnect from our essence, and identify with our creations.

Our responsive thoughts, feelings, and instincts are a reflection of our creation's response to what we have said or done to it, what we have requested of it, and the way we have treated it. This response can come through other people, animals, books, movies, or other experiences in the physical world around us, through people or animals who have passed on, through our spirit guide, or through other sources. It can come directly into our minds and internal experiences, where we can notice it, or we can recognize it when it becomes the content of our dreams or our physical life experience. But, ultimately, everything that we experience—every message we receive in whatever form it comes through whatever messenger from whom we most directly receive it—comes to us in response to what we have initiated ourselves. For we are (each one of us at our common Source is) the Creator, and everything for each of us is a messenger of what we have requested from our creation.

When we identify with Source, we are unlimited, the Creator of everything that we experience, the Source of everything we have and everything we want. When we identify with our creation, we get caught up in and identify with aspects of what it is saying to us about what we are making it think, feel, and want by the way we are treating it; we believe that we are limited, lacking, the product of this world of experiences, and we search outside ourselves for all of the positive attention in every form that we want and need to survive and thrive. Like a husband who works so hard to empathize with his wife that he forgets that his wife's emotions are not his own and that he can actually do something to make her feel better by giving her his positive attention, we as the Creator get lost in our creation's experiences and come to identify with the words it's saying, experiencing these as our own words and losing sight of our true nature as the One who can do something to alter and improve this experience by giving our creation our positive attention.

We are our own father and mother, and we can raise ourselves in a harmonious environment where the male creator part of us listens to and guides the female creation part of us, giving her a clear purpose and direction and encouraging her by bestowing positive attention upon her for fulfilling her purpose well. Alternatively, we can raise ourselves in an inharmonious environment where the male creator part of us ignores, controls, and micromanages the female creation part of us, who is not given any clear purpose or direction and reacts and rebels against being dismissed and treated negatively.

Either way, we will become our parents, identifying more with one or the other at different times in different interactions with the people and the world around us. In the former situation, sometimes we will be the initiating, sharing, listening and guiding one in our interactions with other people and the world around us, and sometimes we will be the responsive, receiving, attending to and differentiating one in our interactions with other people and the world around us. For these will be the dynamics to which we will be accustomed and therefore into which we will naturally fall with others. In the latter situation, sometimes we will be the initiating, ignoring and controlling one in our interactions with other people and the world around us, and sometimes we will be the reactive, dismissed, attention-seeking and rebelling one in our interactions with other people and the world around us. For these will be the dynamics to which we will be accustomed and therefore into which we will naturally fall with others.

In the former situation, we will be inclined to tune into the harmonious experience of life that we have and want to be having. In the latter situation, we will be inclined to tune out of the inharmonious experience of life that we have and don't want to be having.

We are the creator, the creation, and the new creation that is produced from the interaction between the two. We are the male, the female, and the child. We are sharing, receiving, and allowing. We are creating, responding, and harmonizing. We are our own father, mother, child, boss, employee, client, authority, expert, guide, friend, lover, etc. We are the one who is abused as well as the abuser, the one who is fulfilled as well as the source of fulfillment, the one who prays as well as the God to whom the prayers are offered and who ignores or answers these prayers. We have every relationship within and with ourselves. We are everything. Everything is us. Everything is within us. We are the creator and product of all that we experience. We can choose to identify with any part of this spectrum of who we are at any point in time and experience the world from this perspective. We create a purpose for ourselves, fulfill the purpose that we determine, and become the purpose, itself.

Yet, ultimately, we are here, as extensions of Source within Its creation, to learn the language of creation backward and forward, inside and out:

We are here to experience and be part of the world that we've created and that is continually developing to encompass the full creative process in its awareness and manifestation. And we are here to experience what it's like to create the world of our experience and determine and guide the path of its development.

Remembering Our True Creator Nature

In the order of development, first something exists, then we experience this through our senses, and then we experience thoughts, feelings, and instincts about it. In the order of creation, first we express thoughts, feelings, and instincts about something, then we experience it through our senses, and then it exists. We might believe that things are always only occurring in the order of development but, in reality, the reality that we see, hear, taste, smell, and touch always begins in the thoughts, feelings, and instincts to which we've chosen to give our attention and not in "reality". There is nothing but that which we have initiated and created within ourselves. It is simply that we are usually reacting to what we have already created and thereby creating more like that which we have already brought into our experience.

We are the Creator who has gotten lost in Its creation. Just as we can set a goal and then find ourselves experiencing the achievement of it, forgetting at first that we have set the goal, we experience this reality that we have brought into being in its entirety without immediate remembrance of our initiation of it.

The purpose of it all is for us to remember and re-identify with our true Creator nature. For it is in remembering that this goal that we have achieved is one that we, ourselves, have set, that we experience empowerment and fulfillment. It is in becoming aware that the reality that we are experiencing is one that we, ourselves, are creating that we experience the fulfillment of the purpose of existence. From here, we can begin to create willfully what we wish to experience.

Creator Vs. Creation

When we focus too much of our attention and energy on anything, we are being controlling and micromanaging, trying to do the job of figuring out how to get where we want to go and ensuring that we get there rather than letting our internal GPS—the thoughts, feelings, and instincts coming from our creation—take care of this. When we try to do what we are supposed to be letting our creation do, acting from the place of feeling that things won't get done or might not get done if we don't do them and make them happen, ourselves, we end up feeling overwhelmed. So if you are feeling overwhelmed, you are identifying with the role of creator in development order as you focus on the metaphorical pole that you don't want to crash into while riding the metaphorical bicycle of life and try to force the bicycle in some direction other than where you're looking.

In this case, you are trying to navigate the roads of life without listening to your GPS and letting it play its role, and as you try to play the role of both driver/destination-determiner and GPS at the same time, you get overwhelmed because you have to take care of too much at once and don't even know how to get where you're going or how to ensure that you'll get there. It can end up feeling like every little thing you do could lead to irreversible disaster—like you are walking a tightrope over Niagara Falls with all the people around you, and you don't know where you're going exactly but you feel certain that you and everyone around you absolutely needs to do exactly what you believe they need to do at this moment in order to avert something really bad from happening. You are overwhelmed with intense anxiety and fear about all the possible things that could go wrong that you feel you somehow have to stop from happening in order to avoid catastrophe.

In this situation, we force other people and the world around us into the role of a controlled, resistant, rebellious, and defensive creation. We do not get what we want because we act toward other people and the world around us as though they are going to put up resistance and therefore as though we are going to have to force them to do things in order for those things to get done. Whether people are actually resisting and rebelling or not, we push them and micromanage them until they do resist and rebel because we anticipate them doing so and are trying to make sure that they do what we want them to when we don't believe they will. And so as we imagine and anticipate resistance because we are getting it from ourselves, we create it for ourselves outside ourselves in reality.

When we are focusing too much attention and energy on anything and therefore are being controlling toward ourselves, the result is that, from the perspective of our creation, we end up feeling trapped. We are not being allowed any freedom to play our role and fulfill any kind of purpose because our role is being infringed upon by the creator part of us. So if you are feeling trapped, you are identifying with the role of creation in development order as the creator part of you has been focusing on the pole that it doesn't want to crash into and is consequently trying to force you to go a different direction and isn't listening to your directions as you guide it right toward the pole.

Since the creator part of you is trying to play its role and your role at the same time and isn't giving you any clear destinations or positive reinforcement when it *is* providing destinations, and therefore isn't providing you with any clear direction or purpose, there is nothing for you to do that you feel motivated to do. Sometimes, you feel purposeless, like you are wandering, confused, without meaning, direction, or a reason to go on and do anything in particular. You just go with the flow of what you're thinking and feeling and wanting, and you wander around. You are a GPS without any destinations plugged in, or with destinations plugged in but with a driver who isn't listening to any of the directions you're providing, and so you aren't getting any positive feedback that would indicate that you are doing what is wanted of you at all. So at the times that you don't feel utterly directionless, it feels like you have to do quite a lot of work to make nothing happen as it seems that nothing you do is ever good enough to get any positive attention or results. You essentially feel that you have no definitive purpose or anything to work or strive toward or do at all that seems worth striving toward or effectual in any substantial way.

In this situation, we force other people into the role of controlling creators as we defend ourselves and react and rebel against them as though they are forcing us to do things whether they actually are or not. We resist and lash out with pre-emptive strikes and counterstrikes in reaction to what we imagine is their forcing themselves upon us until they actually do start trying to force us to do things that we aren't doing because we really aren't doing them. And so as we perceive and imagine control because we are getting it from ourselves, we create it for ourselves outside ourselves in reality.

In this development-order scenario, you switch back and forth between trying to force things to happen as you fear bad alternatives happening, and feeling forced and controlled and just wanting to do anything else, but with no clear idea of what to do. You oscillate between being overwhelmed with everything you feel you have to do and being trapped by the sense that nothing you do is good enough anyway. This is the experience of life we have when we tell ourselves we have to or need to or should do things and generally focus on where we don't actually want to go. And this happens when we give too much attention to anything and consequently inevitably ignore other things that require our attention.

Alternatively, we could be present to the moment, merely setting our clear destinations by focusing on what we'd like to have happen and then trusting that our internal GPS—the thoughts, feelings, and instincts coming from our creation—will direct us there. We play our role as creator by listening to our creation and guiding it in accordance with its thoughts, feelings, and instincts, and we let our creation play its role of guiding, helping, and directing us toward the destinations that we've set for it. We allow our GPS to fulfill its purpose as we plug in clear destinations that we'd actually like to go to and then listen to the directions that it provides, acting when and how it says to.

In this scenario, we feel present, balanced, in control, attended to, accepted, acknowledged, and like everything we do is significant and good. We feel on top of things and like things simply go our way, that we have a purpose and that we are fulfilling this purpose, and we are fulfilled.

The shift from development perspective to creation perspective is from reactivity to proactivity. In the moment we notice that we are reacting as we may have reacted before and we recognize that we can actually respond differently and determine a different outcome than we may have gotten in the past, we are shifting from the development perspective to the creation perspective, and ultimately from creation's perspective to the creator's perspective overall. We are no longer the product of the world, where things happen to us over which we have no control and where we are just a reactive manifestation. We are the creator, itself, and the entire world of our experience is our creation—the result of where we choose to focus our attention.

At every moment that we notice something consuming our attention or making us feel negative in any way, we have a choice. We can continue to focus on what we are focusing on and allow it to shape our experience in ways that will be reflected back by other aspects of our lives as well. Or we can choose to step into the role of creation-order-perspective creator, respond to this situation with the direction we'd like it to go, redirect our attention to the moment, take a deep breath, and let go. Our now-creation-order-perspective creation will take over from here. And all we need to do is stay present to the moment and listen and go forward, and act on any directions our GPS provides us as we drive along the roads of life.

Sharing, Receiving, Allowing

In the order of development, we allow life to happen and the world to exist, we receive experiences from the world, and then we share these experiences with others. In the order of creation, we create new experiences and share them with the world, the world receives these experiences and comes up with something different from what it receives, and then the world we experience allows these created and differentiated experiences to be manifested through itself.

Ultimately, we are the originators, initiators, and creators of everything that we experience, for the experiences begin anew based on where we choose to focus our attention. Everything is always occurring in creation order, even as we can experience it in development order at the same time. And so it is up to us whether we allow the world to determine the experiences we receive and share with others as we react to it, or whether we create and share new experiences with others through our willful response to what we have experienced and even, eventually, through our proactive creation of something entirely new altogether.

We are always choosing our experiences. And as we increasingly shift into identification with being the creator of our experience, we can recognize this.

Using Your Internal GPS

When you make use of your internal GPS system and set your destinations clearly and get your destinations aligned with each other, you'll experience amazing things. You'll open a book or turn on a television or speak with a friend or meet someone new and very clearly get the answer to the question you just asked. You'll meet the kind of new friend you were intending to meet. You'll have the kind of conversation and connection tonight that you wanted to have. You'll recognize your significant other for whom you've been searching and feel it's right even if it doesn't start out with the magnetic attraction that previous side-street relationships had. Your relationships will improve as you imagined they would. You'll recognize your ideal career and get the kind of income that you've been asking for.

This will all happen as you begin to look with your attention in the direction of where you want to go rather than of where you don't want to go. When you're riding a bicycle, if you look at the pole that you'd like to avoid, you crash into it. And you often likely attempt to control yourself and the circumstances around you every step of the way as you see yourself heading straight toward the pole and do everything you can to avoid going where you're looking. You've got to look where you want to be going if you are to get there. When you notice where you don't want to go, you've got to acknowledge this and then focus your attention on where you'd like to go instead if you actually wish to get where you'd like to go. So, too, it is with life.

Remember: Everything you focus on in your thoughts and feelings is a destination that you are plugging into your GPS and the fuel that drives you toward this destination. As you play out conversations and interactions and experiences in your mind—even if this is the way things played out in the past—you are essentially choreographing and rehearsing the scenes of your life that are to come. You are the writer, choreographer, director, and main character in the play that is your life. So consider what you are writing, choreographing, and rehearsing, and how you are directing everyone and everything in your life to act toward and around you.

Your thoughts and feelings are tremendously powerful. The thoughts and feelings from which you act will determine the outcome of your action. So your true control over your life comes *not* from forcing yourself upon the people and the world around you through your words, tone, behavior, or insistent and forceful thoughts; or from replaying what's wrong or undesirable that needs to be corrected or avoided; or from tuning things out; but from setting clear destinations in your own mind.

Imagine what it would be like to be where you want to be and to have things the way you want them. How would you feel about the situation, about your life, about yourself? What would you be thinking? What would your life be like? How would you view your past (including what is now the present for you) with the new context of what you learned from it and how these lessons led you to where you wanted to be?

If ever you notice yourself focusing with your thoughts on destinations that make you feel bad and that you don't want to be going to, acknowledge these thoughts and feelings, and redirect your attention to where you want to be going.

If you can't actually look fully at where you'd like to be going, that's fine. If you can't imagine what exists outside of the box that you've built up for yourself and seemingly trapped yourself in, then simply poke a hole in the box by opening yourself to the possibility that there could be something beyond this. Just preface what you are saying with "I would love to experience..." or "It would be really nice to experience..." or "I'm open to the possibility that...". Then you will experience different things that you can focus on and magnify.

As soon as you can, begin to imagine what the world could be like outside of your current reality box. Use what you are experiencing for contrast and comparison. Notice what you don't like and imagine what you'd like instead. Notice what you do like and imagine this in your future reality. Until you can imagine and see some idea in your mind of where you're going, you're not going to allow yourself to leave the comfort of the familiar, no matter how unpleasant or undesirable the familiar may be. We don't head into the unknown; we head into realities that we've constructed in our imagination and that we take part in actualizing. These realities can either be more of what we've already experienced and kept focusing our attention on, or they can be great departures from our previous experience that we imagined and made real by looking forward instead of backward or down.

We cannot run away from ourselves. Even if we physically move to a different location, relationship, or job, we will face the same issues we faced in previous places, relationships, and jobs—albeit with different people in each role—until we change our relationship with ourselves and what we focus on and rehearse in our minds as our reality.

Everyone and everything in our lives is merely a messenger reflecting back our own thoughts and feelings. So if ever anyone says or does anything to you that makes you feel bad, ask yourself how you might have been saying or doing this to yourself. Then, once you have identified how the other person's behavior toward you is actually a mirror of your behavior toward yourself, change your behavior toward yourself. When you look in the mirror and you don't like what you see, you don't change the mirror, you change yourself. The entire physical world and everyone and everything within it is a mirror reflecting back your internal focus to yourself. So rather than trying to change what is outside you—which would only lead to anxiety, shame, anger, and other forms of stressful, negative feelings—change what is inside you, and what is outside you will change as well as you are guided toward the appropriate actions to bring about this change.

Look where you want to go, be clear in your focus of attention on that destination, replace any destinations—such as those that evoke doubt, fear, etc.—that aren't in the same direction so that the majority of your destinations are in the same direction, and the whole world will help you get there. Once you decide what you want and you tip the scales in favor of wanting and focusing on your most desired thing more than you want and focus on contradicting things, you will be pulled forward toward what you want.

Understanding The Magic That Fills Our Lives When We Use Our Internal GPS

How can the thoughts we think determine the physical outcomes of our lives? How can we affect other people's actions toward us just by thinking? How can giving attention to a certain thought or emotion give rise to more reasons to think that thought or experience that emotion?

The thoughts we consciously choose or subconsciously allow ourselves to think bring about the emotions that we experience. When we give attention to thoughts of something, we end up feeling emotions corresponding with whether we actually want to be headed to the destination we are focusing on. Our feelings are like a thermostat, a monitor of our thoughts.

So we should check in with ourselves every once in a while and ask ourselves how we're feeling. Then we should ask ourselves what we're thinking about and giving our attention to that is making us feel this way. If we're not feeling good, we should change our thoughts and focus on things that make us feel good.

But why should this matter? Can't we just do what we need to do in life regardless of what we're thinking and feeling? How does our internal world affect our external world?

There are layers to the answer to this. We could explain some of why our thoughts and feelings affect the outcome by pointing out that what we are thinking and feeling immediately comes through in our facial expressions, the volume and intonation of our voices, the wording we choose, our body language, etc. People react to all of this in us whether they're consciously aware of it or not. We basically wear our emotions on our faces and our voices and our bodies and everything else. This alone can explain how our thoughts and feelings could determine whether a job interview or a date goes well or poorly. Feeling good about ourselves and our lives, feeling like we belong in this job or relationship, being confident about this, etc., is much more likely to get us the results we want than feeling bad about ourselves and our lives, feeling like we don't belong in this job or relationship, being insecure about this, etc. Our thoughts and feelings could therefore determine whether we get a job or a relationship.

Our internal worlds can also likewise determine whether people want to be around us or not, and which types of people. Ever heard the saying "Misery loves company"? If we aren't in a good place internally, we will likely attract people to us and be drawn to people who also aren't in a good place internally. And our stresses play off each other. On the other hand, if we are in a good place internally, we attract more of the same, and the happiness spreads and reinforces the happiness in the people around us. Further, most people would rather avoid people who don't feel good about themselves and who therefore bring them down with negative energy and negative talk and actions, unless they are feeling similarly negative. People who feel good about themselves and who bring people up around them with positive energy and positive talk and actions are like people magnets, on the other hand, because we feel good when we're around them and so we want to be around them. We can also notice that people are inclined to group together with other people who think and feel similarly to the way they do about certain things. That's how all groups are formed, from a group of friends to a religion or nation—based on similar beliefs, similar internal ways of operating, and ultimately similar focuses of attention.

The timing in which we do and say things changes depending on how we're thinking and feeling. Even if we're saying exactly the same words or performing exactly the same actions, we're much more likely to get the right timing that will get us favorable results when we're in a good place. This is because when we're in a good place, we're more present to what's going on around us. We are therefore more likely to pick up social and environmental cues that tell us when to speak and act, and we are more likely to listen to these cues and actually adapt our behavior and speech to them.

Basically, the goings-on of our internal worlds determine whether we are more or less in tune with the external world. We determine with our thoughts and feelings whether we are working with the world, against the world, or some combination of the two. When we are aligned internally with our focus on a desirable destination, we are working with the world, and the world helps us forward toward that destination. When we are misaligned internally with conflicting destinations, we feel like we're working against the world and against ourselves, and we essentially are.

Whatever we are thinking and feeling also determines what we notice in the world around us and when. So we likely never even notice the right job opportunity or the right life partner or the answer to our question—let alone act on these opportunities and information—until we're ready to find them.

When we are really in the zone, we begin to transcend any logical physical explanations for how our GPS systems work in relation to everyone and everything else. It truly seems that all of our personal internal GPS systems are coordinating us with each other so that we are interacting with each other even merely through our thoughts and feelings. We don't need to interact physically with people through words and behaviors in order for them to get our message.

This is where Jungian synchronicities and apparently purposeful happenings come in. You think of someone you haven't seen or spoken with in years, and that person calls you that day. You think out a response to an email, and the person responds to your specific response before you even type it up and send it. You learn something that then plays out everywhere around you—in your friends' life experiences and the conversational topics they bring up, in movies you watch at that time, etc. You ask a question and end up involved in a conversation or go to a lecture where you hear the answer you were looking for without your even bringing up the topic. You think something about yourself—be it a compliment or insult—and then someone speaks not just that same thought and feeling but those very same words to you later that day.

How are we to explain people and the world around us responding to us when we haven't even said or done anything more than merely thinking a thought?

The only reason the whole situation seems paranormal is that we think of our thoughts, feelings, and desires as existing inside ourselves—in our minds—separate from and inaccessible to other people and the world around us. However, the reality is that our thoughts, feelings, and desires cannot actually be separate from other people's thoughts, feelings, and desires. This is because there is nothing to separate them.

Our bodies are separated by space and time from other people's bodies, and though our particular thoughts, feelings, and desires might be separated by time—existing in this moment, but not earlier or later—they are certainly not separated by space. Our thoughts, feelings, and desires are not physical things that they could be separated by space. We often think in science of thoughts, feelings, and desires as products of our brains' neural firing. But our thoughts, feelings, and desires actually shape our brains even as they seem also to be shaped by our brains.

Our brains are like computers that have their own processing systems but that connect to the internet for new information, software, and networking with the world outside of their own hardware and software. So if you're like a computer hooked up to the internet, as we all are, there shouldn't be a question of whether other people can access your thoughts, feelings, and desires or not.

Every computer can access every other computer that is hooked up to the internet. Some computers are harder to access, and some files on some computers are harder to access, but everything is accessible. Nothing is truly private. When you think or feel or want something, other people can access this thought, feeling, or want. If you think or feel something about someone, you are affecting that person whether you like it or not. So it is not just your behaviors that get you the reactions you get from other people; it is your thoughts and feelings about those people and about other related topics that get you the reactions you get from other people.

Furthermore, as was mentioned earlier, the way you treat yourself determines the way other people treat you. This is because they have access to this information, and they help you get to the destinations that you are setting for yourself. You are essentially setting the example for everyone around you, getting people and the world around you on your team helping you out as you specify through your internal and external behaviors.

Another way to think about how this all works is to think of you and everyone and everything around you as leaves on a tree. We are not separate from each other, because we are all part of the same tree, and anything that affects the branches or the trunk further down will affect not only the single leaf that is you, but also all of the leaves around you and potentially all of the leaves of the tree. Our choices, thoughts, feelings, and desires are the trunk and branches of the tree, leading not only to the single leaf that is you, but also to every other leaf on the tree. The further along we go in this creative process, eventually to physical actions, the closer we go to the singular, particular manifestation of you as a single leaf. But earlier in the process, where it seems that we are most within ourselves and isolated from the outside world, we are actually very much affecting every leaf around us and even every leaf of the tree of existence.

At the point where the destinations we set seem to intermingle with the destinations that others set and every interaction becomes clearly purposeful, such that we are all messengers for each other, we begin to get at the singular Source of existence who is coordinating all of this—the Source of every one of us, of which every one of us is merely an extension, a projection, a messenger and, in actuality, the Source that we all actually are at our Source. We begin to recognize that we cannot all have our own GPS systems that seem to position us, guide us, and coordinate us so well with one another unless there is something analogous to human-made satellites in relation to which our position is being determined by human-made GPS systems so that we might determine our position on the surface of the earth. Thus, while "GPS" stands for "Global Positioning System" in regard to the human-made version, which tells us our position in relation to the globe, we might recognize that "GPS" could stand for "God Positioning System" in regard to the Source-made version, which tells us our position in relation to the Source of existence and all fulfillment—in relation to our highest, truest nature and selves.

Everything Has A Natural Frequency Of Vibration

Everything has a natural frequency at which it vibrates. This vibration is energy. You may have seen a demonstration at some point where an opera singer shatters a glass. The glass begins to vibrate when its natural frequency of vibration is matched by the sound of the opera singer's voice. When the singer sings loudly enough, so there is enough energy at this frequency, the glass vibrates so much that it breaks. Likewise, a tuning fork begins to vibrate if a piano key that is tuned to match the tuning fork's natural frequency of vibration is pressed. Whenever one thing is around a second thing that is emanating energy at the natural frequency of vibration of the first thing, the first thing will resonate and begin to vibrate with the energy emanated by the second thing.

When we give a thought attention and energy, it produces an emotion that vibrates at the same frequency as that thought. This emotion then gives rise to an instinct that vibrates at the same frequency as the emotion and the preceding thought. And this instinct gives rise to spoken words and physical actions that bring about physical outcomes that support the vibration of the thought, emotion, and instinct that gave rise to them. Just as a piano key, when pressed, can cause a tuning fork to vibrate if its frequency matches the natural frequency of vibration of the tuning fork, if something happens or someone says or does something or simply feels something that has a frequency of vibration that matches that of any of your thoughts, feelings, and instincts at the time, you will resonate as those matched thoughts, feelings, and instincts begin to vibrate within you, energized by the external stimulus.

This is why when something happens it can seem to stir up or reinforce some thought, feeling, and instinct that is already within you (and *only* one that is *already* within you). And this is also why that event or happening can then seem to trigger the arising of a series of memories from the past, all connected by the same emotional vibration.

Imagine a scene in a busy city where many people are and several things are happening. You are standing in this scene, and you just had a miserable day where nothing seemed to go your way. Your emotional vibration will seem to highlight everyone and everything in this scene that matches it and resonates with it. The spotlight of your attention is drawn to the person who walks right into you and doesn't even apologize, the person who shouts some obscenity on the phone nearby, the angry faces and voices of some people arguing as you pass them by, the too-loud music that you don't even like blasting from a bar, etc. This all brings up a bunch of negative thoughts, feelings, and desires. Perhaps you think about how annoying people are, how you feel uncomfortable, overwhelmed, and frustrated, how you wish everyone would just be quiet.

Imagine the same scene in the same busy city where many people are and several things are happening. You are standing in this scene, but now, you just had the most fantastic day where everything seemed to go your way. Your emotional vibration will again seem to highlight everyone and everything in this scene that matches it and resonates with it. Consequently, the spotlight of your attention is drawn to the happy faces and voices of some friendly-looking people nearby, the perfect timing of the light as it changes to allow you to walk just as you get to the intersection, the face of an attractive person who makes eye contact with you and smiles, the beautiful evening breeze as it brushes past your face. This all brings up a bunch of positive thoughts, feelings, and instincts. Perhaps you think about how pleasant it is to be alive, how you feel like you belong here in the world and like you are connected to it and part of it, how you'd love to experience this more often.

The same exact situation can be experienced completely differently based on your natural frequency of vibration at the time based on the thoughts, feelings, and instincts to which you are giving your energy and attention. Further, you will actually be altering what comes to you in the world around you to be experienced by you. In the above situation, for example, you will be more likely to end up in the path of someone else who also isn't paying attention to where he or she is going if you are lost in your own internal negative world and aren't present to the world around you, and you will be more likely to have someone make eye contact with you and smile at you if you are present to your surroundings and already smiling yourself. The former scenario will support and reinforce any negative thoughts, feelings, and instincts you already had that brought about your experience of the situation and drew your attention to it. The latter scenario will support and reinforce any positive thoughts, feelings, and instincts you already had that brought about your experience of the situation and drew your attention to it.

Creating a negative internal vibration by giving your attention to negative thoughts, feelings, and instincts highlights all the negative things and negative aspects of things in your experience and actually brings more negative things to you—things that would make you feel negative—as you feed them with your attention and energy and thereby reinforce them. Creating a positive internal vibration by giving your attention to positive thoughts, feelings, and instincts highlights all the positive things and positive aspects of things in your experience and actually brings more positive things to you—things that would make you feel positive—as you feed them with your attention and energy and thereby reinforce them. This is all because the thoughts, feelings, and instincts that you are giving your attention and energy determine what you experience in the world around you as you draw to you and into your attention those people and things whose frequency of vibration is a match to that of those thoughts, feelings, and instincts.

For the tuning fork, it is as though anything that is vibrating around it almost isn't even there unless it is vibrating at a frequency that matches or is very near to matching the frequency at which the tuning fork naturally vibrates when it is struck. It is the same for us. It is as though anything that is around us that has a very different frequency to that of the thoughts, feelings, and instincts that are existing within us is hardly even there. We are only inclined to draw into our awareness and notice those things that are moving at the frequency at which the thoughts, feelings, and instincts within us are naturally inclined to move. As we increase our own frequency toward the positive, we shift the setting on our experience of life so that we only experience those things around us that match our new, higher frequency.

Therefore, as soon as you shift internally to a different emotional vibration by shifting your focus of attention to different thoughts, feelings, and instincts, you suddenly begin to notice different aspects of everything you've been experiencing—aspects that are resonant with your new frequency of vibration. This reframing changes your entire perspective. Your focus of attention is suddenly drawn to those experiences and aspects of experiences that support your new thoughts, feelings, and instincts, giving you reason to think what you are currently thinking, feel what you are currently feeling, and want what you are currently wanting, in place of whatever you were experiencing and getting support for previously in what you were noticing arising in your awareness.

Life is an experiment that always gets the results you intend to get in it. What you go in with determines what you come out with. You will draw to you people and experiences that prove what you already believe. Shift your beliefs by opening yourself up to the possibility of a different reality than that which you have been experiencing, and your entire experience of reality will change.

If you cannot easily shift your negative thoughts, feelings, and instincts about something, first redirect your attention to something else about which you think and feel at least slightly more positive. Do some other activity if necessary. Take some time to meditate and just focus on your breathing. Go for a walk or a run outside. Read a positive book, watch a positive video, or listen to a positive song. Or simply focus on what you are actually doing in the moment. Then return with your more positive frequency of vibration to the original topic and try again to respond to and redirect any negative thoughts, feelings, and instincts that arise within you. Your higher, more positive frequency of vibration will cause you to notice more positive elements of the original topic and therefore make it easier to shift your thoughts, feelings, and instincts about it in a positive direction rather than simply gather support for your original negative perspective.

Become a vibrational match to what you want, and you will get it. When you set a clear destination and thoroughly imagine what it would be like to be there, you make yourself a vibrational match to thoughts, feelings, instincts, actions, people, and things that can help you get there. They are highlighted in your experience and you are highlighted in theirs; you are drawn to them and they are drawn to you. Bring yourself into resonance with any goal by focusing on the experience of what it would be like to reach it and be there—on what you would be thinking, feeling, wanting, and doing when you are there. The result is that you will be energized by, and drawn to, this goal and anyone and anything that can help you reach it, and it—along with anyone and anything that can help you reach it—will be energized by you and drawn to you as well.

The Peak Experiences Of Life—Glimpses Into The Fulfillment Of Our Purpose

Introduction To The Spectrums Of Life Experience

The purpose of life can be gleaned from the peak aspects of our life experience. When we stop acting from the feeling that other people and the world around us have to change in order for us to have what we want, we begin to experience something very different from our usual reactive, pinball-in-a-pinball-machine-like experience of life. As we learn how to use our internal GPS to create the experiences that we want, and we align ourselves with those experiences by changing our relationship with ourselves, we begin to experience exactly what we want in life. As we begin consistently to prioritize presence and internal creation and imagining of what our destination feels like before we set out with action, our lives are filled with a magical purposeful wonderment.

Our relationship with our own creations—our own thoughts, feelings, and instincts—and with the reflection of these in our bodies, the circumstances of our lives, and the people we've brought into our lives, determines our entire experience of life. We can cultivate a negative relationship with our own creations where we direct them away from ourselves and toward others, judge and dismiss them, or simply tune them out. When we do this, we are not present to our lives, and our experience is filled with stress in the forms of anger and frustration, shame and regret, anxiety and fear. Alternatively, we can cultivate a positive relationship with our own creations where we direct them toward ourselves, accept and acknowledge them, and tune into them. When we do this, we are present to our lives, and our experience is filled with deep fulfillment in the forms of profound and overflowing peace, love, and joy.

There is no single point of experience of life with set motivations that drive us. Our experience is the result of moving up and down a series of spectrums of possible experience, where our motivations differ depending on where we are on the spectrums. These spectrums range from identification with and attachment to our creations and their reflection in the physical world outside us—where we feel that other people and the world around us need to change in order for us to be happy—to our identification with our truest selves as the creators of our lives and ultimately as the Source of all existence—where we recognize that we are in control of the experience of our lives. In the ideal, we recognize that we are ultimately responsible for our experience, and we—and not anyone or anything else—make it whatever it becomes.

Considering what we imagine and focus our attention on becomes our reality, it is useful to have a guide in understanding and imagining what our experience could be like in the ideal and what makes this different from our usual experience so we can understand how to get to a better experience from wherever we are. So here we'll discuss some of the spectrums of life experience from the extreme negative to the extreme positive, so you can see where you are and why you are where you are and how to get from there to where you want to be (and how to get to where you want to be more often).

First of all, it is important to note that all of the spectrums of life experience follow the patterns that we've explored elsewhere in this book, as does everything. This gives us a basis for understanding them.

When we are young children, we are inclined to get frustrated or angry when we don't have what we want or things aren't as we want them to be in the present moment. When we are adolescents, we are inclined to experience shame and regret when we feel that we should have done something different from what we did in the past, which in some way caused us to be perceived by ourselves and others unfavorably. When we are young adults, we are inclined to worry about and be afraid of the future consequences of the decisions we are making.

When we are young children, we are inclined to be particularly attentive to our not having enough food, the right temperature, cleanliness, etc. When we are adolescents, we are inclined to be particularly attentive to our not belonging or being part of the group, to our being left out. When we are young adults, we are inclined to be particularly attentive to our feeling lonely and disconnected from others.

Self-aware choice is where things change and we shift to the capacity for much more positive experiences of life. This is accessible to us when we are younger, but it is accessible to us to a much greater degree, where we are much more in control of our life experience, from the mid-twenties onward. The pivotal factor is our capacity to recognize the relationship between our internal goings-on and our external goings-on. The more we can be present to everything as it is, was, and will be with acceptance of it and with the awareness that it is what we have created with the focus of our attention and with our relationship with ourselves—and that we can create something different by shifting our focus of attention and our relationship with ourselves—the more we can experience the reason we exist in the first place.

Moving Up Levels Of Health

When we have been stressed for an extended period of time, either because we have been dealing with exceptionally straining circumstances (such as the death of a loved one, the end of a relationship, or the loss of a job), or because we have simply been dealing with things reactively, we get less healthy. When we are not stressed for an extended period of time, either because we have had exceptionally relaxed circumstances in our lives (such as a vacation), or because we have been dealing with things proactively and well rather than reactively, we get healthier.

When we are very unhealthy, we get consumed in our personality-related obstacles as we become fixated on things in this world as the source of our fulfillment. We are wrapped up in ourselves and get lost in our own worlds, interpreting the world through our very warped lens. We are concerned with our own survival, and may often end up on the brink of self-destruction. Everything is about us.

At the worst, we tune out reality and go through the motions, but we are empty inside. One step up, we feel reality should be different and we make an effort to change it from our internal place of frustration and rigidity. Another step up, we aggressively try to impose ourselves on the world, control it, and make it what we want it to be from our internal place of anger.

When we are in the average range of health, we try to orient ourselves in relation to other people, attempting to find our role in the world and fit in. Our actions are still often from self-interested motives, as we care about our own social roles and reputations and the way we are coming across to others. Other people are just projections of us.

At the bottom here, we try to meet other people's expectations of us at the expense of meeting our own expectations of ourselves. One step up, we try to distinguish ourselves from others and make ourselves important by rejecting parts of ourselves. Another step up, we try to help others in order to make ourselves feel needed and appreciated when we're not yet fully there for ourselves.

When we are in the healthy range, we recognize and validate other people's perspectives as we come to recognize and validate our own perspective. We connect with other people as other people, and we are able to be genuinely there for them as we are already there for ourselves. We want to help lift other people up and share our positive experience of the world with them, guiding them toward better decisions for themselves in accordance with what they really think, feel, and want. Other people are other individuals who are similar to us in some ways and different from us in other ways and who have their own valid perspectives on the world.

At the bottom here, we begin to trust our own internal guidance rather than simply looking to others for guidance, and we begin to trust that things could actually go right and keep being good as long as we keep listening to our own internal guidance. One step up, we really begin to enjoy ourselves and life, deeply connecting with it, and we face, acknowledge, and address any issues that arise so that we can truly move on from them. At the peak, we delve deeply into each moment of experience fully with understanding, awareness, and profound presence.

As we get healthier, we shift from being motivated away from what we are afraid of experiencing, which we focus on in order to avoid and so end up creating for ourselves, to being motivated toward what we want and would love to experience, which we focus on in order to achieve and so end up creating for ourselves. When we run away from something, we have no specific direction or destination and so can't get anywhere that we can recognize as being where we wanted to be. When we run toward something, we have direction and a sense of purpose, we get where we aim to be going, and we know when we've gotten there because we've already specified what "there" should be like. The goal is to shift from trying to get *away* from what we *don't* want to trying to get *to* what we *do* want. This shift is pivotal to our growth. It requires that rather than focusing on our negative experiences and thereby creating more of them, we instead use them as contrast to provide us with the opportunity to try to imagine and focus on alternative possible experiences that are more positive, or at least to open ourselves to the possibility that something else could happen and that we could experience something different and better.

The Spectrums Of Human Experience

In order to understand all of this better, let's more closely examine the internal landscape of human experience in its various specific spectrums from extremely negative experiences to extremely positive experiences.

The Spectrum Of The Instinctual Stages

The spectrum of the instinctual stages of development is from complete emptiness and powerlessness to complete presence and power.

In the negative, you experience emptiness, powerlessness, and chaos. You might experience this if you just found out that someone you know committed suicide, or that there was a terrorist attack on your country. It feels like you're pulling back into yourself, surrounded by chaos, and nothing you can do can possibly have any positive effect or yield you any control over the situation.

Just under midway up the spectrum, you experience goosebumps on your skin, and just above midway up the spectrum, you experience chills running up and down your spine. You might experience goosebumps if someone jumps out and yells, "Boo!" It feels more bad than good since you aren't ready to be present in your body much at all, and you only feel the energy in your periphery—in your skin. You have been thrown into your body and the world around you much more fully than you were a moment ago, suddenly and unexpectedly and without being prepared for it. You might experience chills, or waves of energy running up and down your body, if you have been stressed lately and you just gave a speech where everyone is clapping and giving you a standing ovation. It feels good but not completely good because you don't feel ready to be present in your body and in the world around you fully since you still feel like there's too much that is wrong and chaotic that you're not in control of there. It's sort of like you're jumping into your body suddenly and unevenly, resulting in waves of energy running up and down.

In the positive, you experience complete presence, power, and harmony. You might experience this if you have been in a good place lately, as due to your taking care of everything in your life in a balanced way, and you just gave a speech and you're getting a standing ovation, or you are now seeing a business that you have been creating really taking form. It feels like your whole body is vibrating with positive, harmonious energy and power. It feels like your presence matters and is positive and good, like you're having a positive impact by being there, and like you're completely in control. It feels like you're immensely powerful, like you're on top of the world.

The key to bringing about the positive version of the experience associated with the instinctual stages is to be present to your own instincts so you can recognize them as harmonious, listen to and accept them so you can recognize them as good, and direct them toward yourself so you can recognize them as powerful.

The Spectrum Of The Feeling Stages

The spectrum of the feeling stages of development is from total helplessness and rejection to total love and self-worth.

In the negative, you feel like a failure, insignificant and helpless. You might experience this if you just closed the door of your car and you realize that your keys are now locked inside, or if you are climbing up stairs and you miss a step. It feels like a sinking feeling of regret located mainly in your heart or chest area and dropping toward your stomach. You feel like you screw things up, like you're not valuable or worthy of being treated well or cared about.

Just above midway up the spectrum, you experience a flow or flush of energy through your body, stemming from your heart or chest area. But it feels like there is a blockage of the flow, and so this results in a feeling of tightness or restriction in the chest or throat area. You might experience this if you have been stressed lately and someone you care about compliments you or hugs you. It feels good but not completely good because you don't feel entirely worthy of being cared about or valued since you don't fully care about or value yourself at this point. It's sort of like a river of energy is flowing through you, but there is a partial dam in the river, restricting the energy from flowing freely throughout your body.

In the positive, you experience complete love, self-worth, value, and acceptance. You might experience this if you have been in a good place lately, as due to your taking care of everything in your life in a balanced way, and someone you care about hugs you, or you just helped someone in need and the person smiles at you with appreciation and thanks you profusely. It feels like the energy of love, value, and self-acceptance is flowing freely through your body. It might feel warm. It might feel a bit like electricity. But it always feels like flushing or flowing energy all through your body and it is feels wonderful—like you're important, like you're loved, cared about, and valued for who you are. It's sort of like a river of loving energy is flowing freely through your body and overflowing from you to everyone and everything around you. You feel such tremendous love and appreciation—directed inward to the point of overflowing outward.

The key to bringing about the positive version of the experience associated with the feeling stages is to be present to your own feelings so you can recognize them as valuable, listen to and accept them so you can recognize them as significant, and direct them toward yourself so you can recognize them as loving.

The Spectrum Of The Thinking Stages

The spectrum of the thinking stages of development is from complete ungroundedness and fear to complete groundedness and awe.

In the negative, you experience incapacitating fear. You might experience this if you have too many things to do and you try to keep them all in your head at once to the point that it becomes entirely overwhelming and confining. It feels like your mind is racing with anxiety, like the gears of your mind are spinning so rapidly that they are out of control and not latching onto anything or effectively processing anything. It feels like the world around you is moving at the torturous pace of your racing mind, and you are moving in slow motion in relation to everything, unable to process or handle it all and keep up with the pace. You feel painfully ungrounded, trapped, and overwhelmed, paralyzed in fear and indecisiveness.

Just above midway up the spectrum, you experience your mind expanding to encompass and comprehend some of the concepts you are trying to grasp. But it feels like you still can't fully grasp everything because it is still too much for you, still beyond the ability of your mind to process entirely as it races with the repetition of thoughts in an attempt to encompass it all. You might experience this if you have been stressed lately and you are looking out over a vast and awe-inspiring landscape or thinking about the concepts of infinity or eternity or God. It feels good but not completely good because you don't feel ready to grasp and encompass the view or the concept fully since you are still preoccupied with and distracted by your own staticky thinking. It's sort of like your mind is trapped in a bottle, unable to break through and expand beyond the confines of its own borders.

In the positive, you experience complete understanding, stability, clarity, and joy. You might experience this if you have been in a good place lately, as due to your taking care of everything in your life in a balanced way, and you are looking out over seemingly endless ocean or sky or land, or reading a profound poem, or thinking about a vast concept like infinity, eternity, or God. It feels like your mind is expanding to encompass everything within its awareness and understanding, seemingly without limits. It feels like a clear-minded knowing without any active thought. You feel like you are experiencing Truth and are amazingly supported by it and free, and you are overflowing with ineffable joy, awe, wonder, and gratitude for the experience.

The key to bringing about the positive version of the experience associated with the thinking stages is to be present to your own thoughts so you can recognize them as trustworthy, listen to and accept them so you can recognize them as fulfilling, and direct them toward yourself so you can recognize them as capable.

The Spectrum Of The Preserving Inclination

The spectrum of the preserving inclination is from being completely uncomfortable in your own body and environment and feeling disgusting and without sufficient time, money, etc., to being completely comfortable in your body and environment and feeling clean and with abundant time, money, etc.

In the negative, you feel like you don't have enough resources to meet your needs and survive. You might experience this if you haven't been spending enough time attending to your own health and well-being in positive ways—sleeping sufficiently, getting necessary work done, eating the right amounts of the right foods, exercising, bathing, earning money, etc. This could be because you have been giving too much attention to this area of life—leading to unbalanced, stressed attention due to insufficient attention to other key areas of life—or because you have been giving too little attention to this area and so are now stressed out and experiencing the results of your having ignored this area of life. Either way, you feel dirty and disgusting in your own skin, overtired, too hot or too cold, overstuffed or starving, surrounded by a mess that needs to be organized and cleaned, lacking in sufficient money and energy, behind on work, and either like you don't want to be around anyone or like you just want the comfort of having your family around. You feel uncomfortable in your own skin and surroundings, like nothing is as it should be, and like you have no control over it all.

Just above midway up the spectrum, you feel like you have reasonably sufficient resources to meet your needs. Your body and surroundings feel somewhat comfortable and as they should be, and you feel somewhat in control of them. You might experience this if you have been stressed and unbalanced in your attention to different areas of life lately but you have just gotten a good night's sleep and gotten some work done, cleaned, exercised, gone for a walk outside where the weather is beautiful, bathed, and are eating a healthy and tasty meal in a well-lit room. It feels good but not completely good because you still don't feel ready to settle into your body and your environment fully since you still feel like there is work to do to get everything as it should be inside and outside of you in order for you really to be comfortable and relaxed. It still feels like you need more money, time, etc., and that you have not yet gotten complete control over the situation.

In the positive, you feel like you have more than enough resources to meet your needs and thrive. You might experience this if you have been doing a great job of balancing your attention to different areas of life lately and you have been getting just the right amount of sleep at the right times, the right amounts of the right foods, the right amount of exercise, sunshine and fresh air. You are getting any work done that needs to get done and feeling like you're earning more than a sufficient amount of money to remain in control of your environment and live comfortably. When you are regularly taking care of work, sleep, eating, cleanliness of yourself and your surroundings, health, family, etc., and you do this in balance with attention to other life priorities, your experience of your body, your surroundings, your belongings, your career, and your family shifts. You are wide awake and extremely lucid, and it feels almost like you're living in a fairytale land where the very air around you is soft and comfortable, your clothes are like soft pajamas that smoothly drape your clean skin, your shoes are like slippers, and the lighting and temperature are absolutely perfect. It feels as though the world around you is a comfortable cushion or even a womb, sustaining and nourishing you with everything that you need so that you can thrive. You feel accomplished and entirely in control of your health and your environment, which feels relaxed, harmonious, and perfect in every way.

The key to bringing about the positive version of the experience associated with the preserving inclination is to tune into, attend to, maintain, and preserve yourself.

The Spectrum Of The Belonging Inclination

The spectrum of the belonging inclination is from feeling like you don't belong anywhere and aren't a part of anything to feeling like you are an important, valuable, integral part of something larger than yourself.

In the negative, you feel like you don't belong anywhere. You might experience this if you haven't been spending enough time attending to being part of something larger than yourself in positive ways. This could be because you have been giving too much attention to this area of life—leading to unbalanced, stressed attention due to insufficient attention to other key areas of life—or because you have been giving too little attention to this area and so are now stressed out and experiencing the results of your having ignored this area of life. Either way, you feel like you don't fit in, like you aren't a part of any group, team, or community. You feel like you aren't significant or valuable to any group of people and like you aren't helpful to or cared about by any group of people. You feel like you are left out, like you have no real role or part in anything larger than yourself, and therefore your actions seem to be insignificant and to have no real value.

Just above midway up the spectrum, you feel like you are somewhat part of some group. You feel like you have some importance and value in something larger than yourself. You might experience this if you have been stressed and unbalanced in your attention to different areas of life lately but you have just spent some time with a group of people and felt somewhat included and part of the group. It feels good but not completely good because you still don't feel ready to accept and include all parts of yourself since you still feel like you wouldn't belong somewhere and really be important, valuable, and appreciated there, and so you still have to work to belong. It still feels like you need to do things to identify or create a role for yourself so that you'll really be wanted in the group.

In the positive, you feel like you are an integral part of the interconnected web of interactions of everyone and everything in the world around you. You might experience this if you have been doing a great job of balancing your attention to different areas of life lately and you have been attending just the right amount to hanging out with groups of people, working with other people toward mutual, larger goals, etc. You feel like you are part of something much larger than yourself, like all of your actions have a higher purpose and greater impact than simply what they seem in themselves because they are magnified and built upon by the efforts of others who are working toward the same goal. When you are regularly participating in group activities such as singing as part of a choir, dancing with a bunch of people, playing as part of a team, or working on a project as part of an organization, and you do this in balance with attention to other life priorities, your experience of being part of something shifts. You come to feel like you don't have to work to be important to any particular exclusive group because you are an invaluable part of the group of the entire world just by being you. You are a vital part of something tremendously greater than you as you work on the same team as everyone and everything else toward the world's accomplishing its goals. It feels like you merge with the group of the world and are on the same side as everyone and everything around you, totally accepted by them as you are and totally accepting of them as they are in the valuable and helpful roles that you and they play in bringing the whole world to greater awareness. You become part of it all, truly belonging, like a necessary cog in the works that plays an irreplaceable role in the interconnected web of interactions with a unique contribution in bringing the whole world to its larger aims.

The key to bringing about the positive version of the experience associated with the belonging inclination is to allow all parts of yourself to belong within you by accepting every part of yourself.

The Spectrum Of The Connecting Inclination

The spectrum of the connecting inclination is from feeling lonely and disconnected to feeling connection and intensity in all of your interactions with everyone and everything around you.

In the negative, you feel lonely and disconnected. You might experience this if you haven't been spending enough time attending to one-on-one connections with other individual people in positive ways. This could be because you have been giving too much attention to this area of life—leading to unbalanced, stressed attention due to insufficient attention to other key areas of life—or because you have been giving too little attention to this area and so are now stressed out and experiencing the results of your having ignored this area of life. Either way, you feel like you don't have anyone to share your life with, like you don't have any really close friends or especially a significant other to whom you can really connect deeply. You feel like you don't have anyone in your life who understands you and whom you understand, whom you can trust and on whom you can depend and who can depend on you, and with whom you can be truly happy. You also fear that you may never find such a person. You feel like your experience of life lacks any real depth or intensity because it is lacking your real connection to it as well as someone with whom to share it.

Just above midway up the spectrum, you feel like you are somewhat connected. You feel like you have someone or some people who somewhat understand you, who are somewhat there for you, and to whom you can somewhat connect. You might experience this if you have been stressed and unbalanced in your attention to different areas of life lately but you have just spent a long time in an intense, enjoyable conversation with someone. It feels good but not completely good because you still don't really feel ready to open up and share yourself with someone and really connect since you still feel like you can't fully trust anyone, including yourself, to understand you. You also generally still feel somewhat disconnected from yourself, so you don't feel ready to connect deeply with the world outside yourself for fear of losing yourself.

In the positive, you feel intensely connected to everyone and everything around you. You might experience this if you have been doing a great job of balancing your attention to different areas of life lately and you have been attending just the right amount to connecting with other individuals and the world around you in extended, deep conversations and interactions. You feel like you are so connected to everything around you that everything seems brighter, clearer, crisper, more vibrant and vivid. When you are regularly engaging in prolonged, intense conversations and interactions with other individuals and the world around you, and you do this in balance with attention to other life priorities, your experience of being part of something shifts. You come to experience the world in crystal clarity, with brighter, more vibrant colors and crisp images that are glowing with intensity. You begin to merge with the other person through the intensity of the conversation and the sense of complete security and understanding in the relating of experiences through the connection. It feels like the boundaries of walls and people lose concreteness and tangibility; your experience merges with the other person's experience as you trust and know with certainty that you are completely understood, that you are discussing and sharing the same thoughts and feelings, that you are on the same wavelength as each other. As you merge with the other person or with some other aspect of the world in prolonged, deep interaction, you are filled to overflowing with the most intense joy and fulfillment as you experience the intense relating and clarity of connection.

The key to bringing about the positive version of the experience associated with the connecting inclination is to be present to, and connect with, yourself.

How To Move Up The Spectrums Of Experience

We can identify key themes in these spectrums of experience that indicate how we can ensure that we'll move toward the higher ends of the spectrums more often and more reliably in our own experience of the world:

1. Be present with your awareness where you are. When you are present and paying attention to yourself and the world around you, your experience is far more positive.
2. Cultivate a relationship with yourself that you'd like to have with others and the world around you. However you make yourself feel is the way everyone and everything will make you feel. So treat yourself the way you want to be treated.
3. Acknowledge, listen to, and respond to what is inside you, because otherwise it will only continue to distract you and take your attention away from what is outside you. Your experience will be filled with lack, nagging, and dissatisfaction if this is what you are creating inside you through lack of acceptance and appropriate acknowledgement of your own thoughts, feelings, and desires. Your experience will be filled with positivity, peace, love, and joy if this is what you are creating inside you through acceptance and appropriate acknowledgement of your own thoughts, feelings, and desires.

Remember: Your thoughts are the destinations you are plugging into your internal GPS system. Your feelings help you gauge whether these are good destinations or bad destinations to be headed toward—whether it feels good or feels bad to go there. Your feelings are also the fuel in the car that motivates you in the direction of the destinations you have specified with your thoughts, and toward more of themselves—toward more reasons to experience the same feelings. Your wants, instincts, desires, inclinations are the directions your GPS is providing you, guiding you toward the destinations you have specified with your thoughts and toward more of the feelings that you are giving your energy to. Your actions get you to those destinations that you have specified with your thoughts, and therefore toward greater justification for the thoughts, feelings, and inclinations to which you have been giving your attention and energy.

Acknowledge the world inside and outside of you for what it all is—the experience that you are creating for yourself—and so pay attention to it, accept it, respond to it, and shift it where appropriate in order to keep yourself on track toward more desirable and fulfilling experiences.

How To Make Life Deeply Fulfilling

In order to make life really fulfilling, we have to exercise and refine our power to create it. That's essentially why we're here in existence—to learn to cultivate a relationship with ourselves, and thereby with the Source of existence and with everything within existence, that we would ideally want to have. The physical life experiences we have are just reflections of our relationship with ourselves along the way, and as we learn to transform our relationship with ourselves, we learn to transform our actions and reactions to the world around us and, consequently, we learn to transform our life experiences.

As we learn to listen to ourselves, we learn what we want in life, and we must assert what we want, align ourselves with it, focus on it, feed it and nothing contradictory to it, until we achieve it. We must set general destinations to give ourselves direction in order to take steps forward, and we must refine and clarify our destinations as we go.

Within our larger destinations, we must set smaller destinations—where we'll aim to reach and set up basecamps along the way toward the peak of the mountain we're climbing. Along the way, we must remind ourselves that we don't need to know where we're going for sure, and we definitely don't need to know how to get there. We just need to decide where we'd like to go in some general form and specify this as clearly as we can at every step of the way based on what we like about past and present experiences that we'd also like in future ones, and based on what we don't like about past and present experiences, which we must use as contrast to determine what we'd like instead in the future.

Even if all you can say at first is what you'd like to feel, then that's enough to begin with. Let the GPS guide you closer to that, and specify the contents further as you go. And let the GPS guide you to your destination even after you know what this is; you don't need to figure out how to get there yourself, and trying to get there without listening to yourself along the way will require a lot of effort and won't get you there. So set your destinations, let go, and address whatever beliefs, and shift any internal dynamics, that come up that aren't compatible with those destinations on the way there.

With destinations to head toward, and alignment with them, come a sense of purpose, motivation, drive, energy, and aliveness in life. When we have somewhere to go that we really want to go to, and we are actually in the process of actively going there, we experience what it really is to be alive, with life in our lives.

If we don't set destinations, we simply drift. If we set destinations and maintain contradictory destinations so that we aren't aligned with getting where we actually want to go, we feel constant tension in life. With contradictory destinations in our GPS, wherever we are and wherever we're going, we're on track in regard to one destination and are going the wrong direction in regard to another destination, so we feel pulled in different directions, never to be fully where we are, and never to be fully satisfied or fulfilled.

So we need to exercise our ability to be always improving our situation in life, always challenging ourselves to learn new lessons by asking for new experiences and going through the process of coming into alignment with getting them. By always determining clear destinations toward which we can and would like to be striving, we ensure that we will live with purpose and direction in every moment of our lives.

Creating Entirely New Experiences

When it comes to asking for entirely new things that we've never experienced before, this is where being present is vital. Asking for something we've never experienced before, or even that we're simply not experiencing now, inevitably results in our reacting by calling upon all of our past experiences that seem to us to be evidence that we can't achieve this new experience. We've never experienced this before, we tell ourselves, so why should we believe we'll experience it now or ever?

The result is that we end up afraid of being disappointed by an experience that doesn't meet our expectations. It seems safer to keep open an option that we really believe can get us where we want to go than to exhaust our options and take the very actions that we believe will actually get us where we want to go. Because what if they don't take us there? What if we do everything we are aware that we can possibly do to be happy with our lives and to get the results that we want, and then we still aren't happy with our lives and we still don't get the results that we want? Or what if we actually get the outward results we want—the relationship, or the career, or the living situation, or the financial situation, or whatever—that we believe will really make us happy and then we're still not happy? What then? It seems like it's almost better just to stay where we are and do what we've been doing or keep trying alternatives to what we really believe will get us where we want to go because then we'll always have the sense of freedom that comes from knowing that there's still the possibility of our getting what we really want. We still have a path that is within our awareness and control to take that could lead us there.

"What if I do what I really believe will get me where I want to go and I don't get where I want to go? What if I put my all—my energy, my time, my other resources and the extent of my capability—into getting what I want, and I still don't get it; what then?" Asking these questions is a recipe for failure and disappointment. We cannot succeed until we fully align with our desired destination because we won't actually put the necessary energy and time into the necessary places in order to reach our intended destination unless we actually believe in the possibility of its becoming our reality. If you say you want something and then add on "But what if I don't get it?" you are making your destination into the disappointment of not getting what you want, rather than keeping your destination as the excitement of actually getting what you want. We can't be adding on to our destination the fear of the possible disappointment that could result if we don't get there and still feel motivated to put our all into getting there.

So we stay where we are in life—where things are familiar and therefore, in a sense, comfortable. And we attempt to optimize our experience of where we are and keep at least one really good and believable option open that keeps us feeling somewhat in control of the possibility of getting where we really want to go.

You can either guarantee that you will stagnate in the maintenance of your past and present experience of life and be disappointed by not getting what you want in life, or you can guarantee that you'll keep evolving and opening new pathways to yourself as you go for how you can always be improving your experience. There will always be new doorways opening where we might have suspected, based on previous experiences and disappointments, that there were only walls. But if we don't step through the first doorway that might really lead us where we want to go, we'll never be able to keep ourselves moving forward, finding out what exists beyond this doorway and discovering what new doorways will reveal themselves to us beyond there.

We need to step out of our current emotional and mental state in order to break out of our creation of the future based on the past and the present. By practicing being mindful of this moment, letting go of the past and our imagined futures and simply being fully here now, we can achieve this. We can truly step out of our identification with our current thoughts, feelings, and instincts about how things are and have been. From the place of our complete presence to this moment, anything seems possible for the next moment.

This is the next level of listening to ourselves, where we come to realize that listening to ourselves means listening to the part of us that is beyond our identifications with the present and past and an imagined negative future. That part of us recognizes that anything is possible, that we can experience anything we ask for, and that part of us really believes this and so can make anything happen. We simply have to shift out of our experience of linear time and into the eternity of now in order to go beyond our reactively entrenched identifications and into the realm of willful choosing from endless possibilities.

From here, we do not state that things will happen, but instead we simply state, "I would love for this to happen. It would be so nice to experience this. It would be great to be, do, or have this and experience all the excitement of this." Then, we aren't seeming to be attempting to control the future outcome, which would require that we do everything and make this happen ourselves when we have no idea how to guarantee this because we've never been able to make this happen before. Remember, control only leads to reaction, resistance, and rebellion and doesn't lead to motivation toward the outcome we actually want.

So, rather than forcing an outcome with a false or hard-to-believe statement of its (future) reality, we say, "I know that all I need to do is set a destination and then let go. I would love for this to happen and to be pleasantly surprised at how I somehow managed to get everything I really wanted, and that's all. Now I just have to listen to my thoughts, feelings, and instincts as they guide me there. It's not up to me to make this happen. It's just up to me to set a clear destination and then listen to the directions, just as with any GPS." There is no fear of possible disappointment here to hold us back in realities where we've been and are. There is just, "I would love to experience this," and then being present to the excitement of that possibility. Then that exciting possibility is what you are fueling into reality.

Shift

No matter what is going on in your life, take a moment to breathe and simply be present to your breathing. Notice what thoughts, feelings, instincts, sounds, etc. distract you from your breathing. Acknowledge these, respond to them with acceptance and positive redirection, and refocus your attention on your breathing.

Open up your body and your mind. Stand up, put your arms up in the air, and look upward. Stand like this for a couple of minutes and be present to your body. Notice your emotional state shift as you do this. Encourage it along by asserting some positive destinations. What would you love to experience? What would be great? What would be fantastic and amazing? Say it out loud. Maybe even shout it. Let the universe know. Let the Source of everything know. Let your higher self know. Let your creation know. And then go about the rest of your day and be present and listen. And you will be guided toward wherever you requested to go.

Do this regularly, and you will learn from experience that your life is entirely yours to create and recreate at will in every moment.

As you shift from identifying with reactive creation to identifying with proactive, willful creator—recognizing that you are the source of everything you can possibly experience, and that you can shift your experience in this moment simply with a request for another experience—your life becomes yours to shape and create as you choose.

It's Time To Let Go, Turn Around, Face Our Fears, And Move Forward

As we travel down the river of life, we are so often inclined to paddle upstream so that we don't have to face all the obstacles that lie ahead, in the direction of all of our hopes and dreams. But we cannot go backward; the river of life is too powerful to allow this. The closest we can get to this is stagnation. We can continue to paddle with all of our energy to stay in place as we keep looking back at where we came from and around at where we are. But this is a stressful and exhausting way to live.

The alternative is to stop putting so much effort into holding onto the past and resisting moving forward. We must let go of the past and the present, allow the river of life to turn us around, and face all of our fears that have kept us from moving forward.

At first, this is often a very difficult experience; we are inundated with all of the thoughts and emotions and experiences that we were avoiding for so long. We may have put so much of our energy into avoiding these things that we don't have nearly as much energy to face them when we finally give up our paddling against the current of life. But once we get the hang of looking toward where we want to be going downstream and navigating the rocks and other obstacles that we face along the way, we experience the flow of life.

Life requires far less energy than we have been putting into it. This is because it is already taking us where we want to go as long as we allow it to, rather than fighting against it, and we simply navigate as we go. As long as we keep our focus on where we intend to be headed—on all of the great experiences that are up ahead and becoming the present in every moment—life's moments become filled with an ineffably deep peace that is imbued with love and joy.

As we cultivate the relationship with ourselves that involves our truly being present to ourselves, addressing our own needs, and accepting, acknowledging, and listening to our own thoughts, feelings, and desires, our relationships with the people and the world around us are transformed. We must go through the process of learning to respond to each negative experience by asking ourselves the questions, "How might I have brought this into my life, and how can I shift those beliefs, thoughts, feelings, and behaviors toward myself and others so that I experience something more positive from here onward?" Further, we must learn to focus on what we want and show gratitude and appreciation for it and, in doing so, request more of it. This applies to every relationship we have—with ourselves, with other people, and with the Source of everything and the entire world.

As you learn to acknowledge what you don't want and then identify and ask for what you'd like instead by shifting your attention to that, and as you learn to ask for more of what you do want by giving your attention to it, you will come to experience your immense power to shape your life experience. For you are responsible for all of it and no one else. Your life experience is your own. And every relationship and experience you have is no more than a reflection of your relationship with yourself and your internal focus of attention. So as you shift your internal dynamic and focus, you will come to get everything that you ask for. For now you have the key, and all you need to do is use it.

Learning Which Direction In Life Is The Right One

On the road of life, one direction leads to darkness, a cliff and ultimately death, and the other direction leads to increasingly idyllic, fantastic, magical, brilliantly bright scenery and ever increasing life.

Those of us who have been all the way down the road to the edge of the cliff with one and a half feet off the edge, staring down into the abyss, searching for some kind of salvation, know that that direction doesn't lead anywhere but death. There is, therefore, no reason ever to go that direction again. Whenever we go that direction, we know we are going the wrong direction.

There is no way not to know that it is the wrong direction because we've already been down there as far as it goes, and after being one and a half feet into the darkest possible death and staring it in the face, we've realized that nothing we're searching for is down the road that way. Therefore, we've realized that if anything we're really searching for actually exists, it must be down the road in the other direction. And we absolutely must try to go down the road that way to find out, because we know we're going the right direction on this road so there's no reason to waver, and there's every reason at first to get as far away from the darkness and the menacing cliff as possible and, after this, to keep going into the obviously increasing light and life and fantastical scenery.

Those of us who have not yet been all the way down the road to the edge of the cliff, and who have not yet stared down into the darkness long enough and deeply enough to eliminate all doubt that this direction won't lead us to anything we actually want, waver and wander back and forth down the road, not sure which direction to go to get where we want to be going. In this scenario, we can

a) continue to waver back and forth down the road aimlessly, confused and unsure about which direction will lead us where we actually want to go, with little clarity, therefore, about when we are going the right direction and should keep going and when we are going the wrong direction and should turn around,

b) travel all the way down the road into the darkness in order to be sure that this is not the right direction toward everything that we truly want, or

c) learn by really listening to ourselves and—only from that place of listening to ourselves so that we know to what else and to whom to be listening and how—paying attention to and learning from other people and the world around us which direction down the road will get us where we want to go and which direction won't.

I would love to save everyone from getting any closer to the cliff than he or she is already because I would never wish that experience upon anyone. And so I urge everyone: Take responsibility for your own experience by recognizing and acknowledging that *your choices*, alone, determine it and can change it; really listen to yourself; and look where you want to go and not where you don't want to go! Looking where you don't want to go in order to be sure to avoid it or correct it doesn't work because wherever you look, you will go!

But we must all experience whatever we need to experience in order to learn what we need to learn at the pace that we need to learn it. No one and nothing but *you* can determine what you need to experience in order to learn how to create what you actually want for yourself. I wish I could help everyone, but I have learned that I can only help those who are ready to learn. And I've come to realize that this is actually a good thing because, in the school of life, everyone is learning at a pace at which he or she is comfortable, and we'll all get where we're ultimately headed eventually.

Allow Yourself To Think, Feel, And Want Again

In order to turn around and head downstream toward everything you truly want, you must allow yourself to think things again, feel things again, want things again. After ignoring, dismissing, and tuning out your own thoughts, feelings, and instincts for perhaps a lifetime or more, this can be very difficult. At first, you are inundated with everything you have been making your thoughts think, your feelings feel, and your instincts want during all the time you haven't been listening. Like a whole bunch of children who haven't gotten your attention in a long time, your thoughts, feelings, and instincts see their chance and they pounce, all talking at once. But it is possible to work through this barrage and learn to listen to them all one by one, acknowledging them and apologizing to them for treating them as you have, and intending to treat them better going forward, and they gradually calm down. And paying attention and listening is the only way to get where you truly want to go. By tuning into yourself and being present to your own thoughts, feelings, and instincts, you can come to recognize that you already have all the guidance you need in regard to where to go from here.

When you allow yourself to think, to feel, to want without suppression, judgment, neglect, and so forth—without modification due to what other people seem to think or feel or want, or due to what you otherwise feel you "need" to do or "have to" do or "should" be doing—you allow yourself to breathe. There is no need to follow old maps or other people's GPS systems when you have your own GPS system with updated maps and turn-by-turn directions. Allow yourself to think, to feel, to want, and you will recognize that it doesn't take great effort to begin imagining and setting new destinations for yourself. And once you set new destinations and you come to experience what it would be like to be there in your thoughts and feelings and instincts, you can finally let go of where you are and move forward to where you want to be.

When you climb a rock wall, you are very unlikely to let go of the rocks to which you're clinging if you haven't yet looked for and found other rocks to grab onto. Likewise, in life, you are not likely to let go of where you are, of the way you've been experiencing and approaching life, when you have no conception or imagining of where you might go instead. It almost doesn't matter how bad where we are is—it usually has to get really amazingly terrible for us to be willing to leap off of our current handholds and footholds without knowing that we'll land someplace safe. Because we have to get to the point that absolutely anything—including death—would be better than where we are before we would be willing to leap from all of our current identifications and risk the death of ourselves and life as we know it.

When you are swimming poorly and struggling to stay afloat, it is unlikely that you'll try a new swimming stroke as long as your head is above water because you wouldn't want to risk drowning. But once you're tired and can't keep your head above water anymore and you're actually drowning—then you are likely to be much more willing to let go of the way of existing that you've known all along and try something entirely new. Because at this point you're going to drown anyway otherwise, so you might as well make one last attempt even if you don't fully believe it will work. It seems worth it at this point.

Ideally, rather than clinging rigidly to what we already know, we learn to turn around and continually refine our identifications and ways of approaching life, being willing to learn new tools and try new things, even when we aren't already drowning—even before life gets so bad that absolutely anything, including physical death, would be better. The fact is that we must allow parts of ourselves to die, in a sense, in order for us to grow and move on. We must let go of the past and the present, of who we were and who we are, of what we've known ourselves and other people and life to be like. It is, therefore, a kind of death that we must learn to welcome and embrace—the kind that recognizes that every moment of experience rises into existence and falls out of existence, that everything is born and dies in every moment. We and everyone and everything around us are continually evolving, flowing with the river of life, and nothing needs to stay the same from moment to moment, because everything is being created anew in each moment. Nothing that is so now must be so in the next moment. It is up to you whether your experience stagnates or whether it continually flows and evolves. It is entirely up to you.

Somewhere along the way of trying so hard to avoid what you fear or to face your fears and create a different reality, you might recognize that faith and fear are essentially the same: They both involve believing in what hasn't happened yet and doesn't already exist in our experience, and they both make real what is believed in. So we get to choose: faith that things will turn out okay and even as we wish, or fear that they won't. Whichever we choose will become our reality.

So allow yourself to think, to feel, to want again. You will conceive of experiences of life that you have never allowed yourself to believe in before, and you will gradually come to believe in them, and they will gradually become your reality. Your life will unfold much more freely, positively, and beautifully than you've ever known. The world of your experience will become so clearly your chosen creation.

Stop chasing what you want in the world outside you and avoiding yourself. Be still, and let your thoughts, feelings, and instincts catch up to you. Rather than seeking what your thoughts, feelings, and instincts want outside you, stay still and give them what they truly want—your positive attention. Listen to them—to yourself—and life will reveal itself to be truly good.

The Learning Process Can Be Easy, Enjoyable, And Positive

We're often inclined to believe that the learning and growth process has to be difficult. "No pain, no gain." However, there doesn't actually have to be pain in order for there to be growth. In fact, what we are working toward, if we haven't reached it already, is a situation where the growth process is enjoyable, positive, and smooth. In this situation, learning lessons isn't a struggle. Life gently nudges us forward, challenging us to grow and expand ourselves because we ask for it to, and our experience of this is positive every step of the way.

When we have an internal dynamic that involves focusing on where we don't want to go, and consequently ignoring, control, rebellion, and disharmony, the growth process is definitely a struggle. In order to learn, we need to be forced or to force ourselves, because this is the paradigm by which we are operating. But when we cultivate an internal dynamic that involves focusing on where we do want to go, and consequently listening, guiding, response, and harmony, the growth process becomes enjoyable, positive, and good. We recognize that we actually always should be following what makes us feel deeply fulfilled, because the path toward happiness is the path of both a positive experience and rapid growth.

We're going up the mountain of life no matter what. It's up to us whether we take the most unenjoyable route possible by internally forcing, whipping, and discouraging ourselves every step of the way, or whether we take the most enjoyable route possible by internally guiding, encouraging, and supporting ourselves every step of the way. In the former scenario, we experience much or all of the world as seemingly working against us as it reflects our own internal resistance to our own control. In the latter scenario, we experience all of the world as working with us as it reflects our own internal alignment with, and eager following of, our own attentive guidance. The choice is ours to make every step of the way.

Whatever choice we make, it will be reflected in every aspect of our bodies, our relationships, our careers, etc. Everything can be difficult and painful, or everything can be easy and painless. For example: Our digestion of food reflects our attitudes and approaches toward life and the learning process.

It could be difficult, uncomfortable, and painful. We could take in things mindlessly, without paying attention to what we do and don't take in. We could take in too much bad stuff that doesn't contain much that we could benefit from. We could take in too little to have what we require to function optimally. We could only partially digest what we take in and integrate very little of what we could benefit from. We could hold onto what we take in for too long or let it go too quickly. We could experience difficulty and pain processing what we've taken in. We could experience difficulty and pain letting go of what we've taken in.

Alternatively, it could be smooth, easy, comfortable, and painless. We could take in things mindfully, paying attention to what we do and don't take in. We could take in just the right amount of primarily, or only, good stuff that contains a lot that we could benefit from. We could fully digest what we take in and integrate everything we could benefit from. We could let go of everything that we take in as soon as we've processed it fully. We could process everything that we take in smoothly, easily, and painlessly, and let go smoothly, easily, and painlessly of everything that is left over after we've processed it all and integrated what we could benefit from.

We ought to set the destination that our learning and growth process is smooth, easy, comfortable, and painless—that we take in our experiences fully, process them fully and integrate everything we can learn from them easily and painlessly, and then let go of the experiences easily and painlessly, taking with us only the lessons we learned from them. If we intend it, our learning process and integration of lessons can be not only smooth, easy, and painless, but also positive, enjoyable, exciting, liberating, expansive, awe-inspiring, and wonderful. This is our choice. Our experience will be whatever we open ourselves to, bring ourselves to believe is possible and, from this place of possibility, request.

Why wait until some nonspecific future time to enjoy yourself? Life is here, now. You're already living it. If you determine to enjoy every minute of the journey, of every part of the learning process that is life, then you will.

What We Must Learn In Order To Treat Ourselves The Way We Truly Want To Be Treated And Set This Example For Everyone And Everything

We must learn to listen to our own thoughts, feelings, and instincts with total acceptance and recognize the true, positive intentions even in our negative thoughts, feelings, and instincts—that they have our best interests in mind and they are always attempting to help us become the best version of ourselves with all of their efforts.

We must learn to step into the shoes of our own thoughts, feelings, and instincts, and experience what they are truly experiencing and saying to us—without our own beliefs and commentary to interfere with our listening—and, only after this, we must respond to them with consideration of where they are coming from.

We must learn to create an open, accepting, loving relationship with our own thoughts, feelings, and instincts so that they feel comfortable with being fully open with us, so that they tell us everything that they're experiencing and hold nothing back from us that we might need to help them and, ultimately, ourselves.

We must learn to allow ourselves and others to go through the experiences that we're going through, at the pace that we're going through them, so that we learn the lessons that we need to learn when we are ready to receive them. We cannot receive the lessons until we are ready, and we must experience whatever we need to experience in order to become ready to receive the lessons—no less, and no more. This is true of all the people around us as well as of us, and so we must recognize that, sometimes, there is nothing we can do to help. We must simply let them (and us) experience their (our) struggles and wait until they (we) are ready to receive the lessons that the struggles are meant to be teaching them (us).

We must learn to love even the struggles—for they are merely challenging us to become the best version of ourselves that we can possibly become.

We must learn to apologize to our thoughts, feelings, and instincts for how we've treated them in the past. And we must learn to forgive ourselves and the messengers of our ill treatment of ourselves, and let go of our past negative experiences and struggles, carrying forward only the positive lessons that we've learned from them.

We must learn to give our thoughts, feelings, and instincts a clear destination and purpose for every moment by focusing our attention on where we'd like to be headed. When we work with them, they work with us, and when we play our role of letting them know where we'd actually like to go, they can and do play their role of guiding, helping, and directing us there.

The Key To Positive Life Experience Creation

Your life is the product of where you direct your attention and in what form—positive or negative. Wherever you look, you go. Whatever you focus on, you get. Your life is your own creation. The key to creating a positive life experience is to give positive attention to all of your creations, and to give more attention to those that you want more of than to those that you want less of.

As you create your life, remember to make use of the tools you are given to gauge what you are creating before your creation is finalized in physical form in each moment. Your thoughts, feelings, and instincts are the tools with which you shape your life, the measure of the quality of what you are forming and the motivation behind your creation, and the detailed directions you need to bring your creation into the physical world, respectively. They are your guides and supporters, your helpers and motivators, and your protectors and directors, here to accompany you in your process of life creation.

As you create and live your life, remember and apply the following:

1) Always set your desired destinations before you act: Include your thoughts, feelings, and instincts in any plans you make and any actions you take, as well as in any changes you make to these plans of action, by proposing what you'd like to be thinking, feeling, and wanting after you experience what you are proposing to bring about.

2) Always listen to and act on your thoughts, feelings, and instincts as they guide you toward the destinations that you have set—the actualization of the proposals that you have presented to them regarding what

you'd like to experience. Give your thoughts, feelings, and instincts positive attention and follow their guidance, be true to their intentions, and act on their directions.

3) Always respond to your thoughts, feelings, and instincts appropriately when they tell you something. If you have lapsed in listening to them, listening to them now might mean getting back on track toward your original destination—going back to your original proposal that you presented to them and deviated from yourself—or it might mean setting a new destination—presenting a revised proposal to them. Be sure always to be aiming to be treating your thoughts, feelings, and instincts better than you have before based on what they say about what you're making them think, feel, and want.

All of your life experience—every relationship dynamic you have with everyone and everything in your life—is nothing more and nothing less than the result of how well and how willfully you apply the above.

Live Fully In Each Miraculous Moment

Life can seem extraordinarily mundane in the moments that we are tuned out and on autopilot. But in the moments that we are tuned in, we experience life with the awe and wonder of a child experiencing it for the first time combined with the awareness that we are creating everything that we are experiencing.

When we are simply reacting to life, trying to control it, and recreating what we've experienced before, life becomes monotonous, dull, and even torturous as our thoughts, feelings and instincts speak louder and louder to us through themes of intensifying experiences in repeated and exhausting attempts to get our attention and be heard and understood. But when we are paying attention, willfully creating our lives, and responding to each experience, every moment increasingly becomes filled with the specialness, miraculousness, and illumination that come with ephemerality and rarity along with the awareness that the contents of each moment are not random or determined by anyone or anything else outside us but instead are chosen and determined by us. Each moment becomes a gift that is different from the last as we grow and change, always setting new destinations and reaching them, always evolving. Each experience is the most wondrous treasure, filled with the fruits of all the lessons we've learned from everything we've experienced before.

In this magnificent conversation with ourselves that we call life, all of our interactions with everyone and everything are simply interactions with ourselves. This is true no matter where we are in our process of development. We can identify with any part of ourselves at any point in time, with any relationship definition—creator, creation, or the result of the conversation between the two; male, female, child; father, mother, sibling, boss, employee, client, lover, friend, etc. But the other end of every relationship we have is us, too. It is all us interacting with ourselves—the people and the world around us simply roleplaying with us, allowing us to experience the other end of the dynamic we have with ourselves. Sometimes we are initiating, sometimes we are responding, sometimes we are harmonizing. Sometimes we are on one end of the relationship, sometimes we are on the other. Though it is ultimately all us playing out the dynamics we have with ourselves, simply switching which role we play in each dynamic with different people and at different times. We move through lifetimes of experience, identifying with different relationship roles within ourselves as we go, evolving in these relationships, and every lifetime is a moment in eternity.

In this moment in eternity, you are here in your journey. You will be someone else experiencing something else in the next moment. So experience this moment fully, focusing on the best parts of it, and thereby bringing into existence what you'd like to experience in the next moment or in some other future moment as you do so.

You Can Be, Do, Or Have Anything, But You Must Experience What It Would Be Like First

Every experience you want is available to you as long as you can create it in yourself. Ask yourself what you'd like to be or do or have. Then imagine what you'd be thinking and feeling and wanting if you already were or were doing or had this.

What we always really want is the internal experience that we imagine we would have if some aspect of our external experience were to change. We often imagine that our fulfillment comes from outside ourselves, and so we place our happiness in the future or the past or alternative versions of the present. But everything you want is ultimately an internal experience—a way of thinking, of feeling, of wanting—and so is available to you right now.

If only I had a relationship, then I'd be happy. If only my significant other did this, then I'd be happy. If only I had the job that I want, then I'd be happy. If only I had the income that I want, then I'd be happy. If only I were further along this process toward the actualization of all that I want, then I'd be happy. This way of operating will keep you forever unfulfilled. This is because when you operate like this, you are experiencing the world from the role of your creation, and yet you are the creator from whom all that you want comes and who is doing the guiding with the focus of your attention.

When you step with your awareness into the role of creator, you recognize that your reactions to the world are unnecessary and won't get you where you want to go because you are the one who can decide that things will go differently. And not from a place of control, where the entire world is on your shoulders, but from a place of attentiveness and guidance, where all you need to do is imagine the destination that you want to reach and allow your creation, with its thoughts, feelings, and instincts, to guide you there. If you focus on what you are reacting to, then you as the creator are guiding yourself toward more of this. If you focus on what you'd like instead, then you as the creator are guiding yourself toward this instead.

If you can create, in your imagination, what you would like to experience, then you can become, end up doing, and end up having everything that would support you in experiencing this. Choose *right now* to be where you want to be internally, and you will end up externally in a place and situation that would support this experience—in the place and situation in which you want to be. And, at that point, the external situation will almost be superfluous, because you will already have everything you wanted from it inside you. That's all anything in this physical world ever does—it merely reflects and supports what you have already created in your internal experience.

When will you experience what you would like to experience if not right now? You never will until you choose to in the moment you're in. And until you choose to direct your attention toward what you'd like to experience, you'll block anything from coming into your physical world experience that would support the internal experience that you'd like to have—delaying your plans, discouraging yourself and others from getting you where you want to go and doing what you want to do and have done, etc.

If you choose to imagine and experience what you wish to experience right now, then this is what will fill your experience of reality as the world—your creation—comes to support what you asked of it with the focus of your attention. All of your words and actions and those of others, and the circumstances of your life, will come to help you keep experiencing this and more of this. If you simply select with your attention what you'd like to experience now, then this is what you will fuel into being—beginning now.

Every Experience Is Perfect

The purpose of every experience is to support the growth of our awareness of the fact that we create everything that we experience as well as our awareness of exactly how we do this.

Therefore, every experience is actually completely perfect as it is, and everything in our lives at the moment is exactly what should be here in the ideal. For it is all what we have created, and it therefore has the capacity to enable us to recognize that we created it and how we did this so that we can more willfully create something even more desirable for our next experience.

There is nothing that needs to change for us to be okay or for things to be good. We can be okay right now and recognize things as good right now in their being exactly what we need to understand that we create our own experience and how.

We are perfect. We are already everything we could ideally want to be. Our lives are perfect. They are already everything we could ideally want them to be. It is simply up to us to choose to recognize this so that we can allow this reality to reveal itself to us.

For what we focus on, we get. So if we focus on what we perceive as the imperfection or undesirability of things as they are, we will get more of this. And if, alternatively, we shift our perspective to recognize that it is all already perfect in the sense that it is the absolute best it could be in order to achieve the aim of raising our awareness of our ability to create whatever we wish with the focus of our attention, then this is what we will get—perfection. So our experiences will shift in order to support this and reveal themselves to us to be perfect, in order to give us reason and support to believe them to be this.

It could not possibly be better if we were simply handed everything we ever believed we wanted, because then we would never recognize that we create what we experience. And so we would be left feeling dependent and powerless, at the whim of someone or something outside ourselves to determine if we get to keep it all.

In this most magical, amazing world, the best possible experience of it all is not truly dependent on what we experience externally or have in any way. It is actually entirely dependent on our awareness that we are fully responsible for and capable of creating our experience of it all however we wish from moment to moment. When we get good things, we need not fear losing them.

For we are the only ones who could possibly determine if we lose them or keep them—based on whether we focus on the fear of losing them or the fulfillment of having them.

We are the creators of our own experience, and every experience is here to demonstrate this and show us this. And so every experience truly is perfect.

Three Forms Of Choice

As with everything else, there are three forms of choice—a male, sharing, proactive, initiative, controlling or guiding form; a female, receiving, reactive or responsive form; and a child, allowing, harmonizing, tuning out or tuning in form.

In the order of development: First we are inclined to allow the choices of others to be expressed through ourselves as we make choices that others would make. Then we are inclined to dismiss, react to, and rebel against others' choices and make choices that others wouldn't make. And then we are inclined to make choices without consideration of others.

In the order of creation: First we are inclined to attend to others and guide them in making their own choices. Then we are inclined to accept others' choices and respond to them positively. And then we are inclined to allow the choices of others to be expressed through ourselves as we tune into a reality that we guided into being.

Shower Everything With A Lot Of Positive Attention, And Only Positive Attention

The world of your experience is your creation. There is nothing within your experience that you did not bring into it with the focus of your attention. You chose it, if not at some point in this life, then in the spiritual realm prior to this life or in previous lives, and you can choose more of the same or something different in any moment. Your creation accommodates your every request. Recognize this, and shower your creation with positive attention—with gratitude, appreciation, love, etc. for its so loyally adhering to your guidance and directing you toward the actualization of your requests of it.

If there is anything in your experience that seems negative, recognize that this is a reflection of where you have given your attention. If anything bothers you, upsets you, angers you, worries you, seems to cause you regret or shame or make you afraid, recognize that this is a reflection of something within your own internal dynamic that you are not liking. Your creation wants nothing but your positive attention. It will do whatever you ask of it, give you whatever you focus on, conform to your will, and reflect back how you are treating it so that you can become aware of this and alter this where you wish to do so.

You are fantastically, awesomely powerful beyond your wildest imaginings. You have complete control over what you bring into your experience. Anything to which you are inclined to react negatively is something that you would ideally address so that you no longer bring anything else like this to you. For everything negative is the result of your focus of attention just as is everything positive.

You shape the world with your thoughts, with your instincts, with your actions. Your creation is your partner in the creation of your next experience. If you work with it and allow it to play its role and fulfill its purpose of guiding you in the direction of what you request of it, it will do so. If you provide it with clear destinations and listen to it, it will prove to be the best companion possible.

You are Source and Creator. You initiate the interaction that gives rise to everything that you experience. You can control and ignore your creation or pay attention to and guide your creation. The former way of initiating your interaction with your creation leads to reaction, resistance, and rebellion, and ultimately clinginess, attachment, and eventually escapism, where you are inclined to tune out from an experience of life that you feel you have no control over. The latter way of initiating your interaction with your creation leads to response, support, and the actualization of what you actually would like, where you are inclined to tune into an experience of life that you are aware that you have control over.

Recognize this, and nothing cannot be changed, nothing is permanent or fixed, nothing is beyond your capacity to shift within your experience. Everything is flowing, changeable, guided, shaped, and molded by your focus of attention. Change how you treat the creation you call "myself" and "my experience" and the whole world of your experience will change in accordance with this to reflect the new dynamic within you.

So shower every aspect of your experience with love and appreciation, say thank you often, tell everyone and everything how much love and joy they bring to you and that you have for them—within your mind, and outside your mind where appropriate. Speak only words of kindness toward every thought, every feeling, every instinct, every part of your body, every person, animal, plant, thing, entity, etc. within your life experience. The result will be equivalent degrees and types of kindness and other positive attention reflected back at you by every aspect of the mirror of the world that is like what has gotten such kindness and positive attention from you and beyond. And so your experience will be filled to overflowing with reasons only to be calm, positive, loving, appreciative, joyous, and grateful.

Creating Our Life Experience

When we stop looking to the physical world in the present and the past for evidence of what is to come in the future, and instead begin to imagine what we'd like the future to be and focus on that, we begin to choose and create a future for ourselves that differs from what we've experienced before. When we stop focusing on how the outside circumstances of our lives (including our bodies and the people and the world around us) need to change in order for us to be okay, and instead ask ourselves what we really want to experience and what we can change about ourselves in order to get this, we begin to get what we want in our lives. When we take full responsibility for our own experience of life and we really listen to ourselves—not just to our words to ourselves, but to the meaning we are trying to convey to ourselves—then we can make our experience anything we want it to be.

Our experience of life is not dependent on anyone or anything other than ourselves and the choices we make in each moment about what we give our attention to. This is the key to shaping our life experience.

When we apply this, our whole experience of life becomes a conversation between us—as we identify with the highest part of ourselves, the Source and Creator of all existence—and our thoughts, feelings, and instincts—our creations. Everyone and everything becomes so clearly a messenger of our own thoughts, feelings, and instincts, giving voice to the parts of ourselves that we may not be listening to in any other form. Our relationships become magical reflections of our relationship with ourselves, and we recognize that when we see dynamics that we don't like, we can change them at their source, within ourselves. We stop looking in the mirror of the world and the events and other people in our lives and insisting that the mirror must change in order for us to be happy with ourselves, and we instead seek to change ourselves so that when we see ourselves reflected back at us, we will like what we see.

Life becomes a mystical and profound learning experience where everything takes on meaning and conveys to us the answers to all our questions, and where the world truly provides us with everything we ask for. All we need to do is pay attention and listen. All the guidance we could possibly seek about how to get what we want is here, within ourselves, and reflected back at us by everything outside ourselves.

Everything we want is available to us in every moment. We need only request what we want by shifting our attention to it, and then listen to and act on the guidance provided to us to access and actualize it.

About The Author

Jonathan R. Wachtel is an international inspirational life guide, speaker, and personality expert. Creator of the JRW Life Guidance System—an innovative and effective approach to helping people actualize their ideal lives—he offers relationship, career, and personal development guidance; family, friends, and couple workshops; and more. He guides people in achieving greater fulfillment in their lives through one-on-one, individualized, life guidance sessions, as well as through group workshops and talks. He aims to inform, inspire, and guide with his written and spoken words and is also the author of *An Experiential Understanding of How All that Is Came to Be*, *There is a Place*, and *Freedom: An Inspiring And Transformative Story Of Self-Discovery*. To find out more about Jonathan, and to contact him, visit www.jonathanrwachtel.com.

www.ingramcontent.com/pod-product-compliance
Lightning Source LLC
Chambersburg PA
CBHW060231290526
45789CB00001B/8

* 9 7 8 1 5 0 0 2 3 2 7 0 2 *